JIHADISM TRANSFORMED

SIMON STAFFELL
AKIL N. AWAN

(*Editors*)

Jihadism Transformed

Al-Qaeda and Islamic State's Global Battle of Ideas

HURST & COMPANY, LONDON

First published in the United Kingdom in 2016 by
C. Hurst & Co. (Publishers) Ltd.,
41 Great Russell Street, London, WC1B 3PL
© Simon Staffell, Akil N. Awan and the Contributors, 2016
All rights reserved.
Printed in the United Kingdom by Bell & Bain Ltd, Glasgow.

A Cataloguing-in-Publication data record for this book is available from the British Library.

978-1-84904-647-3 Hardback

This book is printed using paper from registered sustainable and managed sources.

www.hurstpublishers.com

CONTENTS

CONTENTS

LIST OF CONTRIBUTORS

Christopher Anzalone is a PhD candidate in the Institute of Islamic Studies at McGill University, where he studies political Islam with a focus on militancy and jihadist groups, Shi'ism, martyrdom and the martyr in Muslim discourses, and Muslim visual cultures. He has written extensively on these topics and most recently has published a number of articles on al-Shabab in Somalia and Shi'ite militias in Syria.

Akil N. Awan is Associate Professor in Modern History, Political Violence and Terrorism at Royal Holloway, University of London. His research interests are focused around the history of terrorism, radicalisation, social movements, protest and new media. He has written widely in these areas, both academically and in the popular press. Dr Awan is also regularly consulted in his fields of expertise, having served in an advisory capacity to the UK Home Office, the Foreign Office, the US State Department, the US Military, Council of Europe and the OSCE amongst others. Most recently, he served as special adviser on Radicalisation to the UK Parliament, as academic expert on Genocide to the UK House of Lords delegation to Srebrenica, and as expert adviser on Youth Radicalisation to the United Nations. He is Founder and Chair of the Political Science Association's Specialist Group on Political Violence and Terrorism. He is on Twitter: @Akil_N_Awan

Valentina Bartolucci is a lecturer at the University of Pisa, Department of Peace Studies and Aggregate Researcher at the CISP (Inter-Departmental Centre of Science for Peace), University of Pisa. During 2013–14 she was a Fulbright Research Scholar at the Center for Strategic Communication at Arizona State University, studying jihadist discourses. Dr Bartolucci was awarded her PhD from the University of Bradford. Her latest research project, generously founded by the Veronesi Foundation, concentrates on understanding the growing involvement of women and children in terrorist actions and their manipulation by violent extremist organisations as instruments of propaganda.

Virginia Comolli is a Research Fellow at the International Institute for Strategic Studies (IISS) in London, where she runs the Security and Development programme. She is a member of the European Expert Network on Terrorism Issues and of the Global Initiative against Transnational Organised Crime. She sits on the international advisory board of the African Centre for Peace Building Ghana, and acts as a Project Associate for the International Drug Policy Project at the London School of Economics and a Technical Adviser at the Global Drug Policy Observatory at Swansea University. She is the author of *Boko Haram: Nigeria's Islamist Insurgency* (London: Hurst & Co., 2015) and co-author of *Drugs, Insecurity and Failed States: the Problems of Prohibition* (London: Routledge, 2012). She is currently editing a volume on the strategic implications of transnational organised crime. She is on Twitter: @VirginiaComolli

Jonathan Githens-Mazer is based at the Institute of Arab and Islamic Studies and the Strategy and Security Institute at the University of Exeter. He was awarded his PhD from the London School of Economics in 2005, and graduated from Swarthmore College in 1997. Githens-Mazer's research examines nationalism, radicalisation, terrorism and counter-terrorism, and he has published on these issues in Ireland, North Africa and the United Kingdom. His current book projects include an examination of the appeal of Salafi Islam amongst young gang members in South London, and another that looks at the symbolic role of Islam for nationalism in North Africa. He is an Associate Fellow of the Royal United Services Institute (RUSI).

Donald Holbrook is a Senior Research Fellow at the Centre for the Study of Terrorism and Political Violence, University of St Andrews. He holds postgraduate degrees from the University of Cambridge and the University of St Andrews and completed his PhD from the latter in 2012. Research interests include how beliefs and ideas relate to terrorism and terrorist public relations initiatives. He manages a research project focusing on mapping extremist media.

Elisabeth Kendall is Senior Research Fellow in Arabic and Islamic Studies at Pembroke College, Oxford University. Her current work examines connections between militant jihadist/political movements and cultural production in Arabic. She spends significant time in the field and is the author or editor of several books, including *ReClaiming Islamic Tradition* (with Ahmad Khan, 2016), *Twenty-First Century Jihad* (with Ewan Stein, 2015) and *Literature, Journalism and the Avant-Garde: Intersection in Egypt* (2006, paperback 2010). Dr Kendall also conceived of and edits the 'Modern Middle Eastern Vocabularies' series, which includes the titles *Security Arabic*, *Intelligence Arabic* and *Media Arabic*. Previously, she held tenured lectureships or fellowships at the Universities of Edinburgh, Oxford and Harvard. Before returning to Oxford in 2010, she served as Director of the Centre for the Advanced Study of the Arab World, a UK government-sponsored initiative aimed at building Arabic language-based research expertise.

Nelly Lahoud is is Senior Fellow for Political Islamism at the International Institute for Strategic Studies (IISS)—Middle East. She completed her PhD in 2002 in the Research School of Social Sciences at the Australian National University. In 2003, she was a postdoctoral scholar at St John's College, University of Cambridge; in 2005, she was a Rockefeller Fellow in Islamic studies at the Library of Congress; and in 2008–9 she was a Research Fellow at the Belfer Center for Science and International Affairs, Harvard University. Before taking up her current position, Dr Lahoud was Associate Professor at the Department of Social Sciences at the US Military Academy at West Point and Senior Associate at the Combating Terrorism Center (CTC) at West Point (2010–15); and previously an Assistant Professor of Political Theory, including Islamic Political Thought, at Goucher College (2004–10). Her research interests include terrorism and ideology, and the public narrative of the al-Qaeda leadership. She manages a research project focusing on mapping extremist media.

Simon Staffell is a UK government official, currently serving in the British Embassy in Washington, who has specialised in counter-terrorism, the Middle East and political Islam. His PhD in Politics at the University of Sheffield examined the emergence of al-Qaeda in Iraq and developed a new approach to analysing Arabic language extremist literature published online. He has studied and worked across the Arab world, most recently in a diplomatic posting in Cairo. Prior to joining government, he was a teacher and founded a college programme for the study of Islam and the philosophy of religion.

Martha Turnbull is the Head of the FCO's National Security Research Group.[1] Martha joined the FCO in 2012, having previously worked on terrorism issues at the Ministry of Defence. Martha's research focuses on international Islamist extremism, specifically groups linked to al-Qaeda and the Islamic State of Iraq and the Levant.

LIST OF ABBREVIATIONS

AAB	Abdullah Azzam Brigades
AASE	Ansar as-Shariah Egypt
ABM	Ansar Bait al-Maqdis
AQ	al-Qaeda
AQIM	al-Qaeda in the Islamic Mahgreb
AQAP	al-Qaeda in the Arabian Peninsula
EIJ	Egyptian Islamic Jihad
GSPC	Groupe Salafiste pour la Prédication et le Combat (Salafist Group for Preaching and Combat)
IG	Islamic Group (*Al-Gama'a al-Islamiyya*)
IS	Islamic State (since late June 2014 up to the present)
ISI	Islamic State of Iraq (from 2006 until April 2013)
ISIL	Islamic State of Iraq and the Levant (April 2013 and June 2014)
ISWAP	Islamic State West Africa Province
MENA	Middle East and North Africa
MNJTF	Multi-National Joint Task Force
MUJWA	Movement for Unity and Jihad in West Africa
TWJ	al-Tawhid w'al Jihad
WS	Wilayat Sina (Sinai Province, formerly ABM)

GLOSSARY OF ARABIC TERMS

Ahl al-Bayt	Shia Muslims—lit. People of the house (of the prophet)
Ahl al-Sunna wa-l-Jama'a	Sunni Muslims—lit. people of the tradition and community
al-wala' wa-l-bara'	Loyalty [to believers] and disavowal [of non-believers]
Bay'a	Oath of allegiance
Bid'a	Innovation
Dajjal	Devil
Dawlat al-Islam	Islamic State
Din	Religion
Fiqh	Jurisprudence
Fitna	Discord, civil strife
Hakimiyya	Sovereignty: In Islamist thought, used particularly to denote the sovereignty of God (*Hakimiyyat Allah*)
Hijra	Emigration
al-Ikhwan al-Muslimun	the Muslim Brotherhood
Jahiliyya	*Pre-Islamic 'age of ignorance'*
Khalifa	Caliph
Khilafa	Caliphate
Kharijites or *Khawarij*	a rebellious group in the first century of Islam (7th century CE), who are considered in mainstream Islam to have been heretical and extreme
Manhaj	Methodology
Mujtama'	Society

GLOSSARY OF ARABIC TERMS

Murtadd	Apostate
Nashid	Islamic anthem
Rafida, pl. *rawafid*	Rejectors—a sectarian term against Shia Muslims
Sahaba	Companions—refers in Islamic literature to companions of the prophet Muhammad.
Shahada	Islamic declaration of faith—'there is no god but God and Muhammad is the messenger of God'
Shahid	Martyr
Shari'a	Islamic legal framework
Shirk	The sin of polytheism in Islam
Takfir	Excommunication; to declare a fellow Muslim as kafir (non-believer)
Tawhid	The oneness of God
'Ulama'	Council of religious scholars
Umma	The worldwide community of Muslims
Wilaya	Province

PREFACE

On 12 December 2014, the British Foreign and Commonwealth Office convened a panel of experts to assess how jihadist narratives had evolved in recent years, in the context of turbulent events in the Middle East. The event's aim was to consider the current state of jihadist narratives and to assess their trajectories. A great deal has happened since then, and the conference inaugurated an ambitious project which has expanded in response to the scale of the task.

This volume seeks to take a long view of the trajectories in jihadist narratives globally. A number of excellent studies have already begun the task of understanding the Islamic State phenomenon,[1] mirroring the substantial body of literature that was developed previously for al-Qaeda. This study takes on board the lessons learnt from the counter-intuitive twists and turns that jihadist movements have shown a propensity to take, and attempts to gain a sense of the historical sweep of transitions in the movement, and of trajectories across time and space.

1

INTRODUCTION

Simon Staffell and *Akil N. Awan*

On 17 December 2010, a young Tunisian street vendor, Mohammed Bouazizi, doused himself in gasoline and set himself ablaze in silent protest against the petty bureaucratic tyranny with which Tunisians had been forced to contend for decades. Bouazizi's self-immolation, which captured a mood of impotent rage against authoritarianism and lack of upward social mobility for the youth bulge, sparked historic protests that swept through the Middle East and North Africa (MENA), removing long-rooted dictators from power within a matter of months.

As the protests continued to rage throughout the region, halfway around the world, on 2 May of 2011, an elite team of US Navy SEALs made a clandestine incursion into Pakistani territory, raiding an affluent compound in Abbottabad to assassinate al-Qaeda's infamous leader and global terrorist mastermind, Osama bin Laden. The death of an ageing, cloistered and largely impotent bin Laden nevertheless left al-Qaeda (AQ) bereft of its charismatic and symbolic leader—one who had provided a rallying cry to generations of Islamic militants the world over.

Triumphalism over the end of bin Laden, and by extension the scourge of jihadism, would prove to be sorely misguided. Barely three years later, on the first day of Ramadan at the end of June 2014, Abu Bakr al-Baghdadi, adorned in the regalia of Caliphate-dom, ascended the pulpit of the Grand Mosque in Mosul. As he addressed the congregation, he demanded obeisance from the *ummah* (the global community of Muslims), in his new incarnation as the self-anointed Caliph Ibrahim—ruler of the newly established Islamic State—in recognition of their spectacular success in staking claims to large swathes of territory straddling Syria and Iraq.

These three events have, in their own ways, fundamentally transformed the jihadist movement. They have caused seismic shifts in practice, in narratives and in worldviews. This volume gathers a panel of renowned experts to identify, track and explore the changes that have taken place. We ask how these shifts have come about, and how jihadist narratives and discourses have evolved in the context of these and other turbulent events in the Middle East and beyond. The contributions consider the current state of the jihadist narrative, mapping its trajectories and assessing its impact, not just inside the Middle East and North Africa, but further afield in South Asia and sub-Saharan Africa, and indeed the West too.

The impact of the Arab Spring

Early responses

The dramatic self-immolation of the young Tunisian, Mohammed Bouazizi, in 2011 signalled the advent of the Arab Spring—a social movement that heralded momentous change as it swept through much of the MENA region. Very rapidly, the Arab Spring mobilised a whole swathe of young people in popular local uprisings that sought to remove their autocratic leaders from power through largely peaceful protests. Al-Qaeda and other jihadists were initially blindsided by the advent of this organic, grass-roots and initially largely secular social movement, which was not only directed at the very same opponents that animated the 'near enemy', autocratic dictators who held sway over the Muslim world, but appeared to draw from a similar constituency and support base: the youth bulge throughout the MENA region. Crucially, this was a rejection of the very raison d'être on which the jihadists' recourse to brutal violence was predicated, and as the regimes teetered or toppled, they appeared more and more like impotent bystanders witnessing history from the sidelines.

It initially appeared that the Arab Spring might represent the death knell for jihadists. The fact that the Arab uprisings had been able to oust entrenched dictators like Zine el-Abedine Ben Ali and Hosni Mubarak in less than a month, while jihadist violence had proven unable to affect the balance of power significantly in any Arab country after a decades-long struggle, was incontrovertible.[1] So compelling was this account of dismal failure that commentators intimated that 'the organisation might not survive'.[2] These sorts of sentiments were widespread in the immediate euphoric aftermath of the revolutions, but ultimately proved somewhat naïve and short-sighted. The structural conditions created by the revolutions were to prove more telling for the fate of the jihadist movement than the Arab Spring itself.

It is certainly true that in the immediate aftermath of the uprisings in Tunisia and Egypt, the jihadists were rhetorically floored. A cross-sectional analysis of over 500 jihadist statements released onto forums and via social media between 2010 and 2015 was conducted as part of this study, with texts coded for key themes. This analysis showed that immediately prior to the uprisings, hyperbole and bragging from AQ-inspired ideologues had reached its zenith; one internet forum writer claimed in late 2010 that 'The reality today is that the empire of America is near to collapse and al-Qai'da is on its way to regain the Islamic Caliphate the Almighty God has promised to the nation of monotheism.'[3]

However, the braggadocio and self-aggrandisement that had become a prominent feature of AQ's discourse after 9/11 all but disappeared by the start of 2011. In its place, the jihadist forums were awash with attempts to interpret and reframe political events to suit jihadist narratives, desperate to retain relevance somehow. As one forum post in late 2011 argued, 'toppling of regimes is not a change by itself but it is a blessed step to achieve this change. The ummah's current battle against its enemy is more critical than its battle against the toppled regimes.'[4]

These convoluted attempts to reframe and appropriate events as their own were remarkably unconvincing. The challenge for the jihadists during this period appeared greater than simply the questions of whether or not peaceful protest made their violent methodology unnecessary; it was more a fundamental problem of how they might meaningfully engage with the complex political reality around them, which bordered on an existential crisis. Jihadists were drawn into detailed political commentary and fairly esoteric ideological discussions on these issues. These efforts to make a radical reframing of political events according to jihadist ideology opened up the risk of inconsistencies and contradictions. Many forums, for example, were awash with vociferous debates over whether one should critique the uprisings or support them. One forum participant earnestly appealed for aiding the 'glorious revolutions', recognising the protesters as fellow 'youth of the ummah': 'What then are you waiting for? Save yourselves and your children! The time is ripe, especially after the youth of the ummah took upon themselves the burden of their glorious revolutions, enduring the bullets and tortures of the tyrants.'[5]

Others offered more tentative support, pragmatically arguing that the uprisings might be co-opted for their cause: 'Since the land is in chaos and Qaddafi is helping through his reactions and actions to increase the hatred of the population against him, it will be easier for us to recruit new members.... There is lots of work to do ... we have to help the people fighting and then build an Islamic state.'[6]

Some, however, were far more condemnatory, taking 'principled' stances against the engagement with democratic change: 'Many people in Egypt and in other countries have been misled to the point that many of them do not realise that democratic rule is contrary to Shari'ah.'[7] A Jordanian who had fought in Iraq under al-Zarqawi, was adamant that the uprisings were destined to fail, and the jihadists would then step into the void, reaping the benefits of failure and soured idealism: 'At the end of the day, how much change will there really be in Egypt and other countries? There will be many disappointed demonstrators, and that's when they will realize what the only alternative is. We are certain that this will all play into our hands.'[8]

Irrespective of the fundamental ideological disconnect from the vast majority of the secular protestors in Tahrir Square and elsewhere, or the equivocal attitude towards the uprisings themselves, there was no escaping the fact that these events were the most important to have taken place anywhere in the world for a generation. Whatever response they might merit, they certainly could not be ignored. Indeed, jihadist forums and literature over this early period responded rapidly, but not very effectively, to developments on the ground.

The jihadist ideologues became preoccupied with political commentary—some supportive and others critical of the events—but were left unable to form a consistent and decisive narrative frame that could make sense of the events for the jihadist worldview.

Islamism, democracy and jihadism

The uprisings in both Tunisia and Egypt were not only instrumental in removing entrenched dictators from power, but also brought about unprecedented electoral successes for Islamist groups like Ennahda and the Muslim Brotherhood. Jihadists could not conceivably have accepted or even shown tacit support for this successful democratic transition by their co-religionists, without appearing deeply hypocritical.

As early as 1991, al-Zawahiri wrote his first book, *The Bitter Harvest*, which was a vicious denunciation of Islamist groups for embracing democracy: a reprehensible system of governance as it rejected both the absolute sovereignty of God (*hakimiyya*), and principles of loyalty to the believers and disavowal of disbelievers (*wala wal-bara*). Jihadist attitudes towards the democratic victories of the Arab Spring's Islamists were a little more ambiguous and conflicted. The official ideologues of al-Qaeda obstinately rejected any concession towards democracy, which of course they viewed as anathema to jihadism. On the other hand, they were also acutely aware of the danger of being rendered obsolete by the tremendous new successes enjoyed by the non-violent Islamists.

Fortunately for the jihadists, this apparent quandary was soon resolved by events in Egypt, where the Arab Spring quickly turned into a winter of discontent, paving the way for the old military guard to usurp power through a 'counter-revolution'. If the Arab Spring had been a setback for al-Qaeda and everywhere, the Egyptian military's overthrow of the elected Muslim Brotherhood government on 3 July 2013 would prove to be their saving grace; a powerful validation of everything they had warned against.

Western policy-makers, themselves frustrated by President Mohammed Morsi's leadership, and acutely sensitive to the risk of being accused of interference, had little choice but to acquiesce to Abdel Fattah el-Sisi's (to some degree popular) coup against Morsi's democratically elected government.

For jihadists everywhere, this was irrefutable proof that democracy was a ruse and would never bring about true Islamic political power. Even if believers sold their very souls to win democratic elections, their victories would be meaningless. Only violence therefore could bring about real change. Just days after the coup against President Morsi, in a series of tweets from its official Twitter account, al-Shabaab castigated the Muslim Brotherhood for attempting to gain power and impose shari'ah by following the democratic process: 'It's time to remove those rose-tinted spectacles and see the world as accurately as it is, change comes by the bullet alone; NOT the ballot.' 'They should perhaps learn a little from the lessons of history and those "democratically elected" before them in #Algeria or even #Hamas.'[9]

Al-Zawahiri, behind the curve, made a similar appeal a month later on 4 August 2013, reiterating many of al-Shabaab's arguments.[10] Indeed, Morsi's removal in Egypt provided a lifeline for jihadists everywhere, exonerating their interpretations of events: that the 'near enemy' (local dictators) could never be defeated whilst they were being propped up by the 'far enemy' (the US or the West); the West would never allow believers to come to power, even if they operated legitimately within the existing frameworks; sufficient change could not come through political processes alone without violent jihad; and democracy remained a dangerous illusion and a threat to Islam.

Establishment of the 'Caliphate'

While most commentators and analysts opined that the Arab Spring might represent the death knell for jihadism, there were some early ominous signs of the secular uprisings potentially being subverted. In late 2011, the black flag of the *khilafah* (the Islamic declaration of faith, the *shahadah* in white text written on a black background) began appearing frequently in peaceful protests across the MENA region, sometimes alongside other potent jihadist imagery.[11] At the time—in a prevailing atmosphere of hope that the Arab uprisings might still represent a spring—it was unclear what this black flag phenomenon represented. In hindsight, it was an ominous early portent of things to come: of an era that became less about democratic hope than about the violence of an emergent group calling themselves the Islamic State.

After Morsi's removal and the return of military rule in Egypt, ISIL were able to take up the re-framist jihadist narrative, without being dogged by the contradictions that had beset AQ ideologues for the preceding two years. In August 2013, ISIL spokesman Abu Muhammad al-'Adnani argued:

> Today, our precious Ummah is living in slavery and humiliation. The evidence of this is what is known as the Arab Spring revolutions, in which people went out demanding freedom and dignity. For the armies of the tyrants have humiliated the Muslims and made them slaves to unjust pagan laws.[12]

This worrying trajectory came to a head on 29 June 2014, when ISIL brazenly announced the re-establishment of the Caliphate—the religio-political entity that had historically governed vast swathes of the Islamic world, but which in this new incarnation would now straddle parts of Syria and Iraq:

> As for you, oh soldiers of the Islamic State, then congratulations to you. Congratulations on this clear victory, congratulations on this great triumph.... Now the caliphate has returned, humbling the necks of the enemy. Now hope is being actualized. Now the dream has become a reality.[13]

Evincing global pretensions, IS declared that it was now incumbent on all Muslims worldwide (al-Qaeda and others included) to swear fealty to their new religio-political leader, Caliph Ibrahim, as the self-aggrandising Baghdadi demanded he be addressed.

Most analysts were shocked at the rapid ascension of IS and the establishment of a Caliphate, dumbfounded by both the alacrity and sheer audacity of this event. However, in hindsight we might note that whilst this turn of events may have elicited astonishment, it was not entirely unexpected. Rather, both ISIL and its progenitors—AQI and ISI—having already established a number of 'emirates' in the political vacuum of post-Saddam Iraq, and more recently in civil war-riven Syria, had long articulated the desire to secure political territory as one of their principal goals. As Nelly Lahoud sets out in Chapter 2, ISIL built on the ideology of their forebears. The establishment of a more expansive Caliphate was assumed to be the inevitable next step. For many years, al-Qaeda had itself pointed to an aspirational future Caliphate as their utopian end goal—one which allowed them to justify their violent excesses in the here and now. Islamic State, abetted by the insecurity and tumult in the wake of the Arab uprisings, managed to turn that abstract aspiration into a dystopic reality.

It would be myopic to lay the blame for IS's emergence solely at the feet of the failed Arab Spring. Of course, the uprisings were central to the rise of IS, particularly in the wake of the Syrian uprising, civil war, and brutal suppression by Syrian dictator, Bashar al-Assad. However, the rise of IS also stems in very large part from the emergence of AQI and ISI in Iraq, which of course saw no such uprising. Consequently, the emergence of IS cannot be understood without understanding the fall-out from invasion and occupation of Iraq in 2003; the destruction of the country's infrastructure in its wake; the dismantlement of its military and security apparatus which left insecurity and power vacuums; the rule of a divisive, sectarian Shiite political administration in Baghdad. All of these issues are key to explaining IS's rapid ascendancy.

Irrespective of what the combination of structural factors may have been, IS managed to hijack not only the failing Arab Spring, and the chaos and insecurity of the region, but also the floundering jihadist narrative along the way, breathing new life into the global salafi-jihadi movement. The audacious establishment of a Caliphate in 2014 represented a new era for jihadism and allowed Islamic State to claim to be the rightful new heirs to the jihadist mantle.

Continuity and rupture in the narrative

Whilst it is abundantly clear that the momentous events of the last five years have fundamentally shifted jihadist narratives and discourses, an exclusionary focus on the rupture and change within these narratives would belie the significant continuity that remained within jihadist worldviews. Some key precepts of the jihadist meta-narrative have endured, linking both pre-Arab uprising worldviews with those that developed in the post-Islamic State context, whilst other themes have emerged within the narrative which serve to highlight the clear disconnect between the two.

Historical themes

At the heart of the narrative remains the view that contemporary conflicts are part of a wider historical global attack on Islam and Muslims by non-believers. This notion of a war on Islam has been present since the earliest AQ statements.[14] The adversary in this 'war on Islam' is often blurred into the 'West' or the 'crusaders', drawing on particular historical themes and collective memory. Indeed, the invocation of the Crusades is a constant refrain in the jihadist narrative. AQ have referred to the Americans and their allies almost exclusively as the 'Zionist–Crusader Alliance'. One of al-Qaeda's earliest statements to the outside world in 1998 was presented under the banner of the *World Islamic Front for Jihad Against Jews and Crusaders*.[15] Much of AQ's later propaganda literature continued to perpetuate this narrative—note for example, *The Result of Seven Years of Crusades*, which received a huge circulation after it was released in 2008 on the seventh anniversary of the 9/11 attacks.[16] Concomitantly, jihadists have long sought to portray themselves as chivalrous medieval knights, at the head of the vanguard, opposing these 'neo-Crusaders'. Indeed, the appeal to the valiant holy warrior or chivalrous knight is a recurring trope in much jihadist literature, with Ayman al-Zawahiri's famous text, *Fursan Taht Rayah Al-Nabi* (Knights Under the Prophet's Banner), representing one of the most important examples.[17]

Recent Islamic State propaganda has perpetuated and developed these Crusades analogies. For example, its flagship magazine, *Dabiq*, released issue 4 in October 2014 entitled *The Failed Crusade*, containing the feature-length article 'Reflections on the Final Crusade' (see Figure 1.1). In a striking illustration of the anachronism represented by Islamic State's worldview, the magazine quoted IS spokesman Mohammed al-'Adnani's infamous threat against

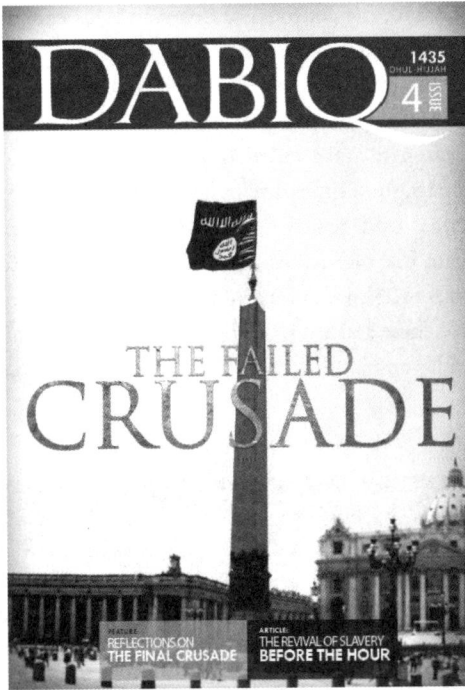

Figure 1.1: Front page of *Dabiq*, issue 4

'Rome's Crusaders',[18] juxtaposed against a photoshopped image of Islamic State's flag fluttering atop the Holy See in the Vatican. In the official IS statement claiming responsibility for the 13 November 2015 Paris attacks, they referred to France as being at 'the forefront of the Crusader campaign'.[19]

Religious identity

Religious identity is another central constant tenet within the jihadist narrative, used tirelessly to dehumanise enemies, as well as delineate insider–outsider status. Jihadist ideologues have always made use of the traditional conservative salafi theological concept of *al-wala w'al-bara*—association with believers and disavowal of disbelievers—particularly when raising the spectre of the corrupting unbelievers. *Takfir*—the pronouncing of disbelief or excommunication of other Muslims—has also been a persistent theme, required to justify deaths of innocent Muslims while still claiming to be fighting for Islam. So pervasive is this desire to demarcate the contours of belief and disbelief that critics often refer to them pejoratively as *takfiris* (excommunicators).

Whilst caustic sectarianism, aligned with the belief that other Muslims are beyond the pale, has always been a prominent part of jihadist ideology, jihadist leaders have often taken a more ambivalent or pragmatic attitude to minorities in the past, sometimes downplaying difference in order not to risk alienating audiences and constituencies. Indeed, al-Zawahiri tentatively rebuked al-Qaeda in Iraq's leader, Abu Musab al-Zarqawi, for fomenting internecine conflict with the Shiite in Iraq in 2005. Pointing out how senseless and counterproductive these actions were, he asked, 'Can the mujahideen kill all the Shia in Iraq? Has any Islamic state in history ever tried that?'[20]

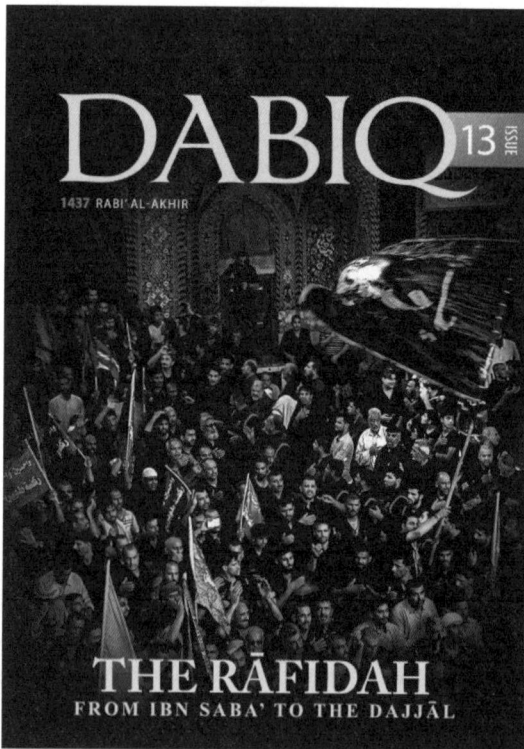

Figure 1.2: Front page of *Dabiq*, issue 13. The *Rafidah* (rejectors) is a common sectarian term appearing frequently in IS propaganda. *Ibn Saba'* is a derogatory reference to Abd Allah Ibn Saba' al-Himayri. *Dajjal* is Arabic for the devil.

IS and the Syrian conflict have replaced AQ's often pragmatic or ambivalent approach to terrorist targeting, with a much more venomous and acrimonious attitude towards sectarian differences. With battle-lines being drawn against the 'Shiʿite crescent', represented by Assad's Alawite regime, Hizbullah, and Iranian-backed Shiite militias, religious sectarian fervour has reached fever pitch. IS have taken the criterion of religious identity to a new extreme, constantly using their sectarian lexicon to denigrate the Shiites as part of their internecine war.[21] The front page of *Dabiq*, issue 13 provides a good example of this persistent sectarian imagery (Figure 1.2) and the magazine contains a number of long sectarian articles. Sectarian ideas are also repeated constantly via IS's social media channels.

The observable difference between AQ's and IS's attacks on the Shiites is perhaps not particularly surprising, considering that IS's progenitors were participants and instigators of the brutal sectarian civil war of 2006–7 in Iraq. Moreover, IS's current success in controlling territory in both Iraq and Syria is predicated in part on a degree of tacit support from some Sunnis in both Iraq and Syria, who were disillusioned by the highly corrupt and sectarian Shiite government in Baghdad, or chafing under the brutal regime of an Alawite dictator in Damascus. In Chapter 10 of this volume, Christopher Anzalone examines in detail the sectarianisation of the post-Arab Spring Middle East.

On 23 June 2015, Islamic State spokesman Abu Muhammad al-ʿAdnani appealed to Sunni grievances at the violence that was occurring against them, in the context of the Iraqi government failing to bring them into the political process:

> Be keen to conquer in this holy month [of Ramadan] and to become exposed to martyrdom ... [bringing] calamity for the infidels—Shiʿites and apostate Muslims. The Sunni people are now behind the Jihadists ... the enemies have been petrified by the daily pledges of allegiance by the chiefs of tribes to the Mujahideen... Needless to say, you all know the kidnappings, evictions, and killings of Sunnis that happen every day in Baghdad.[22]

Thus by peddling and perpetuating sectarian rivalries, IS were able to portray themselves as the crucial vanguard against oppression and disbelief. As one forum participant argued in 2014: '[IS] stands alone in Iraq against the armies of infidelity.'[23]

Schisms

Osama bin Laden, as both friends and foes alike willingly concede, was an able, charismatic and much-respected leader. His death left a gaping void in the movement that was unlikely to be filled by any potential successor. Al-Zawahiri's succession did nothing to ease the loss, and rather reinforced how central bin Laden had been to the whole enterprise. The stark juxtaposition between the lofty, articulate warrior-cleric, who eloquently recited poetry in classical Arabic, with the dour, humourless eye doctor, who spoke haltingly in his guttural Egyptian dialect, made for a rather unflattering comparison for al-Zawahiri, doing little to endear him to the movement.

To al-Zawahiri's credit, he was a better leader than many analysts assumed he would be. Indeed, al-Zawahiri managed successfully to transfer the various al-Qaeda affiliates' oaths of allegiance from bin Laden to himself, in the months following his death, including those of important offshoots like al-Qaeda in the Arabian Peninsula (AQAP) and al-Qaeda in the Maghreb (AQIM). Moreover, he later also increased al-Qaeda's ambit by receiving new pledges of allegiance from al-Shabaab in Somalia and Jabhat al-Nusra in Syria, or opening new fronts, like that of the new offshoot in the Indian subcontinent.

Nevertheless, these successes were not enough to engender loyalty in all, particularly amongst those groups that had shown secessionist tendencies even whilst bin Laden had been alive. Primarily, these were the rebellious Zarqawite strains in Iraq who would later go on to become IS. The first serious schisms and fissures began to appear after Abu Bakr Baghdadi, leader of the ISI, chose to export his particular brand of violence over the border to Syria in August 2011, following the outbreak of civil war. Baghdadi's deputy in Syria, Abu Muhammad al-Joulani, proved highly adept at recruiting and training fighters, and soon established an eminently capable military unit: Jabhat al-Nusra (JN).[24] Baghdadi, however, soon fearing irredentist ambitions, announced that ISI and JN would merge under the new moniker, Islamic State of Iraq and the Levant (ISIL). Joulani was incensed that he had not been consulted, and sensing his power might wane, formally complained to al-Zawahiri, who, seeing the opportunity to reassert his significance, decided to mediate between the two. Al-Zawahiri ruled against the merger, ordered the disbanding of ISIL and allocated the Syrian front to JN as al-Qaeda's official affiliate in Syria. He also appointed an emissary, a veteran of the movement, Abu Khalid al-Suri, to ensure that his wishes were carried out, and to oversee the establishment of cordial relations between the various factions. Baghdadi, showing complete contempt for al-Qaeda Central's authority, not only rejected the order, but promptly ordered al-Suri's assassination in a suicide bombing which would mark the beginning of a brutal internecine war between the various jihadist factions in Iraq and Syria, and drew battle lines amongst jihadists the world over.

The jihadist media space over the past four years has reflected this dispute between those aligned with AQ and those with IS. Schisms and internecine conflict has spread globally, with groups as far afield as North Africa and Indonesia fracturing and declaring their allegiances along IS and anti-IS lines.

The celebration of savagery

On 3 February 2015, IS released a video entitled *Healing of the Believers' Chests*, in which Muadh al-Kasasbeh, a captured Jordanian fighter pilot who participated in airstrikes against IS positions, is shown standing in a steel cage.[25] Clad in an orange Guantanamo-esque jumpsuit, he stands accused of incinerating civilians during the aerial bombardment. Apparently heavily sedated, his face betrays no emotion as his punishment is announced: *lex talionis*, he is to be burnt alive. The video documents the punishment in excruciating detail, as the flames first engulf and then consume al-Kasasbeh, until finally his smouldering corpse collapses to the ground. The video voyeuristically lingers on Kasasbeh's charred face, frozen in a death-mask of agony. The brutality of what takes place is particularly jarring juxtaposed against the slick production values of the video, typical of IS media material.

From beheadings of bound victims with hunting knives, to fighters playing football with decapitated heads; and from throwing homosexuals to their deaths from rooftops, to dragging victims to their deaths behind pick-up trucks, brutal yet meticulously staged savagery has become a hallmark of IS's violence. Later media productions feature even more egregious examples of barbarity, as if increasingly desensitised viewers needed ever more taboo content in their steady diet of this pornography of violence. In the 23 June 2015 production, *But If You Return, We Shall Return*,[26] for example, three separate groups are accused of being spies before they are accorded their horrific punishments: one group is submerged in a steel cage until they drown; the second group are graphically burned alive in their vehicle; the final group are beheaded with explosives.

Although AQ's narrative has always justified extreme violence and attacks that kill thousands, part of their narrative generally demands theological justifications for violence. From the perspective of AQ leaders, violence is an important part, but only a part nonetheless, of the broader ideology. Understandably, they were wary of creating a generation who understood little more than violence, but more importantly, could not contextualise that violence as a 'necessary' aspect of the broader struggle, as opposed to simply revelling in the violence itself.[27] Al-Zawahiri criticised the youthful Jihadist following of al-Zarqawi for their preoccupation with bloodshed and brutality, writing in 2005: 'Among the things which the feelings of the Muslim populace who love and support you will never find palatable, also, are the scenes of slaughtering the hostages. You shouldn't be deceived by the praise of some of the zealous young men and their description of you as the Sheikh of the slaughterers.'[28]

In this pointed criticism, al-Zawahiri was in fact referring to Zarqawi's pioneering of the brutal videotaped beheadings, which he correctly predicted would in fact repulse the Muslim masses on whose behalf the jihadists claimed to serve as the crucial vanguard. In contrast, the IS narrative, which is the heir to the Zarqawite strain of jihadism, does not appear to share this 'ends justify the means' logic, or share concern for legitimacy of targets. In many instances, it almost appears as if death and violence are an end in themselves. Ideology and thought are far less important than the act.

AQ attempted to dissociate itself from IS's propensity for seemingly mindless violence, disavowing the 'shedding of protected blood'.[29] In May 2014, al-Zawahiri released a statement calling on al-Baghdadi to 'put an end to this bloody carnage and be fully devoted to fighting the enemies of Islam and the Sunnis'.[30] However, a closer reading of IS's unfettered violence reveals a twisted logic that should not have come as a surprise to al-Zawahiri. *The Management of Savagery*,[31] published in 2004 by the al-Qaeda theoretician Abu Bakr Naji—a tome that was characterised by NPR as 'al-Qaeda's playbook'[32]—appears to hold the key to explaining IS's rationale for brutality. The text calls for the administration of abominable savagery, and massacres of the enemy in order to terrorise them: 'We must make this battle very violent, such that death is a heartbeat away, so that the two groups will realize that entering this battle will frequently lead to death... Our enemies will not be merciful to us if they seize us. Thus, it behooves us to make them think one thousand times before attacking us.' So the purpose of the violence is not whimsical, random or crazed, but deliberate, strategic and didactic;[33] it terrifies the enemy, whilst simultaneously polarising audiences of the violence.

All of this is germane to the ultimate aim of Naji's text—the establishment of an Islamic State, and his tactics appear to have greatly influenced IS. The text is not only part of the organisation's curriculum, but is widely read among provisional commanders and senior fighters as a way to justify beheadings as not only religiously permissible, but commendable acts.[34] There is little doubt that IS's brutal reputation for savagery was central to the widespread defections amongst the Iraqi security forces, such as those witnessed in Mosul in 2014, even though the Iraqis vastly outnumbered the IS fighters advancing on their positions.

Eschatology, the realised Caliphate and Utopian Project

Some analysts have argued that AQ is an irrational actor, lacking any coherent strategy, captured in Jean Elshtain's claim that 'there is a nihilistic edge to terrorism: It aims to destroy, most often in the service of wild and utopian goals that make no sense at all in the usual political ways.'[35] Whilst their idea of the global Caliphate may have seemed utopian and unachievable, AQ were never nihilistic actors. AQ needed potent religio-political discourses to sustain and legitimise their ideology, which was heavily dependent on acceptance of the achievability of their distant utopian vision. Failure to achieve legitimacy, al-Zawahiri warned, will cause the jihadist movement to be 'crushed in the shadows, far from the masses who are distracted and fearful.'[36] Consequently, AQ narratives always sought to create a narrative gap for their audiences, by pointing out grievances that the entire Muslim *ummah* must respond to, and why AQ were best placed to provide this response.[37] But these narratives, and the clear lack of efficacy in AQ's response, left open more questions than they resolved.

The advent of IS's Caliphate, by contrast, has helped fill that narrative gap for the jihadist movement. IS play on similar grievances to AQ, but in a way that often rejects complex ideological justifications in favour of action. IS's focus is on creating the utopia in the here and now, and they have provided ample evidence of both tangible goals, but also unprecedented material success. This is perhaps the most fundamental divergence in the ideology of al-Qaeda and Islamic State, and the reason for the competitive advantage of the latter in terms of global recruitment over the past several years. Their goal is to contribute to a concrete state, and not an abstract eschatological vision, and since as early as 2006, when the successors to Abu Musab al-Zarqawi—the former leader of al-Qaeda in Iraq—declared the formation of an Islamic state in Iraq, this strain of jihadist ideology began to focus far more obsessively on the task of establishing a physical state and of using any means necessary to achieve this.

While ISIL/IS established territorial emirates in Iraq and later Syria, AQ central leadership continued to talk, hypothetically, about the notion of a

Caliphate. Indeed, IS's forebears were, in one sense, putting into practice what AQ leadership was preaching. In his tenth Message of Hope and Glad Tidings to Our People in Egypt, AQ leader Ayman al-Zawahiri discussed the concept, providing a useful summary of how it is often understood in AQ texts. Most frequently, it takes the shape of a historical reference—'the Jewish occupation of Palestine would not have taken place without the occupation of Egypt and the fall of the Islamic Caliphate'[38]—or as a theoretical or ideological construct—'the West seeks to lead people away from the fundamentals of the Islamic Caliphate and what leads to it'.[39] Al-Zawahiri's 2012 statement on the anniversary of the 9/11 attacks combined both with a millenarian vision:[40]

> ... we should work to establish the Caliphate that does not recognise the national state, national religions, borders that were put in place by the occupiers. We should establish a righteous Caliphate that follows the path of the Prophet and believes in the unity of Muslims' lands, encourages brotherhood between Muslims in their religion, makes everyone equal, removes borders that were put in place by the enemies, spreads justice, imposes shari'ah, supports vulnerable people, and liberates all Muslim countries, including the usurped Palestine, and the threatened al-Aqsa.

This more abstract, eschatological version of the Caliphate, without a clear or tangible set of goals, was evident for example in al-Zawahiri's early attempts to reconcile what was happening in Iraq and Syria in 2012 with AQ's framework.

'This will melt all groups and coalitions of jihad in one pot and turn them into the Shari'ah framework and the solid nucleus of the state of the rightly guided Caliphate, God willing.'[41] This statement was striking in that it bore very little relation to what was actually happening on the ground. Further, by giving credence to the idea of the Caliphate, al-Zawahiri and other writers sympathetic to AQ were inadvertently only preparing the groundwork for ISIL's more concrete plans. Meanwhile, ISIL continued to concern itself with the Caliphate's material manifestation. A typical statement from ISIL spokesman al-'Adnani in July 2013: 'we hereby congratulate the dear homeland for the great victory achieved by the heroes of the Islamic State in Baghdad of the Caliphate during the Vanquish the Tyrants raid, the latest such raid carried out as part of the Tearing Down the Walls campaign'.[42]

As AQ saw the jihadist mantle slipping from its grasp, in autumn 2013, al-Zawahiri felt the need to define more exactly the concept of the Caliphate. He attempted to re-shift the narrative in AQ's favour, presenting them as magnanimous losers in the race towards the Caliphate, whose ultimate aims had only ever been the *ummah*'s eventual success:[43]

Al-Qa'ida wants a Caliph who is chosen by the ummah with consensus and free will. If the ummah established an Islamic rule in any of its regions before establishing the Caliphate system, we will be the first to accept whoever the Muslim ummah chose as the imam who fulfils the shari'ah requirements and rules in accordance with the Qur'an and the prophet's sunnah. This is because we have no interest in power; we only seek the establishment of an Islamic rule.

ISIL, meanwhile, were busy turning the abstract millenarian notion of the Caliphate, propounded by AQ and others, into a present, tangible reality. Central to understanding the difference between IS and previous jihadist movements, therefore, is their differing eschatology. IS propaganda uses popular apocalyptic literature in order to present itself as the fulfilment of divine destiny, to an extent and in a way that had not previously been possible. The name of IS's official magazine, *Dabiq*, is chosen for its significance in apocalyptic literature. As the first edition of the magazine stated, the name:

> is taken from the area named Dabiq in the northern countryside of Halab (Aleppo) in Sham. This place was mentioned in a hadith describing some of the events of the Malahim (what is sometimes referred to as Armageddon in English). One of the greatest battles between the Muslims and the crusaders will take place near Dabiq.[44]

IS propaganda videos have quoted Abu Musa'b al-Zarqawi as saying in 2004 that: 'The spark has been lit here in Iraq, and its heat will continue to intensify ... until it burns the crusader armies in Dabiq'.[45] *Dabiq*'s first issue describes how this will be the first step to the conquest of the world, drawing on classical and contemporary apocalyptic traditions.[46]

IS have therefore shifted the jihadist movement from an abstract future eschatology to one realised in the here and now, claiming that 'the signs of victory have appeared'. In doing so, they tend not to engage in detailed political commentary or explanations of ideological subtleties, instead focusing on how the material facts of conquering territory, securing loyalty and support and amassing wealth bear out the realisation of divine prophecy. It is this combination that was used in a statement entitled 'This is the Promise of Allah', which announced IS's Caliphate on 29 June 2014. After reeling off a list of IS's apparent material successes, including implementing the shari'ah punishments and introducing the *jizya* tax, IS spokesman al-'Adnani stated that there was only one religious obligation that remained, and which could no longer be neglected:

> The signs of victory have appeared. Here the flag of the Islamic State, the flag of monotheism, rises and flutters. Its shade covers land from Aleppo to Diyala. The frontlines are defended.... There only remained one matter, a collective obligation

that the ummah sins by abandoning. It is a forgotten obligation. It is the caliphate. It is the caliphate—the abandoned obligation of the era.[47]

Keenly aware that AQ, or indeed other jihadist groups in Syria, were unlikely to accept meekly this self-aggrandising proclamation and assertion of leadership, al-ʿAdnani attempts to demonstrate the legitimacy of the declaration, hoping to expose the hypocrisy of those who might choose to reject such an ostensibly self-evident case for a legitimate Caliphate:

> We clarify to the Muslims that with this declaration of caliphate, it is incumbent upon all Muslims to pledge allegiance to the Caliph Ibrāhīm and support him. The legality of all emirates, groups, states, and organizations, becomes null by the expansion of the caliphate's authority and arrival of its troops to their areas.

> The Caliph Ibrāhīm has fulfilled all the conditions for the caliphate mentioned by the scholars. He was given bayʿah [oath of allegiance] in Iraq by the people of authority in the Islamic State... The land now submits to his order and authority from Aleppo to Diyala. So fear Allah, O slaves of Allah. Listen to your caliph and obey him.

> So rush O Muslims and gather around your caliph, so that you may return as you once were for ages, kings of the earth and knights of war.[48]

In light of these exhortations, which had shrewdly built on the very narrative AQ had propounded for years, al-Zawahiri could do little but look on in impotent rage at his increasing obscurity. In his 2001 autobiography, *Knights Under the Prophet's Banner*, al-Zawahiri had argued that AQ's most important strategic goal was to seize control of a state or part of territory, as 'without achieving this goal our actions will mean nothing'.[49] Now that IS was doing precisely that, al-Zawahiri had been hoisted on his own petard. Finding himself increasingly irrelevant and acknowledging his profound weakness, around early 2015 he appeared to strike a more conciliatory tone: 'Despite the big mistakes of ISIL, if I were in Iraq or Syria I would cooperate with them in killing the crusaders and secularists and Shia even though I don't recognise the legitimacy of their state, because the matter is bigger than that.'[50]

Most significantly, this shift to an eschatology of the here and now means that IS are purporting to sell a chance to participate in building the promised utopian state. These narratives move beyond appeals to violence, and provide other more nuanced motivations to joining the cause, including state-building, joining a community, escaping persecution and enjoying religious freedoms. The establishment of the Caliphate in June 2014 therefore provided compelling alternative narratives to audiences: undertake your own *hijrah* (emigration)—a journey that paralleled that of the Prophet Muhammad;

escape the religious persecution in your own societies; live under Islamic sovereignty and law; help defend the burgeoning state and community; and ultimately restore the state to its long-lost glory. An image from *Dabiq*, issue 11 exemplifies this message: happy brothers in arms are shown with the slogan '*wala' and bara'* (the concept of loyalty to believers and disavowal of disbelievers) versus American Racism' (Figure 1.3). The messaging in *Dabiq* and elsewhere in IS's social media is very focused on presenting idealised images of establishing the 'Islamic State', such as a detailed article on healthcare in the Caliphate in *Dabiq*, issue 9 that could almost be taken from a brochure for any public or private healthcare service (see Figure 1.4).

Seen as a totality, these are some of the main themes in the recent evolution of global jihadist narratives in response to a tumultuous period. The picture is,

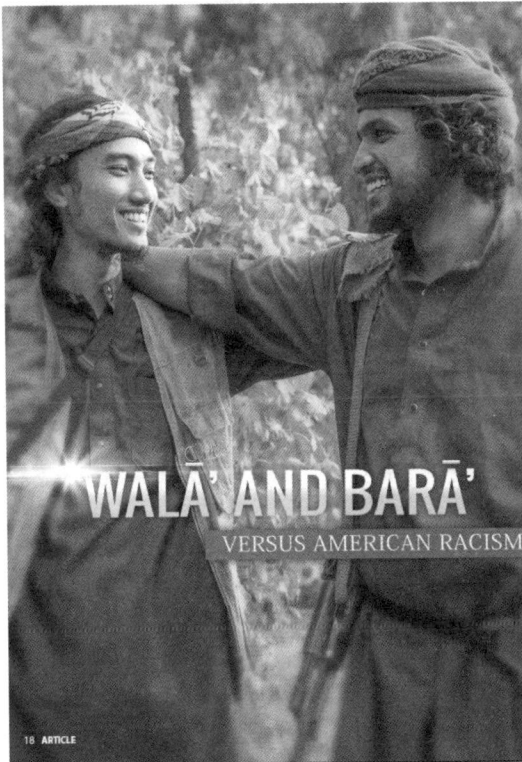

Figure 1.3: Image from *Dabiq*, issue 11

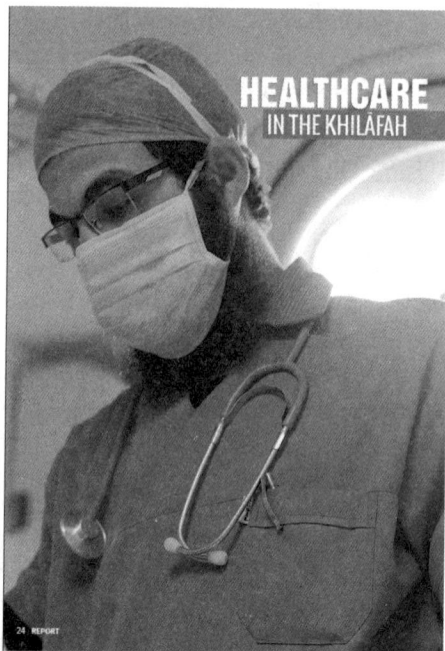

Figure 1.4: Healthcare in the Khilafah (Caliphate)

however, far from uniform across the globe, and the chapters that follow dissect the particularities of how jihadism has transformed in key regions. Indeed, a theme throughout this volume is the tension that has arisen between AQ and IS brands in local and global contexts. Chapters 2 and 3 explore in more depth aspects of the history and leadership of Islamic State, and their divergence from AQ. The next chapters then consider areas of the world where IS have been on the ascendancy in the global battle of ideas (Egypt, Tunisia, Nigeria), other areas where AQ-affiliates have maintained their lead and needed to respond to the challenge of IS (Yemen, the Maghreb), and South Asia, where the Taliban-led jihadist movement has been challenged. In each region, the global jihadist brands have needed to respond and adapt to complex local markets in a time of upheaval, with differing results in each case. Broad themes, sectarianism and radicalisation in the West, are then explored in the final two chapters.

2

THE 'ISLAMIC STATE' AND AL-QAEDA

Nelly Lahoud[1]

The Iraq-based group 'Jama'at al-Tawhid wa-al-Jihad' is the parent group of today's 'Islamic State' and is the only regional jihadist group that was admitted by Osama bin Laden under the al-Qaeda umbrella. Bin Laden and other AQ leaders lived to regret this decision. Much like a trying relationship between a parent and a rebellious adolescent, the group's years under al-Qaeda were difficult for both. This chapter explores the tension in ideology and vision between the two groups, including during the phase when they merged.

The Evolution of the 'Islamic State' through its names

In April 2013, Abu Bakr al-Baghdadi announced that his group, the Islamic State of Iraq (ISI), was thenceforth to be called the Islamic State in Iraq and the Levant (ISIL); he justified the name change on the basis of the group's level of development. In doing so, al-Baghdadi presented an account of the group's evolution, as he and his followers see it, through its name changes over the years. He elaborated that it is 'permissible to cancel the names of jihadist groups and replace them with ones commensurate with their [higher level of] development and nobility ... new names that would make us forget the previous ones despite our affection for them'.[2] In the case of the Iraq-based group, al-Baghdadi explained that when Abu Mus'ab al-Zarqawi, the founder of the group, launched his jihad, he initially did so under the name of 'al-Tawhid wa-al-Jihad', before his group's name changed to 'Qa'idat al-Jihad in Mesopotamia'.[3] This occurred, according to al-Baghdadi, when the group acquired 'a more noble position and higher rank after al-Zarqawi pledged allegiance to Sheikh Usama Bin Laden, the leader of al-Qa'ida'.[4]

In al-Baghdadi's mind, al-Qaeda was certainly not the highest development the group was destined to achieve. As it developed higher in the eyes of its supporters, al-Zarqawi's group again changed its name to 'Majlis Shura al-Mujahidin' when 'the souls of its members grew higher in ranks as they were elevated through jihad'.[5] Then jihad in Iraq, al-Baghdadi continues, reached an even more 'blessed' rank with the declaration of the new name the 'Islamic State of Iraq' (ISI) under the leaderships of Abu 'Umar al-Baghdadi and Abu Hamza al-Misri. Al-Baghdadi proudly remarks that through declaring ISI, these leaders were effectively 'charting a path for us that does not recognise borders, and formulating an [ideological] program that does not discriminate between nations and races'.[6] It was time, he decreed, that ISI and its jihadist brethren, Jabhat al-Nusra, the Syrian-based group, should formally merge, thereby acquiring a higher level of development, to be reflected in the new name, the Islamic State in Iraq and the Levant (ISIL). In his words:

> We commissioned al-Julani, who is one of our soldiers, along with a group, the members of which are ours, and we sent them from Iraq to the Levant so that they may join our cells there. We prepared a work plan and a way forward for them, and we supported them financially and on a monthly basis with half of what is in the treasury. We also sent them men, *muhajirun* and *ansar* [i.e. Syrians and foreign fighters], who are experienced in battle ... thus the authority of the ISI extended to the Levant but we did not make it public for security reasons so that people may see for themselves the truth of this State away from the distortion and falsehood of the media. It is now time that we declare to the people of the Levant and the entire world that JN is but an extension of ISI and part of it ... that is why we now declare that the names 'ISI' and 'JN' are henceforth cancelled, and we combine them under a single name 'The Islamic State in Iraq and the Levant (ISIL).'[7]

As will be discussed below, al-Julani's public rejection of the merger set in motion the acrimonious events that eventually led to al-Qaeda's public dissociation from ISIL. In June 2014, and in a statement entitled 'This is God's Promise', Abu Muhammad al-'Adnani, the spokesman of ISIL, asserted that all the requirements to establish a state have been met. He added, 'Only one matter remains outstanding ... namely, [the establishment of the] *khilafa* (state).'[8] That is why al-'Adnani went on to proclaim 'the establishment of the Islamic caliphate/state', thereby 'annulling "Iraq and the Levant" from the name of the state'. He also announced that the leader of ISIL, Abu Bakr al-Baghdadi, was to be the caliph (*khalifa*). He presented al-Baghdadi to be a descendant of the tribe of Quraysh,[9] one of seven criteria required to qualify for the office of caliph according to classical Sunni scholars.[10] Following al-Baghdadi and al-'Adnani's line of logic, now that the name is ecumenical with the dropping of geographical references, we can expect no further changes to the name of the 'Islamic State'.

Just as the name of the group is considered by its leaders to be closely tied to its identity as it evolved, the name of the group has also been a cause of deep frustration for al-Qaeda (AQ). In February 2014, four months prior to the proclamation of the Caliphate, AQ had released a statement disowning ISIL and its actions, deriding it as the 'group' that calls itself a 'state'.[11] In other words, AQ was indirectly describing ISIL as a group with an aggrandisement complex. In May 2014, al-'Adnani responded and accused Ayman al-Zawahiri, the leader of al-Qaeda, of 'dividing jihadis',[12] dismissing the import of AQ's statement since, in al-'Adnani's words, ISIL 'is not a branch of AQ and it never was one'.[13] He went on to explain that al-Qaeda is a mere organisation, not a state like ISIL.

As the rest of this chapter discusses, the differences over the name reflect a profound ideological divide between IS and AQ, a divide that has existed at least since 1999. In this chapter, the names ISI, ISIL and IS are not used interchangeably; instead, each is used to correspond to the period when the name was used by the group: ISI is used to designate the group between October 2006 and April 2013; ISIL is used to designate the group between April 2013 and June 2014; and IS is used to designate the group since late June 2014 up to the present.

Abu Mus'ab al-Zarqawi and the building of a society (Mujtama')

According to Sayf al-'Adl, one of AQ's military strategists, ideological differences between al-Zarqawi and AQ's leadership were manifest from the start. Sayf relates that when Osama bin Laden and Ayman al-Zawahiri first met al-Zarqawi in Afghanistan in 1999, both of them thought that al-Zarqawi held 'rigid views' in matters of religious doctrine.[14] According to his onetime mentor, the jihadist ideologue Abu Muhammad al-Maqdisi, prior to heading to Afghanistan in 1999, al-Zarqawi's political activities had largely been based in Jordan and revolved around spreading the religious teachings of al-Maqdisi.[15] Al-Zarqawi and al-Maqdisi had met in Peshawar in 1991, and upon their return to Jordan, they led like-minded individuals in spreading al-Maqdisi's writings, which rejected the legitimacy of the political systems that govern Muslim-majority states, including Jordan and Saudi Arabia.[16] Their activities ultimately led to their arrest and imprisonment by Jordanian authorities.[17]

Although bin Laden and al-Zawahiri were reluctant to have an association with al-Zarqawi in 1999, Sayf relates that he convinced them that al-Zarqawi's connections in the Levant might yield dividends in the future.[18] It appears that al-'Adnani was one of these connections; a biography of al-'Adnani posted on a jihadist website claims that he and 35 other Syrians had pledged allegiance to al-Zarqawi in early 2000, before they joined him in Iraq following the US invasion.[19] In 1999, Sayf facilitated the establishment of a training camp in Herat to be run by al-Zarqawi; it was initially funded by a 'brother' from the Hijaz.[20] Perhaps fearing his zealot disposition, AQ did not want to have any official ties with al-Zarqawi then, and Sayf made that clear: 'we do not want from [al-Zarqawi] and those who joined [his group] a complete pledge of allegiance; rather, we want to coordinate and collaborate in the service of common goals'.[21] Al-Maqdisi claims that it was al-Zarqawi who declined to join AQ because bin Laden refused to assign al-Maqdisi's books in AQ's training camps,[22] a claim that al-Zarqawi refuted.[23]

At any rate, within weeks of setting up the camp, Sayf came to realise that al-Zarqawi was not simply acquiring military training, he was also keen on building a complete social structure (*mujtama' mutakamil*).[24] The embryo of al-Zarqawi's society began to take shape in Afghanistan, but Sayf relates that al-Zarqawi had always looked to Iraq as the place where his society would grow and expand. Sayf also relates that al-Zarqawi had established contact with the Sunni Kurdish group Ansar al-Islam which had a presence in northern Iraq, a contact that later proved useful when he had to flee Afghanistan. Thus, when US forces invaded Afghanistan following the 9/11 attacks, it was logical for al-Zarqawi to head to Iraq. The choice of Iraq was not simply because, as Sayf put it, 'we had anticipated ... that the Americans would inevitably make the mistake of invading it',[25] but also because al-Zarqawi wanted to duplicate an episode in Islamic history, with Mosul at its centre. In the words of Sayf, al-Zarqawi:

... was impressed by the personality of the unique Islamic military commander Nur al-Din Zangi [d. 1174] who led the movement for the liberation and [political] change that were to be completed by Saladin [d. 1193] ... I think that what he read about Nur al-Din and the launching of his campaign from Mosul in Iraq [to liberate the al-Aqsa mosque from the Crusades] played a large role in influencing al-Zarqawi to move to Iraq following the fall of the Islamic Emirate in Afghanistan.[26]

Al-Zarqawi managed to move to Iraq after the fall of the Taliban, but did not live long enough to launch a Nur al-Din-like campaign from Mosul. In 2014, al-Baghdadi appears to have taken on the mission that al-Zarqawi had started. On 4 July, when Americans were celebrating their Independence Day, al-Baghdadi made his first public début in Mosul's Great al-Nuri Mosque, built in the twelfth century by none other than Nur al-Din;[27] the choice of place was perhaps designed to pay homage to al-Zarqawi.

Al-Zarqawi's group began operating in Iraq under the name 'al-Tawhid wa-al-Jihad' in 2003 and announced itself in April 2004. Among the operations for which the group claimed responsibility was the operation that killed Sergio Vieiro de Mello, the UN Secretary General Special Representative in Iraq on 19 August 2003.[28] Thus when in October 2004 al-Zarqawi pledged allegiance to bin Laden, seeking to join al-Qaeda, he had already made his presence felt on the militant landscape of Iraq. In the meantime, AQ had suffered serious blows in 2003;[29] thus if in 1999 AQ could afford to set conditions on al-Zarqawi and collaborate with him from a distance and on its own terms, in 2004 bin Laden was willing to compromise AQ's standards and accept him into the fold.[30] In so doing, al-Tawhid wa-al-Jihad acquired a new name, AQ in Mesopotamia (Tanzim al-Qaeda fi Bilad al-Rafidayn).

Judging by the tone of the intercepted/leaked letters by the leaders of AQ, al-Zawahiri and 'Atiyyatullah al-Libi, the inclusion of al-Zarqawi's group under the umbrella of AQ was a regretful one. Al-Libi reminded him that he was a battlefield commander and needed to consult with the leadership of AQ before taking unilateral decisions, not least those that concern declaring a war against Shiites and expanding the war to neighbouring countries. Al-Zawahiri gently but firmly questioned al-Zarqawi's attacks against Iraq's Shiites, reminding him that Iran holds more than 100 AQ detainees and would likely want to respond with retaliatory measures.[31]

Notwithstanding the concerns over al-Zarqawi's statements and actions, AQ's leaders limited their criticisms of the group to internal communiqués and chose not to make it public. It is not clear why in January 2006 al-Zarqawi changed the name of the group to Majlis Shura al-Mujahidin fi al-'Iraq (the

Jihadis' Advisory Council in Iraq). It is possible that he could not ignore the plethora of Sunni militant groups that emerged following the de-Ba'thification of Iraq, or perhaps he was under pressure from AQ to exert some effort towards unity among jihadists, or a combination of both. At any rate, the new name initially brought together six Sunni militant groups,[32] and others joined later. The Advisory Council was headed by a certain 'Abdallah bin Rashid al-Baghdadi, who is reported to be none other than Abu 'Umar al-Baghdadi, who would become the leader of the Islamic State of Iraq.[33] However,[34] it is not reported that al-Zarqawi pledged allegiance to him.[35] Indeed, one finds many statements that were released by the media committee of the Advisory Council, but still bearing the signature of AQ in Mesopotamia, suggesting at least that the latter had a degree of continued autonomy. It is unlikely that he joined the Advisory Council to secede from AQ. If he did, his wife did not think so when she eulogised her husband, welcoming his martyrdom and describing him as 'nothing more than a soldier in one of the ranks of [bin Laden]'s armies'.[36]

The March to 'Statehood'

The killing of al-Zarqawi in June 2006 did not cause his successors to give up on his plan of building a society (*mujtama'*); indeed, they developed more ambitious designs while maintaining the spirit of his vision. Abu Hamza al-Muhajir succeeded al-Zarqawi, and his initial statement suggests that he saw his group to be loyal to AQ, assuring bin Laden that 'we are at your beck and call and at your disposal'.[37] Yet within four months, Abu Hamza pledged allegiance to Abu 'Umar al-Baghdadi's newly formed group the 'Islamic State of Iraq' (ISI), thereby submitting the 'army of al-Qa'ida', as Abu Hamza put it, to the authority of ISI.[38] It is reported that both Abu Hamza and Abu 'Umar had trained in Afghanistan and joined al-Zarqawi's group in Iraq. It is also reported that it was Abu 'Umar al-Baghdadi who served as the intellectual engine of ISI.[39] If it is true that he was the head of the Advisory Council that al-Zarqawi joined, then his influence on the Iraq-based group pre-dates his assumption of its leadership in 2006. The so-called state did not want to limit its activities to militancy, and in April 2007 it announced the appointment of ten ministers, including ministers for health, oil, agriculture and fisheries.[40] In other words, ISI conceived of itself to be in the business of governance.

The declaration of a state in 2006 did not meet the approval of AQ, and judging by internal communiqués, AQ's leaders were highly critical of Abu

Hamza and Abu 'Umar. According to a statement released by al-Zawahiri in May 2014, the proclamation of the ISI was made without any consultation with AQ's leadership, not even with bin Laden.[41] Al-Zawahiri seems keen to highlight AQ's displeasure with Abu Hamza and Abu 'Umar, so much so that he cited an anonymous letter highly critical of both leaders which was captured during the raid that killed bin Laden and was published by the Combating Terrorism Center at West Point, after declassification.[42] The letter which al-Zawahiri cites highlights the 'political mistakes' of Abu 'Umar, and refers to him and Abu Hamza as 'extremists', 'repulsive' and 'lack[ing] wisdom'.[43]

US and Iraqi forces killed Abu 'Umar and Abu Hamza in April 2010, and Abu Bakr al-Baghdadi assumed the leadership of ISI; he has been in charge of the Iraq-based group since then. The challenge that the declaration of the ISI posed to AQ, however, did not end with their death. Two serious implications resulted as a consequence of Abu Hamza's pledge of allegiance to Abu 'Umar. The first concerns the very notion of declaring an 'Islamic state': this entails elaborate conditions, including providing security to the populace residing in the territory of the 'state' and making them accountable to good governance, an accountability that ISI could hardly deliver at that stage, not least given the occupation of Iraq by US forces at the time. It is for such reasons that, in his private communiqués captured in Abbottabad, bin Laden mocked al-Qaeda in the Arabian Peninsula (AQAP) for wanting to declare an Islamic state in Yemen,[44] and urged Somalia's al-Shabab not to take that route.[45] Indeed, al-Qaeda's statement disowning ISIL does not admit that it represents a 'state'; instead, it refers to ISIL as the 'group' that calls itself a 'state'. The criticism is made more apparent when the statement derisively remarks that 'we do not hasten to declare emirates and states ... that we impose on people, then declare whoever disapproves of such entities to be a rebel (*kharij*) [against whom it is lawful to fight]'.[46]

The second serious implication pertains to Abu Hamza's oath to Abu 'Umar when he pledged: 'I hereby enlist under your direct leadership twelve thousand fighters who constitute the army of al-Qa'ida'.[47] Did ISI cease to be under the leadership of al-Qaeda in 2006, and indeed did the pledge by Abu Hamza effectively subordinate bin Laden's authority to that of al Baghdadi? Of course, bin Laden never pledged allegiance to Abu 'Umar, and according to al-Zawahiri's May 2014 letter, Abu Hamza wrote to the leadership of AQ to assure them that the group continued to consider itself to be part of AQ.[48] Nevertheless, because bin Laden did not go public and discredit the group, ISI became a *fait accompli* 'state', acting without consultation with AQ and even against its directions. In an internal communiqué dated early 2011, the American jihadist Adam Gadahn advised the leadership:

> it is necessary that al-Qaʻida publicly announces that it severs its organisational ties with the Islamic State of Iraq, and [to make known] that the relationship between its leadership and that of the State [i.e. ISI] have not existed for several years, and that the decision to declare a State was taken without consultation with the leadership, and this [ill-considered] innovative affirmation (*qarar ijtihadi*) led to divisions among jihadis and their supporters inside and outside Iraq.[49]

Parting ways with al-Qaeda

Why did it take so long for al-Qaeda to disown ISI/ISIL publicly, if the problems between them began in 2005 and worsened in 2006? As noted earlier, in April 2013, al-Baghdadi unilaterally proclaimed the founding of ISIL by declaring a merger between his group and that of Jabhat al-Nusra (JN) in Syria. JN, it should be noted, was the first jihadist group to emerge in Syria in January 2012,[50] and in its nascent phase, it was praised even by non-jihadists for its effective conduct on the battlefield, and its dealings with the populace.[51] It was not organic to the Syrian revolution; instead, its members had fought alongside ISI in Iraq and their move to Syria was initially funded by ISI.[52] The leader of JN, Abu Muhammad al-Julani, publicly rejected the merger and pledged allegiance directly to al-Zawahiri.[53]

In June 2013, al-Zawahiri intervened, annulling the merger and therefore the very concept of ISIL, and appointed Abu Khalid al-Suri—who had fought in Afghanistan and was closely connected to the jihadist strategist Abu Musʻab al-Suri and Ayman al-Zawahiri[54]—a member of the Syrian militant group Harakat Ahrar al-Sham, to serve as an arbitrator between the two groups.[55] Al-Zawahiri's intervention was in the form of a private communiqué to the leaders of the ISI and JN, but it was leaked to al-Jazeera as a typed letter. When ISI continued to operate under its new name, ISIL, and debates among jihadists surrounding the authenticity of the letter ensued, an audio statement of the same letter, with the unmistakable voice of al-Zawahiri, was leaked to al-Jazeera in November 2013, leaving no doubt as to its authorship.

Several reasons may have caused al-Baghdadi to make this unilateral decision: it is possible that he was envious of JN's stardom in the jihadist world, and he wanted to make it known to the world that gratitude is owed to his group; it is also possible that he was worried about his investment in JN, seeing that it was collaborating with militant groups whose agenda was nationalist rather than jihadist;[56] or he believed that the time was ripe to expand his 'state' into Syria. Judging by what happened later, expanding the 'state' would not only make his divorce from AQ public, but it would also fulfil the vision that al-Zarqawi and his successors had set in motion for the jihadist landscape. That is to say, the jihadism of ISIL/IS is not designed simply to fight against the unjust global establishment, as it was with AQ, but it is aimed at creating a just establishment of its own to deliver what al-Zarqawi had started.

Al-Zawahiri may have sensed that the merger that al-Baghdadi was imposing on JN amounted to a coup against AQ, hence his intervention to annul ISIL. Before long, the public dispute developed into a bloody conflict. It is not clear which side initiated the transgression: although ISIL received the lion's share of criticisms in the mainstream media,[57] it is also the case that statements by ISIL in early January 2014 suggest that its members were being harassed, imprisoned and constrained in their movements by other militant groups in Syria.[58] The situation took a turn for the worse in December 2013,[59] when ISIL kidnapped and then killed Abu Sa'd al-Hadrami, the leader of JN in the province of al-Raqqa.[60] The geographical importance of al-Raqqa cannot be exaggerated: its proximity to the border with Turkey makes it critical for the flow of foreign fighters; its economic prospect is assured, given that it holds oil reserves and the Euphrates River runs through it; and it is also in the middle of five strategic provinces (Aleppo, Hasaka, Dayr al-Zur, Hums and Hama), hence serving as a focal point for military expansion. ISIL admitted that it was behind al-Hadrami's killing, justifying it on account of his apostasy (*radda*). The ISIL statement did not provide supporting details.[61] JN claims that al-Hadrami had been duped into pledging allegiance to ISIL, but when al-Zawahiri made his judgement in favour of JN and when al-Hadrami 'saw for himself the crimes and torture of the innocents [ordered] by the [ISIL] governor of al-Raqqa [as a form of punishment] for even the most minor and dubious errors and pettiest causes, he returned to JN dissociating himself from ISIL'.[62] The events allowed ISIL/IS to consolidate control over al-Raqqa.

The other key event that made the divide between JN and ISIL irreparable was the killing of one of the leaders of Ahrar al-Sham, Abu Khalid al-Suri, in February 2014. As noted earlier, al-Zawahiri had nominated al Suri to serve as arbitrator in the disputes between ISIL and JN. In January 2014, al-Suri released a public statement in which he accused ISIL of 'crimes and erroneous practices in the name of jihad'.[63] He further decried the way in which he believed ISIL was degrading those who have 'liberated the country', behaving as if it was a real state while other groups were mere 'platoons'.[64] Soon thereafter, a suicide bomber assassinated al-Suri.[65] The Saudi cleric 'Abdallah al-Mhisni claimed on his Twitter account that prior to his death, al-Suri had told him that ISIL had threatened to send five suicide bombers to kill him.[66]

The assassination of al-Suri created shock waves in the jihadist world. In his eulogy, JN leader Abu Muhammad al-Julani remarked that al-Suri had fought the Syrian regime some 30 years before, which suggests that he might have been a member of the Syrian Muslim Brotherhood that bore the wrath of Hafiz al-Assad's regime in the 1980s, particularly in Hama.[67] Al-Julani also reported that al-Suri knew bin Laden and al-Zawahiri well, as well as 'his jihad companion Sheikh Abu Mus'ab al-Suri,' the renowned jihadist strategist.[68] In a phone conversation from prison in Jordan, the Palestinian-born ideologue Abu Qatada al-Filastini almost choked from distress as he was describing the importance of al-Suri and the respect he commanded in the jihadist world, believing that his death was the worst 'that has devastated us since [the killing] of Bin Laden.'[69] Although ISIL denied any responsibility in al-Suri's killing,[70] one has to wonder whether it was in retaliation to the public statement that AQ had just released and in which it disowned ISIL.

What was the difference between the 'Islamic State' of 2006 and that of 2014?

President Barack Obama remarked that 'ISIL is certainly not a state' according to international law.[71] But while Obama's statement is designed to cut it down to size and highlight that it is nothing more than a terrorist organisation, the group projects itself otherwise. To be sure, IS does not seek membership of the United Nations, to be part of the global community of nation-states. Indeed, it believes the world order to be illegitimate and seeks to redraw today's world map and create a global Islamic state, a Caliphate, akin to that which pre-dates the modern state system. Accordingly, the group is intent on pursuing the acquisition of additional territories beyond Iraq and Syria. Indeed, the designated caliph's address on the occasion of the start of the holy month of Ramadan promises that if the 'soldiers of IS' remain united and commit themselves to being the 'guardians of religion,' they 'shall conquer Rome and seize the earth.'[72]

Yet from a legal perspective, why should the 'Islamic state' of 2014 be any different from that which was proclaimed in 2006 (i.e. the Islamic State of Iraq) or that which was announced in 2013 (i.e. ISIL)? One would think that the intent of establishing an Islamic state is intrinsically universal, an issue highlighted by the jihadist pundit Abu al-Fadl Madi, an opponent of IS. He questioned whether there is anything legally meaningful about it from an Islamic standpoint, and forewarned that even a 'limited air bombing campaign could deny this caliphate all its resources'.[73]

It is perhaps more important to ask what IS could deliver by way of outcomes. An internal communiqué to ISI designed to present an internal critique of the Iraq-based group in the years 2006–7 suggests that the announcement of a state was used by many of the group's leaders 'to cover up their weaknesses (in the military and security [domains]) and took to convincing themselves and others that they should [focus on] building a state and its institutions without paying due attention to military and security matters'.[74] The author laments that the announcement of the state caused that generation of leaders to be 'deluded' by a supposed power in the form of a state.[75] In his mind, this led to a complacency such that:

> we [i.e. ISI] switched roles [with the Americans] ... we virtually became an organized army whose movements are known ... to everyone while America turned into a guerrilla warfare [group] working to assassinate the leaders and the jihadist elites ... we lost the cities, then the villages and [even] the desert became a dangerous shelter ... and found ourselves in a closed circle.[76]

Judging by ISI's internal critique, the declaration of a state in 2006 led to the near annihilation of the Iraq-based group in 2007–8.

The Iraq-based group, however, was resilient enough to survive in Iraq, not through governance, but through sporadic terrorist operations. Its misfortunes changed when militancy in Syria allowed it to expand and grow, not least through the flow of foreign fighters who flocked to Syria from different parts of the world. The group's growth in Syria coincided with the continued political sectarianism in Iraq which alienated Iraq's Arab Sunnis, culminating in the latter's violent clash with and the ultimate expelling of the Iraqi army from Sunni-majority areas, thereby creating a fragile security environment which ISIL was happy to exploit.[77]

Concluding remarks: The ideological divide and more

According to al-'Adnani, the heart of the dispute between his group and AQ concerned the latter's understanding of religion becoming 'twisted' (*din a'waj*) and the deviation in its path (*manhaj inharaf*). He accuses AQ of abandoning jihad and championing 'peace' as a method, and of having swapped the vocabulary of 'jihad' and *'tawhid'* (passion for divine unity) with nationalist expressions, such as 'revolution', 'popularity' and *da'wa* (preaching). Perhaps the most profound criticism he levelled against al-Zawahiri was to accuse him of embracing the 'Sykes—Picot' agreement (hatched by the imperialist powers in 1916) when he asked in his letter that ISI should limit its activities to Iraq, leaving JN to be in charge of Syria.[78] Of course al-Zawahiri did not embrace the Sykes—Picot agreement, but the division of labour he allotted to JN and ISIL pointed to geographical borders that he himself had declared to be illegitimate.

Although al-'Adnani's accusation is directed against al-Zawahiri's leadership, assuring the followers of ISIL that the group is faithful to the path that was set by Osama bin Laden, in another statement that followed, he couldn't help but remark on the superiority of his group over AQ. Addressing himself to al-Zawahiri, al-'Adnani stated: 'should you ever be in a position to set foot in ISIL's Islamic territory, you shall have no choice but to pledge allegiance to it and serve as a soldier to its Amir/leader'.[79] In case al-Zawahiri did not fully comprehend his inferior status in the eyes of ISIL, al-'Adnani explained that he is nothing more than a leader of an organisation and it is not right for a state like ISIL to pledge allegiance to an organisation.[80] The title of al-'Adnani's statement is "Udhran Amiru al-Qa'ida", which roughly translates to 'I beg your forgiveness, leader of AQ'. In Arabic, the title is meant to convey a forewarning that its author is going to raise some criticisms that will be couched as constructive suggestions. But that was far from what al-'Adnani had in mind; instead, he ended his statement with an ultimatum to al-Zawahiri: 'persist with your error ... and let the bloodshed among jihadis continue or admit your mistake and correct it'.[81]

Beyond IS's emphasis on the importance of establishing a state and its superiority complex over AQ, it has also sought to transform the mindset of jihadists who support it. The role that brutality plays is key to the identity that IS is seeking to instil as part of this transformation, which is meant to engender a new jihadist mindset. To be clear, IS does not hold a monopoly on brutality, and even states that champion human rights are known to have engaged in similar practices. Rather, IS's brutality is distinct from that carried out by AQ by virtue of seeking to project it as a norm from which virtue emanates, whereas AQ's leaders did not deny that their operations resulted in the killing of innocent civilians. Although AQ had no qualms justifying their *irhab* (terror) against their enemies as being lawful in Islam, they nevertheless projected themselves as regretful terrorists. They championed the causes of the underdog and saw themselves as their defenders, whereas IS sees nothing regretful about its actions, and the underdog theme seems to have taken the backseat in its discourse. If the underdog wants to be saved, s/he has the obligation to emigrate (*hijra*) to the Islamic State where s/he can aspire to be the bully and do unto others what s/he did not want others to do unto her/him. Thus, if AQ's leaders wanted to show that they and their followers were willing to die for the cause, IS's leaders are keen to highlight that they want to kill for the cause.

3

AYMAN AL-ZAWAHIRI AND THE RISE OF ISIL

Donald Holbrook

Introduction

As a jihadi leader and ideologue, Ayman al-Zawahiri has proven a prolific author of statements, essays and other publications written to elucidate and publicise al-Qaeda's agenda against the backdrop of unfolding events. By 2005 he had overtaken Osama bin Laden in number of communiqués issued on behalf of al-Qaeda each year and invariably offered far denser and more detailed dissections of particular events than al-Qaeda's erstwhile *amir*. Many have indeed argued that al-Zawahiri is better suited as a thinker and deliberator than as the public face of a jihadist movement. Montasser al-Zayyat, who knew al-Zawahiri from his involvement in jihadism in Egypt around the time of Anwar Sadat's assassination, noted that 'despite his strong opinions, he has always been humble, never interested in seizing the limelight of leadership'.[1] These tendencies have become more overt since the death of bin Laden in May 2011.

Unfortunately for al-Qaeda, the death of its charismatic leader coincided with a wave of political uprisings in the Middle East and North Africa (MENA) that together presented a fundamental crisis of legitimacy and, in the long run, spawned rival jihadist entities that would challenge al-Qaeda's appeal among Islamist militant sympathisers around the world. Studying translations of al-Zawahiri's communicative output,[2] this chapter focuses on the way in which he responded to these challenges, using those methods with which he seems most comfortable: the issuance of public communiqués, essays and video statements directed at affected audiences and disseminated via the internet.

This chapter is split into five sections. The first reviews these statements in the context of MENA uprisings and the rise of the Islamic State in Iraq and the Levant (ISIL) from the remnants of al-Qaeda's troublesome pseudo-franchise in Iraq. The second focuses on the aggregate narrative of al-Zawahiri's statements in relation to the MENA uprisings. The third section discusses the way in which these statements framed the rise of ISIL in light of global jihadism in general and the MENA region in particular and expands briefly upon ISIL's rhetorical response. The fourth discusses how the tensions between al-Qaeda senior leadership (AQSL) and ISIL highlight questions regarding legitimate leadership of jihadist vanguards, the role of public opinion in that equation and the way in which al-Zawahiri has sought to exploit and address those challenges. The final section concludes by considering the particulars of al-Zawahiri's most recent discursive emphases in light of his public rhetoric to date, in order to highlight the evolution and, at times, contradictions of this narrative.

AQSL and crises of the MENA region

In a 2007 report on 'Leadership Schisms in Al-Qa'ida', researchers at the West Point Combating Terrorism Center observed that the organisation had 'consistently put its ability to inspire a broader movement over the development of its organisational capacities to pursue strategic military goals'. 'Branding' had prevailed over 'bureaucracy'. Bin Laden and al-Zawahiri in particular, the authors argued, 'preferred press releases over battlefield preparedness'.[3]

This apparent prioritisation was made clear as al-Zawahiri reflected upon the life of bin Laden in his first statement as leader of al-Qaeda. The 'noble knight', al-Zawahiri argued, had seen as his first priority the need to incite the *ummah* to jihad, and his message had been received from east to west and all over the world.[4] Al-Zawahiri himself, as noted, has placed great emphasis on disseminating his thoughts and ideas via different media, primarily online. Figure 3.1 provides an overview of this output for a ten-year period between

2005 and 2014. The focus here is on the statements issued from 2011 onwards where al-Zawahiri grappled with the impact of the MENA uprisings. There was a visible hike in published statements in the first two years of this period, as al-Zawahiri (and other AQSL leaders) raced to respond to these seminal events affecting the key target audience of this message. The number dipped, however, with the emergence of a new and rival jihadist entity in the form of ISIL or the 'Islamic State' organisation.

These statements and publications covered a wide range of topics and focused on a variety of regions, against the backdrop of a new socio-political reality that appeared to be emerging in the aftermath of the uprisings. Figure 3.2 places these statements on a timeline that incorporates key events of the post-revolutionary epoch.

Al-Zawahiri's initial public response to the uprisings came in February 2011 in the form of an address titled 'A Message of Hope and Glad Tidings to our People in Egypt', for which allied jihadist media entities such as the 'Global Islamic Media Front' quickly provided translations in English, French and other languages. Al-Zawahiri ultimately went on to present nine more iterations of these 'Glad Tidings' communiqués over the next sixteen months.

Whilst predominantly focused on his native Egypt, al-Zawahiri used these messages to address audiences across the region, including Tunisia, Jordan, Yemen, Libya, Palestine and Syria. Parts of the 'Glad Tidings' series moved beyond a dedicated focus on the MENA uprisings, meanwhile, to incorporate global and, particularly, US-centric issues. The eighth iteration, for example, contained direct threats to harm the hostage Warren Weinstein, a US contrac-

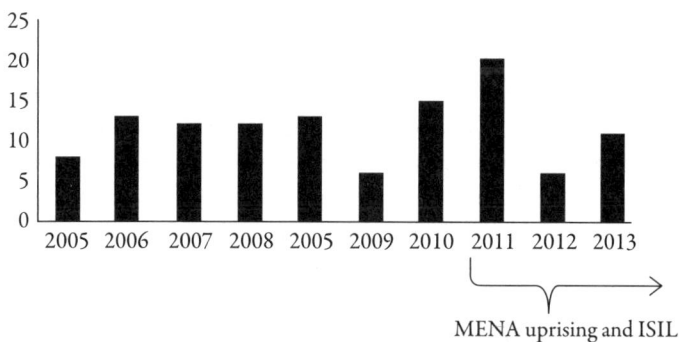

Figure 3.1: Ayman al-Zawahiri AQ statements

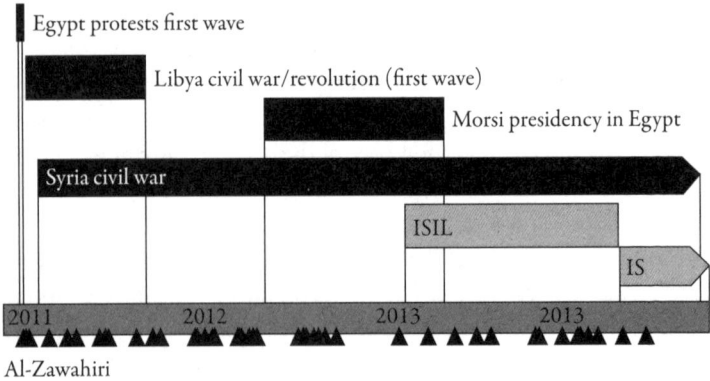

Figure 3.2: Al-Zawahiri statements during MENA uprisings and rise of ISIL 2011–14

tor kidnapped by al-Qaeda in Lahore in August 2011, if the Obama administration committed 'acts of stupidity'.[5]

Several messages were dedicated to developments in other specified countries, such as Tunisia (e.g. 'O People of Tunisia, Support Your Shar'iah', 10 June 2012), Yemen (e.g. 'Yemen: Between a fugitive puppet and his new replacement', 15 May 2012) and Israel/Palestine (e.g. 'Sixty-Five Years since the Establishment of the Occupation State Israel', June 2013). Statements covering (fully or in part) the situation in Syria, in turn, became increasingly prominent as the civil war in the country deepened.

Al-Zawahiri also dedicated statements during this period to particular topics such as democracy or the need to re-emphasise the notion of *tawheed*. Interposed with this politically-focused narrative were eulogies of fallen martyrs and, in particular, reflections of life with Osama bin Laden in a series titled 'Days with the Imam'. Re-emphasising, even claiming ownership over, the legacy of bin Laden seemed increasingly acute with the rise of ISIL, which glorified the late al-Qaeda leader too, whilst developing an agenda independent from al-Zawahiri's publicly articulated wishes and denouncing—even mocking—him through its own propaganda.

The last statement covered in the timeline in Figure 3.2 was a joint statement featuring al-Zawahiri as a confident leader of an organisation that had just opened up a new franchise in South Asia, amidst growing preoccupation in the popular press with the increasing prowess of ISIL in the Levant.

Al-Zawahiri has sought to highlight the significance of two of his publications for the *ummah* that offered, he argued, key guidelines for those who were both affected by the turmoil and eager to improve their temporal and spiritual state. These were his 'Document for the Support of Islam' from November 2012 and 'General Guidelines for the Work of a Jihadi', published in September 2013. Both were unusually succinct and accessible as far as al-Zawahiri's output is concerned and were intended to appeal to a broad audience. Implicitly, the former publication served as a reiteration of al-Qaeda's core agenda in relation to the immediate fall-out from the MENA uprisings, whilst the latter can be seen as a direct response to the rise of ISIL.

Al-Zawahiri and the MENA Uprisings

The MENA uprisings undermined al-Qaeda's core narrative in four fundamental ways.[6]

(1) They showed that the authoritarian regimes in the region could be displaced through public uprising (and resultant pressure on state security services in Egypt, for example) rather than via selective and clandestine jihadism.

(2) Although the uprisings have since contributed to more widespread confrontation and militancy, they were at the time less focused on the use of violence than envisaged in the AQSL discourse.

(3) For al-Zawahiri especially—who had written about the need to topple secular regimes in Egypt for decades—the uprisings appeared, particularly with the subsequent but brief emancipation of the Muslim Brotherhood, to weaken the grievance-focused call to arms by removing some of the chief belligerents.

(4) The uprisings, based particularly on events in Tunisia from where they first spread, raised hopes that politics and society would undergo fundamental changes towards democratisation and gender equality, with concomitant improvement in relations with the West and general stability in the region.

Such developments, of course, would constitute the very antithesis to the AQSL agenda.

In short, the AQSL core narrative seemed dated and its fundamental prognosis proved irrelevant in light of these tumultuous events, at least to begin with. Al-Zawahiri's challenge in the aftermath of the uprisings, therefore, was to exploit the ensuing turmoil and disillusionment in order to frame the revolutions and their aftermath in accordance with the AQSL master narrative.

This master narrative[7] presents violent jihad in the service of God as a constant battle until the mythical Islamist empire has been delivered, simultaneously achieving victory over local and global adversaries, vices and irreligious ideologies whilst establishing absolute social justice based on direct application of scripture and religious law. The MENA uprisings in turn were framed in this context: they presented opportunities and challenges on the road to achieving these ultimate objectives.

Al-Zawahiri's initial response to the uprisings, therefore, was to present them as merely the first step, the initial spark that would have to ignite a far more profound jihadist resurgence aimed at targeting both 'inner corruption' and 'outer invasion'.[8] Internal societal issues and external power-political issues were therefore woven together into a seemingly perpetual grievance narrative which remained equally pronounced in the immediate aftermath of the uprisings.[9] Religiosity was a predictably prominent component of this narrative. Bin Laden, in his last statement, argued that the revolutions were not for 'food and clothing'. They were a far more profound rejection of corruption, indignity and suffering: a cry for Islamic social justice.[10] Al-Zawahiri continued this thread, offering, as usual, more detail. Speaking at length about the *ummah's* territorial integrity and constitutional, legal and judicial reform (especially in post-revolution Egypt), he argued that nothing—in essence—had changed. The old system was still entrenched in the form of a powerful military hierarchy which ensured that treaties with Israel continued to be respected and shari'ah clauses in the constitution continued to be qualified to such an extent that they were rendered purely cosmetic.[11] These dual narrative themes of outer invasion and inner corruption have continued throughout the post-revolutionary period. Al-Qaeda's agenda is both global and deeply—but vaguely—puritanical, which offers plenty of opportunities for criticism and caution.

In the immediate aftermath of the uprisings, for example, the citizens of Saudi Arabia were criticised for failing to match the fervour of their Arab brethren and rise up against family rule[12] whilst those who had taken to the streets elsewhere in the region were warned against the perils of further reliance on mass participation in politics and democratic elections that undermined shari'ah. Condemnation of democracy as a form of vice and anti-Islamic practice is a permanent theme of the AQSL master narrative, but these references became considerably more prominent in al-Zawahiri's output after the uprisings.[13] On the global scene, even if Islamist militant forces in the MENA region could consolidate their power, al-Zawahiri argued, they would still need to take on America and its allies, who were seen as global power brokers for anti-Islamic sentiments worldwide.[14] What was the point of revolution if these issues were left untouched?

For al-Qaeda, the rise to power of the Muslim Brotherhood arguably presented greater problems than the initial revolutions themselves. Al-Zawahiri had been very critical of the Brotherhood and its offshoots such as Hamas for some time, but Brotherhood governments could never be unequivocally condemned or presented as legitimate targets. Brotherhood rule would offer plenty of opportunities to complain and bicker, but could never form part of a conspiratorial rallying call to arms. The Muslim Brotherhood had embraced democracy, which al-Zawahiri detests, and embraced compromise, but they were still Islamists who had spawned revered figures of jihad such as Abdullah Azzam.

Early on in the process of democratisation in Tunisia, al-Zawahiri warned against the spread of a 'modern-day disease' in the form of Westernised Islam void of jihad.[15] Later, as Mohammed Morsi emerged as the president of Egypt, al-Zawahiri focused on two interrelated themes: the precarious process of reform, and continuity of the old order in the form of the Supreme Council of the Armed Forces.

Constitutional and legislative reform was a prominent theme in al-Zawahiri's response to the uprisings already in 2011, but continued throughout the period whilst being adapted to changing circumstances on the ground. Early messages emphasised the perils of entrenching Western-style multiparty democracy in law.[16] Later, whilst the new government in Tunisia was condemned, the Muslim Brotherhood in Egypt was admonished for failing to use its newly acquired executive power to codify the exclusive authority of shari'ah. The Brotherhood had quickly realised that redrafting the Egyptian Constitution would require extensive compromise, which provided al-Zawahiri and other Islamist extremists with plenty of opportunities to decry the dilution of religious law.[17] On the eve of Mohammed Morsi's presidency, al-Zawahiri issued a lengthy statement bemoaning the lack of progress in post-revolution Egypt and beyond, emphasising these legal and constitutional matters. These issues, he argued, were illustrative of a long legacy of subjugation in the Middle East and North Africa, from European colonialism through to more contemporary domination of America and Western democratic legal norms. The Muslim Brotherhood was in power, but temporal supremacy over religious authority was yet to be challenged. A Christian or a Jew could ascend to the height of executive power in Egypt, whilst a Sudanese

Muslim could not, because of the borders imposed by the European colonial powers after they conspired to bring down the Ottoman Caliphate.[18] Later, al-Zawahiri mocked the Brotherhood's attempts at strengthening what limited '*shari'ah* guarantee clauses' could be found in the Egyptian Constitution for continuing to allow all manner of man-made legal norms that contradicted scripture and the spirit of Islamic law, as he saw it.[19]

The revolution, therefore, had to continue and be 'corrected'[20] and 'reclaimed',[21] even where Islamists had managed to gain power. After all, al-Zawahiri asked in a statement from spring 2013, what had the uprisings really achieved? New rulers had taken over but many, he insisted, had been secretly appointed by the same occupation powers that continued to subjugate the region. Islamic movements had failed to achieve meaningful change and they had capitulated in face of an established military elite that retained old power balances and fomented secularism and corruption.[22] These 'military-secularists'[23] had even managed to co-opt much of the religious establishment through bribery or coercion. The culprits, the generals and the military-industrial complex, had been reared on American aid.[24] In Egypt there were 'pretend' Islamists, he cautioned, such as followers of al-Nour party and its founder Yasser al-Borhamy. They were not Salafis but 'Sisi-ists'.[25] They were, in fact, much like the Saudi Royal family: religious on the surface but Americanised at the core.[26] 'Saudi money has many mouths in Egypt and many hands,' al-Zawahiri grumbled, 'some of which are tyrannical and some have no religion, while others are bearded but hypocritical.'[27] The corruptors, therefore, were both local and external, whilst America remained at the heart of this nexus. The corruption itself, moreover, was not only of the tangible sort, as represented for example by a domineering secular military establishment, but also ideational, in the form of global consumerism, which had replaced Arab nationalism as the main disease to plague the region. The uprisings had done nothing to challenge these forces.

The solution that al-Zawahiri offered borrowed, again, from the master narrative which the al-Qaeda leadership has formulated over the years. The *ummah*, al-Zawahiri argued, ought to unite behind the Islamic monotheistic principle whilst taking on external foes and their local lackeys, as well as the unpalatable norms and values that they espoused. Al-Zawahiri articulated these sentiments in an unusually concise communiqué in November 2012, titled 'Document for the Support of Islam'. This statement, which al-Zawahiri has referred to on a number of subsequent occasions, urged Muslims to unite around several key precepts and objectives, including Muslim territorial sovereignty and resource protection, freedom from external influence, implementation of shari'ah rule and supporting the global oppressed. The document's scope was global, ambitious and vague, thus providing a template with which to frame al-Qaeda's continued relevance in the tumultuous aftermath of the revolutions and, al-Zawahiri would hope, to guide the *ummah* after his own passing too.

Yet, the jihadist universe is not a monolith and al-Zawahiri's attempts to retain ownership of its globally focused message would prove futile. With the rise of ISIL, al-Qaeda's narrative—as presented by al-Zawahiri—seemed more tolerant of minorities, more ideologically flexible, much less sectarian but ultimately less potent than that of its new rival.

AQSL and the rise of ISIL

Al-Zawahiri's rhetorical stance in the months and years after the MENA uprisings aimed at responding to challenges to al-Qaeda's credibility that these revolutions evoked, whilst exploiting the turmoil and disillusionment that quickly spread throughout the region to reiterate the core agenda of the global jihadist movement. As events unfolded, especially after the coup in Egypt in July 2013, the initial crisis posed by the uprisings for al-Qaeda seemed less acute. The uprisings, however, had also spawned conflict, especially the bloody civil war in Syria. Some of these developments appeared to offer opportunities for al-Qaeda too, until its half-franchise in Iraq spread into Syria, ignored al-Zawahiri's calls to stay confined to Iraq and expanded its localised 'Islamic State' to form the Islamic State of Iraq and the Levant (ISIL), under the leadership of the enigmatic Abu Bakr al-Baghdadi.

The purpose here is not to trace the particulars of this split or the emergence of ISIL in April 2013 (later the self-proclaimed 'Islamic State' from late June 2014 onwards) or any deliberations behind the scenes between jihadists with a stake in this conflict. Our aim, again, is to reflect upon the way in which al-Qaeda's senior leadership, as represented by al-Zawahiri, publicly responded to another challenge to its credibility that in many ways seemed more severe than that presented by the initial wave of MENA uprisings. Whilst the revolutions made al-Qaeda's agenda seem out of sync with developments on the ground, the rise of ISIL has severely undermined AQSL as a jihadist entity capable of implementing any of its rhetoric in a way that is even remotely comparable to the very tangible gains that ISIL has made over a very short period.

In terms of public discourse, al-Zawahiri has responded to these developments in two ways: firstly, by referring directly to the ISIL leadership through explicit warnings and denunciations; secondly, by developing distinct narrative threads that serve, implicitly, to accentuate differences between the AQSL 'brand' of jihad and that offered by ISIL.

The former approach has been replete with inconsistencies. Thus, al-Zawahiri has, in the first instance, denounced the official 'split' with al-Qaeda and argued publicly that the ostensibly subservient position of the Islamic State of Iraq was retained through the retention of fealty that recognised the overall command of the *amir* of al-Qaeda, who in turn was bound by his pledge to the Afghan Taliban leadership. As late as May 2014, al-Zawahiri continued publicly to claim that al-Baghdadi's outfit was merely a branch affiliated with *Qa'idat al-Jihad* whose members had pledged allegiance to bin Laden, which in turn had passed on to al-Zawahiri as his successor.[28] Whilst ISIL is keen to celebrate the legacy of al-Qaeda's first *amir*, meanwhile, it has clearly ignored al-Zawahiri's insistence that this public profession of loyalty is inherited by the next leader. Al-Zawahiri's repeated 'orders' to ISIL's leadership and other jihadists in Syria to fall in line and respect the boundaries dictated by al-Qaeda's leadership appeared to underline his marginalisation and weakness. Even through his own statements, al-Zawahiri came across as a meek substitute teacher incapable of reining in his class of unruly youths: 'I [...] demand that everyone desist from mutual accusation, and shouting at one another', he implored.[29] He offered 'special advice' to al-Baghdadi, urging him to listen to and obey 'his' *amir*. Bizarrely, al-Zawahiri even referred to the publication, by the US military, of internal documents from bin Laden's Abbottabad compound, to re-emphasise the organisational hierarchy that al-Baghdadi's predecessors had apparently embraced. Abu Hamza al-Muhajir and Abu Umar al-Baghdadi, Abu Bakr al-Baghdadi's predecessors, had made it clear, al-Zawahiri argued, that their cohort was subordinate to al-Qaeda. Their emirate as part of the Islamic State of Iraq (ISI) was merely temporary. Abu Bakr al-Baghdadi himself, according to al-Zawahiri, had assured AQSL in 2010 that the latter had in ISI 'faithful men keen to seek the truth in their path'. 'Faithful men' was typed in bold and underlined in al-Zawahiri's original transcript. Referring to a private letter from al-Baghdadi dated April 2013, moreover, al-Qaeda's leader noted that he had been addressed as 'our *amir*'.[30]

Whilst insisting publicly that ISIL remained part of the al-Qaeda 'family', meanwhile, al-Zawahiri issued several rebukes of the way in which the former organisation had developed as an entity distinct from al-Qaeda. Fundamentally, according to al-Zawahiri, ISIL had erred in terms of methods and social obligation. The former refers to ISIL's excessive, careless and sectarian strategy of violence, whilst the latter concerns the group's experimentation with important and sensitive topics, such as the creation of a caliphate without sufficient consultation, knowledge or authority.[31]

There is a subtler part to al-Zawahiri's discourse since the rise of ISIL, which is no less important in terms of charting an overall course for AQSL in response to a rival jihadist entity. Three elements stand out. Firstly, al-Zawahiri has emphasised (or re-emphasised) al-Qaeda's global scope, which is meant to separate AQSL from what al-Zawahiri insists is a more parochial ISIL, a claim that will become harder to sustain given the latter's ability to spread and inspire beyond its core regions. Secondly, whilst al-Zawahiri has accused ISIL directly of excessive violence, he has also developed an independent narrative that presents moderation as a key component of successful jihadist campaigns. Thirdly, al-Zawahiri has sought to reframe AQSL in looser terms than before, downplaying organisational issues and emphasising ideational and normative components.

Al-Zawahiri continued, as noted above, to peddle the anti-American part of the AQSL master narrative throughout this period, with the added emphasis that this global and ambitious scope, of course, separated al-Qaeda from those preoccupied with mere 'peripheral battles', referring implicitly to ISIL.[32]

On numerous occasions, moreover, al-Zawahiri emphasised the importance of recognising the limitations that had to be respected in terms of the application of violence. Some of these references were in direct relation to ISIL, with others appearing on the surface to be more general, whilst context dictated that these caveats were designed to present al-Qaeda as a more moderate and thus more realistic and sustainable jihadist organisation than ISIL. These limits on jihad, meanwhile, would be governed not only by law and scripture but also by the courts of public opinion. A few months after the emergence of ISIL, for example, al-Zawahiri published a new version of his book *Scent of Paradise* (which glorifies suicide bombings), with added caveats on the need to respect necessary limitations on the applications of martyrdom operations which 'some' had taken too far. Specific appeals were issued to avoid unnecessary attacks on public targets such as markets and residential areas, and stark warnings were communicated to those who operated with excess in the name of Islam: 'those of you who blow yourselves up amongst your brothers, or in their bases, know that you will die alone and you will be buried alone and you will be resurrected alone, and you will find yourself in the hands of your God alone; and you will answer for your deeds alone'.[33] It is a sign of how bad things have become when al-Qaeda's leader issues a 'counter-narrative' seeking to curb violence.

Whilst seeking to retain a semblance of control through these public statements, meanwhile, al-Zawahiri has embraced a deconstructed and ideational conceptualisation of al-Qaeda in favour of group-centric or hierarchical representations. This appeared central to developing a narrative that presented al-Qaeda, or more accurately AQSL, as a vibrant and ultimately successful and relevant player on the global jihadist scene. Central figures might be dead, ageing or under immense physical pressure, but the 'movement' continued to grow. For the 64-year-old al-Zawahiri, this was a particularly important point to highlight. 'Al-Qa'ida is a mission before it is an organization or a group and, in this sense, it is expanding more', al-Zawahiri insisted.[34] The Introduction to al-Qaeda's new glossy *Inspire*-esque magazine called *Resurgence*, which celebrates the establishment of 'Al-Qa'ida in South Asia', notes that *Qa'idat al-Jihad* 'started as a group engaged in Jihad in the way of Allah. Over the years, it has transformed from an "organization" to become a call, a message, and a movement spanning different regions'.[35] Such 'ideational' depictions of al-Qaeda have featured in academic and journalistic discourse for over a decade,[36] but now appear to have been embraced by parts of AQSL, at least some of the time. This combination of themes: a loose ideological movement with an ambitious and global (but hazy) scope that emphasises moderation and discrimination in the application of violent activism appears to highlight core differences with the group-centric, hyper-violent and (principally) regionally-focused ISIL.

The 'Islamic State', of course, has retorted. It accurately claims local successes in terms of territorial control and infrastructure that are beyond the wildest dreams of AQSL. Equally accurately, ISIL has emphasised its ability to appeal to fans and sympathisers globally, whilst building up regional alliance structures to rival al-Qaeda's. Al-Qaeda's Syrian franchise, meanwhile, has been accused of consorting with nationalists.[37] More ideologically, ISIL has accused al-Qaeda and al-Zawahiri in particular of contravening shari'ah, a staple form of delegitimisation within this milieu. Ideologues and propagandists on behalf of ISIL have condemned al-Zawahiri's practice of limiting excommunication of Shia and 'transgressors' (*tawaagheet*) to specific *acts* as opposed to *wholesale* denunciation, which, they argue, conforms to shari'ah and the spirit of the *sahaba*.[38] AQSL's record in shari'ah implementation in the few areas it ever controlled is mocked and criticised. In a competition to present the most 'cleansed' form of religion, al-Zawahiri is presented as someone who 'abandoned the pure heritage left by Shaykh Usamah [bin Laden]'.[39]

Public opinion and righteous leadership

These clashes raise questions about the role of public opinion for jihadist groups and campaigns. Al-Zawahiri himself insisted that the mujahidin must avoid actions that risked alienating the public, even if they were technically legal.[40] Popularity and legitimacy were central to the sustainability of jihad.

The rise of ISIL and the situation in Syria evoked analogies in al-Zawahiri's publications that illustrated the pitfalls of jihad, which centred on the notion of legitimacy and public support. There were lessons, he warned, that could be learned from the demise of the Armed Islamic Group (GIA) in Algeria, or the *fitna* that spread among jihadists after the collapse of the Republic of Afghanistan.[41] Whilst al-Zawahiri has avoided direct *Kharajite* references in relation to ISIL, he has offered another powerful analogy stemming from the same period as the initial *khawaarij*.[42] Abu Bakr al-Baghdadi, he warned, would do well to emulate 'his ancestor' Hassan Ibn Ali, the son of Ali and Fatima, who agreed to relinquish the seat of the Caliph in favour of Muawiyah I, the first *Umayyad* Caliph, in the interest of the greater good.[43] Al-Zawahiri thus combined thorny issues regarding legitimate succession and leadership with more immediate concerns about the role of al-Qaeda in the global jihad. Interestingly, al-Zawahiri has used the Muawiyah analogy before. Montasser al-Zayyat writes that whilst imprisoned in Cairo in 1983, al-Zawahiri confided in the former, arguing that the 'blind sheikh' Omar Abdel-Rahman would be wise to follow the example of the transient Caliph and give up leadership of Al-Gama'a al-Islamiyya in order to pacify jihadist groups in Egypt.[44] Now, 30 years later, the issue of just and righteous leadership of the jihadist movement seems even more pronounced.

Al-Zawahiri articulated his thoughts on operational and tactical matters for contemporary jihad most prominently through the publication of a document titled 'General Guidelines for the Work of a Jihadi' in September 2013, which he has referred to again on a number of subsequent occasions. A number of themes ever-present in al-Zawahiri's discourse, such as the importance of hostage-taking for leverage and attack-planning to maximise economic damage, are highlighted in the 'General Guidelines'. The publication, however, is particularly remarkable for the way in which al-Zawahiri sought to highlight themes that separate al-Qaeda from ISIL. Two points are especially important: (1) the reiteration of al-Qaeda's global scope and apparent reach; and (2) al-Zawahiri's emphasis on moderation in the application of violent jihad. Al-Qaeda's activism, al-Zawahiri argued, was based on two components: the propagation of ideas emphasising the mobilisation and unity of the masses; and 'military operations' through violent jihad. The latter would be focused primarily on the heads of global disbelief in the form of America, its Western allies and Israel. Other 'proxies', such as authorities in North Africa, North Caucasus, Central, South and East Asia and the Middle East presented important and legitimate arenas of battle, but ultimately a set of targets that were secondary, if linked, to the principal external foe. The beneficiaries of this campaign, meanwhile, would not only include Muslims globally but also oppressed non-Muslims the world over.

In pursuing these objectives, however, fighters would have to avoid targeting 'deviant sects' such as Shia or Sufi Muslims unless they posed a direct threat, in which case restraint would still be necessary. Members from these erring sects could not be targeted in their homes or places of worship either, al-Zawahiri emphasised. Christian, Sikh and Hindu communities within Muslim lands deserved to be protected too, he cautioned, whilst non-combatant women and children and the Muslim masses could not be targeted under any circumstances.[45]

Al-Zawahiri has visited the notion of caveats and limitations in warfare before, but invariably defensibly, through his position as a leadership figure forced to respond to outrage provoked by attacks perpetrated by colleagues, allies or affiliates. The rise of ISIL as an independent entity, therefore, has presented al-Zawahiri with the opportunity to frame al-Qaeda as a safer, more sustainable and moderate option in jihad.

Cracks in the narrative

Al-Zawahiri's apparent concern for human life, of course, may be little more than an opportunistic ploy to sustain and promote the 'idea' of al-Qaeda, and contradicts not only his operational legacy as a leader of global and local jihadist outfits but also some of his earlier discursive output on these topics. Al-Zawahiri has spoken openly in the past about the virtues and legitimacy of targeting non-combatants purely because they participate in elections and pay taxes, as have other Salafi jihadist ideologues. His caveats in 'General Guidelines' on protecting women, children and those who 'have not raised arms' in direct acts of hostility may therefore represent something of a break from the past.[46] In his 2008 essay 'Exoneration', for example, al-Zawahiri resisted criticism from a former jihadist colleague by talking at length about the legitimacy (religious and political) of civilian targeting. On regime change in Egypt, he insisted that peaceful mass protests would be futile because the authorities had banned them.[47]

In a 2006 statement, al-Zawahiri compared the efficacy of public protest for regime change to 'treating cancer with aspirin',[48] only to embrace this method later. He even talked about his own participation in demonstrations against the Nasser regime in a recent statement.[49] This does not mean of course that jihad is off the table, but rather that militancy is framed differently, as one of a range of options that a united *ummah*, conscious of its various roles and commitments, will embrace in order to topple corrupt systems of governance and replace them with righteous alternatives.

Yet, al-Zawahiri's talk of movements and ideas appears to contradict his continued preoccupation with hierarchy and control, at least if public pronouncements regarding fealty and legitimate oversight are anything to go by. As leader of al-Qaeda, moreover, al-Zawahiri has been keen to express his dismay over the inconsistencies of the West and other adversaries regarding core issues such as democracy. Why, for example, do Western leaders constantly preach the virtues of democracy when they then embrace a military coup in Egypt that toppled a democratically elected government that was, the story goes, seen as unpalatable because of its association with Islam? Al-Zawahiri's own alternative narrative, however, seems equally replete with inconsistencies.

Al-Qaeda's obituary has been written on several occasions since the 9/11 attacks. Its demise was predicted after the fall of its Afghan haven, the loss of senior leadership such as bin Laden, or after periods of calm. Al-Zawahiri's (and others') attempts at reframing al-Qaeda as an idea is, of course, partly designed to counter such talk. After all, it is much easier to destroy an organisation than it is to destroy an idea. The rise of ISIL, meanwhile, has again prompted many to consider al-Qaeda, at least in the form of AQSL, as dead or marginalised. Ironically, however, ISIL's preoccupation with excessive and sectarian violence, regional control and organisational solidity may indeed present al-Qaeda's leaders with opportunities to present its model as attractive and salient and thus ensure that al-Qaeda, in some form, continues to provoke our anxiety and interest.

4

FROM 25 JANUARY TO ISLAMIC STATE

TRANSITIONS IN EGYPTIAN JIHADIST NARRATIVES

Simon Staffell[1]

Introduction

Egypt is central to understanding transitions in jihadist narratives in every sense. To a large extent the salafi-jihadist narrative was born in Egypt, the birthplace of Sayid Qutb and Ayman al-Zawahiri as well as of many of the Islamist currents of the modern era. This is why the apparent dawning of democracy on 25 January 2011 seemed to hold so much potential to disrupt, or even put an end to, modern salafi-jihadist violence. The argument of Islamists who advocated violence throughout the twentieth-century was that peaceful politics could not bring about results. Surely the crowds in Tahrir Square were proving them wrong? As William McCants put it in 2011: 'The people of the Arab Spring, when allowed to choose their own destiny, have voted against the despotic political vision of al Qa'ida. For the organization's leadership, which spent a generation sowing the seeds of its vision in the region, this is a bitter fruit to reap.'[2]

Sadly, subsequent events have instead taken salafi-jihadist terrorism in Egypt into another altogether more troubling chapter. Despite the historical associations between AQ and Egypt, they have not had a significant impact on this chapter. Instead, local salafi-jihadist groups have grown since 2012 and, particularly since the summer of 2013, most notably Sinai-based Ansar Bait al-Maqdis (ABM). Then, in November 2014, IS gained a foothold in Egypt when the major portion of ABM pledged allegiance to them and renamed themselves Wilayat Sina (WS), the Sinai Province.

This chapter will consider the rise of IS in Egypt, by examining the narratives that accompanied transitions in the jihadist movement in Egypt after 25 January 2011. It will situate these changes in the context of the history of salafi-jihadism in Egypt and argue that this transition, and IS's ability to gain a foothold, were in part due to their global narrative, but more notably were due to the way in which the ABM/WS leadership were willing and able to adapt this narrative to the particularities of the Egyptian context.

Salafi-Jihadism in Egypt before and after 25 January

During the 1980s and 1990s jihadists conducted a long low-level insurgency against the Egyptian state.[3] Al-Gama'a al-Islamiyya (Islamic Group, IG) was the most dominant group, but most believe that it was another organisation, Egyptian Islamic Jihad (EIJ), who assassinated President Anwar al-Sadat in 1981—possibly in collusion with IG—for signing a peace treaty with Israel. IG organised a number of attempts on Hosni Mubarak's life (most famously in Addis Ababa) and carried out a number of deadly attacks on Egyptian government and civilian (particularly Coptic Christian) and tourist targets, including the 1997 attack on a Luxor tourist resort in which 58 tourists and four Egyptians were killed. IG affiliates were also implicated in the 1993 World Trade Center bombing in New York. IG leadership declared ceasefires in July 1997 and then again in March 1999, which largely held, although leader Rifa'i Taha Musa and his followers continued to support violence (demonstrating a historical trend of IG support for, or links to AQ) and signed Osama bin Laden's 1998 fatwa calling for attacks on the US. Following years spent in Egypt's prison cells, the IG and EIJ leadership were engaged in a comprehensive de-radicalisation process, which culminated in a series of recantations. By 2007 over 20 volumes authored by IG leaders had been published to support their new non-violent ideology with both theological and rational arguments.[4] Two of the volumes were critiques of al-Qaeda's behaviour and a third was a critique of the 'clash of civilizations' hypothesis, arguing instead for cultural dialogue. Al-Jihad Organization, the movement that produced Dr Ayman al-Zawahiri as well as the two commanders of al-Qaeda in Afghanistan and Iraq (Mustafa Abu al-Yazid and Yusuf al-Dardri respectively), had also been involved in a de-radicalisation process. Among the results of the process were Sayyid Imam al-Sharif's (Dr Fadl's) two books entitled *A Document for Guiding Jihad in Egypt and the World* and *The Uncovering*. The books were totemic in the anti-AQ former salafi-jihadist movement and so concerned al-Zawahri that he responded in his *Vindication*.[5]

With the exception of a handful of smaller, low intensity, sporadic attacks (most significantly the 7 April 2005 bombing near the Khan al-Khalili bazaar in Cairo, which killed three tourists), jihadist terrorism was largely contained in the Nile Valley after the 1997 Luxor attack. However, it emerged in the Sinai around 2000, partly as a blowback from events in Gaza. The two principal instigators were the group al-Tawhid w'al Jihad (TWJ), founded by Khaled al-Mosa'id, and al-Qaeda affiliate the Abdullah Azzam Brigades (AAB). The Sinai Peninsula presents an appealing combination for jihadist terrorism: in the south of the peninsula, extensive tourism presents high-value Western targets, where jihadists carried out significant attacks at Taba, Dahab and Sharm el-Sheikh between 2004 and 2006, killing at least 145 people.[6] Both TWJ and AAB claimed the attacks, with the former's claim appearing the more plausible.[7] But while the southern tourism industry—so critical to the Egyptian economy—has subsequently been heavily secured, preventing further attacks, it is the north of the peninsula that has proven the more enduring base for Egyptian jihadist activity. In the north of Sinai, the economy has long been underdeveloped and relied heavily on criminal activity and trade through tunnels into Gaza. Proximity with the latter facilitates relationships with Palestinian and Egyptian salafi-jihadist groups, notably with Jund Ansar Allah early on in TWJ's development.[8] Physically, the area is a gateway to the primary enemy of the salafi-jihadists, Israel.

By 2006, however, the threat posed by salafi-jihadist groups in the Sinai was largely dormant, following a concerted campaign from the Egyptian security forces and a large number of arrests. Indeed, prior to 25 January 2011 the Egyptian authorities' decades-long struggle against jihadist groups could claim some success. A combination of imprisonment, ruthless tactics and a sustained and complex effort at countering the jihadist narrative had largely worked. Al-Azhar were called on to unpick the historical and theological aspects (particularly promoting the concept of jurisprudence of consequences, *fiqh al-*

masalih). Hard-line and conservative Saudi-style salafism was very much in the Egyptian popular mainstream, most prominently seen in the tele-evangelism of Mohammed Hassan, but violent salafi-jihadism was largely contained.

The 25 January revolution turned this picture on its head. Although not central to the uprisings, religion quickly came to dominate politics as a unifying force that could consistently mobilise and organise the masses. This was not only about the resurgence of the Muslim Brotherhood, whose leaders had been in prison or in hiding from politics. It was equally about the emergence of a politicised Egyptian salafi movement. Having been predominantly quietist throughout its relatively short twentieth-century history, Egyptian salafism was fragmented and reconfigured. Consistent with his long-standing guidance to avoid political participation, Yasser Bourhami, the influential leader of the Salafi Dawa movement, initially advised against participation in the 25 January 2011 protests. A number of populist salafi sheikhs, such as the hugely popular tele-evangelist Muhammad Hassan, went further and called on people to end the protest to avoid causing the sin of *fitna* (strife).[9] Despite the fact that Hassan had taken a position consistent with that of the Egyptian salafi movement historically, he became an example of the movement's shift, as he was criticised, including by some salafis, for his position on the revolution. Bourhami played a shrewd political game, swiftly pivoting towards participation and founding al-Noor political party (the political offshoot of the Salafi Dawa). Many other prominent salafis followed suit and became involved in party politics, which, they argued, was a lesser evil and a way to try to protect shari'ah from the corruption of secularism, in the absence of a true Islamic state. Instrumentalisation of Islam entered the political sphere in a most dramatic way, and became a dividing line for identity politics. Almost overnight, this meant that the call to conservative or even hard-line forms of religion became a way to mobilise large segments of the Egyptian population.

For most of the two years after the revolution in 2011, this mobilising power seemed most focused on the ballot box. But it also appeared to present opportunities for those salafis who vehemently criticised Muslim Brotherhood and salafi participation in the democratic process; an opportunity which AQ and other jihadists saw quickly. Before the end of 2011, Ayman al-Zawahiri had issued five editions of his series of statements 'A Message of Hope and Glad Tidings to Our People in Egypt'.[10] In late 2011 it was easy to purchase a black flag with the *shahada* (the Islamic declaration of faith) written across it (the 'black flag of jihad') in Tahrir Square. However, AQ did not appear to capture the momentum of the entry of hard-line and conservative salafism into the political mainstream. Instead, a series of local salafi-jihadist groups emerged that were able to respond more quickly to the rapidly evolving social and political flux and, importantly, had local networks and were able to develop locally relevant narratives that would appeal to potential recruits. Radical Islamists released from prisons after the revolution provided a cadre of potential recruits; the country in political flux provided a conducive backdrop for the elements to operate. The Ministry of Interior (MoI) and their National Security Sector arm had for many years rooted out and imprisoned the Islamist opposition, in both violent and non-violent forms. After 25 January the MoI was itself in hiding for a short time, facing public anger at their repressive tactics that had fuelled and symbolised 25 January.

The post-25 January 2011 period spawned a revival of salafi-jihadist activity in Egypt, which became more apparent in 2012. Ansar as-Sharia Eygpt (AASE), headed by Afghanistan AQ veteran Ahmed Ashoush, was initially the most notable group to emerge, and it exploited the post-revolution environment of flux and state in disarray. Ashoush's narrative centred on three themes: continuing the revolution; continuing the battle against state security; implementing shari'ah and monotheism. These themes were close to those covered in al-Zawahiri's messages 'Of Hope and Glad Tidings'. They were also highly popular and resonant themes in the country at the time, and were used by Islamists of all shades to mobilise popular support for the following year, and yet, Ashoush's movement, like al-Zawahiri's messages, had little real impact. This is perhaps precisely because they played to a populist narrative, which was covered in the campaigning of the Muslim Brotherhood and Salafi Dawa—in this sense therefore, the salafi-jihadist methodology did not seem to be required to bring about the kinds of changes for which they were arguing.

As known AQ-affiliates, however, Ashoush's movement did enough to provoke the attention of the security forces: in October 2012 AASE-affiliates were arrested in the Nasr City area of Cairo (what became known as the Nasr City cell).[11] Later, one of those arrested, former army Major Tariq Abu-al-Azm, penned a statement from prison in June 2013 which was issued on the jihadist internet forums. The letter sets out his beliefs about Ansar's goals: striving to implement *tawhid* and an Islamic state; to free the land of Palestine; and to help the oppressed in Syria and Palestine.[12] The addition of these foreign objectives is again in keeping with AQ's global narrative, but again, it was also exploited by the Islamist mainstream who were directing people to the ballot box. Most notoriously, when President Mohamed Morsi, in June 2013, attended a rally in support of the Syrian opposition and called for the removal of Bashar al-Assad. Salafi speakers at the event called for support to jihad in Syria as well as sectarian messages against the Assad regime.[13] In this political backdrop, there was therefore little space for the narrative of these former AQ-linked elements, who were not to prove a particularly notable force, and arguably perhaps would not have done even without the Nasr City arrests.

The Sinai region was the particular focus of new jihadist activity, presenting an appealing combination to be exploited: the Mubarak regime had carried out a heavy crackdown on Islamists in the region, with widespread round-ups and imprisonment leaving festering grievances within the population, particularly those now released from prisons after the revolution. During 2012 and 2013, Sinai increasingly became a permissive environment for the most extreme of the Islamist factions to regroup and launch an insurgency against the state. Many of the salafi-jihadist factions involved appeared to have unclear leadership, organisation, capability or coherence, appearing and disappearing into the sand with frequency. Organisations such as Jund al-Islam (army of Islam), which released its founding statement on the jihadist forums in July 2012 with the aim to 'fully implement the shari'ah of God in all of Egypt, starting with Sinai',[14] Aknaf Bait al-Maqdis (protectors of Jerusalem), Kitaeb al-Furqan (Brigades of the Qur'an), Kataeb Ansar al Shari'ah fi 'Ard al Kinanah (Brigades of the Supporters of Shari'ah in Egypt), all seemed to contain almost fluid groupings of former prisoners, leaders, brought together with ideological hard-liners, some of whom are likely to have had experience fighting in Afghanistan, Palestine or more recently Syria.

Out of this patchwork of jihadist elements, the group that proved to be the most clearly organised and ultimately by far the most significant and enduring was Ansar Bait al-Maqdis (Supporters of the Holy House—Jerusalem, ABM). ABM initially appeared to some extent aligned to AQ, but they were never formal affiliates. Significant early ABM attacks were on the gas pipeline between Jordan and Israel (which have remained the soft target of choice for jihadist groups in the Sinai ever since 25 January 2011) and an attack on Israeli troops in 2012. As their name suggests, ABM focused a large proportion of their narrative on fighting against Israel. However, ABM has largely targeted the Egyptian security forces. After the July 2013 ousting of Mohamed Morsi, these attacks escalated. The northern coastal road between Arish and Rafah experienced intense fighting between the army and the jihadists. ABM also carried out significant attacks outside Sinai, notably an attempt to assassinate the Minister of Interior in September 2013, Ismailia and Mansoura in late 2013, and bombings in central Cairo, the largest on a police headquarters in January 2014.

ABM's language and targeting was careful to demonstrate that it was the state security apparatus—specifically the Ministry of Interior and the Army—who were the foes. ABM do hold a sectarian and *takfiri* ideology, but in contrast to both AQ and IS's ideologies, it is a sectarianism more focused on Copts as 'agents of the West', rather than Shi'a Muslims, and a *takfir* generally used to justify the killing of Muslim members of the security forces, but not civilians. Indeed, ABM showed clear caution to avoid civilian casualties: attacks outside Sinai were consistently carried out in the early hours of the morning; the Sinai insurgency has been directed predominantly at the security forces. ABM's statements and tactics have appeared focused on a desire to keep the Egyptian public on side. After the bombings in Cairo in January 2014, ABM stated: 'We tell our dear nation that these attacks were only the first drops of rain, so wait for what is coming', and asked people to stay away from police and security headquarters; and that 'we try to avoid inflicting harm to the Muslims'.[15]

In November 2014, ABM declared their allegiance to IS and renamed themselves Wilayat Sina (the Sinai Province). The declaration was confused by false starts in June and October, when ABM pledges of allegiance to IS were released on Twitter, only to be denied by the ABM leadership. Some elements of ABM appear to have rejected this pledge, in particular members in the Nile Valley who may have opposed IS affiliation out of concern that an IS strategy of targeting civilians and Western tourists would alienate the Egyptian public and increase support for the security forces.[16] The most notable loss after the affiliation was senior ABM member and ex-special forces officer Hisham Ashmawy, whose allegiance to al-Qaeda and the leadership of a new group called al-Mourabitoun (the fighters) was confirmed in a July 2015 audio recording. Members of the looser coalition of salafi-jihadists operating in the Sinai also rejected the legitimacy of this new IS 'province', arguing that not all of the jihadists in the region had pledged their allegiance to IS.[17]

The remainder of this chapter will consider the shift in narratives brought about by the transition from ABM to Wilayat Sina (WS). It will argue that the IS strategy to gain traction in Egypt, principally through WS, has involved deploying the global idea of a realised Caliphate. However, it has also, and perhaps more importantly, involved real care to appeal to local narratives and to build on the particularities of the salafi-jihadist movement in Egypt, as exemplified by ABM's successes.

From ABM to Wilayat Sina

The realised Caliphate

ISIL spokesman Abu Muhammad al-'Adnani al-Shami was quick to recognise the opportunity presented by the army's removal of Mohamed Morsi in the summer of 2013. In August, al-'Adnani released a statement entitled 'Peacefulness is Whose Religion?', which referred in some detail to the recent events.[18] Characteristic of ISIL messaging, al-'Adnani used sectarian language and focused on the immediate and material situation, urging 'Sunnis in general and our people in Egypt in particular ... to fight for the sake of God'. Al-'Adnani pointed to the failure of the Muslim Brotherhood's attempt to govern, which he claimed did not change the system of 'polytheistic laws'. 'If we wish to remove injustice and gain dignity,' he argued, 'we must shun the earthly, polytheistic laws and empower the shari'ah of Allah, and there is no path to this except through jihad in the cause of Allah.' Freedom from the shackles of humiliation would only come 'with swords, spilling blood and sacrificing one's self, and it is never through peaceful calls or parliamentary elections'.

Al-'Adnani sought to link Islamist anger at the Egyptian army to ISIL's ideological frame. He argued: 'Armies of apostasy and disbelief were only created to protect the tyrants, defend them and steady their thrones.' The army, he claimed, defended sin; 'protecting the banks, which use usury and the whorehouses', and other religions: 'the Jews, Copts, and Christians that fight God and His prophet'. Al-'Adnani uses this as the basis for a somewhat restricted *takfir*, asking whether any sane person could argue 'that it is not permissible to fight this army, even if it were seen as Muslim?'

As in ABM's language, therefore, there is then a clear attempt in al-'Adnani's statement to delineate the targets of the violence that he has claimed is necessary. Outsiders are not described in such brutal and unequivocal terms as is common to ISIL discourse, and al-'Adnani leaves the door open for people to repent and join them. While other Islamist groups are criticised, they are not part of the group marked out for targeting, and indeed he calls on these groups to change their ways and 'renounce the religion of democracy'. He also calls on members of the army to defect and join ISIL. Given the reports of former MB rank and file becoming radicalised towards jihadist groups,[19] and of army defectors supporting ABM and possibly IS,[20] this strategy appears to have had some success. Notably, as indicated above, it is a strategy that persistently did not work for al-Zawahiri and Ashoush's Ansar al-Sunnah in a context where there was a mainstream Islamist democratic alternative.

Al-'Adnani closes: 'In the end, the situation today in Egypt and the world is not the same as it was. The world today with its events prepares for a great incident.' Confronted with the immediacy of this incident, al-'Adnani puts forward ISIL as leaders and guides. This is the heart of the IS proposition: the world has changed, the Caliphate is here and the global ISIL movement are waiting to show Muslims the path to true implementation of Islamic rule.

Contrast the immediacy and simplicity of al-'Adnani's call to action and attempt to set out the intentions of his Caliphate, with a statement from Ayman al-Zawahiri shortly afterwards in autumn 2013. Al-Zawahiri felt the need to define a concept of a Caliphate as seen by AQ:

> Al-Qa'ida wants a Caliph who is chosen by the ummah with consensus and free will. If the ummah established an Islamic rule in any of its regions before establishing the Caliphate system, we will be the first to accept whoever the Muslim ummah chose as the imam who fulfils the shari'ah requirements and rules in accordance with the Qur'an and the Prophet's sunnah. This is because we have no interest in power; we only seek the establishment of an Islamic rule.[21]

Al-Zawahiri was drawn into an abstract theological discussion of the meaning of Caliphate, while ISIL were putting out a very clear proposition for what their material Caliphate would mean for Egypt in practice, and how to sign up.

In a statement on 19 July 2014, prior to their declaration of allegiance to IS, ABM released a statement of principles. The group 'wage jihad so that the word of God reigns supreme', the statement explained, in several ways:

1. We govern with the shari'ah of God the Compassionate, which He imposed on His servants, and without which their lives and faith will never be right.
2. The establishment of an Islamic state in which virtue is propagated, vice is prevented, injustice is alleviated, justice is spread, and shari'ah is applied.
3. The repelling of the aggression of the transgressors against the Islamic Ummah. These transgressors include the Jews, the Christians, and their henchmen in our countries. Their transgression is manifested in the weakening of the Ummah, violation of its sanctities and appropriation of its resources.
4. Working to release Muslim prisoners who were captured unjustly, and avenging those who were killed.
5. All these goals can only be realised by the jihad and fighting that God has commanded us to undertake. He the Almighty said: 'fight them on until there is no more tumult'.[22]

Points 1 (implementation of shari'ah) and 3 (defending the *ummah* and fighting Jews and Christians) are typical populist messages for an Egyptian radical salafi audience. Point 4 is an appeal to local grievances against the security state, Islamist political prisoners being a particular issue, including to a Sinai audience. Point 2 shows that there was already reference to the idea of establishing an Islamic state in ABM's narrative prior to the pledge of allegiance to IS. However, the caveat in Point 5, 'all these goals can only be realised...', suggests that the version of an Islamic state here is an eschatological vision, rather than the immediate proposition and already realised state described by al-'Adnani. The ideal end state is millenarian, and always over the horizon. It is a state with 'no more tumult'—which alludes to the Qur'anic verse (Al-Baqarah, 2:193) and rings of unreachability in the here and now, particularly in the tumult of 2014 Sinai. The distance of these aims is reinforced in the second section of the statement: 'Can we achieve this?' Although the answer is yes—'as long as we follow the Qur'an and the model of the master of creation'—the picture is bleak:

> So we pray for martyrdom for those among us who have been killed. The prophet, may the blessings and peace of God be upon him, said: 'Whoever fought so that the word of God reigns supreme is fighting for the cause of God.' As for those of us who survive the fighting, they will continue in their jihad until they hand over the responsibility to others. We prefer martyrdom over life, and we do not seek this worldly life.

This reads more as a justification for the violence being felt by ABM recruits than as a concrete promise of a realisable state. It is the eschatological Caliphate ever promised in AQ rhetoric, rather than the one that IS claim to have realised. At this point, then, ABM's 'state' ideology was closer to AQ and al-Zawahiri's than to al-'Adnani and IS's.

The allegiance to the Islamic State in November 2014 signalled an immediate shift from this distant eschatological state to the idea of a concrete and achievable one. The statement began:

> God has given us this chance that nobody is permitted to disregard or remain a mere bystander to. This chance is about the establishment of the Islamic state headed by the Amir of Believers Abu-Bakr al-Baghdadi al-Qurashi al-Husayni—may God protect him and make him victorious against the enemies of Islam and Muslims, including Crusaders, secularists, atheists, hypocrites, apostates, and their allies.

The immediacy of 'this chance' is compelling when contrasted with the distant Islamic state promised in the statement of four months earlier. But there is also an immediate challenge to the ABM narrative in the group of enemies listed in the November pledge. The list of 'transgressors' to be repelled in the 19 July 2014 ABM statement are 'the Jews, the Christians, and their henchmen in our countries'. The addition of 'secularists, atheists, hypocrites, apostates' is less resonant to an Egyptian audience, and is more in keeping with the global IS narrative. More significantly perhaps, the group listed in July was more tightly drawn, corresponding to the enemies defined for decades by radical salafi-jihadist groups in Egypt (which incidentally al-'Adnani himself was careful to stay close to in his September 2013 statements). The addition in the November statement of secularists, atheists and even more particularly 'hypocrites, apostates and their allies' rings of a move to a more aggressively *takfiri* violence: justifying the killing of Egypt citizens, even Muslims who are deemed to have apostatised, or supported those who have. This is more akin to IS's ideology globally.

ABM give as the central reason behind their pledge the need for unification, which is of clear relevance to the disparate factions within the Egyptian salafi movement, and the salafi-jihadist groups in Sinai in particular: 'In other words, the interests of human beings are only protected by their unity, and therefore they should be united by one leader.' As discussed above, there appears to have been some internal dispute within ABM about pledging allegiance to IS. In this context, the pledge 'doth appear to protest too much' that it represents the unanimous view of the ABM leadership: 'our top ulema and mujahideen have been unanimous'. The statement sets this unity in the context of the wider region, urging 'our brothers in the Land of the Quiver [Egypt], Gaza, Libya, and the rest of the East and West countries to rely on God, follow our suit and pledge allegiance to the amir of believers'.

The declaration of allegiance to IS appeared to have an immediate impact on the tactics used by ABM. Beheadings were not an entirely new tactic to ABM; they had beheaded captured members of the security forces as far back as 2013, and alleged Israeli informants such as Munayzel Salama as early as 2012. However, after the November 2014 pledge, the number of these incidents increased dramatically: there were eight reported beheadings within the first month of 2015. The range of WS victims also increased. They targeted local Bedouin, generally avoided by ABM, presumably recognising the damage that it would do their local reputation. In August 2015 WS claimed responsibility for beheading a Croatian worker abducted outside Cairo.[23] WS also began to issue the kinds of execution-style videos used by IS.[24] Then when on 31 October a Russian Metrojet aeroplane crashed over the Sinai killing all 224 people on board, IS quickly claimed responsibility.

Balancing global and local narratives

Making the transition from ABM to WS has required incorporating IS ideology into a bloody local insurgency that was already established. In a

9 November announcement of the pledge of allegiance to IS, ABM go into more detail about their targeting and rationale for violence. Their primary target, they explain, is 'the most vehement enemy of the ummah, namely the Jews', on whom they claim they have 'inflicted considerable harm'.[25] This is quite an exaggeration for the few successful ABM attacks on Israeli targets that have taken place—mainly a number of rocket attacks between 2012 and 2014, which do not appear to have led to much damage or any casualties. The most deadly attack was an ABM assault in 2011 on a bus near Eilat, where eight Israelis were killed, which was long before the IS allegiance.

The sense of directly attacking this primary enemy for jihadist groups globally is used to suggest that ABM/WS are helping to establish the Caliphate. However, the glaring problem with this, as Nelly Lahoud has pointed out, is that from the November 2014 declaration of allegiance to IS until mid 2015, WS had not successfully targeted Israel.[26] There is an obvious practical reason for this, given the Egyptian military's focus on border security, declaring the north-east of Sinai a war zone and establishing an exclusion zone with the Gaza border in late 2014. However, given the centrality of Palestine to the salafi-jihadist narrative in general, and to IS/Zarqawite ideology in particular (Lahoud points in Chapter 2 to al-Zarqawi's desire to emulate Nur Ad-Din's campaign from Mosul to liberate al-Aqsa mosque), the lack of any attacks on Israel nonetheless leaves a gap. Perhaps recognising this, WS claimed responsibility for launching three missiles into Israel at the beginning of July 2015.[27]

What IS in fact inherited from ABM was an insurgency against the Egyptian security forces, with roots in attacks against Israel and long-standing confrontation between jihadist-salafis and the Egyptian and Israeli governments. This was built not on IS ideology, but on the local and entrenched politics of the Sinai area. WS have sought to tie the local narrative to a global IS-type one by playing on the link to the great enemy, Israel. WS have asserted that the domestic targets were supporters of Israel: 'their aides and guards among the tyrants and apostates have prevented us from attacking them, and they have come to us with their weapons and their arrogance to pound the earth and completely destroy it'.[28] This last point, however, moves quickly back to the local grievances of the Sinai population against the Egyptian government and military; presumably pounding the earth and destroying it is a reference to the programme of destroying tunnels to Gaza carried out by the military, to the anger of those locals who benefit from trade through the tunnels. In this passage, then, an attempt is made to fuse the parochial jihadist narrative, which plays on the grievances of the people of Sinai (characteristic of ABM), with the vision of a Caliphate being realised, and targeting the great enemy 'the Jews'.

The balance in the 9 November statement leans towards IS's global narrative. The statement covers a breadth of enemies not familiar to ABM narratives. 'There is a ferocious Crusader war against Islam and Muslims, and this war is launched by the Jews and Crusaders as well as their aides among the Arab tyrants, *Rawafid*, and the apostates.' The focus on *rawafid* (rejectors, a sectarian term for Shia Muslims), is not common to previous ABM statements, but is used heavily in IS language. The reference to apostates is not common in ABM earlier language either, and opens up the possibility of a more extensively sectarian and *takfiri* methodology. This statement also pits ABM/WS into a global struggle: 'the largest part of this war has been launched against our mujahideen brothers in Iraq and the Levant, which is the homeland of believers and the best people selected by God in the Earth, and the best soldiers of God are there'.

The call to action in the statement, returns again, however, to local grievances:

> In this context, I do not want to miss this opportunity to send my message to our people in Egypt. What are you waiting for after your dignities have been violated, and the bloods of your sons have been shed at the hands of such a reckless tyrant and his soldiers? When will your swords be unsheathed against your enemies, in order to eliminate such disgrace inflicted on you? Have you accepted the disgrace and humiliation?

The statement goes on to refer specifically to the political context in Egypt, and the failure of the Muslim Brotherhood government's attempt to use democratic means. Like al-'Adnani, ABM/WS make a direct play for disgruntled supporters of Islamist political parties:

> The only way to salvage you from the disgrace and humiliation is that you should wage jihad for the sake of God, and fight against the enemies of God. Prophet Muhammad may God's prayer and peace be upon him—said: 'When people abandon jihad, they will be humiliated.' Therefore, neither the disgraceful slogan of peacefulness, nor the infidel democracy will help you, and you have seen how it has destroyed its advocates and supporters. For you, to die with glory and dignity is better than to live with disgrace and humiliation eternally. Moreover, the happy man is the one who has learned lessons from the experiences of others.

ABM/WS therefore begin their turn to IS ideology quite gradually, clearly recognising the necessity of maintaining a narrative imbued with the worldview and issues of the Egyptian and specifically Sinai population. The appeal to disenfranchised Islamist swing voters shows the extent to which the IS franchise immediately focused on exploiting the particular circumstances found in Egypt. The 9 November statement reads as an attempt to fuse the local to the new global narrative, and ends with a reminder of the primacy of the latter vision: 'finalise your issue, end your division, and support your state. You are part of the state and the state is part of you.'

This early attempt from WS to reconcile the parochial with the global IS narratives was not consistently applied in future statements. On 5 December a statement by WS spokesperson Abu-Usamah al-Masri released on Twitter swings significantly towards local narratives, and almost seems to forget the turn to IS's.[29] The video begins with poetic verses by deceased al-Qaeda leader Osama bin Laden. Although this is not entirely out of step with IS ideology (who claim bin Laden's legacy), it does seem notable in the context of WS's turn to IS and allegiance to Baghdadi being so recent. The video then shows the dead bodies of five men and a caption reads, 'The people of Sinai arrested, executed, and then their cadavers thrown away in the desert.' This strikes at the heart of the Sinai people's grievances against the harsh methods and violence used by the security forces. The remainder of the statement focuses on army aggression against the local population. 'What really saddens us is the killing of unarmed Muslims after being arrested.' 'By God's help and grace, we vow to liberate all the prisoners; this is one of the motives for our jihad. Look at these unarmed people who were killed. Look at how bullets shattered their heads.'

Al-Masri's statement gives a long list of criticisms of the brutality of the army, claiming to have examples of people shot from behind, killed and disposed of in remote areas, expelled from their homes, demolition of homes; the latter in particular being a widespread grievance of the local Sinai along the coastal strip to Rafah, and particularly closest to the Gaza border where many homes were destroyed in order to create a buffer zone in late 2014:

> To the people of Sinai in particular, we say: What are you waiting for? Killing? Here you are being killed. If you are waiting to see your homes demolished, they are already being demolished. If you are waiting for your children to be killed, they have already been killed, and so have your women. Are you waiting for your honour to be desecrated? It has already been desecrated, may God preserve you against such blame! You are known to be people of pride and honour. Do you approve seeing them causing mischief in the land, killing your sons, and saving your women alive so that they desecrate your honour? Would you accept this? I don't think you would.[30]

Al-Masri then moves on to wider Egyptian political grievances:

> To our people in all of Egypt, we say: Here you see the truth. To those who have been looking for security, food, and Egypt's sovereignty and prosperity: Have these

been provided to you? Is the picture today clear enough before our eyes? He who cannot see the situation with his very eyes cannot help himself. Let us not elaborate further. The situation is crystal clear.

The vast majority of the statement then has no emphasis on IS's global narrative. WS fully return to the heart of local political grievances, the humiliation of the local population by the actions of the security forces and the failure of political optimism. The progression of WS statements appears to show learning that local narratives must have primacy if local hearts and minds are to be won over. In keeping with a pattern which became established during 2015, WS refer to IS-type ideology only towards the ends as the resolution to the domestic grievances and turmoil:

> To the people of Sinai in particular, we say: Here is the caliphate established and no one has any excuse whatsoever. The caliphate has been established and its caliph has called on us to join ... The Muslims' caliphate and state is established to implement God's shari'ah and punishments and to protect Muslim honour, lives, and property.

Alongside this persistent focus on local political grievances, WS adopted a hearts and minds strategy. In numerous Twitter messages released via the vast

Figure 4.1: Caption reads: 'Distribution of funds to the Muslims struck by the Army of Apostasy's burning and demolition of their homes: The Islamic State'

IS social operation during 2015, WS have drawn attention to the army demolishing homes, clearing land and launching kinetic attacks harming local civilians, and contrasted this with WS attempting to protect and care for the local population (as part of the IS project). In one Tweet in January, for example, WS claim that in contrast to the 'apostate army', they were 'doing what they can by providing compensation and victory to the oppressed'. 'Your brothers in Wilayat Sinai have undertaken a campaign to bring together those affected and to compensate them with has much as possible. This is what a man with little property can afford to give, and a right of Islam.'[31]

Conclusion

The spectre of IS in Egypt is a troubling prospect both for Egypt and for the region. Given the historical role that Egypt has had in developing the jihadist narrative, if it were to become a true propagator of IS ideology, this would be more troubling still. But thus far this does not seem to have been the case. Aside from the significant practical issue of reconciling the various IS-aligned elements that appear to be in Egypt (ABM elements, Wilayat Sina and IS in the Nile Valley),[32] WS are also pulled in two directions by their need to balance local with global narratives. While the immediacy and power of a realised Caliphate and the brutal sectarianism of IS's worldview have been used in WS messaging, this has consistently been of lesser importance to constructing a narrative that will resonate with the particular concerns of the local population. The path of salafi-jihadism in Egypt is well trodden and there are clearly established lines of what will and won't be tolerated, and what will and won't be considered to work.

There is therefore a tension at the heart of IS's narrative in Egypt—between the global and the local—that may help to weaken it. Despite their apparent success, IS's ideological direction is always pulling them away from the ideas that have allowed them to gain traction in Egypt thus far. Unlike in Syria and Iraq, WS in Sinai do not hold a territory with which they can claim realisation of the Caliphate, or the financial resources to be able to present the trappings of such a 'state' for disillusioned Egyptian youth. WS propaganda therefore lacks a vital part of IS's proposition. As the increased beheadings, the attack on a Croatian worker, the bombing outside the Italian consulate and IS's claim of responsibility for the Metrojet attack appear to show, the pull of IS is likely to be towards increased targeting of foreign targets, and increased violence as spectacle: all to the detriment of Egypt's economy and future. It remains to be seen whether this will be appealing to the rank and file of salafi-jihadist recruits in Egypt, who were radicalised first and foremost by local politics and movements, and not by IS's particular brand of brutality.

5

BEYOND NARRATIVE

HOW AND WHY ISLAMICALLY INSPIRED NARRATIVES OF POLITICAL VIOLENCE RESONATE IN CONTEMPORARY TUNISIA

Jonathan Githens-Mazer[1]

The case of radicalisation and narratives of political violence in Tunisia is a particularly salient one. On the one hand, Tunisia is hailed as the prime example of an Arab Spring success story—the overthrow of the Ben Ali regime in 2011 leading on to a (relatively) inclusive form of democratic transition. At the same time, however, Tunisia has regularly struggled with Islamically inspired violent challenges to this transition, ranging from the storming of the US Embassy in Tunis in 2012, the assassination of two secular anti-Islamist politicians in 2013, and more recently the Bardo and Sousse terrorist attacks of 2015. Additionally, some estimates put the number of foreign fighters from Tunisia fighting in Iraq and Syria at 6,000 individuals—and there is further strong evidence that there is a large presence of Tunisians in ISIL and/or

AQIM oriented strongholds in Libya.[2] How can we understand these significant figures in terms of Tunisian foreign fighter participation? And what is the relationship or tension between Tunisia's role as bellwether for the Arab Spring and the simultaneous apparent appeal of radicalising narratives amongst certain components of its population?

The routes through the Tunisian *rif* (countryside) from Tunis or the major developed cities in the Tunisian *Sahel* (eastern coast from Nabeul to Mahdia) can be depressingly similar: roads pockmarked by deep potholes, punctuated by half-built houses; small towns with traffic controls outside mosques and schools, but not often in residential areas; cows' heads and sheep carcasses hanging outside butcheries to indicate the freshness and quality of meat, which is often too expensive for daily consumption by local residents in the *houmanet* (neighbourhood). At the start and end of each day, cafes are packed with men watching TV, drinking strong coffee and smoking shisha, not least because there is simply nothing else to do. The shopping areas are dominated by kiosks, selling everything from bleach to cigarettes, from yoghurt to batteries, from eggs to cooking oil, with scarce regard for hygiene and even less for refrigeration. Shop fronts advertise mobile companies offering deals on top-up cards, while others hang bumpers and fenders from automobiles—offering quick service for cars that have lost parts via driver error, accident, or the savage conditions of the roads.

These towns are dotted along commercial routes, which provide the means for agricultural produce to be delivered from *rif* to *medina*, as well as providing the bigger cities with cheap labour from the young people desperate to escape the boredom and lack of employment or opportunity in the countryside. The towns are dusty affairs, full of the highs and lows of everyday Tunisian life, where both little and much has changed in the wake of the 2011 revolution. On the one hand, many feel empowered to commandeer what was state land, and to build houses, kiosks and businesses on land previously owned (or at least controlled) by the state, with little fear of policing and redress by local councils and administrations afraid to challenge them for fear of being accused of being like Ben Ali and the former Tunisian regime, and for fear of provoking new episodes of self-immolation and public protest, like those that led to the downfall of this regime. On the other hand, many feel as far from the results of the 2011 revolution as possible—believing that instead of the romantic ideals of wealth, opportunity, employment and freedom, the revolution has, at best, delivered something akin to the *status quo ante*, and potentially something worse: a Tunisia that is open to new security threats from the east (Libya) and from within (with the return of foreign fighters from Syria). After all the struggle, what has it actually all been for?

The departure point for this chapter's consideration of narrative is not to search for the origins of how or why Tunisian Islamically inspired violent political actors justify their activities, but to ask more fundamentally why the narrative resonates with potential audiences. The premise for this question is simple: why does this message resonate with some individuals in a world where there are a multitude of other options for engagement and disengagement? Young people in Tunisia, like young people across the global stage, face a full range of choices of what to do with their lives: from becoming a jihadist, to just hanging out and smoking hashish; from studying at secondary and tertiary educational institutions in order to try to forge a career, to simply accepting one's 'lot in life' without seeking to challenge systemic status quos and class boundaries.

Simple questions, however, are almost always the wickedest, the most complex to research and understand. The Tunisian case is no different. There are many competing reasons why scholars and commentators have suggested that radicalisation has occurred and continues to occur in Tunisia at this moment—ranging from a pent-up genie being released from the bottle in the relative freedom after the 2011 Jasmine Revolution, to the failure of the revolution itself to realise the dreams and promises of so many young people. The purpose of this chapter is not to explore the Islamic basis used to legitimise jihadism among young Tunisians, but rather to understand how and why a narrative of Islamically inspired political violence resonates in cases of violent radicalisation.

This chapter considers the power of jihadist narratives not from their content, but from the potential resonance they have amongst an audience that feels proud to have revolted, but is lost without a clear path for the future. Radicalisation, here, becomes about the appeal of a narrative that makes simple sense out of the complex world, thereby providing straightforward solutions to situations which are complex, long term, and require hard work and delayed gratification; characteristics which are a far cry from the streets of urban centres and towns during the 2011 revolution in Tunisia. To begin to understand this case, the chapter will begin by looking at the role of Islam as a vehicle for expressing symbolic discontent over the past 30 years. It will then look at how differing Islamically inspired violent actors appeal through the application of this history to contemporary problems, and finish by seeking to understand how these narratives can be understood to resonate effectively (i.e.

through 'radicalisation') with some Tunisians today. Throughout, the chapter draws on local research conducted in Tunisia, as well as a more long-term study of the narratives of radicalisation as expressed in the propaganda output of groups such as al-Qaeda and Islamic State.

Some Context: A longer view of Islamically inspired challenges in Tunisia

The role of Islam in Tunisia differs significantly from other countries in the region, especially from the close neighbours Morocco, Algeria and Libya. Islam had played an important part in Tunisia's independence movement—particularly amongst those who formed the *Neo Destour* (the Tunisian New Constitutional Liberal party), which spearheaded the movement for independence during the late 1930s until independence in 1956. The *Neo Destour*, from the outset, was driven by leaders with big personalities, and while they came together in their pursuit of independence from French Protectorate status, they did not entirely share the same view of what an independent Tunisia would look like. Whereas independence resulted from a grand coalition, led especially by Habib Bourguiba (and Salah Ben Youssef), it had popular support from a huge range of Tunisian society, including rich and poor, Islamically observant, and those who considered themselves a product of Western education.

When Bourguiba came to power in 1956, he found himself both trying to muster these differing versions of Tunisian independence into the organisation of the new state, and directly challenged by individuals such as Salah Ben Youssef, whose version of the state differed significantly from his own. This difference manifested itself in a number of ways, particularly in terms of views of Tunisia's role in Pan-Arabism, the role of Islam in 'authentic' Tunisian society, and whether the new state should try to emulate its former colonial ruler (France), or whether it should take on characteristics which were felt, by some, to be more organic (Bourguiba supporting the former view, and others, like Ben Youssef, supporting the latter). In the face of this challenge for the soul of the future Tunisian state, Bourguiba won, and Ben Youssef was exiled and is then alleged to have been assassinated whilst in exile in 1961.

Bourguiba laid a template of secular and largely francophone modernisation for Tunisia from the outset. The Personal Status Law (1957) went further than any other previous piece of legislation in a majority Muslim state (at the time), in trying to relegate Islam to a symbolic rather than observant status—banning polygamy, the headscarf for women, and enshrining equal rights for women and men in law. Furthermore, Bourguiba had abolished shari'ah courts and attempted to convince all Tunisians to ignore the Ramadan fast (famously drinking a glass of orange juice live on TV during Ramadan), and closing Zaytouna Mosque as a centre of Islamic learning (and which had produced many of those who had led the independence movement) to form Zaytouna University, all in pursuit of forming a new 'modern' Tunisia.

In the 1980s, 30 years after the start of Bourguiba's rule in Tunisia, a new Islamist challenge emerged. The Islamic Tendency Movement (MTI) led by Rachid Ghannouchi grew as an opposition to the one party rule of the *Neo Destour* (subsequently renamed the Destourian Socialist party). This Islamist movement was a function not only of its era, a time when young people throughout the Islamic world were inspired by the Islamic revolution in Iran, but also represented a particular challenge to Bourguiba's vision of a singular secular and French-oriented Tunisia. The MTI (which would eventually rename itself Ennahda) was popular amongst those Tunisians who felt that they had not benefited from Bourguiba's relentless pursuit of modernisation, and those who felt that the Islamic identity of Tunisia had been unfairly repressed.

Part of the appeal of Ennahda was the discontent with Bourguiba's regional policies: developing the economies and infrastructure of the coast, particularly the Sahel, from Tunis through to Monastir, in order to generate foreign income through tourism. For those in the interior and further south, in large industrial towns like Sfax and Gafsa, this policy seemed unfair and one-sided. For others, the lack of religious freedom and independence from the state seemed to be symptomatic of a state that benefited the rich and educated the few rather than the many. From the perspective of members of Ennahda, the state appeared riddled with corruption. Bourguiba and his fellow travellers, they claimed, would bend the law to suit their personal political and economical interests. The only fair way to recalibrate the state, from their view, was through Islam: as a vehicle that made all equal before God, and therefore subject to the same rule of law, regardless of class or political privilege.

Bourguiba saw the challenge from the MTI as being fundamentally incompatible with his modern Tunisian state. He systematically cracked down on the movement, arrested its leaders, and refused to recognise its political organisation or agenda. Between 1978 and 1987, MTI was subject to a series of arrests and trials, and its founder and members arrested at various points for crimes related to terrorism against the state, having been accused of being a 'Khomeinist' Iranian-backed movement to overthrow the Tunisian state. With the coup d'état of Zine El Abidine Ben Ali in 1987 (ostensibly due to the failing health of Bourguiba), it seemed initially as though the fortunes of the MTI, now Ennahda, had changed, though these sentiments were short-lived. Ben Ali still refused to licence Ennahda as a legitimate political party, and after Ennahda members ran as independents in the 1989 Tunisian elections (thought to have won between 10 and 17 per cent of the national vote), Ben Ali suppressed the party entirely, arresting some 25,000 members in 1991.

Ben Ali's crackdown on Islamism in Tunisia did not occur in a vacuum. Algeria, which was struggling to contain its own Islamist opposition movement, had expressed deep concerns at the emerging Islamist challenge to the Tunisian state since the mid-1980s. Combined with the First Intifada in Palestine (1987–91), and other events around the world, including the Soviet withdrawal from Afghanistan, which led to the return of thousands of battle-hardened Arab Afghans to their home countries, it seemed as though Islamism was more than a benign reformist movement seeking to reform the state. In the early 1990s, as Algeria descended into its brutal 'Civil War', Ben Ali's suppression of Tunisian Islamists grew even more virulent. His security services resorted to ever more extreme methods, including imprisonment, torture, disappearances and worse.

Throughout the first 65 years of the Tunisian state, the role of Islam was contested, yet latent. Despite Bourguiba's attempt to excise Islam from popular culture and cultural practice, and despite Ben Ali's brutal attempts to repress all forms of religious activism, it remained a part of the Tunisian cultural repertoire, and was alive as a form of religious practice. The independence movement had created a dye for the idea that Islam could provide a vehicle for the legitimate challenge of illegitimate colonial rule and control. This idea was then taken up and refined by Islamists in the 1980s and 1990s as an authentic and legitimate method to challenge what they perceived as the abuse of power in the Tunisian state. Though their attempts failed, their repression at the hands of the state only appeared to legitimise their claims in the eyes of their adherents—and, in turn, Islam was sublimated as a legitimate form of activity to express symbolic discontent against the state.[3]

At the time of the Tunisian revolution in 2011, Islamically inspired political activism therefore held an important symbolic power. Islamism, in revolutionary Tunisia, was (along with strident trade unionism) a vehicle for the rejection of the status quo, which many Tunisians felt was dominated by the abuse of power and unfair economic development—whether in terms of the exploitation of state resources by Ben Ali and his immediate family, or in the form of economic policies that seemed to benefit consistently some regions of

Tunisia at the expense of others. For young Tunisians in 2011, Islamist activism therefore provided one of the most obvious, pre-formed templates to challenge the brutality and corruption of the Ben Ali regime—and to imagine a different basis for the post-transition Tunisian state.

The legacy of Islamism in Tunisia and the historical symbolic role of Islam make it a powerful vehicle for expressing dissatisfaction and protest. For its practitioners and adherents, Islam is a salvific system of revealed truth. From a sociological perspective, it is a resonant and accessible symbolic vehicle for the expression of dissatisfaction with status quos—the status quo of political life, social life, personal life and economic life. It is, by its very definition, a system of beliefs, orientations and practices that challenge social and political orders to reform, or in some cases tear down the system. It is, in essence, an 'off the shelf' template for the popularly resonant expression of dissatisfaction with the institutional status quo, popularly accessible and commonly understood. While this does not mean that all Islamically inspired politics in Tunisia's history are the same—or perceived as the same thing by its proponents and/or actors—it does have the practical effect that for some Tunisians Islam is the primary way to express profound concerns about the state of Tunisian society after the 2011 Jasmine Revolution. In short, in order to understand the narrative of Islamist political violence and its resonance in the Tunisian context, it is essential to understand its wider past and present appeal.

The 2011 revolution and after: the growth of jihadism in Tunisia

Tunisia, bellwether of the Arab Spring, sometimes appears to be teetering on the edge of a chaotic abyss. While it is rightfully hailed as the spark and perhaps only remaining success story of the series of uprisings that swept across the Middle East and North Africa in 2011, Tunisia now faces an increasingly obvious challenge from the threat of jihadist terrorism and political violence. This threat is writ large against profound structural shortcomings: a brittle economy, a fragile transition from authoritarianism to democracy, the incomplete democratic reform of a range of state institutions and, perhaps most significantly, from a youth population that feels that despite bearing the brunt of the revolution against the Ben Ali regime, it still has little to show for it.

For many Tunisian 'youth' (a term which, in this context, can designate anyone from a teenager to a 40-year-old), the romantic ideals of the revolution, of freedom and democracy, seem illusory and intangible: the more they try to grasp the promised pay-off, the further away it seems. For them, the revolution was supposed to be a 'push button'—a single event that would dramatically change their lives, bringing opportunity and prosperity, through the simple act of overthrowing the *ancien régime*. Instead, the revolution now seems to have brought only more insecurity and economic hardship. This is illustrated by the collapse of the tourism sector, which provides the basis for the livelihoods of many Tunisians. At first, fears over the revolution itself kept visitors away, and now, in the wake of the attacks on the Bardo Museum in March 2015 and the beach in Sousse in June 2015, the future of Tunisia as an international tourist destination is in doubt.

Yet, while Tunisia suffers from threats of insecurity and economic uncertainty, it also remains one of the last bastions of pluralistic Islamist inclusion and democratic participation. After the revolution, the Ennahda party returned from exile and has been a key democratic participant in Tunisia's post-regime political life, operating peacefully and inclusively both while in government and now in opposition. The party's existence and persistence in Tunisia's nascent democracy is both an obstacle and a boon to the narrative of Islamic State (IS) in the region. On the one hand, the idea that there can be a form of inclusive and successful Islamically inspired politics in a democratic system represents a threat to the IS narrative that states: socialism has failed, nationalism has failed, authoritarianism has failed, the only remaining option is a purely Islamic form of political organisation of the state. On the other hand, the failure of the Tunisian revolution to deliver fully on economic reform and instantaneously transform the economic fortunes of the youth is used as an argument by IS to demonstrate that Islamist parties in democratic systems are inherently unsuccessful because of the systems in which they operate. This was graphically illustrated in a series of propaganda videos published in January 2016, for example, in which IS calls for more concerted efforts to expand its 'Caliphate' in the Islamic Maghreb. These videos are centred around this notion that the legitimate aspirations of the people of Tunisia and neighbouring countries continue to be disregarded and even suppressed by governing elites—democratic or not—who make common cause with the West. Throughout, they use newsreel material from protests in Tunisia and elsewhere, as well as clips showing politicians meeting with American and European officials.[4]

If chaos and instability are the base primordial ooze for radicalisation and terrorism to emerge and flourish, Tunisia potentially provides a fertile environment for Islamically inspired violent groups to take root and prosper. Evidence for this not only comes in the shape of the 2015 Bardo and Sousse attacks, attributed to Tunisian IS operatives trained in neighbouring Libya, but is also expressed in the apparently massive contribution of Tunisian foreign fighters to the conflicts in Syria, Iraq and elsewhere. According to a United Nations estimate, as of July 2015, more than 5,500 Tunisians had joined IS and other militant groups.[5] So how does the radicalisation process to becoming a jihadist fighter work in Tunisia? And what is the real nature of Tunisian radicalisation?

For Tunisia's youth, ontological crises in identity are part and parcel of everyday life as they are persistently forced to reflect on what the 2011 revolution was for, and what it has actually achieved. In this context, it is little wonder that narratives that provide quick answers to complex and profound problems appear. The chasm between the reality of the hard work required to build a better Tunisia and the desire to have a better Tunisia right now provides the space for those who seek to promote, and recruit for, a narrative of radical violent jihadism.

In addition to this obvious set of structural factors, some argue that the dictatorship of Ben Ali dialectically 'caused' a clandestine turn to conservative Salafism (even before the 2011 revolution) as a response to the long-term repression of Islamism in the country;[6] others hold that unencumbered Islamism in the post-Ben Ali state has created a 'Petri dish' for radicalisation and a growth of resonance of Salafism amongst the disaffected and those who suffered the most and gained the least during post-revolution Tunisia.[7]

Whatever the reason, the rise of Salafi-inspired Islamic practice (sometimes referred to as 'Rejectionists'),[8] and the potential for its rejection of the state as a concept and in practice, are of serious concern for Tunisians and others with an interest in the Maghreb. Questions of how to deal with the salafi demands for full and unadulterated implementation of a literal interpretation of shari'ah-inspired legal codes, as well as the open support for, and even prescription of, the participation in Islamically inspired violence against enemies of Islam in what are perceived as Islamic 'states' go to the heart of the future of Tunisia and the region as a whole.

Against the backdrop of this existential crisis, the Tunisian youth seek answers and solutions. The prospect of hard toil and long-term gain through democratically legitimate economic reform seems a long way off from the heady days of the revolution. Reality has not matched revolutionary romanticism. There is a deep sense of Tunisian nationalism and national identity. However, this does not mean that Tunisians are able to give a clear definition of what it means to be Tunisian, but only that they do not feel Algerian or

Libyan. The space in between remains to be filled. While evidence of the reso-nance of highly conservative or even intolerant forms of Islam in Tunisia remains opaque, there are signs, clearly visible when talking to young Tunisians today, that arguments from this perspective are more present now than ever before, as people see themselves confronted with a host of questions and few answers.[9] If authoritarianism was so brutal and unjust, and fledgling democ-racy seems so ineffective, could the answer lie within Islam? And what kind of Islam: moderate political Islamism, or the jihadist version of a 'truly Islamic' political reorganisation of state and society, through violent means?

Understanding Tunisian radicalisation

There are different forms of Islamically inspired violent radicalisation in Tunisia—none of which have to do with political Islam as is practised inside the contemporary Tunisian state. These different forms largely fall within three categories, though the boundaries between them are permeable and often changing: Salafist, al-Qaeda oriented, and more recently IS/ISIL oriented.

Ansar al-Shari'ah Tunisia/violent Salafism

The Salafist form of radicalisation in Tunisia had its immediate roots in the amnesty and release of a huge array of Tunisians from prison in the wake of the revolution. These prisoners were released as a reaction to the popular sense that because so many had been incarcerated and treated so brutally, the state had to start from a new basis. However, among those released were people who had been imprisoned for forming armed Islamic militant groups within Tunisia, especially the Tunisian Combat Group, a group affiliated with al-Qaeda, and with connections to wider global jihadist networks in Afghanistan and beyond. One of these individuals, Abu Iyadh al-Tunisi, went on to found Ansar al-Shari'ah Tunisia (AST). AST proclaims itself as a Salafist movement, which rejects the idea that Islam can operate within a 'Western' oriented framework—in other words, democracy—and aims to 'Islamicise' Tunisia in its entirety. In 2011, the group was behind an attack on a Tunisian television station that broadcast the film *Persepolis*; it is widely believed to have been the instigator of the attack on the US Embassy in Tunis in 2012; and in 2013 AST was implicated in the assassination of two Tunisian politicians (Chokri Belaid and Mohamed Brahmi), who were strong critics of political Islam and particularly of Salafism in Tunisia. Following AST's designation of a terrorist organisation by Tunisian authorities in 2013, many of its members are thought to have fled to Libya, or to have joined militant groups in Syria.

The Salafist trend in Tunisia has long centred around the city and mosque of Kairouan in the central part of the country. Kairouan holds an important historic and symbolic meaning for Islam in Tunisia. It was one of the first cities established under the *Umayyad* conqueror Uqba Ibn Nafi in 670, and has remained a key religious site for education and pilgrimage in North Africa ever since. For those who are attracted to Ansar al-Shari'ah's Salafist orientation, it makes perfect sense to reject modern innovation and return to the time of the establishment of Kairouan, organising society according to the inherent literal truth of the Qur'an and a limited selection of Hadith. AST's leadership comprises individuals who suffered the worst of the excessive repression of Islamism in Tunisia, especially during the brutal rule of Ben Ali. The lesson for them, in the twenty-first century, is simple: the West, and those allied with the West and following Western political orientations, are the inherent enemy of Islam. The only way to resuscitate and secure Islam is therefore to fight against Western innovation, and especially its manifestations in Tunisia. For some Tunisian Salafis, this does not mean supporting AST or, especially, violence, but rather rejecting worldly politics and Western behaviour. For others, however, this has meant an urge to take up arms and fight for the place of Islam in contemporary Tunisia.

It is fair to categorise AST as a largely network-based organisation, rather than a unitary, strictly hierarchical entity. Various violent confrontations between the Tunisian security forces and AST have appear to be concentrated in specific geographic locations. Take for example the town of Goubellat, near Medjez el-Bab in central Tunisia, the scene of a violent shoot-out between Tunisian Security Forces and members of AST in October 2013. Locals in this area have described the emergence and then growth of Salafism and AST in this town as a specific phenomenon to do with their community and/or mosque, while neighbouring villages and towns did not experience similar support for the group. This, and similar accounts from elsewhere in Tunisia, seems to suggest that AST is a 'who you know' movement, rather than representing a popular trend in Tunisia.

This network-based structure of the group has also meant that it is particularly associated with the Tunisian foreign fighter phenomenon, as it lends itself to clandestine contacts, and its ideological orientation already primes its adherents to a belief in a need to fight for Islam. It is highly likely that more recently those who were previously affiliated with AST not only have a high degree of cross-over with those in Ansar al-Shari'ah in Libya, but may now have drifted into groups and organisations more closely affiliated with IS in Libya.

Al-Qaeda/Uqba ibn Nafi Brigade

AQ has operated for a relatively long period in Tunisia, yet never caught the popular imagination, or posed a fully powerful threat to the stability of the Tunisian state. AQ's most famous operation in Tunisia was the bombing of the ancient synagogue at El Ghriba, on the island of Djerba in southern Tunisia in 2002. Furthermore, the involvement of Tunisians in AQ and AQ-affiliated organisations abroad, while certainly significant, has always remained limited to individuals or small groups, rather than becoming a mass phenomenon. For example, while there is a long history of Tunisians participating in AQ-inspired foreign jihad, including in Afghanistan, the Balkans, Iraq and, more recently, Syria, there is little evidence of the formation of Tunisian *Khatibats* (i.e. Islamist fighting groups made up solely or mainly of Tunisians) in any of these countries. By contrast, there are many cases of fighting units that fought against the Soviets in Afghanistan, or belong to groups such as the Al-Nusra Front in Syria, which are dominated by a specific nationality.[10] Instead, anecdotal evidence suggests that Tunisians have been valued by AQ-affiliated groups around the world for being (relatively) highly educated, competent in multiple languages and therefore able to interact with recruits from many different backgrounds. This has made Tunisians valuable assets within these clandestine terrorist networks in Europe, the Middle East and beyond.[11]

Additionally, the lack of broad popular Tunisian support for AQ is due, at least in part, to ideology. A movement which, in its quest for theological legitimacy, is much richer and more complex than some of its Islamically inspired violent co-travellers has been of limited broad popular appeal to Tunisians. At the same time, national identity, which remains salient across North Africa, but especially in Tunisia, has meant that AQ's regional franchise, al-Qaeda in the Islamic Maghreb (AQIM), which has its main roots in the Algerian Salafist Group for Preaching and Combat (GSPC), has held limited appeal for Tunisian groups. There has therefore been no effective amalgamation between violent Islamist groups in Tunisia and AQIM. Consequently, it should come as little surprise that while some Tunisians are key members of global AQ networks, there is no evidence of wider popular Tunisian support for, or participation in, AQ or AQIM.

The current global competition between IS and AQIM has also affected violent Islamically inspired groups in Tunisia, specifically causing a series of dilemmas not only for AST (facing the question of whether IS or AQIM is more true to the ideals of Salafism), but also for groups like the Uqba Ibn Nafi Brigade, which is operating in the Chaambi Mountains along the western border of Tunisia with Algeria. At various points the group has been linked to AQIM, and is understood to have deep relationships with similar groups on the Algerian side of the border. However, in the past two years there has also been at least one instance in which individual members or a faction of the Uqba Ibn Nafi Brigade pledged allegiance to IS. While the group has since made an effort to reaffirm its commitment to AQIM in almost all its official propaganda outputs, the episode laid bare some of the internal rifts caused by the wider AQ—IS competition.[12]

The question over the Uqba Ibn Nafi Brigade's affiliation is further complicated when considering the group's role in local criminal networks and the political context of the area it operates in. Members of the brigade are regularly engaging in, and profiting from, illegal cross-border smuggling in the region. Disaggregating what is an AQIM/Algerian component from what are 'business' relationships is therefore more difficult than initially appears. The group's primary territory, the Chaambi Mountains, are in close proximity to the urban centres of Kasserine and Sidi Bouzid. Sidi Bouzid was the birthplace of the Tunisian revolution and, like Kasserine, has a population that feels that while it has borne the brunt of the neglect and oppression of the Ben Ali regime as well as the 2011 revolution, it has the least to show for it. Residents regularly complain that although they lit the flame for the overthrow of Ben Ali, their region has received little investment in infrastructure from the Tunisian state; instead, they continue to suffer from state repression. Locally conducted research suggests that groups like the Uqba Ibn Nafi Brigade find some popular support and/or participation in their clandestine smuggling networks in places like Sidi Bouzid and Kasserine.[13] This is not because people in these cities particularly support an al-Qaeda oriented ideology, but rather because they support any group which actively challenges a state they feel is corrupt and inherently against them.

Together, these factors make assessing the relative resonance and/or success of an AQ narrative to recruit members and participants in Tunisia immensely difficult. There is little or no evidence that AQ has been behind the foreign fighter phenomenon in the country, while it is simultaneously evident that its ability to give the state an occasional black eye gives it a form of legitimacy in the eyes of those who feel alienated from, and downtrodden by, the state. Meanwhile, the leadership of the Uqba Ibn Nafi Brigade has been subject to the same kinds of push and pull factors of all Islamically inspired violent organisations around the world, initially having latched on to AQ (via AQIM) as the symbolic leader of Islamically inspired insurgency, but now doubting both its capacity and popularity in the face of the emergence of IS.

IS/ISIL: Foreign fighters, Bardo, Sousse and the Libyan contagion

The draw of ISIL and then IS in Tunisia has, thus far, manifested itself in two different ways: on the one hand, it is a key group, involved in the recruitment of Tunisian foreign fighters for what it portrays as a religiously sanctioned violent jihad in Syria and Iraq; on the other hand, the proximity of an IS presence in the chaos of neighbouring Libya has provided training, leadership and strategic direction for the successful terrorist attacks on the Bardo Museum (March 2015) and in Port El Kantaoui (usually referred to as the Sousse attack, June 2015). Drawing on the power of its global brand, IS is able to portray itself as an organisation that is action-orientated, provides a credible alternative governance structure to ineffective democracy and/or autocracy, and is on the ascendancy throughout the Middle East and North Africa. For young Muslims around the world, including in Tunisia, this idea of an organisation that is about 'doing' rather than 'saying' plays upon romantic visions of what the world could or should be like. Instead of the hard graft of normal life, IS offers (or purports to offer) a life in the mould of the early Islamic heroes who brought Islam, and with it a glorious, prospering civilisation, to the countries of the region.

Tunisia and the foreign fighter phenomenon

Recent estimates by the United Nations put the number of Tunisian foreign fighters in Syria, Iraq, Yemen and Libya at over 5,500, making them the largest single contributor in numbers to organisations like Jabhat Al-Nusra (JN) and IS.[14] Some in Tunisia blame this propensity for Tunisian participation as foreign fighters on the revolution and its aftermath, arguing that it created an overly permissive environment that has allowed Islamists (particularly Salafists) to operate unchecked. While it is clear that the amnesty after the revolution allowed some operators keen to organise violent jihad in Tunisia, North Africa and further afield the space to organise and recruit, such a perspective fails to take into full account how and why their narrative and activities resonate with some Tunisian youth.

In the Tunisian context, especially, becoming a foreign fighter, and more recently and specifically joining the ranks of IS, not only provides an immediate template for making life's daily activities exciting and meaningful, but also provides a quick and simple solution to bypass structural obstacles to achieving simple life goals. One key example is the relationship between IS membership and marriage. In Tunisia, as in other parts of North Africa and the Middle East, marriage is dependent on establishing economic stability and prosperity. Much pressure is put on a young man to demonstrate that he can give financial support to a wife and and future family. In the context of high youth unemployment and lack of economic prospects, achieving this becomes increasingly difficult, putting marriage and family life beyond the reach of many young men. This has also led to an increasing age disparity between men and women in marriage, as men delay getting married until they have achieved sufficient financial stability. Those helping to organise networks for foreign fighter recruitment from Tunisia have recognised popular dissatisfaction with this state of affairs, and often promote the notion that young men travelling to Syria, Iraq or Libya can marry straight away as part of the 'package' of being a foreign fighter. The wives are either separately recruited abroad,[15] or are taken, often by force, from local communities. In Sirte, the main IS stronghold in Libya, for example, public declarations have been issued demanding local residents to give up their daughters to be married to foreign fighters.[16] Wedding celebrations frequently feature in the group's propaganda output. In addition to marriage, young men joining IS also receive financial benefits, not just in terms of salaries for themselves, but also for their families who remain in Tunisia.

It is equally important to remember that for those Tunisians who travelled to Syria in the immediate aftermath of the Jasmine Revolution, it wasn't religion alone, per se, that called them to the front lines. Some were also motivated by a form of revolutionary idealism to help other Muslims in the region to liberate themselves from authoritarian regimes. It is unclear how many Tunisian foreign fighters travelled to Syria in this early period to fight with Free Syrian Army affiliated groups, rather than seeking out groups like JN or IS, which only emerged in the course of the conflict. Furthermore, anecdotal evidence of foreign recruiting networks often includes mentions of individuals who had received funding from the Gulf as financial encouragement to potential recruits to sign up. Here financial incentives not just for the fighters, but also for the recruiters themselves, appear much more relevant than any religious ideals.

While aspects of these various recruitment processes have undoubtedly evolved over the past several years, these nuances are important to understand when dealing with the phenomenon of foreign fighters. Nevertheless, in a context of uncertainty and economic hardship—both widespread after the Tunisian revolution—a life of jihadist adventure offers a degree of religious certainty, a real possibility for economic stability, and immediate prospects of marriage and a family. All of this can be far beyond reach for many except the elites of Tunisian society. This makes joining groups such as IS attractive not just for young men, but also for young women seeking to wed a partner of similar age, rather than those ten years or more their senior. Furthermore, the idea of going abroad for a period has become an important rite of passage for many Tunisian youth, and while some choose to travel to Europe to work (legally or not) and live with family members abroad, others view the idea of being a foreign fighter as a viable alternative.

The importance of Libya

The proximity of the fighting and chaos in neighbouring Libya, along with the long and porous nature of the border, has fundamentally blurred the idea of foreign fighters in the Tunisian context, and provided tactical opportunities for IS to recruit, train and engage with Tunisians. The links between the Bardo and Sousse attacks and recruitment and training networks in Libya are a prime example of this. For Tunisians seeking to join the war in Syria, Libya provides a relatively straightforward waypoint, both in terms of established travel routes and offering opportunities to link up with organisations (even khatibats) affiliated with Syrian jihadist groups. Furthermore, Libya provides an excellent base for attacks on Tunisia itself. Tunisia is a prime target for IS for several different reasons. Tunisia's (relatively) inclusive transition to democracy is a direct challenge to the IS narrative that Islam is incompatible with democratic political practice. Tunisia's pluralistic politics suggest that there is more than one way that Islam can help shape and 'do' politics (i.e. through jihad and eventually the establishment of a shari'ah-based Caliphate), and there is space in contemporary majority Muslim states for political Islam alongside other competing political perspectives. In part, this helps to explain why Islamically inspired violent actors sought to destabilise the Tunisian transition by assassinating outspoken critics of Islamism in 2013. This was clearly meant to create a backlash against Islamism (of all hues), and thereby prove the incompatibility of Islam and the Westphalian model of the state. Tunisia's role as a partner for European states and especially the United States also makes it an attractive target for IS—a lesson first learned from AST's attack on the US Embassy, and more recently the atrocities of Bardo and Sousse, which targeted Western tourists. Finally, if IS were able to open a new front in Tunisia, it would further stretch the West's limited resources and divert attention and capacity away from Syria, as well as take pressure off IS's beachheads in Libya. The opaque and complicated relationship between IS, AQIM and Ansar al-Shari'ah (both in Tunisia and Libya) makes understanding the nuances of this strategy a difficult task, but taken as a whole, the intention is quite clear.

Understanding the narrative and its resonance

The study of radicalisation shows the resonance of a simple narrative in the face of complexity. As individual psychological factors combine with structural elements, and local experiences mesh with global forces, radicalisation and violence offer a simple, resonant and seemingly rational answer that can appear to be the only reasonable and viable option. Considering this process of radicalisation from a holistic perspective, its appeal to the radicalised is evident. The ideas that provide the ideological content for radicalisation come and go—in one case it may be Islam, in another it could be nationalism or ethnicity, and in yet another it might be class or minority status. What remains is that radicalisation offers a simple outlet for action. The study of radicalisation cannot be viewed outside wider studies of asymmetric conflict—not just in terms of the actors' perception of being outmanned and outgunned, but also in terms of a wider sense in which vanguardism is inherently connected to personal and societal salvation. That others are blind to this salvation only makes its adherents more convinced that they have to work harder and believe more strongly in order to achieve their objective: to free the 'lumpenproletariat' from its shackles of a system that inherently makes them blind to the blindingly obvious.

In the Tunisian context, the narrative appeal of Islamically inspired violent radicalisation stems from the sense that the revolution has lost its way. In this context, there are few viable and/or rational alternatives to a form of jihadist ideology presented as Islamic orthodoxy, which in turn demands the very destruction of a system that has proven to be unreformable. The lessons of the revolution, from this perspective, is not that Islam can or cannot overthrow tyranny, but that partial, moderate political Islam will be inevitably be co-opted by the *ancien régime*. In this view, the lack of an economic future, the sense that the revolution failed to deliver instant gratification by changing and easing at least the mundane and difficult tasks of every day life—finding work, earning enough to buy food, eat meat for all meals—become not about the failure of revolutions per se, but specifically about the incomplete nature of the 2011 revolution. Consequently, it is not about what is visible from the outside in terms of a real attempt at post-transition democracy that is politically pluralistic and inclusive, but rather about a perceived failure of moderate Islamism to deliver on the unrealistic and romantic promises for post-revolution Tunisia.

The presence of a historically rooted Islamist challenge to colonialism, and later to Bourguiba and Ben Ali, make fertile soil for such perspectives. They create a basis wherein young Tunisians may not recognise the challenge of MTI and Ennahda as being the forebears of political freedom, but rather the left-over debris from previously unsuccessful attempts at full-blown systemic change and revolution. Islam is seen as a symbolic vehicle for challenging power, whereas specific institutionalised forms of this challenge simply represent historical anachronisms. This history legitimises Islam as the vehicle to express ultimate dissent with the status quo, but is unlikely to act as a barrier or break against the notion that moderate Islamism has failed. In fact, from this perspective the problem becomes not one of ensuring that Islamic perspectives are normalised within the state, but rather that the state itself is fundamentally rebooted to ensure the total social reordering of current social structures.

Young people in the *rif* may not frame this discourse in these terms, but the fact that so many have been willing to travel to theatres of conflict overseas indicates that this is at least one component in their thinking. Even in cases in which some are becoming foreign fighters simply for financial gain, either personal or perhaps in terms of a regular payment of allowances to their families whilst they are fighting in Syria (including death benefits should they become martyrs on the field of battle), the financial incentive can be seen as a symptom of this wider rejection of alternative perspectives. Becoming a jihadist, according to this narrative, is the least worst option as well as the most logical or rational choice. A rise in the popularity of Salafism in the Tunisian context is not just a sign of the ideological potency of the notion that observant Islam is the only true form of the faith; it also represents the inherent perception that other options are not viable or 'real'.

From this optic, two aspects of Tunisian radicalisation become much easier to understand. Contemporary accounts begin to make sense, of debates and infighting in groups like the Uqba Ibn Nafi Brigade between supporters of AQIM and those that are drawn to IS. This is a battle of narratives—a moment of profound sociological change where those supporting and/or participating in Islamically inspired political violence are seeking an answer to which group is actually more resonant to their perspectives on the revolution's failure to deliver. The common denominator is the view that Islamically inspired violence is the only way to generate meaningful social transformation; and it is this acceptance that underpins the willingness of members of such groups to forsake an easy life and engage in clandestine, illicit and bloody activities. The split between them, however, occurs over how such activities will or will not bring about fundamental change to Tunisian society. AQ offers a bottom-up model that offers a clear vision of Islamic intellectual legitimacy (not shared by many Muslims, but coherently argued through the lens of AQ's ideology). IS meanwhile presents a clear roadmap to social transformation through propaganda and writings, backed up by concrete action, emphasising the strength of Islamic governance in creating a new social order. In the specific case of Tunisia, the latter may have more potential for popular resonance among a population that feels that post-revolution governance has yet to deliver on their dreams and aspirations.

The other aspect that becomes inherently clearer is that Western perspectives on the success of post-revolution Tunisia are failing to appreciate the deeper and more dangerous challenges the country faces in the coming months and years. These challenges far exceed the initial shock and need to respond to the Bardo and Sousse attacks in 2015. Seen from London, Washington, Paris and beyond, the story of a (relatively) pluralistic, (relatively) liberal, (relatively) democratic transition from authoritarianism that has effectively included Islamically inspired political actors in a new political culture of the state seems highly successful and highly promising. The bellwether of the Arab Spring seems to provide a shining example (especially when compared to Syria and neighbouring Libya) of what post-transition democracy can and should look like. In this context, the Bardo and Sousse attacks appear to be attempts from outside to destabilise this (relative) success story of the Arab Spring. From within parts of Tunisian society, however, the story is the complete opposite. Here post-transition political stasis, endless compromise and lack of a clear political and economic future dominate as the primary impressions of an incomplete revolution. This notion of incompleteness exists not because democracy is hard, or indeed because organic and legitimate democratic political practice takes time and requires concessions on the part of all parties. According to the radicalising narrative of jihadist Islamism, it is the result of an inherently corrupt state in which participation in the officially recognised political process represents the ultimate form of co-optation into the old system. For young people who feel distant from the wheels of power in Tunis, and who feel that they are teetering the edge of an economic abyss with little prospect of a comfortable life, moderation and compromise seem a cop-out at a moment of deep crisis.

The opening premise of this chapter was that in order to understand a narrative, one must understand its resonance—its basis for popular appeal. In many ways Islamically inspired political activism and political violence, particularly in the latest guise of IS, are one of several vehicles by which young Tunisians voice their dissatisfaction with the inadequacy of the revolution and the contemporary Tunisian state. A chapter about the appeal of trade unionism and the *Front Populaire* would, undoubtedly, share much of the analysis of the current state of thinking and despair amongst Tunisian youth. This ultimately raises the fundamental question, however, of whether it is the power of the narrative that is driving Islamically inspired political violence in Tunisia? Or whether rather the violence is symptomatic of a profound post-revolutionary anomie, and that its perpetrators merely seek and use narratives that rationalise their bloody and murderous activities?

6

AL-QAEDA AND ISLAMIC STATE IN YEMEN

A BATTLE FOR LOCAL AUDIENCES

Elisabeth Kendall

Introduction

Despite vast amounts spent on international counter-terrorism efforts and significant losses inflicted by drone strikes, Yemen's al-Qaeda in the Arabian Peninsula (AQAP) remains one of al-Qaeda's most active and deadly branches. A closer look at some of the jihadist[1] narratives produced by AQAP reveals deep-rooted reasons why it has thus far managed to endure in Yemen and why it may continue to do so, despite the challenges posed both by counter-terrorism efforts and by the expansionist ambitions of the Islamic State (IS) Caliphate. On 13 November 2014, IS officially announced the Caliphate's 'expansion into the Arabian Peninsula, Yemen' with Caliph Ibrahim Abu Bakr al-Baghdadi's acceptance of the oath of allegiance sworn to him in an audio recording by 'Yemen's mujahidin'. Significantly, the Caliph at the same time announced the nullification of all other groups in Yemen.[2] In other words, AQAP ceased to have any legitimacy in the eyes of the new Caliphate. Nevertheless, despite some defections to IS and the self-proclamation of various IS provinces in Yemen, AQAP continues to flourish. How has this occurred?

This chapter argues that AQAP's staying power is explained, at least in part, by its production of jihadist narratives that are culturally attuned to their Yemeni context and adapted to prevailing local conditions. IS, by contrast, has produced little narrative (by the time of writing) that is culturally specific to Yemen beyond savaging the Houthis, tribesmen from Yemen's north who swept down through Yemen's south in 2015. Since the Houthis generally belong to the Zaydi branch of Shiism, they qualify for excommunication and death according to IS's virulent sectarian doctrine, which seeks to reframe what are essentially disputes over power and resources as an existential religious battle of global jihad. However, that local tribal issues predominate over religious issues, at least in Yemen's eastern region close to al-Qaeda's strongholds, is borne out by the results of a comprehensive survey of over 2,000 tribesmen and women conducted by this author in al-Mahrah governorate in December 2012 to January 2013. Only 30 per cent of respondents considered the imam to be 'the most trusted and respected position', as opposed to 41 per cent for the tribal sheikh (and a further 29 per cent for other non-religious choices). Likewise, only 21 per cent of respondents believed that the imam's role was 'to advise on all matters (political, cultural, economic, legal, tribal)', as opposed to 'religious and personal matters only'.[3] This indicates that the notion of an Islamic State Caliphate would be deeply unpopular. It also suggests that attempts to win communities for a jihadist agenda would be more likely to succeed if linked to local grievances, as AQAP has done, rather than engaging immediately and uncompromisingly with the religious ideology of global jihad, as IS in Yemen has done.

This chapter begins by showing how AQAP speaks to local audiences at both practical and emotional levels, rather than through religious ideology: practically, by latching onto community problems such as corruption, poverty and marginalisation and positioning itself as saviour-defender; and emotionally, by deploying traditional cultural materials such as poetry and song. The chapter shows how AQAP narratives resonate strongly with local tribal codes of honour and revenge, and how these can then be harnessed to serve the global agenda of militant jihad. The theological discourses and position statements on which jihad scholars lavish so much attention are important, and jihad devotees like to know that these supporting arguments exist, but ultimately they are unlikely to serve as the major catalyst for winning hearts and hence ultimately minds. Nor are they likely to win the kind of tolerance or even just indifference which are both key to AQAP's survival among a well-armed population. It is useful to remember that for the jihadist project to endure, it requires an infrastructure beyond just recruiting into the mujahidin. A certain degree of community buy-in is necessary for AQAP to survive in its tribal strongholds. This buy-in can range all the way from forging military alliances in the interests of fighting a mutual enemy such as the Houthis, to simply finding enough of a common cause or security vacuum to gain community acquiescence. This occurred perhaps most notably in parts of Abyan and Shabwa in 2011–12 and southern Hadramawt in 2015–16, from which AQAP was again able to spread west. The chapter then explores two key themes that thread through AQAP's jihadist narratives: the celebration of death and the construction of the enemy. It shows how these themes are tuned towards local audiences and how they have developed since the Arab Spring uprising, the emergence of IS and the onset of all-out war in 2015. Lastly, the chapter looks at the relative appeals of AQAP and IS in Yemen. It outlines the potential trajectories of AQAP and briefly suggests ways in which the jihadist threat in Yemen might be countered.

Yemen offers a natural refuge for terrorists, since its topography of deserts, mountains and wadis makes it easy for groups to melt into the landscape when they need to. AQAP emerged in January 2009 when Saudi and Yemeni jihadist movements joined forces following a confluence of circumstances. Chief among these were the increasing crackdown on mujahidin in Saudi Arabia, causing them to flee across the border to Yemen, and the spectacular escape in February 2006 of 22 mujahidin from a high security prison in Sana'a, including charismatic and experienced figures such as AQAP leader Nasir al-Wuhayshi (d. 2015 in a drone strike). This coincided with widespread anger at perceived Western interference in Muslim countries, particularly Iraq and Palestine, and simmering discontent arising from regional neglect, injustice and rampant corruption under the regime of former President 'Ali 'Abd Allah Salih.[4] Since then, the situation in Yemen has deteriorated still further. Today's civil war chaos, government exodus, disintegration of domestic security, numerous prison breaks and burgeoning humanitarian crisis of epic proportions leave Yemen ripe for further exploitation by jihadist groups.

What kinds of individuals might be attracted to such jihadist groups? It is impossible to generalise globally about what makes a jihadist, since this will vary according to geographical and temporal circumstances and the cultural, political and other baggage that these bring. While compelling data-driven research by Marc Sageman appears to explode seductive and popular theories for terrorist motivation such as poor education, economic hardship and sexual frustration, it relies on a sample compiled largely of terrorists who have conducted operations against the US and Europe.[5] It does not therefore speak for how jihad movements operate at a local level inside specific geographies. The levers that entice populations in the West, or for that matter Egypt, Syria, Iraq, North Africa and so on, do not necessarily apply in Yemen. Theories of poverty and poor education cannot be discounted so readily in the context of Yemen. In the absence of a reliable database of Yemen's mujahidin, this research attempts to unravel what motivates local support for jihad through the qualitative analysis of materials produced by AQAP and IS in Yemen, coupled with on-the-ground observation in eastern Yemen during numerous fieldwork trips by this author between 2011 and 2016.

This chapter is therefore concerned with jihadist narratives directed at local audiences in Yemen. Although considerable attention has been paid by the international media to the English-language *Inspire* magazine (2010–ongoing), the brainchild of Yemeni-American AQAP ideologue Anwar al-'Awlaqi (d. 2011 in a drone strike), this was of little importance to local audiences in Yemen where the literacy rate in English is low. The West is of course right to worry about the radicalisation threat posed by AQAP narratives among its own populations. Al-'Awlaqi and his *Inspire* magazine can be traced as the inspiration for home-grown atrocities such as the murder of a British solider in London in 2013. It is also correct that al-'Awlaqi's sermons were downloaded by the bombers of the Boston marathon in 2013 and the perpetrators of the Paris massacre in 2015. However, despite these points, the international reach of AQAP's messaging is being dwarfed by the far more sophisticated media apparatus of the Islamic State. This switch of international interest from al-Qaeda affiliates such as AQAP to IS is evidenced by the flood of foreign fighters joining IS. Nevertheless, a sophisticated English language media apparatus is not what inspires or guides local militants or sympathisers on the ground, and it is on these local audiences that AQAP relies for its ability to survive in Yemen.[6]

AQAP Messaging and the challenge from Islamic State

Working with jihadist materials designed to engage local audiences brings several challenges. First, vast quantities of these are produced, ranging from magazines, official statements, audio recordings and videos—in AQAP's case often through its official al-Malahim and, more recently, al-Athir media organisations—through to auxiliary Twitter accounts, Facebook pages and internet chat forums. Aside from keeping up with the sheer volume, other challenges include assessing the quality and reliability of sources;[7] tracking the changing modes of dissemination, given that websites, Twitter handles, Facebook pages and online posts are constantly being taken down;[8] and situating material chronologically (since original material is not always date-stamped and is often re-posted). Meanwhile, secondary sources, such as monitoring or intelligence analysis organisations, can also prove problematic. They frequently rely on the same consolidated sources of translated materials and therefore repeat one another, which risks generating 'facts' by sheer force of apparent corroboration. Moreover, they tend to be less concerned with translating or reporting on cultural material (such as poems, music and advice), focusing instead on declarations, position statements and doctrinal discussions. This risks blinkering our view of precisely those kinds of jihadist narratives that are likely to resonate more readily with people on the ground.[9]

The main AQAP magazine directed at Arabic-speaking audiences between 2008 and 2011, *Sada al-Malahim* (The Echo of Epic Battles), clearly demonstrates AQAP's use of cultural material to win local communities for the jihadist project. As a mixed content magazine, it could appeal to a range of consumers, including the illiterate to whom it could be read aloud, or, in the case of poems or advice, simply passed on by word of mouth. Large parts of Yemen remain a largely oral culture. In a comprehensive survey of 2,000 inhabitants in east Yemen's al-Mahrah governorate, this author discovered that only a quarter of households contained any book other than the Qur'an and that three-quarters of the population considered poetry (an oral tradition) to be important in their daily lives.[10] Alongside theological, juristic and political articles, *Sada al-Malahim* carries human interest content, such as personal testimonies, letters, memoirs, martyrologies and notices of congratulations to families or whole tribes on marriages, births and even deaths (when a martyr was involved). It also contains religious lessons directed at women in the 'Hafidat Umm 'Ammara' section, as well as tips on cookery and health. Bringing families on board with the jihad is clearly seen as an important strategy for the success of the movement, both for bolstering support and tolerance among the tribes and ensuring a steady stream of willing recruits.

The eruption of the Arab Spring revolution in Yemen marked a change in the types of narratives disseminated by Yemen's jihad movement, as it attempted to turn domestic unrest to the service of the global jihadist agenda. The popular uprisings appeared to take AQAP media production by surprise and it took time to react. *Sada al-Malahim* ended abruptly in January 2011 and its successor, *Madad*, emerged only in September 2011. The opening issue referenced public queries about the recent lack of output from AQAP's al-Malahim media organisation and promised to respond to current events with a forthcoming video entitled 'Umma Wahida' (A Single Islamic Community).[11] This video demonstrates AQAP's attempt to harness the uprisings for its jihadist project, offering analyses of the uprisings based on its own central position in unfolding events in which it claimed an instrumental role. In *Madad*, AQAP constructs links between immediate domestic events and the global jihadist project, with headlines such as "Ali Salih kills 13 revolutionaries, and America supports that".[12] The paper tries to get on side with youth activists protesting against the Salih regime in major cities, sympathising with their apparent side-lining in the Gulf Initiative but reminding them that democracy is not the solution. AQAP's Fahd al-Qus' (al-Quso) al-'Awlaqi (d. 2012 in a drone strike) explains: 'The democratic game is rejected by us on the basis of Shari'ah, because it is based on the rule of the people by the people and also based on majority votes. And this is a contradiction with Allah's exclusive right to rule His creation.' As usual, America is blamed on the basis of its backing for an election process, thus thwarting the Yemeni people's purported desire to 'rule by the Islamic Shari'ah instead of the choices of the American regency council'.[13]

The Arab Spring thus led AQAP to adapt its narrative for local audiences. The broader cultural narratives presented in *Sada al-Malahim* were replaced by a Robin Hood-like propaganda narrative that positioned AQAP as the saviour of local communities. This was disseminated through *Madad*, which was much shorter but more frequent than *Sada al-Malahim*, and through a series of short films called "'Ayn 'Ala al-Hadath' (Eye on the Event). This more expedient media strategy was designed to match the urgent pace of developments on the ground as AQAP took advantage of the chaos to entrench itself in the southern governorates of Abyan and Shabwa, declaring various towns Islamic emirates.[14] For this exercise, AQAP adopted a clever rebranding strategy, calling itself Ansar al-Shari'ah (Partisans of Islamic Law). Having distanced itself from any negative baggage associated with the global al-Qaeda brand, Ansar al-Shari'ah focused hard on winning local hearts and minds for AQAP through claiming to fix everyday practical problems, ranging from infrastructure and utilities to education and meting out justice. AQAP's narrative included personal testimonies to illustrate how its Islamic rule solved problems caused by years of neglect and endemic corruption. One man tells how he turned to AQAP after his land was stolen and the state courts refused to assist him without heavy bribes.[15] At times the narrative can be wholly implausible. AQAP claimed that its introduction of shari'ah law punishments in Ja'ar in 2011 had been welcomed by locals and that a man who had his hand amputated for theft stated that he was honoured to have been the first to have shari'ah law implemented on him.[16] AQAP's 'Eye on the Event' video series also contains several such testimonies. The first in the series sets the tone by filming the mujahidin clearing flood damage and building roads.[17] Although IS has used similar community engagement tactics in Syria and Iraq,[18] this has not yet been the focus of IS in Yemen.

This narrative of positioning the mujahidin as protectors of the local community has persisted and evolved. Although the Yemeni military finally managed to oust AQAP from control in central southern governorates in June 2012, the narrative flared up again in Hadramawt in 2015. Again, AQAP was able to take advantage of a chaotic situation to seize control, this time resulting from the Houthi advance and subsequent Saudi-led coalition bombing campaign. In April 2015, AQAP overran al-Mukalla, releasing around 300 mujahidin from prison, seizing military equipment and robbing the central bank. As it had done in 2011–12, AQAP introduced strict elements of Islamic law, including the banning of the popular narcotic qat. However, this time round, AQAP appears to be accepting a more accommodating approach to local governance. Although elements of Islamic law have been enforced intermittently, AQAP has refrained from full-scale enforcement. The evidence suggests that it has entered into an alliance with local tribes to run Hadramawt, handing over control of infrastructure to the Hadrami People's Council and undergoing another rebranding exercise with an even more local flavour: Abna' Hadramawt (The Sons of Hadramawt). Given that al-Mukalla witnessed periodic street protests against AQAP, it is unclear whether this flex in strategy is a conscious choice or a forced compromise. Either way, this localised model was rolled out further towards the end of 2015 with AQAP's spread west to reclaim the territory of its former emirate in Abyan, this time calling itself Abna' Abyan (The Sons of Abyan).

AQAP needs to steer a difficult line between avoiding a bloody confrontation with local populations and satisfying the mujahidin of its commitment to Islamic rule. This is particularly tricky in the face of challenges from IS. The IS magazine *Dabiq*, for example, featured a photo of al-Mukalla with the caption 'The City of al-Mukalla, where al-Qa'ida made no effort to implement the Shari'ah after taking over'.[19] These kinds of criticisms appear to have pushed AQAP periodically to take a less conciliatory stance, particularly when rumours circulated of AQAP members from within its Hadramawt stronghold defecting to IS.[20] It may be pressure from IS that led AQAP in July 2015 to release a three-part series of testimonies entitled 'Why We Chose al-Qa'ida', which plays up its community popularity. Moreover, following heavy swipes at AQAP's weak implementation of shari'ah made in videos by three separate provinces of IS in Syria and Iraq in mid-November 2015, AQAP released a feature-length film, *Hurras al-Shari'ah* (The Guardians of Shari'ah), in December 2015. This film justified AQAP's long-term strategy and stressed its continuing commitment to and dominance of global jihad. More generally, the narrative accompanying AQAP's local strategy became more militant during 2015. A series of films released by AQAP in Hadramawt starting in 2014, *Min al-Midan* (From the Field), takes a significantly more combative approach and displays a hardening in sectarian rhetoric (discussed in the section below on constructing the enemy).

Since the start of 2016, however, AQAP has refocused once again on its community development and social agendas, learning no doubt from experience what works best among local populations. AQAP's new al-Athir media agency, launched in January 2016, has focused overwhelmingly on the dissemination of materials depicting the proactive ways in which AQAP works to improve the lives of ordinary people. The 'Eye on the Event' film series has been resurrected after a three-year gap to showcase activities ranging from fixing utilities and cleaning streets to renovating hospitals and combating mosquitos. It even afforded a rare glimpse of child indoctrination with footage of AQAP hosting an ice cream eating competition, Qur'anic quizzes and sing-alongs for young boys.[21] A new newspaper, *al-Masra* (a name signifying Jerusalem), was launched in January 2016 with a significantly more global jihadist outlook and professional presentation style than its predecessor, *Madad*. Yet *al-Masra* still celebrates local news and successes—and, importantly, in early 2016 it explicitly articulated the new AQAP media priority of publicising community development work undertaken or facilitated by the jihadists.[22] One full-page article replete with photographic evidence of good works is potently headlined, 'How Do Areas under Ansar al-Shari'ah Control Compare with the Rest of Yemen's Cities?'[23]

Since the emergence of IS, AQAP video production has become somewhat slicker and perhaps better able to engage angry young audiences. This may simply be a result of natural evolution, but it may also in part reflect an attempt to avoid being eclipsed by IS. AQAP even introduced a travelling cinema to ensure that its films could be screened in Hadramawt's coastal towns.[24] The 'From the Field' series, with its snappy action-oriented films, is a long way from the more familiar AQAP videos providing religious guidance in classical Arabic from a talking head. For example, in 2011 AQAP outlined its position on the Arab Spring in *Hisad al-Thawrat* (Reaping the Revolutions), in which Ibrahim al-Rubaysh (d. 2015 in a drone strike) spoke at the camera for 28 minutes in classical Arabic, more heavily focused on criticising America than envisioning the future state. These kinds of narratives appear less capable of engaging local audiences. IS commented directly on the long-winded nature of AQAP video output in its magazine *Dabiq*. The IS magazine criticised AQAP ideologue Harith al-Nazari's rebuttal of Yemen as an IS province: 'he rambled on in his hollow statement ... The portion of Amir al-Mu'minin's [Caliph Abu Bakr's] statement that concerned the dissolving of parties and the current situation in Yemen did not exceed one minute in length. Al-Nazari, however, responded with a statement that was half an hour long.'[25] More recently, AQAP has launched various new video series focused on religious guidance, such as *Mafahim* (Concepts) in 2015, somewhat more expertly produced, resurrecting top names like Anwar al-'Awlaqi (d. 2011 in a drone strike) and Sa'id al-Shihri (d. 2013 in a drone strike) in much shorter clips of less than ten minutes, but they are no match for the action-packed dramas emanating from IS in Syria and Iraq.

AQAP's use of cultural traditions, such as poetry, continues to be a core part of its narrative appeal to local populations, but this use has evolved. AQAP's handling of poetry as a means to engage local audiences prior to the Arab Spring has been well documented elsewhere.[26] The evolution in AQAP media strategies since 2011 and the growing shift from magazine format to video and social media mean that poetry is no longer deployed as frequently in written form. The brevity required for social media, particularly Twitter, does not totally preclude the spread of written poetry, since links are frequently posted to such content hosted on sites like gulfup.com and justpaste.it.[27] However, whereas previously we found poetry peppered throughout the pages of *Sada al-Malahim* (one fifth of the pages featured verses of poetry), its most widespread consumption now is as music, either in sung poetry sessions or as *nashids* (anthems). Videos featuring violent operations or celebrating martyrs generally have a constant background soundtrack of rousing jihadist anthems.

Poetry is useful for engaging audiences at an emotional level at moments of great tension. It can encapsulate a message in a memorable and catchy way that can disseminate quickly, particularly when converted into a *nashid*. In July

2014 when al-Qaeda and its global leader Ayman al-Zawahiri in particular were coming under attack from IS for failing to recognise the new Caliph, AQAP leader Nasir al-Wuhayshi released an audio recording in which he paid tribute to al-Zawahiri. The tribute was followed by a poem that al-Wuhayshi claimed al-Zawahiri had sent him in early 2009.[28] The contemporary-style poem entitled 'Brother in Islam, Come!' was perfect for conversion into a moving *nashid*, which would quickly disseminate AQAP's important message: Muslims should not to be distracted by rivalries amongst themselves but stay focused on the bigger picture—fighting Western 'crusaders'. The third verse in particular poeticised AQAP's stance:

> Listen not to the hatred of malevolence
> Listen to the appeals of help from the minarets
> For they have buried their claws into the heart of Jerusalem
> Surrender not its sanctuary or devotees

Poetry also features as part of AQAP's engagement strategy in other ways, ranging from highly formal to informal occasions. At the highly formal end of the spectrum are productions such as the AQAP video released to comment on the death of its leader Nasir al-Wuhayshi (d. 2015 in a drone strike), which ends with Khalid 'Umar Batarfi reading a long poem featuring traditional mono-rhymed verses in classical Arabic. At the other end of the spectrum we find poetry used to engage with people as a natural part of a relaxed informal occasion. For example, AQAP threw a party after its suicide bombers had facilitated the escape of 29 inmates from Sana'a central prison in February 2014. The celebrations included a traditional sung poetry session mercilessly satirising the head of the state security apparatus.[29] The poem constantly sings out the refrain 'Ibn al-Qamish [head of the state security] has been vanquished' before a delighted crowd of what some sources claim to have been around 400 AQAP militants and sympathisers.[30]

AQAP Narrative themes

Celebrating death

There are numerous themes running through the narratives of AQAP. Two recurrent themes that play an important role in their attempts to win local audiences for the global jihadist project are celebrating death and constructing the enemy. Glorifying fallen mujahidin through celebrating their deaths as the ultimate achievement of their lives is key to ensuring a steady stream of willing fighters. This is particularly important in view of the large number of deaths by drone strike. This remote-control assassination sits awkwardly with tribal honour codes of dying gloriously in battle, but AQAP's martyrdom narratives are able to reframe such 'passive' deaths as heroic acts. As one AQAP narrative tells us, 'Speaking about martyrs and martyrdom revives and nourishes hearts... We live their life stories step by step, so that we take their path and follow in their footsteps.'[31] Even after the closure of the AQAP magazine *Sada al-Malahim* and the shift towards news bulletins and videos with the start of the Arab Spring, the written series of martyrdom narratives persisted. 'Shuhada' al-Jazira' (Martyrs of the [Arabian] Peninsula) ran to at least 16 booklets up to June 2014, demonstrating the crucial importance of celebrating death as a means to embolden existing mujahidin and encourage new ones.

The martyrology genre fits well with oral traditions on the Arabian Peninsula stretching back to pre-Islamic times, when tribal heroes were celebrated through the poetry of *ritha'* (lament), *madh* (praise) and *hija'* (lampooning the enemy). Martyr poems appear regularly in *Sada al-Malahim* and tap into well-established tropes capable of elevating even careless teenagers, rumbled and gunned down by the security services before getting anywhere near an operation, to the level of heroes of old.[32] This is done by associating them with time-old symbols of power such as torrential floods, thunder, lightning and drawing parallels between them and famous warriors of the original Islamic conquests. Early attempts to do the same on video meet with mixed results. While poetry and story-telling can construct idyllic images of martyrs relaxing in the gardens of Paradise in the arms of beautiful virgins, film documentary risks exposing a more brutal reality. One such example is a grainy video from 2009 entitled 'Rabish wa-l-Qasas al-'Adil' (Rabish and the Just Punishment, 2009). This tells the story of the assassination of Muhammad bin Rabish, a security director in Ma'rib. The four martyrs in the video are not the glorious heroes of his 2009 assassination (he was blown up by parcel bomb) but rather the wretched victims of a 2007 operation for which he was deemed responsible. The shaky footage shows one of the 'martyrs' post operation with a badly mangled face. This is just the kind of material that al-Qaeda ideologue 'Atiyyat Allah al-Libi (d. 2011 in a drone strike) advised excluding from media production in his 2010 pamphlet on jihadist media guidelines.[33]

In line with the evolution of AQAP's overall media strategy for engaging local audiences, the martyrdom narrative has shifted increasingly to video, with feature-length film series such as 'Rakb al-Shuhada' (Convoy of Martyrs) from 2012, which can deal with twenty martyrs at once, to the series of shorter videos 'Wa-Yattakhidhu Min-kum Shuhada' (And He Takes Among You Martyrs) from 2010, sometimes with written transcripts. The latter series is designed to celebrate a single significant martyr—with the exception of the initial release when there was clearly a backlog of martyrs to deal with. Several useful strategies present in the above-mentioned 2009 martyrdom video were picked up and developed in future video productions. For example, the 2009 video attempts to tap into tribal codes of honour and pride by ensuring that the name of each martyr's tribe appears in the on-screen credits as well as in the voice-over. In later films, such as *Convoy of Martyrs 1*, in which twenty smiling martyrs appear in turn to the swish of clashing swords, this naming of each tribal affiliation has the added effect of making AQAP appear broadly popular among the tribes and therefore well-protected. The 2009 video also makes a primitive attempt to locate the martyr's image in an artificial haze of green, presumably meant to resemble the gardens of Paradise as the destination of the gory remains pictured. Better effects were introduced over time. By 2011, the green haze had metamorphosed into graphics of luxuriant foliage dripping with dew drops, among which the carefully constructed image of a smiling martyr hovers radiantly.[34] Unlike the poetry, however, which evokes images of welcoming virgins promising sexual gratification,[35] the film footage falls short of creating such graphic scenes on screen.

Finally, just like the poetry, the martyrdom video appeals to local pride by situating the contemporary martyr at the end of a long and glorious tribal warrior tradition. The 2009 video cuts to footage of impressive landscapes and praises various tribes, such as the Nahm of Hadramawt, for their ancient warrior lineage that continues to provide AQAP with brave mujahidin. More sophisticated expertise has enabled this tribal engagement strategy to be refined. The 2015 martyrdom film for 'Ali bin al-Aqra' (Lakraa') al-Kazimi al-'Awlaqi (d. 2014 in a drone strike), a prominent leader of Ansar al-Shari'ah in Abyan, is designed to provoke tribal outrage and wounded pride. After linking the martyr to the historical glories of his tribe, the film cuts to images of wretched contemporary living conditions in dilapidated stick huts, juxtaposing this with glossy footage of impressive oil infrastructure that 'robs the wealth from under them'. This plays powerfully to the desires of frustrated youths to join in and 'do something'. Many of the films end on an emotional high with the lingering on-screen caption 'Join the Convoy', which suggests the kind of camaraderie and group identity offered by becoming part of the broader jihadist project.

The martyrdom narratives also engage local audiences for the global jihad by drawing parallels between their historical struggles and today's jihadist cause. The 2015 martyrdom film for 'Ali bin al-Aqra' (Lakraa') al-Kazimi al-'Awlaqi cuts to footage of the tribe's rebellion against the British in the 1960s to provide local evidence for the idea of an ongoing struggle against the global crusader enemy. The tribe's honour and responsibility are also linked to the plight of Muslims globally by inserting footage of dead babies and Muslims being mistreated, including at the hands of the Israeli police, all to the background music of rousing *nashids*.[36]

Constructing the enemy

This brings us to a second key theme of jihadist narratives in Yemen: constructing a coherent enemy that can play to al-Qaeda's global agenda whilst still appealing to locals by resonating with their immediate grievances and historical concerns. The ultimate enemy is America and the West who are blamed for propping up secular Arab regimes to serve their own selfish desire for oil and power, thereby preventing the possibility of just rule in Muslim countries through the application of shari'ah law. Again we see the deployment of culturally attuned materials, like poems and *nashids*, to instil the idea of this global enemy among local populations. The advantage of such materials is that they can reach even those who are illiterate and technologically isolated. Moreover, unlike the doctrinal and juristic materials, cultural production can telescope a complex political landscape into a simple apocalyptic battle between good and evil that is easy to understand and difficult to refute. On the side of good are the virtuous mujahidin, defenders of the people, whom jihadist narratives implant into the popular imagination through the deployment of age-old tropes of lions, heroes, knights and warriors. On the side of the bad are America, the West, Israel, the Yemeni regime, other Arab regimes, the military and, by vague extension, their 'clients' and 'allies'. Cultural production glosses over the doctrinal debates about which Muslims merit excommunication and blurs this rich range of enemies into convenient stigmatised images of crusaders, Zionists, infidels, dogs and ants. The power of such narratives lies in the illusion they create of reflecting the world while in reality they are actively structuring it in people's minds.

AQAP narratives have also attempted to play to local audiences, particularly in Yemen's south, by blurring local enemies such as the Houthis with the Western crusading enemy of global jihad. Several AQAP ideologues explicitly claimed Houthis to be conniving with America to occupy Islamic lands,[37] presumably helped along by rhetoric emanating from various Gulf states reacting to the growing rapprochement between America and Iran. This narrative became more difficult to sustain in Yemen after America backed the Saudi bombing campaign against the Houthis in March 2015. As a result, the sectarian dimension to the narrative increased, justifying the Houthis as enemies on purely religious grounds, without necessarily requiring association with the crusading West, although the Houthi—US identification persisted in some quarters[38] and was given a new lease of life following the start of concerted US airstrikes against AQAP targets in March 2016.[39] Analysts frequently draw a neat distinction between al-Qaeda and IS, based on the idea that the former is focused on 'the far enemy' (America and the West) and the latter on 'the near enemy' (Arab regimes and Shiites). Daniel L. Byman, for example, writes that al-Qaeda 'considers Shi'a Muslims to be apostates but sees their killing to be too extreme, a waste of resources, and detrimental to the broader jihadist project', namely the fight against the US and its allies.[40] This reflects the position outlined by al-Qaeda's global leader, al-Zawahiri, particularly in relation to his disapproval of al-Qaeda in Iraq's brutal targeting of Shiites under al-Zarqawi (d. 2006) in the mid-2000s, out of which, of course, IS evolved. However, it is perhaps an overstatement for Yemen today.

The sectarian dimension to AQAP's narrative became more prominent with the turmoil that accompanied the 2011 uprising and the increasing Houthi influence that this threatened. One opening headline from AQAP's *Madad* in 2011, for example, reads 'Shaykh Ibrahim al-Rubaysh: The Houthi Microbe is like cancer; it can only be treated by cutting it out.'[41] As early as 2011, al-Rubaysh was calling on Sunnis everywhere to fight jihad against the Houthis. Houthis were framed as the enemy on religious grounds, accused of 'spreading their Shi'ite perversity, fables and innovations among the Muslims'.[42] Hence the killing of non-combatants was permissible, and *Madad* celebrates three suicide bombers who blew themselves up in Houthi crowds in 2010, reportedly leaving hundreds of non-combatants dead.[43] AQAP's attempt to harness local tribal concerns to its increasingly sectarian narrative can be seen in its claim that its targeting of Houthis in 2012 'met with a lot of satisfaction from the honourable tribes of Ma'rib after the Houthi attempt to spread followers in their areas to propagate the Rejectionists' devious beliefs'.[44] It is of course far more likely that both the Ma'rib tribes and the Houthis were battling over territory and resources, not religion.

The sectarian dimension to AQAP's rhetoric has increased dramatically since 2014. There are likely to be three reasons for this: the natural hardening of its existing narrative following the Houthi takeover of the capital Sana'a in

September 2014 and subsequent advances; an effective strategy for 'selling' a jihadist agenda to southern tribes fearful of Houthi incursions; and a reaction to the whirlwind rise of IS which has publicly criticised AQAP for its weak sectarian stance and tried to muscle in on AQAP in Yemen. IS has seized on the Houthi advances to criticise AQAP as ineffective and to position the new Caliphate as the natural solution for Yemen's Sunni Muslims. IS slammed AQAP's video denial (released 21 November 2014, featuring Harith bin Ghazi al-Nazari) of allegiance to Caliph Abu Bakr, blaming AQAP's continued allegiance to al-Qaeda's al-Zawahiri for obstructing Yemen's sectarian battle against the Houthi scourge.[45] It attempted to undermine the credibility of AQAP by offering only two interpretations of AQAP's behaviour: either AQAP's weak sectarian stance was facilitating the Houthi advance, or its gradual recognition of Houthis as apostates was evidence of its hypocrisy since it contravened al-Zawahiri's guidelines.[46] AQAP's ratcheting up of its sectarian narrative in its construction of the enemy may in part be a response to the risks of defection brought by such criticisms from IS. Hence AQAP framed its 'From the Field' video series, launched in 2014, as a project to 'defend Sunnis from Houthi Rejectionists' despite the fact that it is set in Hadramawt, far from the Houthi front line. What the series in fact records are operations against the Yemeni military, which it describes as 'Houthi-ised'. The fact that attacks on Yemen's military are now justified on the grounds of being linked to Shiism rather than to America marks a distinct shift in AQAP's narrative in the direction of IS's extreme sectarianism. This brings us to the broader issue of how AQAP is dealing with the emergence of IS in Yemen.

AQAP versus Islamic State in Yemen

Assessing IS appeal in Yemen is difficult. To what extent do AQAP's official spokesmen really reflect or control attitudes within the organisation as a whole? And, conversely, how far can the actions of particular AQAP cells be taken to represent the approach of the group as a whole? AQAP leaders initially tried to adopt a neutral position towards IS, with two notable exceptions.[47] The start of the US-led coalition bombing campaign against Islamic State in mid-2014 elicited an AQAP statement of solidarity 'with our Muslim brothers' against 'the crusade'. As we have seen, this changed in November 2014 after a group calling itself 'The Mujahidin of Yemen' released an audio recording swearing allegiance to the IS Caliph.[48] IS accepted this oath and publicly nullified AQAP in the process.[49] The denial of the oath by AQAP's leadership in turn elicited a furious response from IS.[50] This dispute clearly reveals divisions between key AQAP leaders and at least some of their rank and file. IS itself stated that its supporters in Yemen came 'from the soldiers and leaders (not including the top-level leadership)'.[51] These divisions have been acknowledged by al-Qaeda itself. Leadership figures from Jabhat al-Nusra in Syria as well as AQAP referred to the rift caused by IS among Yemen's mujahidin.[52] Even Ma'mun Hatim (d. 2015 in a drone strike), a jihadist media activist and strong early advocate of IS in Yemen, revealed in his Twitter feed that he considered the Caliphate's move on AQAP untimely and unhelpful.

Nevertheless, IS narratives of violence appear to have found approval among AQAP's more radical militants, and this suggests that AQAP's leaders may not be in full control of their movement. The gruesome beheading in August 2014 of up to 14 Yemeni soldiers by AQAP in Hadramawt, for example, bore the hallmarks of an IS copycat operation. Senior AQAP spokesman Nasr bin 'Ali al-'Anisi (d. 2015 in a drone strike) acknowledged that 'some of our brothers were influenced by seeing scenes of beheadings that were spread recently'.[53] This marked a violent departure from previous AQAP narratives. An AQAP film from 2009, by contrast, showed seven captured Yemeni soldiers being treated to a religious lecture and assured that 'the door of repentance is still open'.[54] This violent 'turn' is compounded by the fact that Jalal Bal'idi al-Marqashi (d. 2016 in a drone strike), who allegedly orchestrated the Hadramawt beheadings, had himself previously demonstrated compassion. Whilst leading Ansar al-Shari'ah in Abyan in March 2012, he assured 73 captured soldiers that they would be treated well, saying: 'You will eat from the same that we eat and be clothed from the same quality of clothing with which we clothe ourselves.'[55] His hardening attitude can be glimpsed in a short video from October 2013 in which, having swapped his traditional dress for military fatigues, he complained bitterly about the maltreatment of mujahidin by the state security. The hardening attitude among AQAP cells in Hadramawt is also evidenced by the film series 'From the Field', with its open celebration of violence (fighters gloating over bloodied corpses) and its firm focus on the military aspects of operations. This, together with the fact that the operations are attributed to Wilayat Hadramawt, makes it tempting to view this as an IS phenomenon. Yet Wilayat Hadramawt is a name that AQAP had announced as early as 2012[56] following its expulsion from Abyan and should not be taken as evidence of association with IS. Moreover, the films bear the insignia of AQAP's al-Malahim media and carry the concluding AQAP caption, 'O Aqsa, We Are Coming'.

While the above does not evidence IS expansion, it does indicate that a range of attitudes currently exists *within* AQAP and that the top leadership may not be wholly in control. The 'From the Field' series, for example, contravenes media guidelines set out by al-Qaeda ideologue 'Atiyyat Allah al-Libi (d. 2011 in a drone strike). Originally published in 2010, their re-release in April 2015 by an al-Qaeda associated media group suggests an attempt to rein in a perceived uptick in brutality that may have arisen among AQAP rank and file, although it is unclear whether this arose out of rivalry with or sympathy for IS. The guidelines advise jihadist media to avoid exaggeration and refrain from using images of executions or mujahidin taking pleasure in lethal operations.[57] Interestingly, IS's Caliph Abu Bakr was also reported to have issued media guidelines in July 2015 instructing Islamic State media to tone down their images of overt brutality in order not to alienate the broader Muslim public.[58] Even if the latter report is true, the jihadist horror genre has gained a momentum that will be difficult to stop.

The AQAP leadership has clearly tried to steer away from the alienating effects of extreme brutality in a bid to maintain broader support. Nasr bin 'Ali al-'Anisi referred to the Hadramawt beheadings as 'individual acts' and 'a big mistake'.[59] AQAP even apologised publicly for its attack on a Ministry of Defence hospital in 2013. This apology again suggests that AQAP does not have full command and control, stating of the attacker: 'We did not order him to do so, and we are not pleased with what he did... We offer our apologies and condolences to the victims.'[60] AQAP was also quick to dissociate itself from IS's devastating spate of mosque bombings, which began with the double bombing of Friday prayers in Sana'a on 20 March 2015, resulting in over 135 Muslim deaths and injuring over 350 further Muslims. It restated its commitment to 'avoid targeting mosques, markets and crowded places',[61] earning an angry response from the Caliphate whose magazine *Dabiq* called AQAP 'two-faced'.[62] Perhaps even more significantly, given its religious dimension, AQAP also denied any link to the 4 March 2016 attack on a Catholic-run old people's home in Aden that killed 15, including four nuns, stating 'this is not our way of fighting'.[63]

AQAP narratives have thus tried to strike a balance between eschewing extreme brutality to maintain broader support whilst ramping up militant sectarian rhetoric to keep the rank and file on side. Nevertheless, it is clear that defections to IS have occurred. For example, dozens of armed fighters from AQAP's Ansar al-Shari'ah in Lahj reportedly drove through the city of al-Hawta in late February 2015 brandishing IS flags, pinning notices with IS headers to shops and demanding that residents declare allegiance to IS.[64] So, how popular *is* IS in Yemen? One estimate placed the number of IS militants in Yemen in July 2015 at between 250 and 300, owing to increasing defections from AQAP.[65] However, despite indisputable indications that fault-lines exist within AQAP, there is also a risk that analysts and media buy into IS rhetoric creating the illusion that it has gained more traction than it actually has. Does a group of disgruntled youths waving a flag in front of a camera and pledging allegiance to the Caliph make them a province of the Islamic State? Does the local dissemination of identical photocopied announcements of new Islamic State provinces in Hadramawt, Aden and Lahj testify to a significant IS expansion, or just wishful thinking?[66]

AQAP's response to the self-proclamation of various new IS provinces around Yemen in late February 2015 is instructive. It reveals that IS uses money to recruit and that some AQAP fighters had indeed defected, causing ill-feeling, for example, by rejecting invitations to discuss the situation and refusing to return their AQAP weapons and cars. But it also implies that IS in Yemen had no clear leader at the outset, that it was gaining little traction in the tribes, and that its recruits were being coordinated from Syria by someone called Jamil al-Zahiri.[67] It is also important to note that the claiming of attacks by an Islamic *wilaya* (province) does not automatically signal the presence of IS. AQAP has a history of using the term *wilaya* to claim territory for Islamic rule, as distinct from the term *muhafaza* (governorate) used by the secular state. Despite the proliferation of 'emirate' ('*imara*) in many media reports concerning AQAP-held territory in Yemen's south in 2011–12, the term *wilaya* was already widely used in AQAP's own media output. Hence it is natural (rather than derivative of IS practice) that AQAP today should also refer to Wilayat Hadramawt, Wilayat Abyan and so on. Moreover, IS official media in Iraq and Syria have shown little interest in the seven or more self-proclaimed provincial IS affiliates in Yemen outside Wilayat Sana'a, raising the possibility that domestic political players may be seeking to exploit the IS label to their own advantage. Thus there appears to be little evidence up to the time of writing of a centrally coordinated strategy by the Caliphate itself to proliferate the number of IS provinces in Yemen much beyond the notion of Wilayat Sana'a.

There are several reasons why IS nevertheless continues to attract support among a certain sector of Yemen's jihadist community. First, it offers victory. It has enjoyed a meteoric rise in Iraq and Syria, while AQAP could not even prevent the Houthis from sweeping through Yemen. Second, it offers money.

This is suggested by AQAP's complaint that IS is winning over young men with offers of wealth.[68] Third, it offers identity. The IS brand represents a heady mix of violence, power and piety. Its global community ideology is accessible to anyone with an internet connection and may also be being spread by Yemeni mujahidin returning triumphant from Syria and Iraq to assist in Yemen's current war.[69] A further factor pushing some AQAP militants towards IS may be leadership issues within AQAP. Guiding figures from the Islah party (Yemen's religious party) with close ties to AQAP disappeared to Saudi Arabia to watch the civil war play out.[70] More significantly, many key AQAP leaders, including some who stood up to IS, were picked off by drones in quick succession just as IS began to emerge on the scene in Yemen.[71]

While IS may have found support among the most radical of Yemen's muja-hidin, it appears to have found little traction within Yemen's tribes.[72] This may be where AQAP's strategy of culturally attuned engagement targeting local communities gives it the advantage. The first IS video from Yemen, released in late April 2015, does not suggest much of a threat to AQAP and appears somewhat alien to local culture. It features eighteen men in matching beige uniforms and sandals in a desert pledging allegiance to IS and vowing to fight the Houthis. It is a sophisticated production, beginning with the dramatic and highly symbolic act of planting the Islamic State flag in the (presumably) Yemeni desert to three cries of 'Dawlat al-Islam' (Islamic State). The men per-form carefully choreographed military exercises in unison, in a manner remi-niscent of a dance routine, to the soundtrack of a stirring *nashid*, clashing swords, gunfire and desert winds. When this author showed the film to tribes-men from Yemen's eastern deserts, the reaction was one of bemusement. They puzzled at the synchronised routines, the pronunciation of certain words and the inexpert way in which some of the men handled their weapons and had tied the headscarf such that it would not offer protection from the desert. This suggests that foreign influence was involved in this production. Likewise, a video posted by IS Wilayat Shabwa at the end of April 2015 entitled 'The Cleansing of the Rejectionists (Houthis)' is unlikely to have engaged local audiences beyond the most radical mujahidin. It evidences a level of brutality highly unusual for Yemeni jihadist videos. The video begins with wailing cap-tive soldiers who are lined up and beheaded. A second group of soldiers is blindfolded and shot. Subsequent IS videos are less sophisticated productions but appear more authentic to the Yemen context. Both Wilayat Shabwa and Wilayat Sana'a posted videos in May 2015 featuring the popular tradition of sung poetry. The Wilayat Sana'a video, entitled 'Nawafidh Min Ard al-Yaman'

(Windows from the Land of Yemen), features a group of men, this time dressed as Yemenis might naturally dress (under their combat jackets), sitting on the ground enjoying a sung poetry session laden with threats against the Houthis. The video then cuts to shaky footage of primitive assassination operations against alleged Houthis in less than heroic circumstances—with one victim sleeping and another cowering behind a container. Even with the addition of traditional ingredients like sung poetry, it is unlikely that the kind of gratuitous brutality being marketed by IS in Yemen will find widespread appeal. This is borne out by the video testimony of one defector from IS in Yemen who explicitly criticized IS for 'lacking respect for Muslim blood'.[73]

Conclusion

The lightning rise of the brutal Islamic State with its expansionist ambitions has several possible outcomes for Yemen's jihad movement. Three of the more plausible outcomes, all of them negative for Western counter-terrorist efforts, are: (1) AQAP shifts its allegiance from al-Qaeda to IS, either en masse or gradually; (2) AQAP escalates its barbarity to compete with IS; (3) AQAP distances itself from the barbarity of IS, meaning that the most radical mujahidin will splinter off to IS and that AQAP may gain broader support by appearing as the lesser of the two evils in fighting off Shiite/Houthi expansion, whilst at the same time implementing community development projects where the state has failed. As has been shown above, at the time of writing, the first outcome seems unlikely given AQAP's efforts to entrench within local communities by marketing itself more as protector than overlord, albeit with some exceptions. The second outcome has taken place to a limited extent, in that AQAP has been at pains to highlight its periodic meting out of shari'ah punishments in the light of criticism from IS, and its narrative has adopted a more extreme sectarianism. This escalation is unsurprising given the polarisation that civil war generates, and it may be exacerbated by the loss of some of AQAP's guiding voices—both by drone strikes in the case of militants, and by voluntary exodus to Saudi Arabia in the case of previously influential figures from Yemen's Islah party. The third outcome appears most probable, although broader support for AQAP will likely wane as it increasingly becomes a target of the coalition in 2016 (as opposed to a tacit ally in 2015). Long term, however, AQAP's tribal strongholds will only disappear if credible alternatives to its community development work are found. Meanwhile, there is little evidence to suggest that IS enjoys widespread support even within Yemen's jihadist community, and no evidence at all to suggest that the broader population of Yemen subscribes to the idea of a Caliphate. The main risk is that sectarianism is allowed to take root amid ongoing instability. Yemen is not a naturally sectarian country, but this may change as both AQAP and IS use the war and its aftermath as an opportunity to pin the local Houthi enemy onto a global jihadist agenda. The jihadist narrative, helped along by sectarian rhetoric emanating from Saudi Arabia and picked up by the international media, risks turning what were essentially political and tribal disputes over territory, resources and power into a long-term cycle of bloody sectarian violence.

AQAP's staying power in Yemen may in part be due to its culturally attuned narratives that appear to have given it the advantage over IS. AQAP practises a dual-stranded engagement strategy—emotional and practical—to win local hearts for its global agenda. As we have seen, it does this in a culturally specific way: emotionally, by harnessing local traditions of poetry and song, and practically, by positioning itself as the saviour and defender of local communities, for example by the use of brands like Ansar al-Shari'ah, Sons of Hadramawt or Sons of Abyan. Both strands of local engagement play off tribal codes of honour/disgrace, pride/shame or revenge/compassion. It is these local narratives that can strike a chord with Yemeni communities. While the militants themselves like to know that the doctrinal discourse of global jihad supports their actions (and al-Qaeda has produced this in significant quantities), this dry material does not have the immediacy and heady emotional appeal of the cultural material—photos of dead children to avenge, peaceful smiling martyrs to emulate, green meadows of Paradise to aspire to. And all this is imbued with a local flavour and interspersed with rousing poetic verses, many of them easily converted to anthems—suited to journeying, or long evenings around the campfire. IS, by contrast, has not yet attained the same level of cultural attunement in Yemen. Its first highly choreographed video release from Yemen seems culturally remote. Although subsequent video releases from IS Yemen gained in cultural credibility in terms of dress, setting and their showcasing of sung poetry, this is unlikely to be sufficient to offset the abhorrent levels of barbarity and indiscriminate violence, at which even AQAP has baulked.

How can we respond to the persistence of jihadism in Yemen? Military action is unlikely to be the solution because assassinations, particularly by drone strike, incite angry cycles of revenge, and leaders are easily replaced. Policing the internet is only a small part of the solution because ideas live on in the popular imagination. Jihadist cultural production is especially potent because film and photo images are branded into the collective memory, while the circulation of jihadist poetry and *nashids* persists in oral tradition. Therefore, we need to shore up our existing expedient strategies with the propagation of counter-narratives that engage at a culturally specific level, as AQAP itself does. This is unlikely to succeed unless those narratives are produced locally, albeit perhaps with sensitive external facilitation.

Scholars today are waking up to the idea that speaking to emotions may be at least as important as speaking to minds through ideological argumentation. It does not, however, follow that economic imperatives are therefore less of a priority than some counter-terrorism experts believe.[74] One must ask: would the emotional appeal of militant jihad still hold if locals were able to get on with their lives in a stable and secure economic environment with the possibility of education, jobs and advancement based on meritocratic criteria? Put more bluntly, alleviating misery and creating aspiration means that attaining Paradise through death can await its natural moment instead of appearing to be an immediate practical solution. Hence, counter-narratives should be coupled with a long-term strategy to remove the underlying reasons for joining radical groups or even just tolerating them.

Some communities, such as those in Yemen's far eastern al-Mahrah governorate are already trying to initiate basic social programmes to reduce their youth's vulnerability to AQAP outreach activities.[75] And they are coupling this with a positive narrative that publicises inspiring initiatives and engages local concerns through their community newspaper *Sawt al-Mahrah* (The Voice of al-Mahrah). Although this is funded by an international grant facilitated by this author, the content is generated locally and gives voice to al-Mahrah's marginalised communities. As long as international attempts to 'fix' Yemen continue to interact with the same old leaders and elites, who claim to speak for 'the people' but without engaging seriously with deep-seated local concerns, vulnerability to militant jihadism will remain. This is particularly the case in Yemen's outlying tribal areas where AQAP is most easily able to spread its influence and dig in.

7

INSIDE THE PROPAGANDA MACHINE
OF AL-QAEDA IN THE ISLAMIC MAGHREB
AND ITS EVOLUTION FOLLOWING THE RISE
OF ISLAMIC STATE

Valentina Bartolucci

Introduction

Recent events have shown in dramatic ways that violent extremist organisations (VEOs) have increased their appeal around the world. More than ever, it is therefore vital to delve deeper into understanding this phenomenon by systematically analysing the rhetoric used by such organisations to persuade and recruit new members. The strategic communication of VEOs has evolved dramatically in the past few years, driven by multiple factors including the changing geopolitical landscape, the ubiquity of new social media and, crucially, the rise of the so-called Islamic State (IS). This chapter examines the evolution of al-Qaeda in the Islamic Maghreb (AQIM) in relation to IS by showing that the two movements have always had different worldviews and, consequently, very different communicative strategies and discourses. To this end, this chapter presents the results of a detailed analysis of texts produced by AQIM and of an analysis of the visual propaganda of IS.

While not as well known as other jihadist groups, AQIM presents an important case study, being one of the most vocal and active terrorist groups in North Africa. Although there is a fairly extensive body of literature on the organisation, most of it deals with its history and tactical operations.[1] Conversely, IS is far better known internationally, both for its activities in Iraq and Syria and more recently for having carried out terrorist attacks in various countries. Its precipitous rise, methods of operations and immense propaganda machine have resulted in an intense scrutiny by the media, policymakers and the public at large.[2] Furthermore, its unprecedented appeal has already resulted in tens of thousands of people from over a hundred countries joining it it thus far, with more feared likely to follow.[3]

The centrality of communication to AQIM's political strategy has long been evident; nevertheless, academic works that systematically analyse its discourse are few and remain marginal in the literature.[4] As for IS, while it is true that it has 'revolutionized jihadist messaging', still 'for too long, the immensity of Islamic State's propaganda machine has obscured a rational understanding of it'.[5] The present work seeks to contribute to fill this gap by systematically analysing AQIM and IS official discourses in order to explore the use of the particular words and grammatical forms to establish meaning, identities, interests and behaviours.[6]

The first section of this chapter briefly outlines the theoretical and analytical framework guiding the research and provides the reader with information on the data collection and analysis. The second and third sections constitute the core of the paper. The second section presents the results of a detailed textual analysis of AQIM official discourse, performed through the lens of Critical Discourse Analysis. The analysis reveals a fascination for violence and death as well as growing global aspirations, as evidenced by frequent references to the 'Zionist—Crusader Alliance'. References to historical figures that resonate in the Maghreb are abundant in the corpus, helping to bridge local and international grievances. The third section presents the results of an analysis of the IS visual communication strategy. The analysis reveals that there is more to IS messaging than the widely publicised images of violence and brutality. While IS's communication strategy is driven by a desire to outrage hostile audiences, perhaps more important is their attempt to offer very positive images of happiness and fulfilment living in the Caliphate.

Methods of analysis

This study has been carried out through the prism of Critical Discourse Analysis (CDA), a mode of research traditionally associated with the academic field of applied linguistics. CDA seeks to complement the linguistic analysis of texts with an interdisciplinary approach directed at the deconstruction of the whole socio-political and historical contexts in which discourses are embedded.[7] Specifically, CDA aims at critically investigating structural relations of power, control and domination as constituted, expressed and legitimised in discourse.[8] It does this by challenging the neutrality of language and devoting particular attention to exploring the implications deriving from the use of particular words and grammatical forms in specific contexts.[9]

The AQIM corpus for analysis is made up of 106 official statements bearing the 'signature' of the organisation, for a total of 166,711 words. These constitute all the AQIM texts that could be retrieved from a database of texts from Islamist extremist groups compiled by the Center for Strategic Communication (CSC) at Arizona State University.[10] The texts were originally released by AQIM in Arabic, then translated into English by researchers at the CSC. The texts were created and disseminated by AQIM with the clear intent to reach the widest possible audience, although at times only minimally circulated. Texts including secondary information about the organisation, such as news or reports on AQIM, are not part of the corpus. All texts were first coded and, subsequently, software was specifically designed for this corpus.[11] The computational analysis helped identify patterns of discourse, concordance and collocations. The data were categorised by year in order to identify trends in the discourse; however, the raw data could be misleading as the number of texts produced per year varies greatly (for instance, there are 34 documents for the year 2010 and only 8 for the year 2012). In order to bypass this issue, the data were standardised by dividing the number of occurrences by the total number of texts. The fragments of texts reported in this chapter have been selected based on how they reveal a pattern of discourse. All quotes have been reproduced faithfully to the originals. The texts in bold are words, phrases or passages worth emphasising for the discussion. The computer-aided textual analysis was subsequently enriched by a manual analysis. The period of analysis goes from 27 January 2007 (when the organisation previously known as *Groupe Salafiste pour la Prédication et le Combat*, GSPC, formally pledged alliance to al-Qaeda) to the end of December 2013 (when the database was accessed by the author for the last time). This analysis has been updated to include official statements posted by the organisation on its Twitter account, managed by the El Andalous Establishment for Media Production—AQIM's media arm—which were checked daily by the author until 15 December 2015.[12] As will be explored, some of the most notable features of the AQIM discourse in the corpus include the 'us vs. them' representation, the strategy of predication, the construction of the 'evil other', and arguably the most important feature, a negative self-representation.

The full body of IS strategic communication is vast, with new material being released in multiple languages and published every day. For the analysis of IS visual communication presented in this chapter, the corpus is made of 120 images published in one of IS's key official media publications *Dabiq* magazine, over the course of seventeen months, starting with the self-proclamation of its leader Abu Bakr al-Baghdadi as 'caliph' on 29 June 2014.[13] The images were regrouped under various themes, the most important being: Brutality; Death; Conquest; Mercy; Victimhood; Belonging; Hope; Apocalyptic Utopianism.[14] The choice of visual propaganda is due to the fact that the great majority of what the Islamic State media apparatus produces is visual imagery, and this material seemed to provide a useful insight for comparison with the AQIM texts analysed in the first part.[15]

AQIM's discourse

AQIM strategic communications are well designed. In the texts analysed, there is a constant quest for legitimisation of the organisation and its actions. This is achieved in three ways: 1) through a drastic polarisation between 'us' and 'them' (enemies of God, enemies of Muslims, the apostates, the slaves of America and the agents of France); 2) through the vilification of the enemy; and 3) through a highly negative self-representation.[16]

The 'us' versus 'them' representation

The first rhetorical device, dividing the moral 'us' and the immoral 'them', is commonly adopted in political communication.[17] In AQIM's official pronouncements, the polarisation of 'us' ('the lions of Islam', 'the lions of Al Qaeda', 'the martyred heroes', 'the martyrdom-seekers') and 'them' (AQIM enemies) clearly emerges. The 'us versus them' polarisation oversimplifies a complex topic, reducing it to a binary opposition using condensational symbols. The following fragments are illustrative of such a binary discourse:

- God judges between us and them.
- We encourage you to learn lessons, return to your senses, and to stop killing or capturing the Muslims to satisfaction of the crusader infidels.
- Indeed, the lions of Islam have lain in wait for the enemies of God and employed every stratagem against them.

The frequent use of third-person plural pronouns in the corpus (*they, them*, 1,848 times) is also significant, as it further suggests that AQIM is defining itself by reference to an oppositional group. Furthermore, a frequent usage of third-person and of first-person plural pronouns (*we, us*, 1,502 times) indicates that the speakers are addressing an audience that they think share the same worldview, while at the same time attempting to bring more people closer to their ideology. See for instance the following extracts:

- The mujahidin will bring dark days upon them, God willing, making them forget the elation of the false dreams and aspirations that they promoted in their media.
- Here are the masses of Muslims chanting 'we are all Usama'.
- We seek the satisfaction of God in all our acts. God guides us to the righteous path.

Finally, the common usage in the AQIM texts of exclusive or contrast words such as *except, but, exclude* and *without* further signals the intention to make a distinction, to separate 'us' from 'them'.

- But we now tell them that time has changed [...] we are more alert and aware of all the schemes with the pockets of hypocrisy and treason that are being plotted against us.

The strategy of predication: constructing an evil 'other'

The second rhetorical device that AQIM commonly adopts may be described as a strategy of predication, in which the objective is to label actors in particular ways—in this case negatively.[18] A discursive *self*, in order to make sense of its identity, necessitates a discursive *other*.[19] In the texts analysed, not surprisingly, the 'other' is represented in highly negative terms and there is a remarkably high rate of anger or hostile words. In the book *Faces of the Enemy*, Keen shows how enemy images can be historically categorised within certain archetypes, such as enemy as animal, enemy as torturer of prisoners, enemy as barbarian.[20] Such archetypes can be easily found in AQIM's portrayals of the enemy.

In the texts analysed, the *other* is frequently represented as *animals* commonly associated with negativity or even repulsion, such as rats that have to be killed to cleanse the earth, pigs, monkeys, apes, snakes and dogs. The following statements are illustrative of this:

- By God, the nation has lost lions of Islam, trustworthy men, and swords that startle the brothers of the monkeys and the pigs.
- To the Jews, Christians, and their apostate dogs, we say: Rejoice in what will befall you, and dig your graves (God willing), for the descendants of Tariq Bin-Ziyad are racing to martyrdom.
- To Shaykh Abu-Muhammad, who, like a lion, attacks the terrified rats to cleanse the earth.

Rats are usually seen as particularly loathsome, and invariably associated with destruction, disease, the spread of plague, and repulsion. Similarly, the image of the snake suggests that the enemy is by nature poisonous, hostile, vicious and potentially lethal. Monkeys are used to emphasise the inferiority of the enemy, and representing someone as such is used to express their disbelief. Pigs are considered the dirtiest animals in Islam, and in large parts of the Muslim world dogs are seen as impure and unclean.[21] Associating the enemy with these kinds of animals is tied to words commonly used when speaking of wiping out diseases or infestations. Furthermore, in those circumstances, the need for destruction encompasses the whole as it would be ineffective and ludicrous to try to separate the individual from the mass.

In some speeches, the other is not only represented as inhuman, but is even reduced to a parasite. Humans are represented as parasites in the sense that they live at the expense of others. Parasites, indeed, cannot live independently—they need a host to live, grow and multiply, gaining strength at its expense. Usually, they are small, they reproduce very quickly and, crucially, they are characterised by their mass—their sheer numbers make them a threat. In this sense, the enemy is seen as dangerous and repugnant. The image of a parasite brings with it the idea of creatures that are hard to kill and, once killed, are able to return more strongly than before. Images, such as that of hordes of rats, underline the enemy's resilience and its ability to spread. Representing the enemies as these kinds of animals dehumanises them, implying that the only conceivable solution is to eliminate them.

Other representations reinforce the de-humanisation of the enemy. In several extracts, the enemy is represented as *desecrator of innocents, women, and children* and as *torturer of prisoners*. The following extracts are examples:

- The scene of the innocent, completely unarmed, sick, women, and children who were killed, [...] the barbaric torture [...] are all hard evidences which clearly indicate that it is a profligate and unjust Crusade [...] under the slogan: 'Destroy Islam and annihilate its people'.
- The recent hostilities, arrests, and torture carried out by the forces of injustice and oppression, and their crusader masters, against the pure Muslim young men in our beloved Mauritania will not pass without punishment.
- [...] the striking and killing of innocent and defenceless Muslims, in collusion with the Zionist Arabs, with Zionist support, American trickery, and continued European [involvement].
- They [Muslim captives in Uganda] have been subject to torture and humiliation.

As evident in the extracts above, the enemy is represented as vicious and cruel, and its actions invariably denoted as brutal and destructive. Furthermore, while the other is represented as *impure*, and an aberrant subject that is inherently bad, AQIM's supporters and affiliates are represented by contrast as innocent, unarmed, defenseless and *pure*. The question of purity/impurity is particularly important. Purity is connected with cleanliness, and is an essential aspect of Islam. The human analogue to impure animals like dogs and pigs is the *kafir*, the infidel, apostate or unbeliever (as opposed to the true Muslim). A *kafir* can become *tahir* (pure) only if he/she converts to Islam. See, for instance, the following fragment:

- In addition, they have sworn to God that they would not be happy or satisfied and would not halt using their swords until they cleanse the Islamic Maghreb of the impurity of the impure apostates and their Crusader masters, who are rancorous men with their vile man-made laws.
- Praise be to God, the Almighty and All-Powerful, Champion of the pious and Disgracer of the impious.

The enemy is also represented *as criminal, aggressor and greedy*. For instance:

- If Muslims do not rise up and shake the dust of humiliation and shame, this criminal authoritarian gang [the French and the Americans] will remain to make you experience afflictions, humiliation and enslavement.
- [...] the criminals who have the blood of innocent Muslims on their hands.
- This action came to foment the hatred of Muslims toward your continuous crimes and repeated aggressions against Islam and its people.
- The result was a déjà vu defeat that left dozens of killed and wounded among the ranks of the money worshippers who are driven by monetary rewards.

Non-Muslims, unbelievers and apostates—all engaged in a war against Islam—are represented as vicious criminals, deprived of any sense of honour, killing women, innocents and even elderly and sick people without discrimination. They do this not because of beliefs, but to conquer lands, steal resources and collect more money. They are *barbarian*, destroyers of a culture; they are rude and uncivilised:

- the Americans tossed him into the sea much as evil pirates and gangs do with their victims, as the primitive, most backward savages do with their enemy.

The 'other' is depersonalised; either not fully human or the very personification of evil. The enemies are represented as deniers of God, enemies of God, infidels, evils, evildoers, worshippers of evil. The United States of America, seen as the epitome of evil, is depicted as the 'chief of non-belief', the 'nursery of evil', and as the producer of all the bad things in the world:

- His [Bin Laden] sword still drawn against America, the chief of non-belief, the nursery of evil, the source of vice, the pinnacle of vileness, the epitome of injustice, and the emblem of savagery. He, God bless his soul, was poison to America.

Hyperboles abound in the discourse and work very effectively to portray the 'other' as evil.[22] As clearly emerges from the above discussion, the enemy is represented in highly negative ways and is dehumanised. Such representation of the 'other' reflects a worldview that essentially consists of two pairs of binary oppositions: human/not human. What is remarkable here is that this strategy of negative other representation is not accompanied by a positive self-representation. On the contrary, in the AQIM texts, the organisation's own members are often depicted in a highly negative way.

AQIM self-representation

The third strategy that AQIM adopts in its quest for legitimisation is a highly negative self-representation. In contrast with many political discourses in which the 'forces of goodness' are fighting against the 'forces of darkness' (see for instance President George W. Bush's discourse on terrorism), in this case 'the lions of al-Qaeda' linguistically represent themselves in highly negative terms, by describing their own actions as brutal and destructive and themselves as forces of destruction and death.

- We confirm to the sons of our ummah that the strikes of the mujahidin and their blows *will continue to kill* the slaves of America and the agents of France.
- 8 *Jumada al-Thani* [29 April 2012]: By God's grace, they were able to kill five police officers [...]; 11 Jumada al-Awwal 1433 [2 April 2012]: In the area of Hayzur, Faidh El Botma Municipality, Djelfa Province, an explosive device planted by the mujahidin detonated against a military truck. As a result, five soldiers were seriously wounded.

In many other speeches, similar actions are praised:

- In this clash, the lions of monotheism killed more than 30 soldiers and wounded others.
- [We] will continue to kill the slaves of America and the agents of France.

This rhetorical move conveys the image of a strong organisation able to carry out successful attacks and kill a high number of enemies. Furthermore, the device of over-lexicalisation works effectively in further stressing the 'evil' connotations attributed to the enemy.[23] Faced with such aberrant subjects on the ground—the 'other' who is not fully human, if not the very personification of evil—dialogue is not even conceivable. Rather, violent actions are not only legitimised when faced with such an enemy, but also framed as necessary and unavoidable and guided by God himself. The struggle against non-Muslims, infidels and apostates is framed as an act of revenge against 'the Crusaders' that for years have 'inflamed' the rage of Muslims. Violence is represented as the last option: negotiation was attempted but in vain.

- For three years we have been willing to negotiate, and our demands were clear and legitimate. Nevertheless, these demands were sometimes rejected, snubbed, and ignored; other times we were provoked by the French government.

The struggle (jihad) thus becomes a duty, a call that all Muslims need to listen to—and God is not neutral in this struggle. On the contrary, the battle is fought 'with God's support'.

- *Jihad* was a duty since Andalucía fell to the hands of the Christians, and this ruling has not changed till this day. *Jihad* has been a duty since 1492 C. E. [...] *Jihad* will remain a duty until we restore every part that was Islamic to the land of Islam and the hands of Muslims.
- Jihad in the cause of God is the only solution.

- By the will of God the Almighty, our battle with them is naught but a matter of patience [...] God fulfills His promise and supports His army.
- We will continue on his path, hold onto the truth, fight the Christians and their followers, the Jews and their supporters, and the apostates and their cronies until God judges between us and them. He is the fairest of judges.

The struggle is elevated to a cosmic battle between 'right' and 'wrong', between 'us' and 'them'. This rhetorical tool implies 'a dogmatic control of the truth which require[s] the speaker simply to exhort audience approval or action, not to deliberate upon which course of action to take'.[24] The abundance of religious references helps 'sanctify' AQIM's actions, framing them as supported by God himself. For example, in the following extracts:

- The ongoing war between truth and evil is comprised of a group of battles and subsequent stops.
- For 19 years the battle of truth against falsehood has worn on between two factions. One fights for God, relying on Him to champion his religion, defend the weak, and liberate the lands of Islam. The other is made up of nonbelievers, the sons of France. This group is supported and sponsored by the Crusader West.

Conflations and terminological slippages

Conflations and terminological slippages are common in the AQIM discourse. 'The West' is represented as a monolithic category, comprising European states, the US, as well as their 'friends' or 'slaves'. France and the US are very often mentioned together to represent the worst evil, deserving annihilation. The West is depicted as infidel, unbeliever, racist, cruel, bloodthirsty, crusader and greedy, as seen in the following extracts:

- We would like to assure you that the strikes and attacks of the mujahidin will continue to inflict massive calamities upon the slaves of America and the proxies of France.
- We confirm to the sons of our ummah that the strikes of the mujahidin and their blows will continue to kill the slaves of America and the agents of France. [...] The United States, France, and the infidel West have not and will not accept any real change that does not serve their interests in Tunisia...
- France, the mother of evils, and its mercenaries have drowned in the sands of Islam's greater Sahara desert. France will pay for its arrogance, injustice, and war against Islam and its peoples.

The analysis also reveals that the specificity of the US and France, as well as any differences in their foreign policies, are ignored. On the contrary, the two states are discursively represented as having the same political agenda, the same foreign policy and a common goal, the destruction of Islam and the domination of the Muslim world.

- The repeated assaults on the mujahidin by killing or capturing them in order to satisfy the United States and France's Sarkozy are part of a wrong and oppressive policy that goes against all legal principles and reason.
- We have no doubt that in the future the United States and France will play the same filthy role in Tunisia.

AQIM and IS

After several months of 'silence', presumably due to the rise of IS and internal disagreement over the future stand of the organisation, during 2015 AQIM started to threaten to stage attacks in France via its official Twitter account.[25] This is confirmed by an audio statement by Abu Yahya al Hammam, a senior AQIM leader, stating: 'we will seek revenge for the rest of our lives, and days and nights will not pass without our taking revenge against those who oppressed us. You have occupied our land, you have disrupted our shari'ah, you have assaulted our honor and dignity, you have shed our blood, you have looted our wealth and fortunes, and you have disturbed our security. We will treat you in kind.' He added: 'You have only tasted a bit of what you made the Muslims taste in the past decades.'[26]

In January 2015, AQIM praised the Islamic State for the 'heroic and rare' attack that caused the death of 12 people in Paris in what is known as the Charlie Hebdo massacre and urged Muslims to follow this path to further 'humiliate France'.[27] On 8 December 2015, a Tweet was posted urging 'Muslims in #Azawad, Neighboring Countries to Implement the Shari'a, Fight Against French Crusaders'.[28] Recently, the organisation released several statements on Twitter calling for the dismantling of apostate governments; eulogising a number of commanders who had lost their life in 'treacherous ambushes'; and offering 'condolences to the families of the martyrs'.[29] Finally, when considering the IS impact on AQIM's strategic communication, it is worth underlining that some AQIM members in leading positions have expressed support for IS with multiple messages of congratulations to the group for its military gains,[30] with some of them also calling for reconciliation between the two groups.[31] However, in other statements AQIM officially rejected the Islamic

State declaration of a Caliphate, refusing any alliance with the group.[32] These contradictory statements can be interpreted as evidence of internal rifts emerging within AQIM over the stand to take with regard to Islamic State.[33]

IS

Dabiq is a glossy periodic magazine, aimed at attracting a global audience by showing images with a strong visual and emotional impact.[34] It is a very professionally crafted and graphically well designed magazine, widely disseminated on the internet in English and other languages as a PDF document. Images are a key part of the magazine, and aim to demonstrate visually the magnitude of the threat posed by the Islamic State, as well as how the role of the organisation goes beyond simple military or terrorist objectives, to function as a proto-state seeking global support from all pious Muslims.

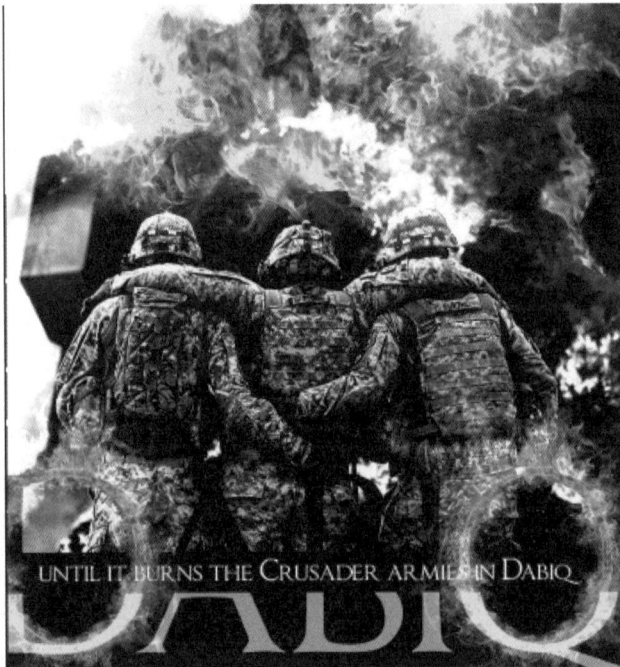

UNTIL IT BURNS THE CRUSADER ARMIES IN DABIQ

Figure 7.1: 'The return of Khilafah', *Dabiq*, issue 1

In every issue, a lot of attention is devoted to the ideological justification for the organisation's warfare, but also to rally support for their 'state' consolidation project. As such, there are frequent images of brutality and death as celebrations of its glorious achievements. An image showing American soldiers burning in flames (Figure 7.1)[35] is of particular note.

This and similar brutal and shocking images are designed to intimidate enemies but also help to gratify supporters, and to provoke outrage from the international media and over-reactions from hostile policy-makers. Connected to this are images of conquest, which help convey the idea of IS's grandiose plan to conquer the entire world. Emblematic are the highly symbolical images showing the black flag of IS flying above the obelisk at the centre of St Peter's Square in the Vatican and an image of the flood, through which IS attempts to be seen as the organisation that will lead the Muslim community into worldwide domina-

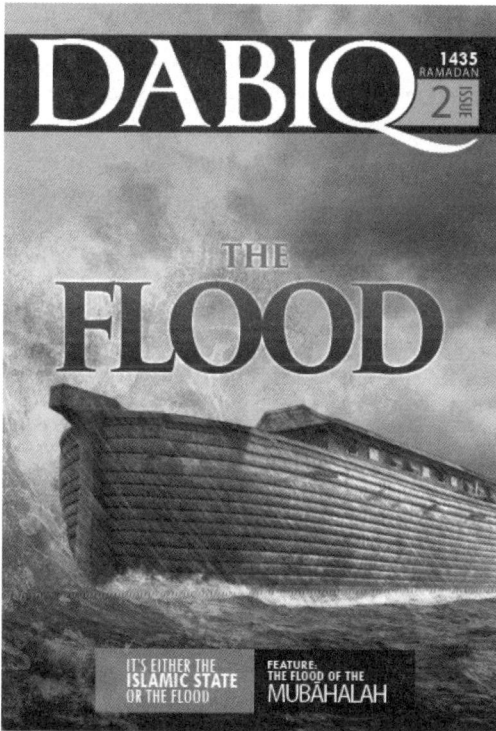

Figure 7.2: 'The Flood', *Dabiq*, issue 2

tion. Each of these images is steeped in and accompanied by an attempted religious justification (see Figures 1.2 and 1.1 in Chapter 1).[36]

Contrary to a common assumption, however, brutal and shocking images are not the core of the IS communication strategy. In tandem with brutality, images of mercy and victimhood are prominent. Important in this regard are the use and manipulation of children as tools of propaganda. Presenting children as victims, most famously the image of a dead child on the shore in Figure 7.3,[37] is contrasted with a constant and pressing call to all believing Muslims to migrate to the Islamic State to support the establishment of the Caliphate. A great deal of attention is devoted to showing how the organisation consolidates its power in the territories it controls, rallying support for its 'state'-building and 'state'-consolidation projects through a dichotomous ideological framework and through framing its self-perception in terms of an apocalyptic battle between good and evil.

The theme of belonging, although distinct, is also closely connected to the themes above and is arguably one of IS's most powerful draws to new recruits, particularly those from Western states. Through the regular publication of photos of fighters from all around the world relaxing with tea; warriors singing and smiling all together; and 'brothers' having good times in parks in what is a very carefully branded *camaraderie*, IS emphasises the idea of brotherhood in the Caliphate and conveys a positive image of inclusiveness, serenity and happiness. As such, this theme is strictly connected to the theme of hope.

The final theme that the group exploits is that of apocalyptic utopianism, which is arguably the broadest and most important theme of IS strategic communication. The images under this theme include children being taught how to recite the Qur'an, functioning hospitals, the establishment of shari'ah courts, the implementing of justice through punishments, collecting taxation,

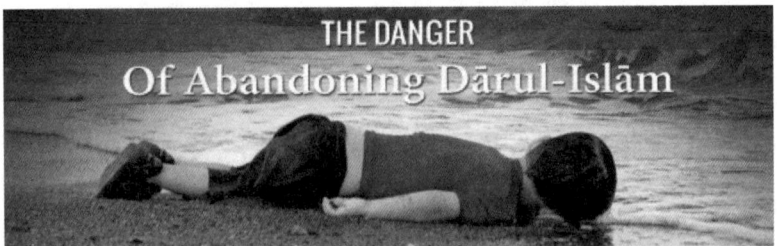

Figure 7.3: 'Of Abandoning Darul Islam', *Dabiq*, issue 11

dispensing *zakāt*—in other words a functioning and happy society. The magazine format, content and style is structured by contrasting images of brutality perpetrated by IS members to reach the organisation's goals with images showing the delights of living in the Caliphate. Through it, IS wants to show that a real Caliphate is actually a functioning society and a realistic response to a decadent Western society. In other words, its members are fighting for a better world, a world that offers real happiness, a world promised by Allah. At the core of the theme of apocalyptic utopianism lies the ultimate goal of restoring Islam's glory by becoming the world's dominant political and social order. This *new world* will result from a definitive and apocalyptic battle, which is coming and will destroy the current state of affairs.[38] At the end, it can thus be argued that, although apparently paradoxical, the Islamic State sends out a positive message: by joining Islamic State you are headed to heaven in the afterlife and you will have a glorious current life, up to martyrdom. This is the heart of the success of the IS communication strategy.

Concluding remarks

The CDA analysis of AQIM discourse focused on the construction of 'an evil other' (the West and the apostates), on al-Qaeda in the Islamic Maghreb's negative self-representation and on conflations and terminological slippages. Results reveal that while the strategy of predication is a very common rhetorical strategy adopted to put 'the other' in a negative light, in AQIM discourse the construction of an evil 'other' is particularly well designed. A lot of effort is put into representing the enemy as intrinsically evil, using various metaphorical associations (e.g. enemy as animal, enemy as torturer of prisoners).

What is of particular interest, however, is the fact that the negative *other* representation is accompanied by a similarly negative *self*-representation. Indeed, the AQIM discourse stands out for its focus on martyrdom and death. In its discourse, the organisation promises spectacular violence and eternal glory to its members. AQIM fascination with violence and death is at the core of its communication strategy, offering potential members a coherent worldview with two choices: continue to be humiliated and suffer, or join AQIM and fight. The discourse operates at two interconnected levels: the first is the general level of the *ummah* presented as an undifferentiated whole in a state of sufferance and humiliation; the second is the personal level centred on the individual who has the opportunity of becoming a hero by joining the organisation. Through violence, he/she can redeem him/herself and revenge the entire *ummah*, bringing salvation through destruction and death. The rhetorical strategy of negative self-representation seeks to ensure support for an organisation that appears successful in carrying out its aims and taking new affiliates through this journey of personal ritual cleansing violence. Nevertheless, it can also be argued that the purpose of AQIM's communiqués listing its organisational successes is not solely to boast about its actions to others, to enlarge its recruitment pool, or to generate a maximum of publicity about the organisation in order to facilitate fund-raising. Crucially, it is also—and perhaps centrally—about persuading members or sympathisers that AQIM actions are justifiable, appropriate and necessary to pursuing the organisation's cause. As such, it looks as if AQIM applauds and glorifies itself not only to attract new people but also to rationalise its violence and motivate its members to further action on behalf of the group.

By contrast with AQIM's use of negative self-representation, IS put a great deal of effort into maintaining a positive image, as seen in the analysis above. IS's political messaging—besides brutality, conquest and death—propagates messages of mercy, victimhood, belonging, hope and, most important of all, apocalyptic utopianism. Some of IS's themes are common to AQIM's, but with important differences which are mainly due to the two organisations' profound ideological divide. Indeed, the stated primary goals of AQIM are to fight against corruption, bad governance, injustice and political oppression, and its affiliates are ready to die for this cause, whereas the goals of IS are to create a new world order, with the violence it advocates having the stated purpose of building a new and better society. Thus, while both narratives show a fascination for violence and death, the IS strategy is much more positive: often brutal but with many more images of an idyllic society. As such, recruitment to the Islamic State is sold as a means of participating in God's project on earth. Furthermore, what makes IS's strategic communication different from that of AQIM is a higher degree of flexibility, a quicker responsiveness to current events, as well as the quantity, quality and regularity of the propagandistic material which is disseminated.

It is probably too early to assess the impact of the growth of IS on AQIM strategic communication. What can be said is that following the rise of IS, AQIM was forced to adapt in order to survive in a more competitive communicative environment than before. This adaptation has resulted in a certain 'modernisation' in its persuasive strategy through a higher online presence on Twitter, the multilingual content of its messaging, as well as shorter and more 'media-friendly' messages. The rise of IS has also had an impact on the quantity and quality of the messages disseminated by AQIM, with numerous and more sophisticated texts, films and images distributed by the organisation on a weekly basis. Finally, the rise of IS has resulted in the emergence of internal frictions within al-Qaeda in the Islamic Maghreb, with far-reaching consequences. On the one hand, these deep internal rivalries may result in the weakening of AQIM and, potentially, its demise (although it is still premature to talk in this terms). On the other hand, the rejection by some AQIM leaders of IS's outrageously aggressive nature and the attempt to present itself as a less 'radical' alternative, together with a new emphasis on the 'far enemy', could conversely create an environment that enables AQIM to endure and expand. Meanwhile, instability and violence continue to plague North Africa. More research is thus urgently needed to enable better comprehension of the impact of the rise of IS on AQIM's communication strategy, as well as its evolution in response to a changing geopolitical landscape.

8

BOKO HARAM AND ISLAMIC STATE

Virginia Comolli

When in March 2015 Nigerian Abubakar Shekau pledged allegiance (*bay'ah*) to Caliph Abu Bakr al-Baghdadi, Boko Haram became the latest, and arguably the deadliest and most infamous group, to align itself to ISIS. Although the implications of this development are yet to become fully apparent, Shekau's move marked an interesting inflection point for Boko Haram's narrative trajectory. In addition, it inaugurated a new phase in the group's internationalisation process. This was, indeed, only the latest step in a process that had begun over a decade earlier and that included interactions with the likes of al-Qaeda in Pakistan, al-Qaeda in the Islamic Maghreb (AQIM) and its affiliates in the Sahel region.

The ensuing chapter aims to trace how a group that was set up as an isolated sect in northern Nigeria came to reach out to international jihadists in the al-Qaeda network, later switching their allegiance to what had become, arguably, the most 'successful' violent jihadist militant group in the world. A long list of unanswered questions remain, including the extent to which alliances had been formed for opportunistic reasons rather than ideological alignment.

129

Boko Haram: Origins and evolution

Boko Haram is a multifaceted violent Islamist group that has been waging an insurgency within Nigeria since 2009, engaging in both terrorist and criminal actions. It has proven capable of capturing and holding territory, and expanding its reach beyond Nigeria's borders into Niger, Chad and Cameroon—countries that have also provided a significant number of recruits. The latter appear to come predominantly from Kanuri and Hausa-Fulani ethnic groups, and although early members included educated middle-class men as well as the disadvantaged, over time it had become clear that the group attracted mainly young, unemployed and disenfranchised individuals.

What is important to note about Boko Haram is that it is hardly a new occurrence—despite the clamour generated by bold attacks and mass abductions, such as the one inspiring the #BringBackOurGirls social media campaign that made the group internationally notorious in 2014–15.[1] On the contrary, its emergence fits within a well-established pattern witnessed in northern Nigeria, particularly from the 1970s onwards, whereby Islamic ideology would be distorted by charismatic preachers and exploited as a force for social mobilisation. In so doing, preachers would capitalise on the feelings of socio-economic neglect and political marginalisation, which were and still are widespread across northern Nigeria, where the highest levels of unemployment, severe poverty and illiteracy are found. There, religious movements became vocal critics of corrupt government and religious elites who, in their view, had gone astray. They also rejected any Western influence. While doing so, groups would present their interpretation of Islam as the solution to societal evil and would engage in confrontation with the authorities. Large-scale riots by the Maitatsine resulted in thousands of deaths in Kano in the 1980s.[2]

In the twenty-first century, groups such as Boko Haram benefit from greater ease of communication, which facilitates interactions and knowledge exchange with more sophisticated foreign groups, as well as coordination within one's group. Similarly, they can access more sophisticated weaponry.

Slightly diverging accounts exist over the origins of the group commonly referred to as Boko Haram (which loosely translates from the Hausa language to 'Western civilisation is forbidden').[3] Yet, most accounts appear to converge on the Alhaji Muhammadu Ndimi Mosque in Maiduguri, the capital of Borno state, as the place where, between the late 1990s and early 2000s, a group of students, headed by charismatic preacher Mohamed Yusuf, became highly critical of the city administration, the federal government and the religious establishment.[4] They did not limit themselves to criticising the Nigerian state: Yusuf set out an Islamic altenative to it, as explained by Hussein Solomon.[5] In 2002–3, Yusuf and his followers set up base in the far north of the country in Yobe state, basing their religious community in the village of Kanama, close to the border with Niger. At this point many names were used to describe this isolated community based on Salafist principles and looking to the Taliban for inspiration for their own societal model: Nigerian Taliban, Muhajirun and Yusufiyyah were among them.[6]

Skirmishes with the security forces and the destruction of the Kanama base prompted Yusuf's return to Maiduguri and the establishment of the Ibn Taymiyyah mosque. The naming was not casual and indeed is worth reflecting over. Thirteenth-century Sunni theologian Ibn Taymiyyah had inspired many ultra-Salafist movements, as well as Mohamed Yusuf's own preaching. Salafism is characterised by a literalist and puritanical interpretation of the Qur'an and hadiths and the desire to rid Islam from external/non-Muslim influences, not necessarily through violent means. Taking this a step forward, ultra-Salafists are vehemently against innovation—a sentiment to be enforced also through violent jihad.[7]

While this description fits Yusuf's group well, those earlier years saw little violent activity—often analysts speculate that Yusuf was just waiting for the groups to be strong enough before embarking on sustained violence; indeed, Boko Haram was thought to have gone underground between late 2004 and 2008. It was only in the post-Yusuf era that the group capitalised on the anger generated by the killing of its leader to embark on an insurgency against the Nigerian state.

Another key element to be observed concerning Boko Haram's ideological drive and narrative is Yusuf's admiration not only for the Taliban but also for al-Qaeda and Osama bin Laden. Equally, Yusuf looked up to Islamists in Algeria, the Salafist Group for Preaching and Combat (GSPC), later rebranded as al-Qaeda in the Islamic Maghreb (AQIM). This was evidenced in his preaching:

> We are yet to establish a pure Sunni Islamic sect that will be ready to take on igno-rance and secularism. The few we have that are functioning are al-Qa'ida and the Taliban, whose ideology and theological foundations are purely Sunni in nature. Finally, we have other groups emerging in Algeria, all of them have missions com-mitted to the spread of Islam and I hope you understand all these.[8]

Boko Haram and al-Qaeda

The post-Osama bin Laden era—up until the establishment of ISIL in 2014—has been heavily characterised by what can be described as the regionalisation of jihad, a trend whereby the appeal of establishing a global Caliphate, as articulated by bin Laden, had in the main faded away. Instead, religiously motivated groups across several developing regions were the product of localised sets of priorities and grievances. Their agendas, as a result, were equally domestic in spite of ad hoc collaborations with foreign groups such as al-Qaeda branches and affiliates. This trend could be witnessed in the context of the Malian crisis as well as in the case of Boko Haram.[9] Yet, those localised groups have been far from completely detached from foreign and more internationalised outfits, and although formal partnerships were not always on the cards, various forms of cooperation have had significant implications on the ground. This was particularly evident in the tactical sphere with the adoption of more sophisticated techniques such as, in the case of Boko Haram, the introduction of hitherto absent suicide attacks in 2011.[10]

Boko Haram had made contact with al-Qaeda in Pakistan well before launching a sustained campaign of violence. Through the 2006 arrest of suspected Nigerian Taliban from Kano, Mallam Mohammed Ashafa, evidence was collected suggesting that funds from al-Qaeda in Lahore, Pakistan, had made their way into Boko Haram's coffers for the planning and execution of attacks against Americans in Nigeria. The same Ashafa was charged with recruiting fighters to be sent to GSPC training camps in Agwan, Niger;[11] although, as noted by Marc-Antoine Pérouse de Montclos, evidence was not always conclusive.[12] Additional reports also pointed to training received in Mauritania and Shekau's own interaction with al-Qaeda in Saudi Arabia around 2010–11.[13] It was indeed under Shekau's leadership from 2010 that links between Boko Haram and al-Qaeda in the Islamic Maghreb (AQIM) became more evident and culminated in the participation of Boko Haram and, in larger numbers, its offshoot Ansaru in the conflict in northern Mali in 2012–13. Here militants fought in support of AQIM and its local affiliates, Ansar al-Dine and the Movement for Unity and Jihad in West Africa (MUJWA).

The partnership with AQIM, in which Boko Haram was undoubtedly the junior partner, allowed the Nigerians to acquire funding, weapons and new training, e.g. in bomb making. Exposure to AQIM also led to the adoption of kidnaps for ransoms, first carried out by Ansaru and later by Boko Haram itself.

From the point of view of understanding Boko Haram's narrative trajectory and al-Qaeda's influence, it is worth pausing on the genesis and character of Ansaru. It is the latter, in fact, that appeared to represent the more internationally-minded current within the Nigerian insurgency, and one perhaps less concerned with establishing an Islamic state in northern Nigeria.[14] The origin of the group can possibly be found in internal fractures along ethnic tensions and disagreement over the redistribution of ransom money. However, the indiscriminate targeting of Muslims perpetrated by Boko Haram was a likely motivation behind the splintering.[15] In fact, and in line with AQIM's stance, Ansaru has been known for distributing leaflets condemning Boko Haram's indiscriminate killings of locals, and indeed the group had shown a preference for targeting foreigners. This is reminiscent of AQIM's leader Abdelmalek Droukdel cautioning Ansar al-Dine against ruthlessly implementing *hudud* corporal punishment and shari'ah law in northern Mali, as such practices and 'wrong policies' would undermine public support.[16]

A greater closeness between Ansaru and AQIM can also be deduced from the individual experience of senior elements within the group. Ansaru's suspected leader, Khalid al-Barnawi, was believed not only to have trained with AQIM but also to have fought under the leadership of prominent AQIM Commander Mokhtar Belmokhtar in the mid-2000s in Mauritania and Algeria.[17]

Bearing these considerations in mind, one could speculate that despite Shekau's several references to and praises of al-Qaeda, as indicated in a number of videos issued by the group,[18] opportunism and the desire to acquire additional skills and funds, rather than a true alignment of narratives, were guiding those interactions. Given the pressure under which AQIM and its affiliated jihadists in Mali found themselves following the French-led operation Serval (January 2013) and subsequent international counter-terrorism efforts in the Sahel, it can be argued that they are in a less favourable position to provide support for the likes of Boko Haram. In addition, Boko Haram's own efforts to diversify its funding base through a variety of criminal activities place the Nigerians less in need of relying on AQIM. In this context of opportunism, ISIS's appeal stems partly from the significant gains in Iraq and Syria that have given ISIS global fame. Aligning one's movement to such a successful group would likely increase prestige and standing in the jihadist arena, not to mention it opening new opportunities and facilitating the acquisition of resources.

Boko Haram declares a state

The year 2014 marked a significant turning point in the history of Boko Haram, which arguably had found in the rise of ISIS an important catalyst and source of inspiration. It was in fact at this time that the group carried out its first successful attempts at territorial control. When the state of emergency was put in place in Borno, Yobe and Adamawa and a large military offensive was launched against the group in May 2013, concerns over Boko Haram's ability to control areas around its camps had already emerged and arguably were behind renewed Nigerian military impetus. But the events of 2014 were on a different scale: judging by the location of captured towns and villages, it was apparent that Boko Haram was effectively attempting to encircle Borno's capital city of Maiduguri.

Boko Haram released a video on 24 August 2014 announcing the establishment of an Islamic state in Gwoza, Borno state, roughly two months following ISIL's own announcement on 29 June.[19] The timing of Shekau's declaration was considered indicative of ISIL's influence and signalled a significant tactical shift for the Nigerians, who were transitioning from hit-and-run attacks to the physical occupation of territory across north-eastern Nigeria and border regions with Cameroon and, starting in February 2015, Niger and Chad.[20]

Expanding beyond its hideouts in the Sambisa forest and Mandara Mountains, Boko Haram seized substantial areas in Borno, Yobe and Adamawa states, propelled by an expansionist drive reminiscent of ISIS's capture of Tikrit, Mosul and other Sunni territories in 2014.[21] In late August and early September, reports emerged that the group had taken Buni Yadi and Bara in Yobe state, Madagali in Adamawa state and Gwoza, Banki, Gamboru-Ngala, Ashigashiya and Kerawa in Borno state.[22] The Archbishop of Maiduguri, Oliver Dashe Doeme, claimed that Boko Haram had captured 25 towns in north-eastern Nigeria in mid-September.[23] By then, Shekau's 'state' was thought to cover an area the size of Ireland.[24] Subsequent estimates by Michael Nwankpa indicate that the group controlled over two-thirds of Borno state between July 2014 and March 2015.[25]

It is interesting to note that Boko Haram's actions had not gone unnoticed by ISIL. Notably, al-Baghdadi praised Boko Haram's abductions in Chibok,[26] and used them to justify the capture and enslavement of 7,000 Yazidi women.[27] Practices such as this, alongside the systematic rape of Alawite, Christian and Shiite women and the implementation of sexual slavery, were indeed similar to Boko Haram's mass abduction of girls and forced marriages.[28]

Shifting towards ISIL: Manifestations

The increased sophistication of Boko Haram's media propaganda since 2014 is possibly the clearest manifestation of ISIL's influence over the Nigerian group and how the former has shaped Boko Haram's social media propaganda.[29]

Boko Haram's media group, al-Urwah al-Wuthqa, launched the group's official Arabic-language Twitter feed on 18 January 2015. This was a major milestone for Boko Haram's propaganda campaign, which had not hitherto featured any official social media presence.[30] The Twitter account has been used as a propaganda tool, barring some disruption following suspension of the original account by Twitter. The feed has posted a stream of short statements about Boko Haram's activities reminiscent of ISIL's one-line tweets. Furthermore, the account was immediately promoted by key ISIL media operatives, such as Abu-Malik Shaybah al-Hamad, claiming to be in contact with the Boko Haram general command.[31]

Interestingly, Boko Haram videos released via Twitter resemble the more polished style of ISIL's media productions, featuring the same choreography, lens angles, professionally designed graphics, slow-motion techniques, Arabic-language jihadist anthems, and high-quality opening sequences typical of ISIS productions.[32] Boko Haram has also recycled titles for its video productions that have already been given to ISIS.[33] Perhaps taking inspiration from ISIS footage of infamous 'Jihadi John' holding a knife behind British, American and Japanese hostages, a Nigerian militant is shown standing behind two victims with a knife in the 2 March video titled *Harvest of Spies*.[34]

These comparisons can be taken even further. Although Boko Haram is not new to beheadings, only a few execution videos were released until relatively recently.[35] Additionally, more slickly crafted productions differ considerably from the group's earlier offerings, often shot with hand-held cameras and posted sporadically on YouTube.[36] The increasing sophistication and the use of multiple languages, including English, Arabic, French and Hausa, suggest that Boko Haram may have benefited from the support of ISIS media operatives.[37] At the same time, ISIL's symbolism has made its way into Boko Haram's productions: the ISIS *rayat al-uqab* flag has been both incorporated into Boko Haram's logo and featured in its videos.[38] In June 2015, Boko Haram released a video under the new name *Wilayat West Africa*, Islamic State West Africa Province (ISWAP).[39] This was the first time since the group had announced its rebranding in April.[40]

Why have Boko Haram and ISIL converged?

Undoubtedly the alignment between Boko Haram and ISIL is a source of concern, and it is no surprise that it made headlines worldwide, given the deadliness and brutality that have characterised both groups. However, it is worth reflecting on the motivations that may have driven both sides to come together.

From the point of view of al-Baghdadi, Shekau's pledge boosted ISIL's global profile at a time when the group's momentum appeared to have come under threat.[41] In fact, upon accepting Boko Haram's *bay'ah*, ISIS had experienced several major setbacks in Kobani, Syria and Tikrit, Iraq showing how waging a war on multiple fronts had strained the group's resources and capabilities.[42] Furthermore, Boko Haram's support presented ISIL with the opportunity to establish its first foothold in sub-Saharan Africa—an important step towards fulfilling al-Baghdadi's goal to establish a global Caliphate by exporting its pan-Islamic ideology of holy jihad to the second most populous Muslim country in the whole continent.[43]

Similarly, the March pledge of allegiance came at a time of operational weakness for Boko Haram.[44] Its increased tempo of attacks in both Nigeria and neighbouring countries has prompted a stronger military response in the form of a Multinational Joint Task Force, including elements from Nigeria, Niger, Chad and Cameroon. The troops, together with private security contractors hired by Nigeria in January 2015 (and causing no little controversy), were capable of driving militants from north-eastern territories that they had controlled since mid-2014 and forced them to retreat to the Sambisa forest, one of its last major hideouts.[45] In light of this context and the position of military weakness in which Boko Haram found itself, it can be speculated that Shekau sought ISIL's support in order to regain operational momentum.[46]

Nevertheless, taking a step back and assessing the broader picture, there could be more to this pledge than a sign of desperation. The alliance is unlikely to be simply a reaction to the more aggressive (and fairly successful) military push against Boko Haram. Rather it should be understood as the culmination of a months-long process. Already in June 2014 Shekau had pledged support for al-Baghdadi and his Caliphate, paving the way for a future alliance. Then, Boko Haram was far from being cornered. On the contrary, it was most likely experiencing its operational peak to date.[47] Moreover, although Boko Haram is currently facing the toughest challenge of its six-year insurgency, the MNJTF—an enhanced African Union-mandated version of which has been repeatedly delayed—is yet to secure a decisive victory. Nigerian troops are attempting to penetrate the mine-infested Sambisa forest, terrain that is much better understood by their opponents.[48] Attacks have also continued unabated, including in the Chadian capital N'djamena and in conjunction with the Eid celebration marking the end of Ramadan in July.[49] The MNJTF is also facing its own internal challenges, not least given Nigerian distrust of its regional partners.[50]

Boko Haram's opportunism may provide an alternative explanation for Shekau's *bay'ah*. Following in the footsteps of over 30 jihadist groups worldwide,[51] Boko Haram's declaration of support for al-Baghdadi's Caliphate might have been prompted by the operational benefits that such an alliance could yield. There has been speculation that Shekau is seeking funding, weapons and even foreign fighters through closer alignment with ISIL,[52] but there is as yet little evidence to substantiate such claims, although reports have emerged suggesting Boko Haram was experiencing supply shortages. Notably, and perhaps in an attempt to earn some favours, in October 2015 Boko Haram/ISWAP reached out to al-Shabaab, urging Somalia's militants to side with al-Baghdadi. In doing so, the Nigerians stressed the importance of being united in their struggle to help defeat infidels around the world.[53]

Significant differences remain

Despite the preceding discussion, one should resist the temptation to lump Boko Haram and ISIS together, and instead acknowledge that differences remain in terms of goals as well as tactics and capabilities. While over time Boko Haram has evolved and taken a broader international outlook, its identity remains, at its core, domestic. The beginning of attacks in Cameroon as of Autumn 2014 and then in Niger and Chad starting in February 2015 indicated that countries that had been previously regarded by Boko Haram as safe havens had become part of the battleground and targeted for inclusion into Shekau's 'state'. Yet, rather than trying to capture foreign countries, Shekau's attempted move into Niger, Chad and Cameroon was most likely prompted by the desire to take control over communities across national borders with shared ethnic and religious identities and, in particular, those within the ancient Kanem-Borno Empire.[54] In other words, it seems unlikely that Boko Haram planned to expand beyond those territories in an attempt to control other African countries.[55]

The extent to which the two groups have proved capable of establishing semi-functioning 'states' varies considerably. Arguably, this is not a mere function of capabilities. Instead, in the Nigerian case the planning for such a state appears to have failed to feature in Shekau's strategy—at least judging by the dearth of provisions made to that effect.[56] Despite its brutality, ISIS has demonstrated both the intent and capability to impose shari'ah law and order in its captured territories, and in spite of the fact the Caliphate is unevenly administered—with tighter control in its 'capital' Raqqa than in other areas—ISIL runs Islamic courts, repairs roads, dictates educational policy and polices traffic in parts of Syria.[57]

In Nigeria, it is unclear whether Boko Haram had the ability or desire to govern its north-eastern territories. The clearest indication of attempted governance by shari'ah law was the introduction of Emirs in its captured areas. Namely, Commander Muhammed Daniuma was named Emir of Bama, and other Emirs were reportedly appointed in Gwoza, Damboa and elsewhere in Dikwa.[58] Little further evidence of the group's attempt at creating a state through effective governance existed. According to Ambassador Alhaji Baba Ahmad Jidda, the secretary to the Borno state government, as of September 2014 'government presence and administration [was] minimal or non-existent across many parts of the state, with economic, commercial and social services totally subdued. Schools and clinics remain[ed] closed.'[59] In Mubi, an Adamawa state city renamed by Boko Haram 'Madinatul Islam' (The city of Islam) in November 2014, residents reported that Boko Haram wanted everyday life to resume:

> They asked us to go about our normal business without fear of being killed. They warned shop owners to come back and open their shops; if not, the shops would be opened by force. The insurgents are now holding public courts and preaching at the emir's palace and threatened to marry off girls in for a dowry of N2,000 to N5,000 [US $10 to US $25].[60]

Unsurprisingly, 'everyday life' was intended as one based on shari'ah law in an environment in which physical punishments such as hand amputations and beheadings were routinely administered to those failing to comply.[61] In sum it appears that the only service promised by Boko Haram to locals has been security provision.[62] Even then, however, Boko Haram did not live up to ISIL's 'standards'. Reports indicate that whereas brutality and disproportionate punishments remained behind the façade of bureaucracy and infrastructure built by ISIS, by assuming monopoly over violence, ISIL prompted a decrease in banditry and other forms of criminality. Conversely, the establishment of the Boko Haram 'state' in Nigeria—which prioritised the implementation of Islamic law over the setting up of government departments and the running of services—only increased fear among the local population and generated chaos and displacement.[63]

Together with governance, the establishment of a strong economic basis is key to the running of a functioning state. ISIL and Boko Haram share some similarities on the economic front, but the two operate on very different levels. This is partly a by-product of different circumstances, for example, the presence of oil fields in ISIL-controlled territories, in contrast to north-eastern Nigeria, an area with very limited economic opportunities. In addition, although Shekau has increased Boko Haram's riches through robberies, kidnaps for ransom and extortions, these activities have had little or no impact in terms of imposing governance and running a state.[64] No evidence indicated that funds had been used for social welfare provisions, the building of infrastructure or the setting up of businesses. Again, the use of coercion as the main tool of state-building indicates that unlike ISIL, little long-term planning had gone into Shekau's strategy which, regardless of the effectiveness of the counter-insurgency campaign, raises doubts over the sustainability of Boko Haram's state.

Conclusions

Since its inception in the early 2000s, Boko Haram has undergone a major transformation: from remote non-violent sect into infamous insurgency and proscribed terrorist organisation. For all its domestic agenda and focus, the group has also not shied away from making contact with foreign terrorist organisations with whom the ideological fit was not always perfect. Boko Haram's narrative (and conduct) has been moulded over time in response to changing leadership, external influences and evolving circumstances. As for the latter, Shekau's lot has demonstrated great resilience and the ability to adapt to new operating environments. This is true in tactical terms, for instance moving the fight from rural to urban theatres and vice versa, as well as with regard to narratives, showing a level of opportunism that possibly outweighs any ideological affinity Boko Haram may have with al-Qaeda or ISIL.

In practical terms, and given Boko Haram's fragmented, cell-based structure, it is yet to be seen to what extent the pledge to ISIS would be widely accepted, prompting the group to act as a genuine proxy to ISIL in the region.[65] Similarly, it is unclear whether the rebranding into ISWAP was endorsed by Shekau.[66] Narrative-wise, there is also lack of clarity. On the one hand the alliance may facilitate Boko Haram's foreign recruitment—ISIS spokesman Abu Muhammad al-'Adnani had even called for fighters to join

Boko Haram if they could not travel to Syria;[67] on the other hand, Boko Haram's local focus may reduce its appeal abroad (after all it never attracted foreign fighters from outside the region) and may even cause frictions with al-Baghdadi's international plan.

For sure, the convergence between the two groups has been a productive propaganda exercise, and it cannot be excluded that Boko Haram might in the future interact with other ISIS sympathisers in North Africa—which would be more practical than direct cooperation with those based in the Middle East. Indeed, beginning in the summer of 2015, a number of reports, on the main unverified, have indicated the presence of Boko Haram/ISWAP fighters in southern Libya and in the city of Sirte, suggesting contacts with Islamic State's branches in the country. Yet, it is too soon to establish with any certainty the extent to which an alliance of this sort is sustainable and reflects a genuine alignment of narratives.

9

LOCAL AND GLOBAL JIHADIST NARRATIVES IN AFGHANISTAN

THE IMPACT OF THE DECLINE OF AL-QAEDA AND RISE OF 'ISLAMIC STATE'

Martha Turnbull

Introduction

The South Asian jihadist movement has long been torn between local and global objectives, embodied respectively in the Taliban and al-Qaeda. The Taliban have for two decades now sought to balance the pragmatic and ideological drivers for support to al-Qaeda, with local imperatives. This context is essential to understanding how global transitions in the jihadist movement have impacted on South Asian jihadism.

This chapter explores the evolution of the jihadist movement in Afghanistan in its historical context and since the Arab uprisings in 2012. It argues that, for a number of reasons, the 'Arab Spring' narrative and the first revolutions in Libya, Tunisia and Egypt had little impact here. The rise of

Syria as the premier jihad of choice, and the emergence of the Islamic State of Iraq and the Levant (ISIL) and its Caliphate, have however had a significant impact. IS and the Syrian war pose an unprecedented challenge to the Afghan jihad: they challenge its relevance, its popularity and, most importantly, they undermine the narrative of the groups that have dominated the terrorist landscape for the past three decades. In addition, they are polarising the jihad and creating direct confrontation between those who support the Afghan Taliban and those who support ISIL. In the process, they are pushing the Taliban and AQ closer together, forcing the former to make greater use of the latter in its public messaging and ensuring that a political process in Afghanistan (with public condemnation of AQ at its centre) looks increasingly unlikely.

Part One: Islamist extremism in South Asia

Afghanistan: a melting pot for extremism

The anti-Soviet jihad in Afghanistan in the 1980s became a melting pot for extremism, with links developed between groups in this era still of crucial importance today. During this time, Afghanistan became a focus for Sunni extremists who believed that violent jihad was an Islamic duty and that the armed invasion of a Muslim state justified war against an 'infidel' aggressor. Abdullah Azzam became the main ideologue of the mujahidin in Afghanistan, calling for a multinational Islamic force to establish a 'pure' Islamic state.

In 1984 Azzam set up Makhtabh al-Khidmat (MAK) to disseminate propaganda and draw in recruits. His partner in this endeavour was Osama bin Laden who had travelled to Afghanistan and was mentored by Azzam. Together, Azzam and bin Laden connected MAK to a growing and complex array of global networks based on familial, tribal and ideological connections. The result was 'a new transnational network of committed and battle-hardened jihadis'.[1] As the anti-Soviet jihad drew to a close, Azzam and bin Laden agreed to use MAK as a 'base' (Arabic translation: al-Qaeda) to support and defend Muslims elsewhere. AQ began its development from concept into reality.

In November 1989 Azzam was assassinated in a bomb attack in Afghanistan. It is still not known who killed him. His death left bin Laden free to develop AQ alone, relocating the group to Saudi Arabia, Sudan and then, in 1996, returning to Afghanistan once more. As bin Laden was travelling the world and building a name for himself and his group, the Afghan Taliban rose to power in Afghanistan in the mid-1990s. The Taliban were influenced by traditional Pashtun society, Deobandism from 1980s refugee camps in Pakistan, as well as a significant Salafi influence, in part from Saudi Arabia. The consequence of this mixture, during the 1990s, was a form of governance at the extreme end of what was acceptable in the already conservative Pashtun south of the country.

By the late 1990s, Afghanistan had become a retreat in which violent Islamists from all over the world came to train, develop strategies and cement links and alliances. The Taliban welcomed other groups, allowing them to set up bases in Afghanistan in return for support against the Northern Alliance. In AQ's case, this 'support' was both manpower and funding: by one estimate, two-thirds of AQ's budget at this point was passed to the Taliban.[2] The Taliban had created a self-styled 'Islamic Emirate' which was recognised as a state entity by three countries in 1997: Pakistan, Saudi Arabia and the United Arab Emirates. With control over the majority of the country, the West's growing problem with bin Laden and AQ became the Taliban government's problem. Despite negotiations[3] between the Taliban and the US in the late 1990s, the issue of what to do with AQ proved to be an intractable one.

During this period, relations with AQ were a subject of considerable debate within the Taliban movement. Pragmatists saw bin Laden and his 'Afghan—Arab' followers as trouble. Not only culturally and religiously different, their political objectives of waging international jihad were at odds with the Taliban's, which confined its jihad to within its own borders; it even desired international (including Western) diplomatic recognition. Indeed, from 1998 relations between the Taliban and AQ grew increasingly strained, a result of AQ's open and confrontational rhetoric towards the US[4] and the East Africa Embassy attacks of that year, which resulted in the US launching cruise missile strikes against AQ camps in Afghanistan.[5] Bin Laden's pledge of allegiance to Mullah Omar in 1998 was in part an attempt to assuage Omar's anger that his orders were being ignored. In the meantime, bin Laden continued to develop AQ's training camps in Afghanistan.

Yet there was also no shortage of Taliban hardliners who approved of AQ and were prepared to overlook bin Laden's indiscretions because he was helping to bankroll the Taliban's fight against the Northern Alliance. Mullah Omar was the ultimate arbiter in this debate and, despite his misgivings, came down on the side of the hardliners. Tribal norms of hospitality and perhaps a degree of ideological sympathy are likely to have played their part in informing Omar's decision-making.

The 9/11 attacks increased the strain on AQ's relationship with its Taliban hosts, who were unsighted on bin Laden's plan. Whilst we know that Omar fundamentally misjudged US intentions at the time, surrendering bin Laden to non-Muslims would have been too damaging to the credibility and legitimacy of the Taliban movement to contemplate, thus sealing Omar's ousting from power and the fall of his regime. For Omar, 'the issue of Usama [was] no longer the issue of an individual, but an issue of the glory of Islam'.[6]

In the years that followed the Taliban's overthrow, the group has rarely mentioned AQ, knowing that advertising their links would be counter-productive to their cause. Instead, the Taliban emphasised the Islamo-nationalist character of its insurgency and objectives of re-installing Islamic governance and expelling foreign forces. In doing so, the Taliban implicitly distanced itself from the global agenda of AQ.

Whilst the Taliban and AQ have remained organisationally and politically distinct,[7] there is of course some collaboration on the battlefield. AQ's footprint in Afghanistan, although now significantly diminished from its pre-9/11 heyday, is mostly focused in the east. But the importance of this support has declined and for the most part when AQ operates alongside the Taliban it is in small numbers, with units subordinated to the local Afghan commander. With very few AQ foot soldiers actually inside Afghanistan, AQ has had only a negligible influence on the Taliban's resurgence, and even less impact on the course of the insurgency more generally.

Part Two: Responses to the 'Arab Spring'

Before their collapse in 2001, the Taliban banned all forms of media apart from their propaganda radio show, *Voice of Sharia*. In the immediate aftermath of the Western military intervention in Afghanistan, the Taliban's engagement with the media was limited; however, as the insurgency grew, so did their engagement with international media. Today the Taliban fully embraces modern technology, including social media and the internet.

Although their method of output has changed, the content of the messages has largely remained the same. Since its inception, the Afghan Taliban has retained an overwhelmingly local focus, despite its dalliance with a number of global jihadist groups. Although it occasionally offers comment on key external developments, its policy is largely focused on its nationalist support base. A statement in June 2013 provides a perfect example of this approach:

> The Islamic Emirate of Afghanistan simultaneously follows military and political actions and aims which are limited to Afghanistan. The Islamic Emirate never wants to pose harms to other countries from its soil, nor will it allow anyone to cause a threat to the security of countries from the soil of Afghanistan.[8]

This statement encompasses many familiar themes: a nationalist narrative; local objectives; and a desire to be left alone. There is, however, one external theme which received frequent mention in Taliban statements: the role and activities of the United States. A March 2012 statement neatly summarises the significance of the US in propaganda terms: 'the Afghan issue has two main dimensions; one is internal and the other external. The external dimension is associated with Americans and the internal dimension is connected with the Afghans themselves.'[9] For the Taliban, the US is a bigger enemy than the Afghan government. It believes that without the support of the US, the Kabul government would fall in the same way as the political system collapsed following the withdrawal of the Soviet Union. Although other 'enemies' are sometimes referenced, including the UK, France, Germany and Canada, it is the US that garners the most attention. Outside the International Security Assistance Force (ISAF) coalition members, the Taliban has historically made little reference to other countries.

So with this background, it was always going to be difficult to translate developments affecting the Arabs of North Africa into a meaningful message for the Pashtuns of southern Afghanistan. This perhaps explains why the Taliban did not offer much comment on the developments, largely remaining silent. That said, the Taliban was quick to react to the fall of Hosni Mubarak, praising 'the victory of the popular uprising in Egypt'[10] in February 2011. Its narrative echoed that of AQ and many other Islamist extremist groups— encouraging Egyptians to avoid compromise, and to take the opportunity to create a Muslim state.

Characteristically, however, the message quickly sought to weave these events with themes much closer to home: it compared Mubarak's repression of the Egyptian population to that of the US-led coalition in Afghanistan, noting that 'the atrocities that you commit against the Afghan people today will soon usher in a revolution and the vessel of your arrogance will drown surely following inception of a popular uprising.'[11] The message also noted Mubarak's fall from power as a warning for the Afghan government: the US, apparently, could not be relied upon to provide unending support.

The Taliban's narrative was not a major departure from the messaging issued before the Arab Spring. It was supportive of 'success' elsewhere which reduced Western influence, but cautious not to stray far from the 'so what' for the Afghan people. It tried to use the example in Egypt to give hope to its Afghan supporters, but did not embark on a media campaign in the same way that other groups (most notably AQ) did. For the Taliban, the Arab Spring prior to the emergence of ISIL was a comfortable time: it was able to ride the wave of enthusiasm generated by political change thousands of miles away with minimal effort and no competitor at home. This was not to last.

Part Three: The rise of ISIL

As other chapters of this book have outlined in detail, ISIL had been quietly gathering momentum and territory in the Levant since 2011. In February 2014, it became the first and only AQ affiliate group to be excommunicated from the fold. On 29 June 2014, ISIL announced the creation of a new 'Islamic State', with Abu Bakr al-Baghdadi as its Caliph. This announcement was an attempt to present ISIL/IS as the most powerful Sunni Islamist group in the world, and in so doing it challenged the authority of AQ and the Afghan Taliban. The Taliban's status as providers of the model Islamic Emirate and Mullah Omar as the 'Leader of the Faithful' was being challenged in an unprecedented manner. To make matters worse, an IS-aligned media campaign was launched which increased public pressure on the Taliban to account for Omar's whereabouts, his religious credibility and his relevance to the current jihad. In January 2015, ISIL announced the creation of Islamic State Khorasan Province: for the first time in its history, the Taliban was forced into fighting a rival Sunni extremist group on its own doorstep.

The rise of ISIL and the pull of Syria

In early 2012 IS was widely perceived to be winning, and had made quick and spectacular gains in the Levant. These well-publicised battlefield victories were juxtaposed with the Taliban's 20-year struggle in Afghanistan with no end in sight. The fight in Syria was benefitting from a 'bandwagon' effect,[12] while the long-running fight in Afghanistan continued to be largely neglected by international jihadists. The Afghan Taliban seemed to confirm this in January 2014, commenting that the appeal of Syria may lead to more fighters leaving Afghanistan and returning to their home countries. A few weeks earlier, in an interview with Asharq al-Awsat, Afghan Taliban spokesman Qari Yousuf Ahmadi spoke of the mass exodus of foreign fighters from the region as a result of the popularity of other conflicts, noting that:

> Before the Taliban came to power in Afghanistan, there were a few hundred Arab Mujahideen living as guests here, fighting and sacrificing for the sake of the nation. At the time, it was unfeasible for them to return to their homelands because of the

oppression and persecution awaiting them there. But recently, the vast majority have returned to their homelands, especially after the events of the Arab Spring.[13]

Not only were some foreign fighters seeking to leave Afghanistan to join ISIL/IS, others were avoiding travelling to the country for jihad in the first place. In neighbouring Central Asia, the rise of IS has had more impact on the appeal of jihadist narratives than did the conflict in Afghanistan or the Arab Spring. More Central Asians have travelled to Syria and Iraq than Afghanistan. Many were recruited in Russia where the offer of a steady income and potential glory of becoming *shadid* (a martyr) in Syria is a tempting prospect for some disillusioned young migrants. As a new brand, ISIL can appeal to Central Asians in a way that the Taliban cannot. Recruitment and travel to Syria is also easier than crossing the heavily militarised border into Afghanistan.

Perhaps sensing that the tide was turning against them, the Taliban began the first of a series of pronouncements on IS's rise. On 13 July 2014, the Taliban's leadership issued a response to IS's announcement of the establishment of their 'Islamic State', in which they tentatively tried to distance themselves from the group. Without specifically mentioning IS, the Taliban called for Muslims to 'stay away from extremism in religion' and for the 'various jihadi groups, intellectuals and esteemed scholars' to convene 'consultative *shuras* ... in order for them to settle their disputes'. By not naming IS, the Taliban were able to keep their distance, and claim to refrain still from meddling in the affairs of other groups.

But Baghdadi's claim to have established himself as Caliph clearly posed something of a challenge to Mullah Omar's position as 'Amir-ul Mo'mineen' (Leader of the Faithful), the title he had used since 1996. It introduced a degree of competition into the jihadist mix which extended beyond IS's dispute with AQ. IS's behaviour towards other groups was becoming increasingly hostile, with significant military aggression shown on the ground in Syria and Libya, and public messaging used to support its narrative. The Taliban could have taken a tougher line, but whilst Omar notionally remained in control of the group, the core of the Afghan Taliban movement at both the leadership and local levels did not change its political or military strategy, despite the success of the IS brand. The leadership probably saw itself as sitting fairly comfortably within an Afghan Deobandi Islamic tradition and constituency that had considerable regional strength and depth, unthreatened by IS's Salafism and its fight in Iraq and Syria.

Sectarian narratives and the establishment of ISIL's South Asian presence

The pull of sectarian narratives has clearly had an impact on the resonance of the Taliban. IS has consistently sought to frame the war in Syria and Iraq as a fight against Shia Islam. In Afghanistan, the Taliban have not framed the fighting there as Sunni versus Shia since the late 1990s, with the Taliban offensive in Mazar against the Shia Hazaras. The Buddhas of Bamian (located within Hazara territory) were destroyed and a number of well publicised massacres occurred. The post-2001 Taliban have positioned themselves as a nationalist group and even gone as far as strongly condemning bomb attacks against the Hazara in Afghanistan, which were likely perpetrated by Pakistani groups.

On the other side of the border, sectarian attacks in Pakistan have killed or injured more than 500 people each year for the past twelve years. Although there has been an increase in attacks between the Deobandi and Barelvi Sunni sub-sects, the majority of violence has been directed towards Pakistan's Shia minority.[14] The underlying motive for sectarian violence is the historical differences within Islam itself which continue to divide the two sects; but, somewhat ironically, it was under the secular regime of Zulfiqar Ali Bhutto that this consensus started to fracture. The genesis was the success of the anti-Ahmadi movement, which, through an effective pressure campaign, managed to achieve an amendment to the constitution in 1974, which in effect declared the Ahmadis to be non-Muslims.[15] Whilst Shias had been a part of this movement, its conclusion greatly encouraged Sunni sectarian leaders, who then turned their attentions to excluding the minority Shia community in much the same way.

It was General Zia ul-Haq who proved to be the catalyst that allowed sectarianism to flourish. His policies, which effectively aimed to 'Islamise' Pakistan, but with a distinct Sunni flavour, gradually marginalised the Shia and brought into sharper focus the differences between the two sects. The Iranian revolution in 1979 and anti-Soviet jihad in Afghanistan were also seminal events in determining the course of Pakistani sectarianism. The former gave rise to fear of the increasing power of the Shia, and the latter saw the beginnings of the proxy war between Saudi Arabia and Iran.

With the Afghan Taliban seeking to distance itself from sectarian violence altogether and a rising number of sectarian attacks in Pakistan, there was a ready market in South Asia for IS's brand of sectarianism, including ultra-violent attacks on minority groups. IS's announcement of its South Asian branch ('IS Khorasan Province', IS-KP) in January 2015 was not, therefore, a surprise. ISIL had sent representatives to the region in the spring of 2014 who had sought to build support for the group from disgruntled members of AQ and the Taliban.[16] In its announcement of the group, IS called on its supporters in South Asia to abandon disunity and factionalism to unite under a new umbrella. The message also sought to appeal to those fighting for nationalist causes: 'you have fought the English, the Russians, and the Americans, and upon you today is a new fight'. It was engaging in direct confrontation with the Taliban, even mimicking their nationalist narrative to maximise its appeal. In seeking to challenge the Taliban's authority, IS-KP quickly found itself with an additional enemy: alongside the remnants of the ISAF coalition and the Afghan government, IS-KP was forced to fight a Taliban counter-offensive. IS-KP resorted to dirty tactics: it claimed to have assassinated Taliban spies, captured Taliban fighters and killed the Taliban shadow governor of Nangarhar.[17] Perhaps recognising that it did not have the military might to overpower the Taliban, IS-KP adopted terrorist tactics to obscure its limited capabilities.

The leadership of IS-KP is predominately Pakistani, mostly individuals formerly aligned with the Pakistani Taliban (TTP). Leadership divisions and power struggles within the TTP will continue into the foreseeable future, meaning that IS-KP will be able to maintain a steady stream of Pakistani recruits. Despite its large Pakistani membership, IS-KP does not have a stronghold in Pakistan and so has been forced to operate mainly in Afghanistan. In Afghanistan, its members are mostly disaffected former Taliban members looking for an alternative master. Many are young and attracted to ISIL's simple narrative of success. The group claims it is active in Kunar, Nuristan, Logar, Farah, Nangahar and Helmand provinces. In reality, its presence is nominal in every province, despite its estimated 1,000 to 5,000 members.[18] Although IS-KP is affiliated to IS, there are some key differences between the two groups. Most Afghan insurgent commanders who have defected to IS-KP appear to be motivated not by ideology, but by the hope that their new flag of convenience will bring them more money and power. It is likely that these commanders gain from not having to pay a cut of their criminal profits to the Taliban. For the most part, the Taliban commanders who have defected to IS-KP have not yet modified their tactics. They use sectarian language in their propaganda videos, but they have not yet conducted the sort of widespread sectarian violence seen in Syria and Iraq.

Since its inception, IS-KP has suffered numerous leadership losses at the hands of the Afghan or coalition militaries. Despite the setbacks that IS-KP has faced, the Taliban appear to be concerned by the threat they pose. They have redirected resources towards countering it militarily, executed alleged IS-KP spies and on 16 June published an angry letter to al-Baghdadi warning him not to provoke them by operating in Afghanistan. The letter,[19] authored by then-Deputy Leader Mullah Mansour, demanded that Islamic State fight under the Taliban's banner in Afghanistan and end divisions amongst jihadists throughout the world. According to Mansour, 'the Islamic Emirate stresses the unity of jihadist ranks in Afghanistan, because maintaining the strength of the jihadist ranks is an obligation'. In support of his argument, Mansour outlines the religious credibility of the Taliban, including:

> The country's 1,500 Ulema [the religious council of scholars in Afghanistan] [who] have chosen, and pledged allegiance to, the leadership of the Islamic Emirate of Afghanistan in accordance with sharia, and famous religious scholars of the world … and famous jihadist leaders like Sheikh Osama [bin Laden], may God have mercy on him, have announced their support and allegiance to the lawful Emirate.

Mansour went on to discuss the damage created by IS sowing discord in other parts of the world, noting that 'Islamic groups and personalities have rendered heavy sacrifices in very tough conditions in various parts of the world'. 'They have made these achievements after suffering great hardships and rendering sacrifices; therefore, we advise you not to create such difficult conditions for Islamic movements in any part of the world that, God forbid, affect their operations and discipline and that may lead to differences among them. In the end, due to differences over the modalities of operations or difference of opinion, they start killing each other.' Mansour's statement ended with a clear threat to IS: 'God forbid, if people, who claim to be affiliated with you, create serious troubles for the Islamic Emirate; it will lead to anger among Muslims against you.'

Mansour's statement broke all the rules to which Taliban public messages had previously adhered: it referenced the group's relationship with AQ directly; it addressed grievances which had little connection to the jihad in Afghanistan; and it contained a punchy threat to another Islamist extremist group. The Taliban had been pushed into direct confrontation with IS and Mansour was clearly in no mood to seek a compromise.

Mansour's statement was just the first in a series of messages which indicated a new, emboldened Taliban that was not afraid to tackle the growth of IS. On 11 August 2015, the Taliban issued another critical statement. The message condemned IS-KP for brutally killing tribesmen with explosives—an act that was shown in a video released on 9 August 2015—and ordered local officials in Nangarhar to find and punish the perpetrators. In an English statement posted on its website, the Taliban declared that this 'un-Islamic act where innocent civilians are martyred after being charged with apostasy merely for aiding the Islamic Emirate, can never be justified'. According to the IS-KP video, the tribesmen had negotiated with the Afghan Taliban and Afghan government to fight IS-KP, and engaged in battle with the group in Momand Dara district of Nangarhar.

Other insurgent groups have been forced to take sides in this rivalry. The Islamic Movement of Uzbekistan and some smaller insurgent groups have pledged support to IS-KP, with bigger groups such as the Haqqani Network and the Pakistani Taliban remaining loyal to the Afghan Taliban. The IMU had issued several pieces of propaganda in support of ISIL throughout 2014 and 2015. On 6 August its leader, Uthman Ghazi, and its fighters formally pledged allegiance to Abu Bakr al-Baghdadi. Later, on 7 September, IS-KP released a video message congratulating IMU on their allegiance to ISIL. The two groups appear to have remained separate entities, with no indication that a merger is imminent. For the IMU, IS's popularity amongst Central Asian jihadists may be a driving force behind their affiliation.

Part Four: The Taliban after Mullah Omar

Despite the changing nature of its relationship with AQ since 1996, the Taliban has still retained ties with its old friends. Recent months have seen a plethora of public messages of support between the two sides, indicating that the relationship may be closer than ever, despite the loss of bin Laden and, more recently, Mullah Omar.

On 30 July 2015, the Taliban confirmed that its leader had died. The statement, attributed to the Shura Leadership Council of the Islamic Emirate and family of Omar, stated that he was 'a leader and chief, faithful to his Islamic Ummah' who 'presented a realistic example for empowering the sharia of Allah for the entire world'. His cause of death was an unspecified illness. He had died on 23 April 2013, but the Taliban had chosen to keep the news a secret for fear of creating disunity in jihad.

The AQ affiliates were quick to respond to the Taliban announcement. Three AQ affiliates—al-Qaeda in the Arabian Peninsula (AQAP), al-Qaeda in the Islamic Maghreb (AQIM) and Al Nusra Front (ANF)—released a joint eulogy for Omar. The eulogy came in a statement posted by ANF on Twitter on 5 August 2015.[20] The three groups praised 'Emir of the Believers' Omar for harbouring Osama bin Laden and refusing to turn him over to the United States after 9/11, and also lauded his bringing together jihadist factions in Afghanistan under the banner of the Taliban.

Al-Shabaab issued their own message of condolence on 13 August 2015,[21] similarly praising Omar's refusal to hand bin Laden over to the US and his creation of a safe haven for foreign fighters in Afghanistan, noting:

> Mullah Muhammad Omar had taught the Ummah the meanings of honor, manhood, and faithfulness. He harbored immigrants, comforted the local supporters, and revived in the Ummah the creed of loyalty and disavowal. He made the principle of brotherhood deeply-rooted among them when he refused to turn over his immigrant Muslim brothers, and on top of them, the martyr of the Ummah, as we consider him, Sheikh Usama bin Laden, may Allah have mercy on him, to the state of disbelief, America, and its henchmen. He even sacrificed his property and his state for their sake, in accordance with the words of the Prophet.... In that in which there is no doubt is the tree of contemporary jihad, in which the Ummah sits under its shade today and has planted its seed in the rugged mountains of Khorasan. A period of time has passed for the Ummah where jihad cannot be mentioned without bringing to mind the land of Khorasan, the land of Mullah Omar and his companions.[22]

Al-Shabaab encouraged fighters in South Asia to keep fighting, stating: 'From here, we call on our mujahideen brothers in the cause of Allah in the land of Khorasan to continue their jihad against the disbelievers and apostates, until Islam prevails over the entire land, and the banners of polytheism and apostasy are brought down.'

Although both the messages from AQ's affiliates were too quick to include mention of Omar's successor, Mansour, the speed and urgency of their release shows the relevance that Omar and the Taliban still have in much of the word of jihadist movements. Indeed, whilst it may seem as though the Levant is the current centre of gravity, we should not lose sight of the significance of the 'Khorasan' in jihadist ideology (especially the Islamic apocalypse) and the important role it has played in the history of Islamist extremism. Khorasan refers to a historical region that encompassed north-eastern Iran, southern Turkmenistan and northern Afghanistan. It was established as a region by the Sassanian dynasty, the last Iranian empire before the rise of Islam, at some point in the third century. Its name literally means 'The Land of the Sun', a reference to its eastern location. After the region was taken over in an Arab conquest in the seventh century, Khorasan became a part of the Umayyad Caliphate, and with that, part of early Islamic culture. Notably, a widely discussed (though disputed) hadith speaks of how 'black banners will come out of Khorasan' in the end times. The prophecy tells of a massive army of non-

Arab Muslims marching on Jerusalem to prepare the way for the return of the Mahdi, the figure in Islamic apocalyptic narrative who signals the end of time and the global triumph of Islam.

A number of jihadist groups (including AQ and IS) have self-identified as the group prophesised to defeat the Christians in the final battle. The prophecy has been widely used as a driver for participation in jihad, including in AQ's black flag which was probably chosen in homage to the prophecy. The hadith predicts an army of 70,000 rising up within the Khorasan before marching on the Middle East: it is therefore imperative that jihadist groups maintain a sizeable foothold in the region if they want to weave the apolcalypse into their narratives.

On 13 August 2015, the final piece of the AQ jigsaw arrived in the shape of a message from AQ leader Ayman al-Zawahiri. It was distributed on Twitter and contained a pledge of allegiance to Mullah Mansour, telling him: 'We are your soldiers and your supporters and a brigade of your brigades.'[23] This message was unique for two reasons. The first was its method of distribution, utilising Twitter instead of the usual method of Deep Web extremist forums. The second was the speed with which it was issued. Although not released until 13 August, the message was dated 1 August, just two days after the original Taliban announcement. It was the first message from al-Zawahiri for over a year.

Given his problems with IS and the need for a counterweight to Baghdadi, it was perhaps not surprising that al-Zawahiri sought a rapid pledge of allegiance to Mansour. Al-Zawahiri sees the Taliban as AQ's best bet in presenting a challenge to the self-styled Caliphate of IS and the global jihad, despite the fact that the Taliban is fundamentally a nationalist movement. Al-Zawahiri's reference to Mansour as 'leader of the faithful' alludes to his religious credibility (and is the same title as previously used by Omar). This is of critical importance in contesting Baghdadi's claims as Caliph.

The next day, Mansour himself spoke publicly for the first time since being chosen as Omar's replacement. He thanked all those who had pledged allegiance to him, including al-Zawahiri:

> I want to wholeheartedly thank all those respected brothers who have sympathized with us in this critical juncture of the Islamic Ummah, have sent messages of condolence about the passing away of Amir ul Mu'mineen or have pledged allegiance with us as the new Amir (leader) of the Islamic Emirate and servant of the Muslims. Among these respected brothers, I first and foremost accept the pledge of allegiance of the esteemed Dr. Ayman al-Zawahiri, the leader of international Jihadi organiza-

tion (Qa'idatul Jihad) and thank him for sending a message of condolence along with his pledge and pledge of all Mujahideen under him.

Mansour's announcement marked a shift in how the Taliban positioned itself in relation to AQ. Historically, references to AQ in Taliban messaging tended to be limited to bin Laden in relation to his role in fighting against the Soviets. In recent years, the topic of AQ and bin Laden has been almost completely avoided. For Mansour, the statement was an attempt to bolster his position as the newly appointed leader. He would have been keen to accept the pledges of allegiance he had already received, a significant number of which came from the global AQ movement. And in the short term, AQ and the Taliban have more in common than in recent years: both groups are fighting against IS-KP and the disunity that Baghdadi's Caliph/Caliphate announcement has created. Both groups, therefore, share an interest in minimising the appeal of IS as a common enemy.

Although the strengthened AQ—Taliban relationship helps to create a united front against the newly created IS-KP, the manner in which Omar's death was covered up by both groups has damaged their credibility. Despite facing significant pressure to confirm Omar's whereabouts in recent months, the Taliban had continued to insist that he was still alive and well, including in Mansour's 16 June criticism of IS. Al-Zawahiri toed the same line, including re-pledging his allegiance to Omar in September 2014. He was either complicit in the cover-up, or woefully uninformed about the inner workings of the Taliban. Either option is damaging.

IS-KP has not maximised the impact of this own goal. It had already accused the Taliban of being religiously deficient, but has not sought to embark on a media campaign to discredit Mansour. It probably expected to profit more from the announcement of Omar's death than it actually has, particularly given the internal rifts this created within the Taliban senior leadership. For now at least, Mullah Mansour appears to have weathered the storm.

The Taliban and AQ: closer than ever?

The emergence of IS, especially IS-KP, has forced the Taliban to deepen its ties with AQ, including in its public statements. It has also been forced to fight a new enemy in its heartland of southern Afghanistan. Mansour has been the driving force behind the Taliban's narrative on IS: the message he has created is uncompromising, increasingly hostile and unforgiving. He may be seeking to target the younger generation of Talibs, a demographic that is more international in its outlook, more likely to devour ISIL's social media output, and potentially more susceptible to groups peddling a global jihadist narrative. For this generation, the much-revered Islamic Emirate of the 1990s is nothing more than legend, with the Taliban having struggled to regain its near-full control of Afghanistan since the 2001 invasion. ISIL and its Caliphate is seen as the only current example of a functioning 'Islamic State', multiplying its attractiveness. And even those who can remember the Emirate may struggle to idolise it in the same way since the arrival of ISIL's Caliphate: the Emirate, in comparison, was 'confined to a relatively marginal area of the globe and had limited capability to project influence or power beyond the frontiers of the remote locations which they controlled'.[24]

Although the Taliban may believe that a closer alliance with AQ will help to defeat its new enemy, IS-KP, it may also be using its links to AQ to draw a line under the faltering Afghan peace process. Disconnecting AQ and the Taliban has always been one of the US red lines for a negotiated peace settlement in Afghanistan. Although this position may have softened with the weakening of AQ and the rise of ISIL as a bigger concern, it had long been viewed as an unrealistic aim.[25] Although still nationalist at its heart, Mansour's Taliban is not afraid to boast about its ties with AQ, and, in doing so, a negotiated peace settlement in Afghanistan now seems a very long way away.

For AQ, the primary benefit of a closer relationship with the Taliban is the access it provides to a safe haven in eastern and, in a more limited way, southern Afghanistan. It provides an opportunity to recover from the relentless threat of drone strikes and Pakistani military action in Pakistan's tribal areas. It also helps AQ to offset Baghdadi's claims to be the rightful Caliph, by allowing them to present Mansour (rather than AQ leader al-Zawahiri) as the better candidate.

AQ has always needed the Taliban more than the Taliban has needed AQ. But the rise of IS-KP has forced the Taliban into a new position where its links to AQ can be a useful bulwark against a new upstart group and the distraction of a long-running peace process. A new era in the AQ/Taliban relationship has begun.

10

IN THE SHADOW OF THE ISLAMIC STATE

SHI'I RESPONSES TO SUNNI JIHADIST NARRATIVES
IN A TURBULENT MIDDLE EAST

Christopher Anzalone

Introduction: Gradual sectarianisation of the 'Arab Spring'

The outbreak of mass protests and then civil war in Syria against the government of Bashar al-Assad and the Syrian Ba'th party during the spring of 2011 into 2012, affected a clear shift in how many Twelver Shi'i[1] political actors saw the 'Arab Spring', the wave of popular protests that began in Tunisia in the winter of 2010. At the beginning, as popular protests swept Tunisia's Zayn al-'Abidin bin 'Ali and Egypt's Hosni Mubarak from power, a number of the Middle East's most prominent Shi'i Islamist parties and leaders claimed that Tunisians and Egyptians had been 'inspired', three decades later, by the Iranian revolution. Iran's supreme leader, 'Ali Khamenei, and Hasan Nasrallah, the secretary general of Lebanon's Hizbullah, initially attempted to harness the Tunisian and Egyptian uprisings as a rhetorical weapon to use in their political competition with the United States, European countries and their regional allies such as Saudi Arabia.[2] This early embrace by the region's powerful Shi'i Islamists, however, did not last. The repression of popular mass protests in Bahrain, and the rise to prominence of Salafi and anti-Shi'i Sunni political parties and armed groups across the region, led to increasingly hostile and even conspiratorial views of the Arab Spring among Iranian officials and other Shi'i Islamists. The wave of uprisings, they said, was yet another 'Western' and 'Zionist' plot against the world's Muslims, and in particular, opponents of the US-led order in the Middle East and North Africa.

This chapter will consider how the Arab Spring was sectarianised. It will do this by considering the ways in which a sectarian frame can be used to mobilise people towards radical or even violent aims. It will then consider how the various actors involved in the conflicts in Syria and Iraq have used sectarian identities in these ways: first considering the development and variety of sectarian views within Salafi jihadist movements, and then setting out the range of counter-polemics, and mobilisation to violence, of Shi'i political actors. The chapter will then describe how particular aspects of Shi'i historical narratives have been used by militant actors in Syria and Iraq to mobilise support. Finally, the role of intra-Shi'i dynamics in armed mobilisation in Syria and Iraq will be explored.

Framing sectarianism: identities and social mobilisation

The reification of communal identities is a process of framing frequently used for social and political mobilisation by different actors. Historically, sectarian identities and divisions have been used both within a single community as well as in struggles and competitions for resources and power between different communities or sects.[3] Modern sectarianism, particularly between Sunni and Shi'i Muslims, far from representing primarily 'ancient hatreds' and divisions, instead rests to a great degree on contemporary political and military conflicts. The evolution of sectarianism in Syria since 2011, and Iraq since the 2003 invasion and toppling of Saddam Hussein, has been guided by political, military and social developments on the ground. Historical divisions do, of course, play a role in the evolution of Sunni and Shi'i sectarian rhetoric and ideologies today, providing a narrative, conceptual vocabulary and frame that seeks to mobilise individuals based on an 'us vs. them' paradigm.[4] Sectarian identities are particularly salient in environments with multiple ethnic groups or sects where there is significant competition for power and resources.

Identifiers such as religious affiliation, tribe or clan, and linguistic group become ways to differentiate between 'us and them', allowing social and political entrepreneurs to turn these identities into mobilisation frames, which draw upon cultural idioms meant to garner support and drive social mobilisation.[5] In order for frames to mobilise their intended audience(s) successfully, they must resonate with people's existing beliefs and identities.

The concept of 'framing', the creation of interpretive lenses through which people perceive world events and through which they develop a sense of group and self-identity, provides a useful framework for understanding the development and devolution of sectarianism in the conflicts in Syria and Iraq. In order to attract new members, as well as to maintain internal solidarity among existing members and supporters, Sunni jihadist groups such as the Islamic State (formerly ISIL) and Jabhat al-Nusra and Shiʻi paramilitary organisations, as well as regional governments and religious figures both inside and outside Syria and Iraq, portray the conflicts in both countries as essential to the survival of their specific groups, the Sunnis (*Ahl al-Sunna wa-l-Jamaʻa*) or the Shiʻis, who see themselves as the 'true' followers of the Prophet Muhammad's family (*Ahl al-Bayt*). The expression of these two sets of mobilisation frames and narratives play off one another, influencing the evolution of the narratives and worldviews of the other community. To achieve 'frame resonance', mobilisation frames draw on the 'toolkit' of cultural, in this case 'Islamic', symbols, idioms, beliefs and worldviews in order to achieve frame resonance and successfully portray social mobilisation and activism as a moral duty.[6] These mobilisation frames, however, only have resonance within particular social, political and economic contexts. The severe upheaval in Syria and Iraq provided such a context. The development of sectarian narratives in each community during a conflict influences the parallel development and contours of the sectarian worldviews of other communities, which respond by constructing and deploying their own counter-narratives.

In the case of the Arab Spring, the steady devolution of the protests in Syria in the face of brutal government repression and the increasingly public participation of pro-Assad Iran, Hizbullah and Iraqi Shiʻi militias have contributed to a rising level of sectarian rhetoric across the region. In Egypt, politically mobilised Salafis[7] were able to influence the country's Muslim Brotherhood (*al-Ikhwan al-Muslimun*)-controlled government during its time in power from 2011 until June 2013, challenging its religious credentials and pressing for increased implementation of a black-and-white interpretation of the shariʻah.[8] To appeal to a Salafi and popular Islamist base, the Ikhwan government increasingly publicly supported, or at least did not condemn, Egyptians joining various Syrian armed rebel groups, and it condemned Shi'i allies of al-Assad.[9]

The influential Qatar-based Egyptian preacher and religious jurist Yusuf al-Qaradawi[10] also publicly condemned Iran, Hizbullah and other Shi'i Islamists for their support of the Syrian government.[11] He had previously also condemned the popular protests in Bahrain for being 'sectarian'.[12] The intervention by Arab Gulf countries led by Saudi Arabia against Bahrain's protests in March 2011, and the continued support for the island nation's al-Khalifa ruling family from the US and many European governments, despite the brutality of its crack-down—which included mass arrests, the killings of demonstrators, and tor-ture—increased the disillusion of many Shi'is to the Arab Spring. The rise to power of Salafi political parties like Hizb al-Nur in Egypt was alarming to Shi'is, already a super minority among the world's Muslims, with the exception of Lebanon, Iraq, Bahrain and Iran. The strong tradition of vitriolic and often violent anti-Shi'ism within the Salafi current of Sunni Islam was the major cause of these feelings of unease. Shi'is' worst fears came to pass in June 2013 when Hasan Shehata, Egypt's most prominent Shi'i preacher, and three other Egyptian Shi'is were lynched in the village of Zawiyat Abu Musalam near Giza by a mob after allegedly insulting historical figures revered by Sunnis.[13] Shehata was eulogised by many Shi'i religious scholars, politicians and Iranian state-owned media outlets such as Press TV and al-'Alam, as well as by Shi'i militias in Syria and Iraq.[14] These and similar events were seen as evidence of the growing existential threat to many Shi'i communities in the region.

Sunni sectarian polemic

Salafi Anti-Shi'ism and Salafi Jihadism

IS, Jabhat al-Nusra and some Syrian Islamist rebel groups such as Harakat Ahrar al-Sham (Movement of the Free-born of Syria) draw upon a repertoire of anti-Shi'i polemic, a discourse that sees Shi'i Muslims as being guilty of heretical religious innovation (bid'a) and polytheism (shirk) because of their elevation of the twelve Imams, and to a lesser extent their families, and Fatima, the Prophet Muhammad's daughter.[15] Existing hostilities towards Shi'i beliefs and ritual practices, such as shrine visitation and intercessory prayer to holy figures such as the Imams (shafa'a), are combined with social, economic and political grievances to create a particularly potent militant Salafi (or Salafi-sed) rhetoric and mobilisation frames that these groups use to try to convince

Sunni populations that Shi'is, in the form of Iran, the Iraqi central government, and groups such as Lebanese Hizbullah and Iraqi Shi'i armed groups and Islamist parties, pose a threat to the survival of Sunnism and Sunni communities.[16] The development of a Sunni anti-Shi'ism in Syria by groups such as the Syrian *Ikhwan*, and even mainstream Sunni religious scholars like the regime-aligned Muhammad Sa'id Ramadan al-Buti, has been profoundly influenced by the political alliance between the Syrian Ba'thist government and Iran, as well as suspicions regarding Iranian interests in the region, including the promotion of Shi'ism, real and imagined.[17]

Al-Qaeda and the Shi'is: hostile ambivalence

The al-Qaeda Senior Leadership (AQSL) approach to Shi'i beliefs and practices has been to consider them as *bid'a* if not outright *shirk*; yet they have not preached open and indiscriminate warfare against Shi'is. Al-Zawahiri and other senior AQSL leaders, including *Shaykh* 'Atiyyatullah (Ibrahim al-Mishtaywi al-Misrati) and Abu Yahya al-Libi, were opposed to the blanket targeting of Shi'is by Abu Mus'ab al-Zarqawi, the founder of Jama'at al-Tawhid wa-l-Jihad and al-Qaeda in the Land of the Two Rivers, the precursor organisations to the Islamic State (IS).[18]

Rather than Shi'i theology and *'aqida*, AQSL leaders more frequently condemn Shi'i actors such as Iran and Hizbullah for political actions such as failing to oppose and even cooperating with the United States in toppling the Afghan Taliban government in Kabul and invading Iraq in 2003. In a 2009 video interview produced and released by AQSL's official media department, the al-Sahab Media Foundation, al-Zawahiri asks rhetorically if a single Shi'i grand *mujtahid* has called for military resistance (*al-jihad al-'askari*) against the Americans in Iraq, and if not, why not.[19] Al-Zawahiri has also ordered members of AQSL and its regional affiliates not to target Shi'is generally, but rather only those groups or segments who target 'the Sunnis' (*Ahl al-Sunna wa-l-Jama'a*).[20] Although he refers to them as 'deviant sects' (*al-firaq al-munharifa*), he wrote in a series of guidelines for al-Qaeda fighters that even if attacked they must restrict their response to targeting those segments from these sects that are openly belligerent and engaged in attacking Sunnis.[21]

Similarly, influential Salafi jihadist religious scholar Abu Muhammad al-Maqdisi publicly criticised al-Zarqawi's targeting of Shi'is generally in Iraq as well as his group's filming of executions, including beheadings. The complex relationship between al-Zarqawi and Maqdisi is explored in Chapter 2 in this volume. Stung by his former teacher's criticisms, al-Zarqawi and his supporters attacked al-Maqdisi for not having actually fought jihad despite his voluminous writings supporting military action against 'apostate' (*murtad*), tyrannical (*taghut*) regimes in the Muslim world and their Western backers.[22]

The opposition of many Sunni jihadist leaders and strategists such as Osama bin Laden, al-Zawahiri and Abu Mus'ab al-Suri to targeting Shi'is generally is due to their concern that the mujahidin will become bogged down in sectarian, inter-communal conflict, which is trivial compared to the need to combat apostate governments in countries such as Saudi Arabia, Pakistan and Egypt along with their foreign backers, chief among them the United States, France, Britain, Germany, India and Israel. The internal tension within the global jihadist current has long been that between those Sunni jihadists who are more puritanical and exclusionary in their religious views and those who seek to create a global jihadist movement that is as large and inclusive as possible.[23]

Two regional AQ affiliates, Jabhat al-Nusra in Syria and al-Qaeda in the Arabian Peninsula (AQAP) in Yemen, have stronger anti-Shi'i views than AQSL. The former was founded by jihadist veterans from Iraq—including the group's leader, the Syrian Abu Muhammad al-Jawlani—who likely brought home with them more pronounced anti-Shi'i views. The 'Alawi identity of the ruling al-Assad family and extensive Iranian state support for the Syrian regime has also fuelled sectarian views, particularly of rank-and-file Jabhat al-Nusra fighters. The founding membership, including senior leaders, of the Yemen-based AQAP included a large number of Saudi Salafi jihadists, and their anti-Shi'i ideology plays a significant role in the group's war against the Yemeni Zaydi Shi'i Houthi movement and its supporters.[24]

IS: Jihadist anti-Shi'ism at its most extreme

IS and its precursor organisations[25] represent the most extreme expression of Sunni jihadist anti-Shi'ism. Guided by the ideology laid down by its founder, al-Zarqawi, the group sees all Shi'is as legitimate targets and frequently carries out brazen and bloody attacks in Shi'i-majority areas of Iraq and against both Shi'i civilians and combatants.[26] IS leaders and ideologues such as its *amir*, Abu Bakr al-Baghdadi (the 'caliph' Ibrahim ibn 'Awad al-Samarra'i), spokesman Abu Muhammad al-'Adnani, and chief shari'ah official and *mufti* Turki al-Bin'ali,[27] justify their extreme anti-Shi'ism and blanket targeting of Shi'is, whether they are actively fighting the group or not, by drawing upon anti-Shi'i positions of past scholars. This includes the medieval Hanbali jurist and religious scholar Ibn Taymiyya (1263–1328), the nineteenth-century Najdi Salafi Muhammad ibn 'Abdullah ibn 'Abd al-Latif Al al-Shaykh (1848–1921), a descendant of Muhammad ibn 'Abd al-Wahhab (1703–92),[28] whose writings are also used by the Islamic State in shaping its creedal ('aqida) views, the great hadith compiler and muhaddith al-Bukhari (d. 870), and the medieval Qur'anic exegete (mufassir), historian and jurist Ibn Kathir (d. 1373).

Iraqi soldiers, police and other members of the security forces and the fighters in the armed groups founded and controlled by the country's various Shi'i Islamist parties and paramilitary groups and 'ulama in the shrine cities are described in IS discourse in a variety of derogatory ways, each drawing upon historical sectarian polemics. The Iraqi army and Shi'i militia forces are labelled the 'Safavid Army' (al-jaysh al-safawi) after the Shi'i Safavid dynasty that ruled what is now modern-day Iran from 1501 to 1732, the 'fire worshippers' (al-majus) in reference to the Zoroastrians of pre-Islamic Iran, and the 'rejectors' of true Islam (al-Rafida or al-Rawafid).[29] Shi'is generally are portrayed as posing a greater threat to Islam than Christians, Jews or other non-Muslims because of their claim to be Muslim, which has historically allowed them their treacherous betrayal of Sunnis and alliance with non-Muslim aggressors such as the Ilkhanid Mongols and the European Crusaders.[30] Modern Shi'is are compared to historical Shi'i 'villains' such as 'Abdullah ibn Saba, the seventh-century heretical 'founder' of Shi'ism in Salafi and other Sunni anti-Shi'i discourses; Nasir al-Din al-Tusi (d. 1274), a famous Shi'i polymath who was patronised by the Ilkhanid ruler Hulagu following his conquest of Iraq and Iran and who is accused of encouraging the sacking of Baghdad by Mongol forces; and Ibn al-'Alqami, the chief minister (wazir) of the last 'Abbasid caliph in Baghdad, al-Musta'sim bi-llah, whom he is accused of betraying. In an attack on Shi'i shrine visitation, the Islamic State also uses hadith narrated from the Prophet Muhammad by 'Ali ibn Abi Talib, commanding the destruction of raised tombs and pictures and drawings to prevent polytheism.[31]

Religious justifications are not the only dynamic to the Islamic State's anti-Shi'i rhetoric and messaging. The group also draws extensively on the deep well of Iraqi and Syrian Sunni grievances against their governments and the regional activities of Iran and Shi'i Islamist groups such as Hizbullah, chiefly their strong and continued backing of the Syrian regime. At the centre of IS public messaging is a claim to be the 'defender' of Sunnis, the only actor willing to combat Shi'i expansionism and avenge Shi'i persecution of Sunnis.[32]

In connecting Shi'is in modern times to historical 'villains' such as Ibn Saba, al-Tusi and Ibn al-'Alqami, IS creates a propaganda narrative of (alleged) historical Shi'i perfidy towards Islam and (Sunni) Muslims. The contemporary behaviour, therefore, of parties such as Hizbullah, Iraqi Da'wa party and the Iranian state is put into a 'historical' context in which Shi'is have always and will continue to seek to harm Sunni Muslims while promoting their own deviant religion, which, according to IS, is nothing more than a gross perversion of 'true' Islam. Dialogue and rapprochement are thus not options in the IS narrative because Shi'is by their very nature will continually seek to undermine and harm Sunnis, no matter what they claim. Thus, Sunnis are never safe and are in need of an always vigilant protector against Shi'i violence. IS claims to be such a protector.

Sectarianism rising

The Syrian civil war as catalyst

Sectarian identities were further entrenched as the participation of Shi'i fighters in Syria on the side of the government became increasingly public in 2013. Hasan Nasrallah, the secretary general of Hizbullah, publicly admitted and defended the party's backing of al-Assad in a speech broadcast on the Lebanese Shi'i Islamist party's satellite Al-Manar television channel, leading to strong condemnations by Sunni religious and political leaders, including al-Qaradawi and the rector of Egypt's al-Azhar seminary, Ahmad al-Tayyeb.[33] Egyptian government officials from the *Ikhwan* responded by announcing that Egyptians who travelled to Syria to fight against al-Assad's regime would not be prosecuted.[34] Public criticisms of Hizbullah and other Shi'i actors also increased. This marked a significant shift from the Egyptian *Ikhwan*'s previous history of relative ecumenical views toward Shi'is, which were supported by the movement's founder, Hasan al-Banna, and one of its most influential supreme guides (*al-murshid al-'amm*), Hasan al-Hudaybi.[35] Unlike the Syrian *Ikhwan*, whose members developed strong anti-Shi'i views in large part because of their conflict with the Alawite al-Assad family and the Syrian regime, Egypt's Brotherhood does not have an extensive history of anti-Shi'ism. Even Sayyid Qutb, its most revolutionary ideologue, did not propagate conflict with the Shi'a, focusing instead on 'reviving' Islam in the country to turn back the tide of the 'modern *Jahiliyya* (pre-Islamic age of ignorance)'.[36] Increasing sectarianisation of the Syrian civil war has been a windfall to those rebel factions whose religio-political ideologies include stronger Salafi leanings, including Jabhat al-Nusra, Harakat Ahrar al-Sham and the Islamic Front umbrella.[37] Syrian Salafis, however, are not the only ones who have adopted a harder anti-Shi'i line. Mainstream Syrian Sunni scholars, such as the prominent Damascene Sunni religious scholar and preacher Usama al-Rifa'i, who was assaulted by regime supporters inside his mosque in August 2011, have also publicly condemned Shi'ism more generally as the civil war has dragged on.[38] Al-Rifa'i differentiates between Iranians/Persians and Shi'is, noting that many of the greatest Sunni scholars, including Abu Hamid al-Ghazali (d. 1111) and Fakhr al-Din al-Razi (d. 1210), were Iranian.[39]

Iran, for its part, remains the Syrian government's chief regional ally and backer. It continues to provide political and military support including shipments of arms and ammunition and military advisers and soldiers from its elite Revolutionary Guards Corps (IRGC). State-owned media outlets have unabashedly portrayed all the Syrian opposition and all Syrian rebel groups as 'Wahhabi/Salafi', thus justifying the Iranian state's support for al-Assad and his regime as a part of an existential 'defence' of Shi'ism and Shi'is against the hordes of Wahhabism. The Free Syrian Army rebel militia umbrella has been described as a 'terrorist army' by Press TV and other Iranian state-affiliated media outlets since before the rise to prominence of IS in Syria in 2013. The Syrian opposition and rebels are also portrayed by Iranian state media, Hizbullah, and many Iraqi Shi'i Islamists as being tools of Western and Israeli ('Zionist') imperial designs on the Middle East and North Africa and the wider Muslim world.[40] Hizbullah's Nasrallah has proposed his own spin on the George W. Bush administration argument of 'fighting them over there' so that 'we don't have to fight them here', arguing that the party's involvement inside Syria is necessary to prevent the outbreak of sectarian conflict in Lebanon.[41] The destruction or bombardment of several shrines and tombs by some Syrian rebel groups and the rise of the strongly anti-Shi'i Jabhat al-Nusra and IS have played into the narrative that the Syrian conflict is at its heart a sectarian one in which the al-Assad regime is the 'defender' of the country's minorities, rather than a cynical manipulator of the fears of minority communities.[42]

The Shi'i shrine complexes of Zaynab bint 'Ali ibn Abi Talib (*Sayyida* Zaynab) and Sakina bint Husayn have been besieged, with the former becoming a major base for the Syrian government and Iraqi Shi'i militiamen fighting alongside government forces. The threats, both real and created, to shrines and the killings of prominent Shi'i figures in Syria such as Nasir al-'Alawi, the director of the Zaynabiyya seminary in Damascus, have been used by the Syrian government and its Shi'i allies such as Hizbullah and the Iraqi Shi'i militias active in the country to attract Shi'i fighters both domestically, regionally and even internationally.[43] These events have inflamed public opinion, not only among members of pro-Assad Shi'i groups, but also of Shi'is generally, who share a particularly strong reverence for the line of the Prophet Muhammad's family that includes the twelve Imams and members of their families.[44] There is, however, a clear attempt by the Iranian state, Hizbullah and other Shi'i Islamist groups and figures to steer Shi'i public opinion generally towards a hyper-sectarianised narrative of the Syrian conflict, a project that has benefited greatly from the rapid sweep of IS in western Iraq in June 2014.[45]

The Shi'i sacred topography of Syria

The construction, expansion and promotion of Syria's Shi'i shrines from the late 1970s onwards by the Syrian and Iranian governments is intimately tied to regional politics and particularly to the development of the political alliance between the governments of the two countries.[46] Funding for the expansion of the shrines, particularly the *Sayyida* Zaynab shrine and its surrounding district and the shrine complex of 'Ammar ibn Yasir and Uways al-Qarani in Raqqa, which was destroyed by the Islamic State in March 2014, has come from a combination of Iranian and Syrian government funding and coordination as well as donations from wealthy Shi'i businessmen from Arab Gulf states, Iran and Pakistan.[47] The economics of the *Sayyida* Zaynab shrine and the surrounding area have also played an integral role in the development of Syria and specifically Damascus as a major transnational pilgrimage destination since the 1980s.[48]

Despite the relatively recent emergence of Syria's Shi'i shrines as major destinations of transnational pilgrimage and uncertainty, including among Shi'is—about their historical authenticity, with regards to whether the holy figures after whom they are named are actually buried inside—the shrines of *Sayyida* Zaynab and others have been imbued with legitimacy, through their consecration to the holy figures as well as through social processes of sanctification involving miracle and dream stories (in which they are said to engage in intercession on behalf of those who seek their help in connecting with God).[49]

There has been a Shi'i presence in Syria from the early centuries of Islam, and Shi'i institutions have been there since at least the fourteenth century.[50] Until the outbreak of mass protests against the Syrian government and their eventual evolution into a civil war following government repression, there were a multitude of Shi'i institutions in the country. These included hospitals founded by various Shi'i grand *mujtahids* (*marja' al-taqlid*, plural: *maraji'*),[51] including Iran's supreme leader 'Ali Khamenei and the late Muhammad Sadiq al-Sadr, father of Muqtada al-Sadr and a widely revered Iraqi jurist who was assassinated in 1999 by the Iraqi Ba'th party.[52] Before the outbreak of the Syrian civil war, there were twenty Shi'i seminaries operating in Damascus and near the city of Homs, the largest of them being the the oldest seminary (*hawza*) in Syria, named after Grand Ayatollah Ruhollah Khomeini and the Zaynabiyya *hawza*, funded by the Iranian government and affiliated with the Shirazi clerical family and its network of followers and institutions.[53]

There was competition between the followers of Khamenei, the Shirazi clerical network, and Muhammad Sadiq al-Sadr in the *Sayyida* Zaynab district, over defining 'authentic Shi'ism' in terms of ritual practices, particularly with regard to the legitimacy of *tatbir*, a cathartic ritual in which individuals cut their heads in mourning for Husayn ibn 'Ali, the third Shi'i Imam, and many of his family and companions who were killed in battle against a much larger Umayyad army in 680 at Karbala, Iraq. These debates are coupled with divergent political views of each group based on the views of their *marja'*.[54] Photographs published online, primarily on Facebook accounts of the Shi'i militia groups in Syria, show some fighters participating in *tatbir*, which suggests that at least some of the Shi'i fighters in the *Sayyida* Zaynab area are individually affiliated to the Shirazi network of *mujtahids* rather than Khamenei or the late Grand Ayatollah Muhammad Husayn Fadlallah, both of whom have spoken against the bloodletting rituals.[55] Recruitment advertisements and calls have been broadcast on al-Anwar, two satellite television channels broadcasting from Kuwait and closely affiliated with the Shirazi network.[56]

Up to the outbreak of protests in 2011, the largest numbers of Shi'is in the *Sayyida* Zaynab area were Iranians or Iraqis, many of them refugees seeking to escape the war, or Iraqis whose families had originally settled in Iraq's Shi'i pilgrimage and education centres, such as the southern cities of Najaf and Karbala.[57] Some of the members of Shi'i militias operating in Syria have reportedly been drawn from segments of these communities, as well as the small Syrian Shi'i community.

Fighting for Zaynab alongside al-Assad: Shi'i foreign fighters in Syria

The mobilisation of Syrian and non-Syrian Shi'i fighters to defend the 'holy places' (*al-muqadassat*), the Shi'i shrines in Syria, began in earnest in 2012. The first reports of growing numbers of Shi'i foreign fighters, mainly from neighbouring Iraq, first appeared in the autumn of that year, including media interviews with individual fighters as well as videos posted online by fighters themselves.[58] Iraqi government officials also acknowledged that there were recruitment drives by Iraqi Shi'i parties to man their militia units inside Syria.[59] The first major armed Shi'i group in Syria was Liwa' (Brigade) Abu al-Fadl al-'Abbas (LAFA), which included fighters from a variety of nationalities, including Afghan Hazara and Lebanese, but was composed mainly of Iraqi and Syrian Shi'i fighters.[60] The militias, as well as the Hashd al-Sha'bi (Popular Mobilization Forces) umbrella in Iraq, are eager to demonstrate that their ranks include not only Shi'i Muslims but also Sunnis and non-Muslims.[61] The vast majority of the militias active in Syria, and to a somewhat lesser extent within the Hashd al-Sha'bi umbrella, are, as of this writing, Shi'is, and some of the Sunni fighters siding with the government initially participated in the battle against Islamic State as part of tribal militias, rather than as fully integrated units within the Hashd umbrella.[62]

The total number of Shi'i fighters in groups aligned with the Syrian government is unclear, with unverified high estimates of up to 10,000, though this estimate includes members of Hizbullah, which is said to have between 3–5,000 fighters inside Syria or along the border with Lebanon, as well as Iraqi fighters, who likely number another 3–5,000, though this number has declined significantly since IS's sweep across western Iraq in the summer of 2014.[63] The early numbers in the autumn of 2012, however, were much lower, probably numbering in the high hundreds before recruitment drives in Iraq and Iran began to accelerate throughout 2013. According to an anonymous Shi'i fighter in Syria interviewed by the Associated Press in October 2012, an estimated 200 recruits from Iraq arrived in Syria. Many arrived on pilgrimage buses on which weapons and other military materiel were also transported.[64] Recruitment and deployment of new fighters and the formation of new armed groups and units within larger, existing groups continued throughout 2013 and into 2014, though many of the Iraqi Shi'i fighters were recalled to Iraq beginning in the spring of 2014 in order to combat the expansion of IS there. IS's 2014 sweep led to an increase in the number of Iraqi Shi'i fighters in Syria returning home to help fill the ranks of Iraqi Shi'i paramilitary units being formed by the country's Shi'i Islamist parties and movements like the Badr Organization, 'Asa'ib Ahl al-Haqq (League of the Righteous), Kata'ib Hizbullah (Brigades of the Party of God), the Supreme Islamic Iraqi Council, and the Sadr Movement. Some Iraqi Shi'i fighters, however, remained in Syria and Iraqi recruits began to travel back there in the spring of 2015. Hizbullah also maintained and even increased its involvement inside Syria during the second half of 2014 into

2015, arguing that it must do so to combat the Islamic State and Jabhat al-Nusra in border areas such as the Qalamoun Mountains.[65]

LAFA and other Shi'i paramilitary groups operating alongside Syrian government forces were largely recruited, organised and trained by existing Iraqi Shi'i socio-political movements and parties, mainly 'Asa'ib Ahl al-Haqq, Kata'ib Hizbullah, the Badr Organization, the Supreme Islamic Iraqi Council, the Movement of the Party of God, Harakat Hizbullah al-Nujaba, and the Sadr Movement of Muqtada al-Sadr. The involvement of these groups and the armed units they dispatched to Syria is verifiable from martyrdom announcements and other statements, videos and photography produced and published by them and their supporters as well as press reports.[66] Fighters in militia photography and artwork are often shown posing with photographs of Bashar and Hafiz al-Assad, Nasrallah, and paintings of Shi'i holy figures. Some artwork depicts Bashar and Nasrallah as 'pious' with light emanating from the pages of the Qur'an onto their faces, demonstrating the close ties between the Syrian government, and specifically the person of Bashar, and the Iraqi Shi'i groups operating in Syria.[67]

LAFA includes smaller field units, all of which are named after historical figures revered by Shi'i Muslims, including units named after Imam Husayn's son 'Ali Akbar, al-Qasim ibn Hasan (the son of the second Imam), Sayyida Zaynab, twelfth Imam Muhammad ibn Hasan 'al-Mahdi' (the *Mahdi*, a messianic figure in Shi'i eschatology) and Malik al-Ashtar, a supporter of Imam 'Ali.[68] The naming and mobilisation frames of the Iraqi groups inside Syria demonstrate their strong Shi'i identities, but LAFA also has some non-Shi'i fighters, including Christians, Sunnis and Druze, whose numbers, though not known precisely, are probably low.[69] Other Iraqi Shi'i armed groups operating in Syria and Iraq also draw their names from historical figures and idioms revered by Shi'i Muslims, such as the twelve Imams.

Shi'i groups highlight attacks by some rebel groups on Syrian Shi'is, and the destruction or shelling of some Shi'i shrines, mosques and centres (*husayniyyat*) inside the country, as reasons for social and paramilitary mobilisation. These include the shrines of Hujr ibn 'Adi al-Kindi and Sakina, one of Imam Husayn's daughters. Hujr was another of the prophet's companions who supported 'Ali and served as one of the first Imam's battlefield commanders. In May 2013, his shrine in the town of 'Adhra about 20 kilometres east of Damascus was destroyed by Syrian rebel group Liwa' al-Islam (Brigade of Islam). Sakina's shrine in Damascus has been damaged in fighting between the Syrian government, its Shabiha militias, Shi'i armed groups and Syrian rebel groups.[70] A 'wanted' poster was published online by LAFA showing four of the rebels present during the exhumation of the body and the destruction of the shrine.[71] One of the alleged perpetrators is shown in another photograph after being captured, executed and beheaded by brigade militiamen.[72] The threat to Syria's Shi'i shrines and communities are seen by Iraqi, Lebanese and other Arab Shi'i fighters as being intimately connected to the ongoing insurgency and conflict between Sunni and Shi'i actors in Iraq. Indeed, many of the Iraqi fighters in Syria publicly proclaim and display their national identities as well as their identity as Shi'is both in battle and in and around the shrines. The collapse of the Syrian regime and the victory of largely Sunni opposition and rebel groups is seen as a disastrous potential outcome, one that will empower groups such as IS and Jabhat al-Nusra, which pose a threat to the region's Shi'is.

Mobilising historical memory and individual piety: Framing sectarian conflict

For their mobilisation frames and narratives the Shi'i paramilitary groups in Syria and Iraq draw upon the historical memory of Islamic history as seen by the Shi'a, chiefly a deep reservoir of cultural idioms from Shi'i history. This view of history revolves around a strong sense of persecution and hardship as a minority community within the wider Islamic world, where the Shi'a are far outnumbered by Sunnis. Feelings of being besieged are coupled with passionate reverence for the honour of the *Ahl al-Bayt* and specifically the line through Fatima and the twelve Imams, who, according to Shi'i historical narratives, were subject to persecution and even assassination during their lifetimes. Shi'i militiamen, party and group leaders, and *'ulama* in Syria and Iraq frequently invoke the honour of the *Ahl al-Bayt* and in particular certain figures such as Imam Husayn, Abu al-Fadl al-'Abbas and *Sayyida* Zaynab in their discourse against the Islamic State, Jabhat al-Nusra and Syrian rebel groups. By doing this, they link themselves to the sacred past and tap into a historical memory of persecution and bravery, the latter from past heroes such as Abu al-Fadl al-'Abbas, which in turn is used as a key part of their media operations and recruitment drives. By tapping into historical figures and motifs they are able to also draw upon popular passions and reverence for the *Ahl al-Bayt* among Iraqi Shi'is and Shi'is generally.

At the heart of these historical frames and narratives is the Karbala tragedy, the martyrdom of Imam Husayn and many of his supporters and family members in a battle with a much larger Umayyad military force in 680. The survivors, including Husayn's sister, *Sayyida* Zaynab, were taken in chains by the victorious Umayyad force to the seat of their ruler, the caliph Yazid ibn Mu'awiya, in Damascus, where they were subject to additional humiliations and persecution. The commemoration of the Karbala events during the first ten days of the lunar month of 'Ashura, followed by the 'Arba'in commemorations forty days later, is at the centre of the Shi'i year and occupies an important part of Shi'i popular cultures, societies and the public sphere.[73] Invocations to the suffering of the defeated at Karbala thus provide the emotional and cultural resonance among target audiences, for example potential recruits, which the Shi'i armed groups are attempting to reach.

Shi'i armed groups in Syria and Iraq all state that at the heart of their purpose is the defence of the honour of the *Ahl al-Bayt* through the defence of the shrines and other holy places dedicated to them. Popular images in Shi'i historical accounts and stories of the bravery of figures such as Husayn and his half-brother, Abu al-Fadl al-'Abbas, are drawn upon by contemporary Shi'i fighters as exemplary models of masculinity and heroism.[74] Fighters frequently invoke the names of these revered figures during battle and present themselves as being at their command, as demonstrated in popular slogans such as '*Labbayk ya Husayn*' ('at your command, Husayn!') and '*Labbayk ya Zaynab*' and willingness to sacrifice their lives for the Prophet Muhammad's family (*Ahl al-Bayt*).[75/76] In this section, the historical and cultural importance of some of the most popular references used by the Shi'i armed groups in Syria and Iraq will be surveyed and their importance to the mobilisation frames explained.

Sayyida Zaynab

The sister of the third Shi'i Imam, Zaynab bint 'Ali ibn Abi Talib, is referred to as 'our lady' (*Sayyida*) Zaynab by Shi'is, an honorific noting not only her identity as a member of the *Ahl al-Bayt*, but also her vital role in propagating her brother's message and the purest form of Islam (Shi'ism) after his martyrdom at the hands of the Umayyad governor of Iraq, 'Ubaydullah ibn Ziyad, the Umayyad commander 'Umar ibn Sa'd, and ultimately the Umayyad caliph, Yazid ibn Mu'awiya.[77] Zaynab is remembered and heralded most for the defiant speeches she is said to have delivered in front of 'Ubaydullah and Yazid in which she excoriated them for their persecution of the *Ahl al-Bayt* and distortion of Islam.[78] Modern readings of Zaynab, beginning in the 1950s and 1960s, portray her as an active participant in the events surrounding Karbala, unlike earlier accounts.[79] She is even portrayed as a kind of 'co-hero' alongside her brother, Imam Husayn.[80]

Shi'i fighters in Syria and Iraq, however, have reverted to older descriptions of her as more 'feminine' and 'passive', in short chiefly as a victim rather than a heroine, and describe themselves as Zaynab's 'guardians' and 'defenders' (*hurras*). They refer to her Syrian shrine and her humiliating imprisonment by the Umayyads between Karbala and Damascus centuries ago, and vow that 'Zaynab will not be taken captive a second time' (*lan tusba Zaynab marratayn*). Each Shi'i fighter is described as a new Abu al-Fadl al-'Abbas who will defend Zaynab's honour and sanctity in the face of unbelieving hordes. Historical villains such as the Umayyads are compared to contemporary Salafis, 'Wahhabis' and other Sunni opponents, including the militias of the Free Syrian Army (FSA) umbrella.[81] Syrian Sunni rebel groups are not differentiated from IS and Jabhat al-Nusra. All of them are described by the Shi'i groups as 'Wahhabi/Salafi' and are labelled *nawasib*, a term used by Shi'is to describe those critical of Shi'ism who thus also allegedly hate the *Ahl al-Bayt*. Contemporary Sunni enemies are equated with historical villains in the Shi'i historical narrative such as Mu'awiya ibn Sufyan, his son Yazid, and other persecutors of the *Ahl al-Bayt*. For example, after he was filmed taking a symbolic bite from an organ of a slain regime soldier, Syrian rebel commander Abu Sakkar was compared to Hind bint 'Utba, one of the Prophet Muhammad's most bitter enemies who, according to some Islamic historical accounts, is said to have eaten the liver of Hamza ibn 'Abd al-Muttalib, the uncle of the Prophet Muhammad and one of his greatest warriors, after he had been slain at the Battle of Uhud in 625 on her orders. She is reviled by Shi'is for her actions, though she converted to Islam after the prophet took control of Mecca in 630, and is thus accorded some respect by Sunnis.[82]

Abu al-Fadl al-'Abbas

The half-brother of Husayn, Abu al-Fadl al-'Abbas, is noted for his heroism as the Imam's standard bearer during the Battle of Karbala, as well as for his attempt to get water from the Euphrates River for Husayn's young daughter Ruqayya. Despite receiving the offer of a pardon from 'Ubaydullah ibn Ziyad, according to some accounts, al-'Abbas rejected it and remained by Husayn's side.[83] In an earlier period, notions of al-'Abbas's masculinity and bravery also made him a popular model for Iraqi tribesmen who began gradually adopting Shi'ism during the nineteenth century.[84]

In Syria, Shi'i fighters frequently use the slogan, 'We are all your 'Abbas, O' Zaynab' (*kulluna 'Abbasak, ya Zaynab*). The contemporary fighters see themselves as modern-day versions of al-'Abbas, the great hero who fought until his last breath and sacrificed himself in defence of 'true Islam' as embodied by his half-brother, Husayn. By invoking al-'Abbas, Shi'i militia recruiters and leaders seek to tap into notions of masculinity and courageousness, primarily among men and in particular Shi'i youth. Indeed, in the discourse of Shi'i militias in Syria and Iraq those individuals who fall in battle, whether against IS or other groups, are described as having 'sacrificed themselves in defence of the Holy Sites' (*istashida fi al-difa' 'an al-muqaddasat*).[85] Martyrs and their deaths are 'presented' to God as offerings or even symbolic sacrifices (*qurban*) in 'defence of Islam, the Holy Places, the nation' and they are said to have embraced danger and martyrdom willingly and with joy, often being referred to as 'the joyful martyr' (*al-shahid al-sa'id*).[86] The martyrdom discourses of Shi'i and Sunni armed groups are remarkably similar in terms of language, terminology and metaphors used, and even visual presentations, though the former include references to the Twelve Imams and other historical holy figures absent in the media output of the latter.

The twelve Imams and other members and supporters of the Ahl al-Bayt

The twelve Imams, whom Shi'is regard as the designated successors of the Prophet Muhammad as the leaders and guides of the Muslims, have also been invoked to encourage social and armed mobilisations in Syria and Iraq. The first and third Imams, 'Ali and his son, Husayn, and the twelfth Imam, the 'Mahdi' Muhammad ibn Hasan, have each had Shi'i militias in Syria and Iraq named after them. These include *Kata'ib al-Imam 'Ali* (Brigades of Imam 'Ali),[87] *Kata'ib Sayyid al-Shuhada'* (Brigades of the Commander of the Martyrs, referencing one of Husayn's honorifics)[88] and *Katibat al-Mahdi al-Muntazar* (Brigade of the Awaited Mahdi). 'Ali's famous sword, Zulfiqar, has also been adopted by an Iraqi Shi'i militia in Syria, Liwa' Zulfiqar (Brigade of Zulfiqar). According to Shi'i beliefs, the twelfth Imam is currently in the state of mystical concealment, the 'greater occultation' (*al-ghayba al-kubra*) and will emerge from it at a divinely appointed time to fight apocalyptic villains, reward sincere Shi'is, punish those who falsely claim to love and follow the *Ahl al-Bayt*, and usher in a period of justice before the Day of Judgement.

Other members or supporters of the *Ahl al-Bayt* have also served as the reference points for the naming and mobilisation frames of Shi'i militias. Among them are 'Ali Akbar, Qasim ibn al-Hasan, Malik al-Ashtar and 'Ammar ibn Yasir. 'Ali Akbar was the teenage son of Imam Husayn who was killed with his father at Karbala, said to have recited the call to prayer on the morning of the day he was martyred.[89] Qasim was the son of the second Imam, Hasan, who according to popular Shiʻi elegiac collections such as the sixteenth-century *Garden of the Martyrs* (*Rawzat-i Shuhadaʾ*) is referred to today, particularly in South Asian Shiʻi ritual cultures, as the 'bridegroom of Karbala' because he married Imam Husayn's daughter Fatima al-Kubra on the morning of the day he was killed.[90] At first forbidden from fighting, he succeeds in getting his uncle's permission to enter the battle after finding a written instruction from his father to do so. Immediately after being wed, he leaves for battle, replying to pleas from Fatima that he not go with a promise that their wedding feast will be on the Day of Resurrection, on which she will recognize him by a sleeve he tears before leaving for the battlefield.[91]

Malik al-Ashtar was one of the Prophet Muhammad's companions (*sahaba*), also a loyalist of Imam ʻAli, fighting alongside him at the Battle of the Camel in 656 against the rebelling forces of two other companions, Talha and al-Zubayr and ʻAisha, one of the prophet's widows. Malik was later appointed by ʻAli, then the caliph, as governor of Egypt, but was poisoned while travelling to take up the post on the orders of ʻAli's rival, Muʻawiya ibn Abi Sufyan, who would become the first Umayyad caliph. Upon hearing of Malik's death, Muʻawiya reportedly crowed that he had cut off ʻAli's two 'right hands', referring to Malik and ʻAmmar ibn Yasir, another companion of the prophet loyal to ʻAli, who had been killed previously at the Battle of Siffin between the forces of Muʻawiya and ʻAli.[92]

In the 1990s and early 2000s, the Iranian government, with the permission of the Syrian regime, funded the construction of a large double shrine complex for ʻAmmar ibn Yasir and Uways al-Qarani, built in an Iranian/Central Asian architectural style. The shrine complex displaced older, local shrines to the two companions who were the focus, particularly the latter, of devotion by locals.[93] Hagiographies published in Beirut and Baghdad since the Second World War placed increasing importance on the two as Shiʻi martyrs and partisans of Imam ʻAli.[94] Similarly, the shrine of *Sayyida* Zaynab in Damascus became increasingly Shiʻi, transforming from a local shrine to one of international prestige and the destination for increasing numbers of Shiʻi pilgrims, many of them from Iran.[95] The shrine construction, in addition to its religious purposes, was also a profoundly political act meant to solidify ties between the Iranian and Syrian governments; it demonstrated the power of the Syrian state to impose itself locally, particularly in Raqqa, which, unlike Damascus, has had no significant local Shiʻi community historically.[96] The shrine complex was the centrepiece of conferences on anti-Zionism organised by the Iranian Cultural Centre in 1997 and 2000, and has also served as the point for the sale and distribution of Shi'i literature and recordings of lectures as well as being the site of lectures and classes about the twelve Imams and their supporters.[97]

By drawing upon resonant historical narratives and popular notions of piety, masculinity and nationalism, particularly in the case of Iraqi Shi'i mobilisation to fight IS inside the country and particularly among Shi'i youth, the party/group leaders and recruiters are attempting to portray volunteering in one of the militias as a sanctified religious duty. Enlisting is also portrayed as a way to avenge historical wrongs by fighting the 'descendants' of villains in Shi'i historical narratives, such as Yazid and Mu'awiya. By doing so, the recruits are able to achieve a cathartic release to counter the sense of continual persecution and impending eradication at the hands of hostile enemies, leading to a sense of empowerment in the face of perceived global hostility or ambivalence towards Shi'is, Shi'ism and, in the case of Iraqi Shi'i Islamist parties and armed groups, the fate of the Iraqi nation-state.

Intra-Shi'i dynamics, the Mujtahids and armed mobilisation in Syria and Iraq

Many of the Iraqi Shi'i groups in Iraq that are heavily involved in the recruitment and deployment of fighters in Syria are part of the broad and discordant Sadrist current in Iraqi Shi'i politics, that is, groups who base their legitimacy in part on a claimed connection to the late Ayatollah Muhammad Sadiq al-Sadr (1943–99), recognised as a *marja' al-taqlid* by his millions of followers (*muqallidun*), who was assassinated in Najaf with two of his sons by the Iraqi Ba'th.[98] He is known among his followers as 'the second Martyr al-Sadr' (*al-shahid al-Sadr al-thani*) in reference to the honorific of Zayn al-Din al-'Amili, a famous Levantine Shi'i hadith scholar (*muhaddith*) and jurist who was executed by the Ottomans in 1558 and is known as 'the Second Martyr' (*al-shahid al-thani*).[99]

A populist religious scholar and jurist, he had during his lifetime a large following in both southern and central Iraq, particularly in the shrine city of Kufa, where he preached from the city's central mosque, and in the poor district of Baghdad known today as Sadr City, formerly Revolution City and Saddam City.[100] Sadiq al-Sadr and his aides built a large grass-roots social network of mosques, *husayniyyat*[101] and other institutions in these areas. Following the collapse of the Iraqi Ba'thist government in the face of the massive US and British-led coalition invasion of the country, the martyred grand ayatollah's son, Muqtada, and his supporters mobilised by using this grass-roots network, becoming a powerful social and political force.[102]

Initially the broad Sadrist current was largely, if somewhat nominally, directed by Muqtada, but since 2003 it has become increasingly fractious and segments of it broke away to form new groups or to promote their own identities as grand *mujtahids* (grand ayatollahs, *maraji' al-taqlid*, singular: *marja' al-taqlid*). They remain connected, even if loosely, however, by their claims of representing the 'true' legacy of Muhammad Sadiq al-Sadr. These groups include the mainstream Sadr Movement (*Tayyar al-Sadr*) led by Muqtada, Grand Ayatollah Kazim al-Ha'iri, 'Asa'ib Ahl al-Haqq, Grand Ayatollah Qasim al-Ta'i, and other, smaller Sadrist splinter groups.

Competition between these groups and personalities is centred on their rival claims to social, religious and political authority based on their claims to represent Muhammad Sadiq's intellectual legacy. One way for those with smaller numbers of followers to compete is by harnessing popular pieties and hyper-communalism in the form of sectarianism to win more followers from among those individuals who are more interested in engaging in counter-polemics with Sunnis. Some, such as some followers of the Shirazi network of *mujtahids*, even engage in proselytisation aimed at other Shi'is who do not follow their *marja' al-taqlid*. The adoption of more overtly sectarian rhetoric by some younger, less established religious and political figures is a means through which they hope to solidify a place for themselves as self-declared new *mujtahids*. They also hope to attract potentially greater numbers of followers and thus gain more revenue from religious taxes such as *khums*, the one-fifth share due to the Imam which is collected, during his occultation, by the *'ulama*. This inter-generational competition among different segments of the *'ulama* has also historically occurred in other places, such as in India during the 1930s when a distinct Indian Shi'i identity began to form vis-à-vis the majority Sunnis.[103]

Among the most active supporters of Iraqi Shi'i armed mobilisation in Syria have been Qasim al-Ta'i (b. 1970), a self-declared grand *mujtahid*, and 'Asa'ib Ahl a-Haqq, a Sadrist splinter group that emerged in 2006 after its founder and current leader, Qays al-Khaz'ali, broke away from the Sadr Movement's armed wing, the Mahdi's Army (*Jaysh al-Imam al-Mahdi*).[104] Both have challenged Muqtada and other Iraqi Shi'i political and religious leaders for influence over the country's Shi'is. They draw upon the alarm of Shi'is generally, in both Iraq and around the world, at the rise to prominence and power of Salafi political forces in countries such as Egypt, the continued influence of Saudi Arabia and its Salafi *'ulama*, and the rise of virulently and violently anti-Shi'i armed groups such as the Islamic State and Jabhat al-Nusra in the wake of the abortive Arab Spring.[105] Recruits and other supporters of Shi'i armed mobilisation in Syria have created and deployed mobilisation frames to convince their target audiences of their fate and the fate of Shi'i communities in countries such as Lebanon and Iraq. The danger in Syria is portrayed as an existential threat to the region's Shi'is.

Al-Ta'i, a former student of Muhammad Sadiq, formerly served time in prison during the Ba'thist period. Under the late ayatollah, al-Ta'i studied jurisprudence (*usul al-fiqh*). After the Muhammad Sadiq's assassination, al-Ta'i studied *usul al-fiqh* under a number of other jurists including Grand Ayatollahs 'Ali al-Sistani and Muhammad Ishaq Fayyad in Najaf.[106] Previously a relatively minor figure, al-Ta'i has adeptly used the issue of the danger to the Shi'i shrines in Syria in his mobilisation calls to increase his standing among a segment of Iraqi Shi'is. He has visited the besieged shrine of *Sayyida* Zaynab, delivered lectures and dispensed religious advice and support to Shi'i fighters there; then in December 2012 he established a representative office in the *Sayyida* Zaynab district to the south of Damascus.[107] His office in Iraq has also organised and sponsored events there to support armed groups such as LAFA in Syria and has been thanked by Shi'i fighters there.[108]

The most explicit juridical support for armed mobilisation in Syria has come from Grand Ayatollah Kazim al-Ha'iri, another former *hawza* student of Muhammad Sadiq who is an Iraqi grand *mujtahid* residing in the Iranian seminary and shrine city of Qum. He has issued at least two responses to questions about his religious juridical opinion on the permissibility of Shi'is travelling to Syria to 'defend the holy places'.[109] In a juridical opinion (*fatwa*) dated 18 November 2013, al-Ha'iri responds to a question from a group of individuals who follow him as their *marja' al-taqlid*, stating that the question of fighting in Syria 'is not just a question of Syria or a question of defending [the shrines of] *Sayyida* Zaynab and *Sayyida* Ruqayya, peace be upon them, but a question of confronting unbelief in its entirety (*muwajahat al-kufr kullahu*), unbelief targeting the light of Islam'. In a shorter fatwa dated 25 May 2013, he also states that the defence of the 'light of Islam' is not only permissible but required, though he does not include specific mentions of the Syrian Shi'i shrines.[110] In both, al-Ha'iri closes by noting that it is also obligatory to avoid serving under a 'corrupt leadership' (*wa la budd min al-taharruz 'an al-'amal tahta zill qiyadatin fasidatin*).[111] This 'corrupt leadership' is not specified, though it is possible that he is referring to the Syrian government. In the November 2013 fatwa al-Ha'iri references the authority (*wilaya*) of the 'leader of the Muslims' (*wali amr al-muslimin*), Iran's supreme leader 'Ali Khamenei.

'Asa'ib Ahl al-Haqq took advantage of the unclear position of Muqtada—his mainstream Sadr Movement—regarding fighting in Syria, by adopting an aggressive strategy of recruitment of fighters to dispatch there.[112] The group benefits from its close alliance with Iran, which has provided it with material and logistical support for its activities in both Syria and Iraq. More recently, it is attempting to become a political force by creating a political wing to compete in local and national elections.[113] By invoking the legacy of the martyred Muhammad Sadiq al-Sadr and adopting a position and image of strength against the 'enemies of Shi'is' in Syria, the group and specifically its leader, al-Khaz'ali, have tried to woo Muqtada's followers. After the Islamic State's sweep across western Iraq during the summer of 2014, 'Asa'ib Ahl al-Haqq has repositioned itself as one of the main Iraqi Shi'i groups providing fighters to aid the national army, police and other security forces in the Popular Mobilization Units (*al-Hashd al-Sha'bi*, PMU) paramilitary umbrella organisation.

'Asa'ib Ahl al-Haqq's secretary general, Qays al-Khaz'ali, formerly a chief aide to Muqtada al-Sadr, has said that the ongoing battles in Iraq and Syria are one conflict rather than separate conflicts.[114] A charismatic leader with a reportedly magnetic personality, al-Khaz'ali was imprisoned in Iraq by US military forces between 2007 and late 2009 or early 2010, and ever since his release has been at the forefront of collective Iraqi Shi'i Islamists most closely aligned with Iran.[115] He has alleged that the US is 'not serious' in its anti-IS campaign, but his group has threatened to treat US military advisers, Marines and special forces deployed to support Iraqi government forces as enemies.[116] In remarks at a mass celebration marking the tenth anniversary of 'Asa'ib Ahl al-Haqq's founding, al-Khaz'ali alleged:

> What is happening generally in the region and what is happening in Syria in particular is a conspiracy in the full sense of the word. It is intended [by the US, European states, their Arab allies, Israel] that Syria be the nucleus for starting the fire of sedition and discord (*fitna*) in every region and especially in Iraq. And despite all of their reservations concerning the Syrian regime not being a democratic regime in governing our sister country, Syria, over the decades, the strangest and most amazing thing is that the monarchical, hereditary regimes and the ruling dictatorial regimes in the Arab world are the ones calling for democracy in Syria. And it is even stranger that the U.S., Britain, and France, who claim to be fighting terrorism, are supporting the military option and the armed opposition, whose

takfiri views were fully displayed recently when the so-called Free [Syrian] Army dug up and desecrated the shrine of the Prophet's companion Hujr bin 'Adi.[117]

He also noted how the West, despite calling for democracy, has turned a blind eye to events in Bahrain despite there being, he said, no '*takfiri*' or armed groups among the (largely) peaceful popular protests for democratic governance.[118] The group has also accused 'foreign powers' of causing sectarian violence in Iraq and does not differentiate between the diverse array of Syrian rebel groups, accusing them all of being '*takfiri*' and in league with the West, Israel and Sunni Arab states in forwarding their projects of 'imperialism and Zionism.'[119]

In the midst of Iranian state support and the support of Iraqi groups and religious figures such as al-Ha'iri, al-Ta'i and 'Asa'ib Ahl al-Haqq, Iraq's most revered and influential resident grand *mujtahid*s, the grand ayatollahs al-Sistani, Fayyad, Bashir Najafi and Muhammad Sa'id al-Hakim, did not support the mobilisation of Shi'is to fight in Syria.[120] The aggressive expansion inside Iraq of the Islamic State, following its victories in Syria during the first half of 2014,[121] was seen as a clear existential threat to the Iraqi nation-state and specifically Iraqi Shi'is. In response, al-Sistani, Fayyad, Najafi, al-Hakim and other Shi'i *mujtahid*s in Iraq, such as Muhammad Taqi al-Mudarrisi, issued calls for the government to redouble its efforts to defend the nation; they supported, in juridical terms, the collective struggle (*al-jihad al-kifa'i*) against the Islamic State.[122] Importantly, al-Sistani's *fatwa* calling for volunteers to the national security forces was addressed to all Iraqis and not only Shi'is, continuing the grand *mujtahid*'s history of promoting Iraqi national unity and opposing the division of the country by ethnic group and sect.

In response to their calls, tens of thousands of Iraqi Shi'is volunteered to join armed units formed by existing groups such as the Badr Organisation, 'Asa'ib Ahl al-Haqq, Kata'ib Sayyid al-Shuhada (Leader of the Martyrs' Brigades, referencing an honorific of Imam Husayn), the Sadr Movement (the 'Peace Battalions,' *Saraya al-Salam*) and Kata'ib Hizbullah, as well as newly formed paramilitary groups such as Kata'ib al-Imam 'Ali (Brigades of Imam 'Ali). The PMU remains a largely Iraqi Shi'i grass-roots force, though as of June 2015 growing numbers of Sunni Arabs, primarily from tribes and clans opposed to the Islamic State and its tribal allies, are joining groups within the paramilitary umbrella.[123] The PMU, with coordination and strategic leadership provided by the IRGC and with US air power and military support for the Iraqi army, contributed significantly to the recapture of Tikrit in late March 2015 and has been deployed in other areas of the country, including the restive governorates of Anbar, Babil, Diyala and Saladin, where the Islamic

State maintains a strong presence. It remains to be seen, as of this writing, whether the strong grass-roots support and organic formation of the fighting units that make up the umbrella organisation will also take hold among Iraq's Sunni Arabs more broadly.[124] Tensions between PMU and other Shi'i militia forces and Iraqi and Syrian Kurdish forces dramatically increased following the retreat of IS from Sinjar in November 2015 following reports that Kurdish fighters were persecuting and expelling Iraqi Shi'i Turkmen and Arabs and looting their homes and businesses in a land grab.[125]

It remains unclear at present whether the Iraqi central government will be able to control the groups within the PMU in the longer term, or whether the groups will be answerable more to other actors such as Shi'i religious leaders in the shrine cities of Najaf, Karbala and Kufa and the IRGC, particularly after the IS threat subsides.[126] PMU, militia and Islamist party leaders such as al-Khaz'ali, al-'Ameri and Muqtada al-Sadr are taking political advantage of the Iraqi central government's reliance on their manpower in the fight against IS and have increasingly demanded more financial autonomy and support as well as political concessions.[127]

Al-Sistani has also publicly cautioned PMU fighters, warning them not to perpetrate abuses and other crimes against civilians or Iraqi Sunnis generally, which has occurred in some instances despite his earlier calls for unity, demonstrating that despite his influence, his authority has its limits.[128] In 2006 and 2007, following multiple bombings of the al-'Askariyya shrine in Samarra by the group known today as the Islamic State, al-Sistani issued a series of statements calling for patience and forbidding acts of retaliation against Iraqi Sunnis. His words, however, were trumped by powerful political players such as the Iran-backed and aligned Badr Organisation,[129] led by Hadi al-'Ameri, and segments of the Sadrist *Jaysh al-Imam al-Mahdi* engaged in counter-sectarian violence against Iraqi Sunnis. His and other voices of unity and reason were overshadowed by virulent and overtly violent and sectarian voices.

In his most recent public call, al-Sistani warned Iraqis fighting in the various anti-IS forces and particularly those engaged in military jihad, one of the 'pillars of the religion', as mujahidin to uphold the conditions and regulations governing warfare in the name of God. Just as God has made jihad one of the foundations of Islam and has favoured mujahidin over those who do not fight (*al-qa'idin*), he wrote, He 'has also placed certain conditions and a mode of conduct for *jihad*' on those engaged in it.[130] This proper conduct should be modelled, according to the grand *ayatollah*, on the Prophet Muhammad's own actions and Qur'anic directives and prohibitions on 'extremism', the mutilation and desecration of the dead, even enemies, killing women, the elderly or children, and cutting down trees or razing crops.[131] Mujahidin should also follow the example set by 'Ali ibn Abi Talib who, even when faced with the brutality and extremism of the Kharijites, did not deviate from the regulations governing proper conduct of military jihad. Indeed, he resisted calls from the Kharijites when they were still within the ranks of his own forces to harm the families of enemy combatants or loot their property. It is the first Imam's example also that the PMU and other Shi'i fighters should follow, al-Sistani stated.[132]

Grand Ayatollah Bashir Najafi, in a statement, proclaimed his support for those fighting against the 'enemies of humanity, the *takfiris* [those who declare other Muslims to be apostates]'.[133] The 'martyrs who fell on the battlefield' are a source of pride for the Muslims who 'cherish and honour' the blood they have spilled defending the nation and Islam.[134] He prayed for God to raise 'scores of martyrs' and grant them places alongside others who have 'sacrificed themselves' in defence of Islam, just like the third Imam, Husayn bin 'Ali.[135] He also praised the parents of those 'martyred' for encouraging their children to the 'field of glory, dignity, and high honour', the path of jihad.[136] Najafi, one of the four *marja' al-taqlid*s in Najaf, previously endorsed the '*shari'a*, national, and moral duty' of deterring IS through 'defensive *jihad*' (*al-jihad al-difa'i*).[137] Muhammad Sa'id al-Hakim, one of the other four grand ayatollahs in Najaf, echoed Najafi's support for those fighting the jihad against IS and also called for the mujahidin to abide by the regulations for warfare set down by the Qur'an and the *sunna* of the Prophet Muhammad and the Imams.[138]

Conclusion

The rise of IS, Jabhat al-Nusra and powerful Salafi Syrian rebel groups such as Harakat Ahrar al-Sham and Jaysh al-Islam have alarmed Shi'is in the Middle East and the wider world, fuelling the rise of Shi'i armed groups in the region and particularly in Syria and Iraq. The extreme and brutal violence of IS and some other Sunni jihadist and some Syrian and Iraqi rebel actors have resurrected images of persecution and repression from the recent and distant past for many Shi'is, and it is this emotional response and real fear of a renewed existential threat that have enabled Shi'i Islamist actors to be successful in recruiting scores of thousands, of mostly young men, to enlist in an array of armed groups. Recruiters for these groups have designed mobilisation frames and recruitment calls that tap into this fear while also providing a way to glory and the fulfilment of personal piety by 'defending' the *Ahl al-Bayt* against

'Wahhabi' hordes who seek to defile their shrines and eradicate their followers, the Shi'is.

IS, Jabhat al-Nusra and other Sunni armed actors similarly have crafted narratives of persecution, in this case of an empowered minority community, the 'Alawis in Syria and the Shi'is in Iraq, running roughshod over a Sunni majority. This persecution is so severe, according to their mobilisation narratives, that an armed response is the only possible solution, the only way to defend Sunnis from Shi'i repression. Like their Shi'i opponents, IS, Jabhat al-Nusra and other Sunni actors draw upon their particular vision of history in order to explain and justify their strategies and actions, connecting contemporary Shi'i enemies to historical 'traitors' and 'villains' of old, such as Ibn Saba, Ibn al-'Alqami and Nasir al-Din al-Tusi.[139]

Both Shi'i and Sunni groups and religious and political figures not only draw upon particular hyper-sectarianised readings and interpretations of history, but also contemporary narratives and realities of persecution and repression. Their competing mobilisation frames, which are dialogic and formed in relation to the frames of rival groups and communities, draw upon 'religious' motifs and language as yet another way, in addition to political grievances, of justifying their armed response, often shockingly brutal, to perceived existential threats. All-out war is necessary, many of these actors argue, because it is the only way to ensure the survival of their respective communities. Their discourse is neither wholly 'religious' nor solely 'political', but rather is a combination of both; it is a comprehensive argument justifying certain actions that draw upon motifs of both 'religious' requirement, permissibility and sanctity, as well as of contemporary issues of persecution and political alienation.

11

THE IMPACT OF EVOLVING JIHADIST
NARRATIVES ON RADICALISATION IN THE WEST

Akil N. Awan

In announcing the re-establishment of its so-called Caliphate in June 2014, IS also revealed its global pretensions by declaring that it was now incumbent on all Muslims worldwide to swear fealty to its leader, Abu Bakr al-Baghdadi, or Caliph Ibrahim, as his new regnal moniker demanded he be addressed. Unsurprisingly, the backlash from within the Islamic world against this flagrant usurpation of power and authority has been overwhelmingly negative, with the vast majority rejecting any such claim to legitimacy. Nevertheless, the resurrection of even a notional Caliphate has resonated with a small but significant minority of Muslims, leading to many thousands of young men, in search of a cause, flocking to the IS banner. Indeed, IS has drawn foreigners from every corner of the globe, willing to fight and die for its nascent Caliphate. Some estimates place the number of foreign fighters who travelled to Syria and Iraq to join violent extremist groups (the overwhelming majority of whom will have joined IS) to be anywhere between 27,000 and 31,000 individuals, originating from no less than 86 different countries—a truly glo-balised mobilisation on an epic scale.[1]

As realisation gradually dawns upon the international community of the grave consequences for both state and society, should citizens decide to take up arms with brutal and extreme outfits like IS, the international community has scrambled to instate strategies for dealing with this worrying recruitment of fighters. Most prominently, in September 2014, US President Barack Obama chaired a special meeting of the UN Security Council in which he asked member states to pass a resolution establishing an international legal framework to help prevent the recruitment and transport of would-be foreign fighters from joining terrorist groups. As expected, United Nations Security Council Resolution 2178 on Foreign Terrorist Fighters passed unanimously.[2]

Many states have shown grave concern about their own citizens joining IS, but understandably also about the dangers inherent in the inevitable influx of returnees once the conflict is over. Fighters returning from the front lines, brutalised by the ravages of war and potentially suffering from post-traumatic stress disorder, may prove incapable of easily slipping back into their respective host societies. More ominously, some will also have engaged in horrific sectarian or other violence or egregious human rights violations that have become hallmarks of the conflict. The social media accounts of some Western jihadists, Tweeting images of grisly executions and selfies with severed heads, or the prominence of individuals like Jihadi John, the Briton who became infamous for brutally beheading American and British hostages, are testament to the barbarity many fighters have not just been immersed within, but have positively relished. Naturally, these revelations will prove all the more troubling should these men choose to return home. Indeed, a small minority have already brought violence back with them, as recent examples have shown. Mehdi Nemmouche carried out sadistic violence in Syria before returning to Belgium, where he carried out an anti-Semitic attack on a Jewish museum in Belgium that left four people dead in May 2014.[3] But most strikingly, the multiple attackers who wrought carnage in Paris in November 2015, and Brussels in March 2016, appear to have been French and Belgian natives who had been directed by IS, and some of whom had recently returned from Syria.[4]

This attendant surge in terrorist activity amongst Western jihadists has understandably caused great concern in their host countries, as signs of foreign fighter blowback brings the violence of Raqqa, Homs and Mosul to the streets of London, Brussels, Paris and New York. Potential solutions have ranged from revoking citizenship, exclusion and prosecution, to deradicalisation and rehabilitation, with many Western states showing uncertainty over precisely how they should deal with their errant sons and daughters who choose to return home once the conflict has lost its glamour and appeal, or indeed might have been directed to return and attack their home soil.[5]

However, these measures are by their very nature reactive, dealing with the consequences instead of addressing the underlying root causes of the problem. Rather, in order to stem the flow of willing young recruits to IS, we must understand and address the appeal that IS holds for impressionable youth in Western societies. Why does the narrative of IS appear to resonate with them? However, considering that recruitment in the West by militant Islamist groups is certainly not a new phenomenon, and that IS has simply usurped al-Qaeda's role as the organisation of choice for Western jihadists today, we must also consider the narrative's appeal in its broader context, highlighting in particular the continuity and change within the narrative peddled by both groups. This chapter attempts to answer precisely these questions by providing a fuller, more nuanced understanding of some of the motivations for joining jihadist groups, and explores the relationship between individual motivations and larger jihadist narratives, particularly as those narratives have shifted with the ascencion of IS.

What is the narrative? Join the caravan

At the heart of IS's appeal is the alluring simplicity of its narrative, which is composed of two main strands. The first strand, which sits at the core of all jihadist narratives and originates with al-Qaeda, compels Muslim audiences to view contemporary conflicts through the prism of a wider historical global attack on Islam and Muslims by a belligerent 'Zionist—Crusader Alliance', in response to which the jihadists claim to serve as the sole and crucial vanguard.[6] This narrative, as many commentators have recognised, has remained remarkably coherent and consistent over time.[7] As bin Laden put it:

> The people of Islam had suffered from aggression, iniquity and injustice imposed on them by the Zionist-Crusaders alliance and their collaborators; to the extent that the Muslim's blood became the cheapest and their wealth as loot in the hands of the enemies. Their blood was spilled in Palestine and Iraq. The horrifying pictures of the massacre of Qana, in Lebanon are still fresh in our memory. Massacres in Tajikistan, Burma, Kashmir, Assam, Philippine, Fatani, Ogadin, Somalia, Eritrea, Chechnya and in Bosnia-Herzegovina took place, massacres that send shivers in the body and shake the conscience.[8]

In addition to making the case for the legitimacy of a violent response, bin Laden also offered the opportunity to reply to the enemy in kind, often presenting his own role as merely an instigator who had *awakened* the *ummah* to the reality of their predicament. At the end of 2001, Osama bin Laden concluded after his escape from Tora Bora in Afghanistan that 'God willing, the end of America is imminent. Its end is not dependent on the survival of this slave to God. Regardless if Usama is killed or survives, the awakening has started.'[9]

It is not difficult to see why bin Laden's emphatic challenges to the *ummah* in the past, to recognise the assault and stand up in defence of their faith, lands and people, might strike powerful emotional chords with Muslim audiences everywhere. Indeed, the hundreds of individuals who have heeded bin Laden's fervent calls thus far are surely testament to the alluring potency of this narrative. However, beyond the involvement in violence and terrorism, AQ were unable to offer any other real motivation for 'joining the caravan of Jihad'.[10] There were some attempts made at offering armchair jihadists the opportunity of contributing to the war effort, without actively fighting on the battlefront—what I have previously referred to as the 'virtual jihad'.[11]

In 2002, Osama bin Laden famously wrote to Mullah Omar that '[i]t is obvious that the media war in this century is one of the strongest methods; in fact, its ratio may reach 90% of the total preparation for the battles'.[12] With this increasing recognition by the jihadist leadership of the critical need for engaging in the 'media battle', various jihadist ideologues attempted to legitimise this activity, often by drawing upon historical or religious precedents. Abu al-Harith al-Ansari's categorisation of the types of warfare sanctioned by the Prophet Muhammad, for example, cites 'media warfare' as a legitimate endeavour,[13] whereas Muhammad bin Ahmad al-Salim's highly popular text, '39 Ways to Serve and Participate in Jihad', extols 'performing electronic jihad' as 'a blessed field which contains much benefit'.[14] Perhaps the most infamous jihadist ideologue in the Anglophone sphere, Anwar al-'Awlaqi, also offered alternative opportunities for engaging in jihad. These included 'fighting the lies of the Western media', 'following the news of jihad and spreading it', 'spreading the writings of the mujahidin and their scholars' and 'establishing discussion forums that offer a free, uncensored medium for posting information relating to jihad'.[15]

The contemporary jihadist strategist and a key proponent of a decentralised, leaderless jihad, Abu Mus'ab al-Suri, even acknowledged the underlying reasons why this mode of action might be appealing in his seminal *The Global Islamic Resistance Call*. Al-Suri conceded the existence of large numbers of individuals within the ideological support base who were nevertheless unwilling to engage in actual violence themselves. Addressing these individuals directly, al-Suri proposed a number of alternative modes of non-violent action to support the jihad, one of which entailed the 'media or informational battle'.[16]

However, despite these lacklustre attempts at accommodating other modes of non-violent jihad, the appeal of jihadism remained limited. Indeed, Muslim audiences have largely remained immune to the cajoling messages of violent global jihad, with large swathes of the Muslim world in fact having repudiated the message outright.[17] As al-Zawahiri laments, 'we should realize the extent of the gap in understanding between the jihad movement and the common people'.[18] Al-Qaeda did attempt to provide some sort of distant utopian vision of an aspirational future caliphate, as a means of justifying and drawing supporters to their violent excesses:

> we should work to establish the Caliphate that does not recognise the national state, national religions, borders that were put in place by the occupiers. We should establish a righteous Caliphate that follows the path of the Prophet and believes in the unity of Muslims' lands, encourages brotherhood between Muslims in their religion, makes everyone equal, removes borders that were put in place by the enemies, spreads justice, imposes sharia, supports vulnerable people, and liberates all Muslim countries, including the usurped Palestine, and the threatened al-Aqsa.[19]

However, this abstract notional Caliphate also lacked any real mobilising potency—at least until IS appeared on the scene. Since June 2014, this second part of the narrative—IS's own unique addendum to the already heady mix—claims that the Caliphate has now been re-established, thereby restoring glory and honour to the downtrodden Muslims once again. As IS spokesman Abu Muhammad al-'Adnani ecstatically announced in June 2014:

> As for you, oh soldiers of the Islamic State, then congratulations to you. Congratulations on this clear victory, congratulations on this great triumph.... Now the caliphate has returned, humbling the necks of the enemy. Now the caliphate has returned, in spite of its opponents. Now the caliphate has returned; we ask God to make it to be upon the methodology of prophethood. Now hope is being actualized. Now the dream has become a reality.[20]

The obvious corollary to the establishment of the Caliphate was that it was therefore now incumbent on every Muslim to make *hijrah*, or emigrate to the new Caliphate. Hijrah is an important theme in Islamic literature and stems from the emigration of the Prophet Muhammad from Mecca around AD 632 in order to escape religious persecution, and move to Medina where he founded a religious community and burgeoning city state. It is of central importance in the Islamic canon and indeed is considered such a seminal event that the Islamic or Hijri calendar begins from this date. In the past, a number of Islamist militant groups have also employed the trope of *hijrah* in justifying their secession from mainstream Muslim society. This was most evident in the Egyptian jihadist group founded by Shukri Mustafa, *Takfir wal hijrah*, who chose to secede from wider Egyptian society during the 1970s in order to preserve their religious integrity and avoid moral and spiritual corruption through association with the *jahiliyya*[21] society around them.[22]

The establishment of the caliphate in June 2014 therefore provided compelling alternative narratives to audiences: undertake your own *hijrah*—a journey that paralleled that of the Prophet Muhammad; escape the religious persecution in your own societies; live under Islamic sovereignty and law; help defend the burgeoning state and community; and ultimately restore the state to its long-lost glory. Clearly these multiple narratives moved beyond al-Qaeda's appeals to violence alone, and provided other motivations for joining the jihadist cause. Indeed, many foreign fighters who travelled to Syria prior to the announcement of IS's Caliphate and ended up joining al-Qaeda affiliated groups soon switched sides to IS. Take, for example, the case of Israfil Yilmaz, a former Dutch soldier and one of the oldest and best-known foreign fighters in Syria due to his social media presence, who joined the fight to topple President Bashar al-Assad of Syria in 2013. He remained fiercely 'independent' until mid 2015, when he decided to join IS. When asked by journalists about why he made the choice after previously keeping his distance, he replied:

> Ask yourself which other group is implementing the sharia as complete as possible? Ask yourself which group is fully taking care of the affairs of the people as complete as possible? No other group but the Islamic State, so me joining the Islamic State was just a matter of time, for they are able to govern the people and implement the sharia on a large scale—protecting the Muslims, their wealth, health and religion.[23]

In addition to the patent appeal to foreign fighters from the West, we have also witnessed cases of numerous young women travelling to join IS—the 'jihadi brides' phenomenon, as it has been labelled by tabloid media, also a number of families with elderly parents and young children in tow, clearly not drawn by the violence, but something much more profound. This is the utopian narrative of belonging and sanctuary, of new beginnings and state-building which has proven so important to IS's success. Western media have focused almost exclusively on IS's media output, which purveys the pornography of violence, deliberately targeting Western audiences and sensibilities. However, the overwhelming majority of IS media content is in fact centred around depictions of blissful civilian life in the 'utopian' Caliphate, and therefore offers an additional compelling narrative.[24] Take for example the images in IS's flagship English language magazine *Dabiq* and elsewhere in IS's social media catalogue, which focus on presenting a positive utopian image of the Caliphate by highlighting a wide range of activities that take place under its jurisdiction, from health care to taxation, and from festivities to blissful married life and the roles of both men and women who choose to join.

These narratives are important to the recruitment of Western jihadists, but they are not in and of themselves sufficient to account for the rise of the foreign fighter phenomenon, particularly amongst young Muslims in the Western diaspora. One way of conceptualising this problem is to view the narrative as one of the important pull factors that offers something—an appeal—but it is the individual's context and their personal circumstances that are central to whether or not this narrative resonates on an individual level. The narrative has to find fertile ground to take root. And, of course, we have to consider the role of individual agency here too. Very few individuals whose context and circumstances intersect with a resonant narrative become de facto jihadist automatons. Consequently, it is likely a combination or interplay of these elements that ultimately manifest as a desire to join jihadist groups or move towards violent extremism, and (with a few minor exceptions) these elements have remained largely constant between those who were drawn to al-Qaeda in the past and those who are drawn to IS today, as I will illustrate below.

Reconfiguring identities

To Western audiences inured to depictions of jihadists as either evil, bloodthirsty savages or deranged, religious zealots, there must be something inherently incongruous and deeply unsettling about recognising the essentially altruistic sentiments behind the actions of many jihadists. However, as discomfiting as this revelation may be, it is nevertheless important to recognise that many individuals who gravitate towards jihadism often do so for largely selfless reasons, being sincerely compassionate to those they see themselves as helping.[25] Indeed, empathy for fellow Muslims inculcates many potential radical Islamists with a profound sense of duty and justice, which finds effective expression through the conduit of jihadism. The role and value of altruistic appeals within the broader jihadist narrative has remained remarkably potent and consistent amongst jihadist groups over the years. Indeed, it is perhaps best illustrated by the detailed cases of numerous young men who were drawn to al-Qaeda's calls to violence. Take for example the case of Umar Farouk Abdulmutallab, a Nigerian graduate of University College London, who failed to detonate explosive-lined underwear on a trans-Atlantic flight in 2009, on behalf of al-Qaeda in the Arabian Peninsula (AQAP). He justified his actions to US prosecutors by stating: 'I carried with me an explosive device onto Northwest 253, again, to avenge the killing of my innocent Muslim brothers and sisters by the U.S... to save the lives of innocent Muslims.'[26]

Similarly, Mohammed Siddique Khan, the ringleader of the 7/7 bombers in 2005, attempted to justify his actions by pointing to British tacit support for injustices perpetrated against his 'fictive kin'.[27] In his posthumously released 'martyrdom' video testament, later released by al-Qaeda and in which al-Zawahiri also appeared, Khan repeatedly invoked a communal identity in which he identified the subjugation of *his community* as being principal amongst his grievances:

> Your democratically elected governments continuously perpetuate atrocities against my people all over the world. And your support of them makes you directly responsible, just as I am directly responsible for protecting and avenging my Muslim brothers and sisters. Until we feel security, you will be our targets. And until you stop the bombing, gassing, imprisonment and torture of my people we will not stop this fight.[28]

We may dispute the notion that Western jihadists comfortably ensconced within the West hail from 'occupied', 'oppressed' or 'subjugated' communities, but to do so would be to ignore the communal and supra-national nature of radical Islamist discourse, and the widely held perceptions of Western domination and hegemony in the Muslim world more broadly. Indeed, one of the cornerstones of jihadist discourse has been the rejection of a more parochial conceptualisation of community that is predicated upon the traditional ambits of ethnicity or nationalism, in favour of a global community of belief instead. As an example of the championing of this global community of belief and purpose, the *ummah*, the *Global Islamic Media Front*, a prominent media organ of al-Qaeda, stated in 2005, 'The [battle]front does not belong to anyone. It is the property of all zealous Muslims and knows no geographical boundaries.'[29]

Clearly it is this radically reformulated global community of belief that many incipient jihadists clearly see themselves as identifying with, first and foremost. But how do we explain this confusing dislocation and melodramatic sense of duty to a nebulous and disparate body of peoples ('my Muslim brothers and sisters', 'our children in Palestine', 'our mothers and sisters in Kashmir'), who ultimately become the object of their altruistic sacrifice? This is despite the fact that they often have little direct connection to, or identification with them, in terms of ethnicity, nationality, language, culture or customs, to name but a few salient markers of identity. Moreover, this attitude is all the more perplexing when juxtaposed against the feelings of indifference and open hostility displayed towards their victims, with whom they often *do* actually share many facets of their identity. And this should not simply be dismissed as a type of post hoc rhetoric used retrospectively to justify violent actions. Rather, as the examples of at least the initial influx of foreign fighters to Syria have shown, the profession of humanitarian grounds is often genuinely expressed. Take for example Israfil Yilmaz's response when asked in an interview with CBS about his motivations for fighting:

> I would fight anybody, even if it was my own father that was bombing these people, I would fight him and kill him myself... So I felt the need as a person, as a human, and, of course, as a Muslim, because it was the Muslims that were getting crushed in Syria, that I had to stand up and do stuff.

> We left everything behind, when we migrated, everything, everything, our families our friends, basically our future.[30]

How then do we explain this appeal? This disconcertingly misplaced identification can be partially explained through a process I describe elsewhere as 'dual cultural alterity':[31] essentially a double alienation or double sense of otherness that results in a staunch repudiation of, or at least a distinct lack of identification with, both *minority* (ethnic or parental) culture, and *majority* (mainstream or host society) culture, as a result of being unable or unwilling to fulfil either group's normative expectations, and thus is likely to inspire feelings of uprootedness and lack of belonging.

Minority culture may be relegated to obsolescence for a number of reasons, including the imposition of conservative socio-sexual mores; a profound sense of alienation from one's family; and the presence of cultural power structures, which can have the ostensive effect of divesting youth of any real tangible control over their own lives.[32]

The disenchantment with majority culture, on the other hand, is less clear-cut, particularly as many, by virtue of being raised in a pervasively Western environment and having imbibed many of its values and cultural norms, display a remarkably easy immersion into majority culture (particular popular, mainstream youth culture), prior to their radicalisation. However, clearly this comfortable embedding is disrupted at some point and is gradually superseded by disillusionment with majority culture, as a result of perceptions of hedonism, consumerism, racism, inequality and the general imposition of conflicting core value-systems from the 'host' society, which may render the individual unwilling or unable to perpetuate assimilation into the predominant paradigm.

Cherif Kouachi, one of the gunmen in the Charlie Hebdo attacks in Paris, was described by his lawyer in 2005 as 'a confused chameleon',[33] aptly summing up the cultural schizophrenia that can be borne out of a 'dual cultural alterity'. Examining identity through the lens of self-categorisation theory[34] shows that the self may be defined at different levels of abstraction, depending upon differing circumstances; at times it may be in terms of individual uniqueness, whilst at others in terms of specific group membership. The salience of a communal identity, for example, may arise during periods of perceived group crisis or threat. For incipient jihadists, these flashpoints may have been evoked by a range of contemporary events, including the Iraq war and the wider Global War on Terror; the new securitised landscape that places an inordinate scrutiny on Muslim organisations and institutions, or profiles young Muslim men; the banning of the veil and other European sartorial restrictions on Muslim women; the provocative publication of Danish and French cartoons of Muhammad deemed offensive to Muslims; and the resurgence of the Far Right and its convergence with the rise in Islamophobia in the US and Western Europe more generally.[35] In some scenarios, this new communal identity provides an emphatic rejoinder to the experiences of dislocation and lack of belonging in the West, and by extension the identity offered by their own society, which these individuals feel has already rejected them anyway.[36]

IS has shrewdly attempted not just to capitalise on these feelings of alienation, but hopes to nurture them more actively by creating conditions in Western societies that are conducive to these outcomes. In the wake of the January 2015 Charlie Hebdo attacks, the February issue of IS's flagship magazine, *Dabiq*, wrote of polarising the world by destroying its greatest threat, the 'grayzone': that liminal space in which young Frenchmen could be both Muslims and good citizens of the Republic, without any inherent contradiction. IS anticipated that provocative terrorist attacks, like the ones in Paris in January and November of 2015, would goad the French towards over-reaction and create a climate of fear and hostility, further alienating French Muslims from wider society, and 'further bring division to the world and destroy the grayzone everywhere'. Western Muslims would then be forced to make 'one of two choices': between apostasy or IS's bastardised version of belief. The article even cited, rather approvingly, George W. Bush's central dictum that underscored the Global War on Terror: 'The world today is divided into two camps. Bush spoke the truth when he said, "Either you are with us or you are with the terrorists." Meaning, either you are with the crusade or you are with Islam.'[37]

Naturally these sorts of confused crises of identity and belonging can prove incredibly useful for jihadist recruiters, as they can easily be co-opted by and yoked to the jihadists' utopian narrative of a global fraternity or community of believers—the *ummah*—which does not recognise colour, race or nationality, and claims to be equally besieged from all sides. Indeed the Islamic State's narrative exemplifies this message. Issue 11 of *Dabiq* shows happy brothers in arms alongside the slogan '*wala and bara*' (the concept of loyalty to believers, and disavowal of disbelievers), juxtaposed against its opposite, 'American racism'. It is this radical interpretation of the religious community of believers then, that becomes the sole locus of identity and belonging. Consequently, in the absence of an appealing cultural paradigm from either parents or mainstream society, the individual simply resorts to a cultural entrenchment that assumes a religious hue by default, transforming religion from religion per se into the principal anchor of identity.

Those who buy into this identity reconfiguration narrative should be thought of as the 'born again' variety of believer. They have much in common with religious converts found in all faiths. Indeed, it is no accident that Islamic converts are disproportionately represented among Western jihadists.[38] Recent terrorist attacks carried out in Ottawa, Quebec and New York were the work of recent converts to Islam, as was the hostage crisis in the kosher supermarket in Paris in January 2015, which played out alongside the siege that led to the death of the Kouachi brothers and was undertaken by Amedy Coulibaly, who declared allegiance to IS before his death. With little previous religious socialisation, no effective spiritual counterweight in their immediate circle, and a desperate desire to prove their religious credentials, the born again variety are far more likely to accept totalitarian visions of Islam, with the proverbial zeal of the converted.

Consequently, religion not only provides an emphatic rejoinder to Western identity, but is also interpreted *de novo*, without the perceived cultural accretions of the Islam associated with their parental or ethnic identity, thereby constructing a legitimate identity outside both minority and majority cultures. Take for instance the case of Umar Farouk Abdulmuttalab, who wrote in the final text messages to his devout father back in Nigeria, 'I've found a new religion, the real Islam'; 'You should just forget about me, I'm never coming back'; 'Please forgive me. I will no longer be in touch with you'; and 'Forgive me for any wrongdoing,

I am no longer your child.'[39] Olivier Roy argues that globalised radical Islam is particularly attractive to diasporic Muslims, precisely because it legitimises their sense of deculturation and uprootedness by refusing to identify Islam with the pristine cultures of their parents, pointing to a strong correlation between deculturation and religious reformulation.[40]

Religious Motivations and Rhetoric

This leads us on very usefully to one of the enduring myths that has surrounded jihadists for many years: the ascendancy of religious motivations over other more 'worldly' concerns, and it is easy to understand why this might be the case. Many of these individuals themselves employ starkly religious language, and invoke religious texts that promise 'other-worldly' rewards as compensation for 'this-worldly' sacrifice, including, amongst other things, the guarantee of eternal Paradise, and most famously, the lascivious offering of 72 heavenly virgins.[41]

Take for example Muhammad Siddique Khan, who tempers his earlier altruistic but 'secular' motives by introducing a sacred dimension to his rationale:

I and thousands like me are forsaking everything for what we believe. Our driving motivation doesn't come from tangible commodities that this world has to offer… With this I leave you to make up your own minds and I ask you to make dua to Allah almighty to accept the work from me and my brothers and enter us into gardens of paradise.[42]

Umar Farouk Abdulmutallab presents a similarly curious mix of secular and sacred motives, by first providing a very careful reasoning of his participation in jihad as constituting not only a religious duty, but a virtuous deed:

In late 2009, in fulfilment of a religious obligation, I decided to participate in jihad against the United States. The Koran obliges every able Muslim to participate in jihad and fight in the way of Allah, those who fight you… Participation in jihad against the United States [sic] is considered among the most virtuous of deeds in Islam and is highly encouraged in the Koran… If you laugh at us now, we will laugh at you later in this life and on the day of judgement by God's will, and our final call is all praise to Allah, the lord of the universe, Allahu Akbar.[43]

Consequently, it becomes extremely difficult, if not impossible, to delineate that which is genuinely 'religious' from other more secular factors, particularly if all we have to base this on is the overtly sanctified and highly-stylised discourse of the individuals themselves. Thus, whilst we must give credence to their stated *sacred* intentions, and their own attribution of meaning to their actions, we must crucially also be cognisant of the post hoc attribution of meaning and validation to these acts.[44] To put it differently, religion may not provide the initial motive, but it does provide the motif or stamp of approval. Take the example of a young man who wants to go to Syria to fight for any reason that is *not* explicitly religious. It is not enough just to fight and even die like a jihadist, but to be accepted by that community (and indeed not to end up beheaded as a member of a rival group), you need to walk, talk and behave like one of them too. The highly stylised genre of video 'martyrdom testaments' which suicide bombers record prior to their deaths provides a very good example of this sort of conformity. It is no accident that they all look and sound pretty much the same, as they need to display certain religious tropes and conform to established archetypes to be conferred with the status of martyr by the wider community. Amedy Coulibaly had no tangible contact with IS leaders, but nevertheless unilaterally declared allegiance to the group in a hastily assembled 'martyrdom video', which bears an uncanny resemblance to 'officially sanctioned' videos.

One recent telling example of this sort of religiosity tacked on at the end is the case of Mohammed Ahmed and Yusuf Sarwar, two young British men from Birmingham who were jailed for travelling to Syria to join and fight alongside a jihadist group in 2013, in response to what they saw as their religious duty. But it was the reading material they purchased to accompany them on their trip, the books *Islam for Dummies* and *The Koran for Dummies*, which prove most revealing about their lack of religious literacy and motivation.[45] This characterisation appears to hold equally true for the violent men who attacked the Charlie Hebdo offices. The Kouachi brothers, as orphaned children of Algerian immigrants, were raised in foster care, and certainly not as pious Muslims. Rather, as the French newspaper *Libération* reported back in 2005, Cherif led a decidedly non-devout and hedonistic lifestyle, smoking marijuana, drinking alcohol, listening to gangster rap, and had numerous girlfriends. Indeed, during his trial in 2008 for helping transport jihadist fighters from France to Iraq, Cherif's lawyer described his client as an 'occasional Muslim'.[46] Similarly, a number of those who committed the Paris 2015 attacks showed an equally indifferent attitude towards religion, smoking marijuana, drinking alcohol and partaking in other activities that ran contrary to central tenets of the Muslim faith.[47]

Now, this is not to exonerate religion in any sense. Religion has historically been responsible for a great deal of violence, and religious texts and doctrines often appear to condone death and destruction. However, unlike believers, academics tend to understand religion in epiphenomenal terms, as products of social, economic, political and other factors that offer solutions to something. So what does religion offer a solution to, in the case of Europe's jihadists?

Transforming losers to martyrs

In addition to the timely identity reconfiguration offered in the face of a dual cultural alterity, this particular form of religiosity also offers meaning and purpose to the lives of those who desperately lack it. It appears that for an increasing number of aspiring jihadists the appeal of al-Qaeda or Islamic State does not stem from altruistic identification with a community of victims, but rather results from an egoistical desire to overcome an unbearable ennui born largely of underachievement. In these instances, the turn to jihadism serves as an emphatic rejection of the banality and monotonous inanity of daily life, providing, perhaps for the first time, a sense of being part of an elite group that compensates for the shortcomings of one's own trivial existence;[48] or, as Sageman suggests, 'martyrdom lifts them from their insignificance'.[49]

Anthony Garcia, one of the failed 2004 'Bluewater bomb' plotters, appears to epitomise this motif. Garcia left school at the age of sixteen with few qualifications and no discernible ambitions, instead drifting peripatetically from one menial job to another. Prior to his arrest, Garcia had been working night-shifts stacking shelves at a local supermarket, but spent much of his time daydreaming about becoming a jihadist fighter, with the jihadist fantasy clearly providing a form of escapism from the daily tedium and drudgery of his otherwise uneventful life.[50] Indeed, for others like Richard Reid, the 'shoe bomber' who tried to detonate an Atlantic flight in mid-air in December 2001, martyrdom offers not just an escape from underachievement, but also from a life plagued by incarceration and petty crime.[51]

In the case of the Kouachi brothers, and the Paris 2015 attackers, jihadism potentially offered a rejection of and escape from the banal and inane drudgery of daily life in the French *banlieues*, which for many French Muslims is a depressing mix of unemployment, crime, drugs, institutional racism and endemic cycles of poverty and disenfranchisement. For example, although France's Muslim population is around seven to eight per cent of the whole, Muslim inmates constitute as much as seventy per cent of the prison population in France.[52] This disparity by a factor of ten is all the more troubling considering that prisons are often cited as being one of the key environments in which radicalisation takes place.[53] Consequently, any attempt to explain why France is the largest exporter of Western jihadists to Islamic State has to acknowledge the clear and striking role played by the presence of gross structural and socio-economic inequalities.

Contrast these feelings of boredom, purposelessness and insignificance with the offer of redemption through the image of the chivalrous warrior, recasting the individual as some sort of avenging hero. Following the Charlie Hedbo attack, Islamic State's official radio station praised the Kouachi brothers, validating their transformation from petty criminals and nobodies into heroes of Islam: 'We start our bulletin with France. Heroic killed 12 journalists and wounded ten others working in the French magazine Charlie Hebdo, and that was support for our master (Prophet) Mohammad, may Allah's peace and blessings be upon him.'[54]

It is only via the redemptive prism of the chivalrous jihadist warrior, through which his heroic sacrifice recasts him as the community's champion, that the individual then discerns a mechanism to reclaim agency, purpose, self-esteem and manhood. Muhammad Siddique Khan's martyrdom video emphatically refers to his coterie of martyrs as 'real men', pointedly distinguishing them from the emasculated individuals who 'stay at home'.[55]

The appeal to the valiant holy warrior or chivalrous knight is a recurring trope in jihadist literature, and indeed it is no accident that Ayman al-Zawahiri's most important work is entitled *Knights Under the Prophet's Banner (Fursan Taht Rayah Al-Nabi)*,[56] shrewdly seeking to exploit traditional Muslim male sensitivities around chivalry, honour, shame and sacrifice. The astute framing of this loss of dignity as being somehow sinful offers up the prospect of redemption and absolution through sacrifice and martyrdom.[57]

Muhammad Siddique Khan exemplifies the transformative power offered by the martyr's mask, undergoing the ready metamorphosis from children's learning mentor to heroic avenging soldier:

> I am directly responsible for protecting and avenging my Muslim brothers and sisters... And until you stop the bombing, gassing, imprisonment and torture of my people we will not stop this fight. We are at war and I am a soldier. Now you too will taste the reality of this situation.[58]

More recently, the Islamic State's propaganda machine has orchestrated a savvy and highly sophisticated media campaign, producing material that shrewdly seeks to exploit these tensions. Recent social media agitprop from IS included the telling phrases: 'Sometimes people with the worst pasts create the best futures' and 'Why be a loser when you can be a martyr?'

Conclusion

As IS continues to draw young Muslim men from every corner of the globe to its nascent Caliphate, it is clear that their broader jihadist narratives are continuing to resonate at some level, even with a small but significant minority of young men and women born and raised in the West. This significant exodus of foreign fighters from many European states will no doubt continue to haunt us long after the Islamic State meets its inevitable demise, through the inevitable foreign fighter blowback syndrome. Indeed, it appears likely that as IS loses ground, it will lash out in desperation, as we have already witnessed in the spate of terrorist attacks over the last year.

If we are to address this pressing security issue of recruitment and blowback proactively, rather than simply attempting to deal with the returnees, it is important not just to understand what IS's appeal is, but also crucially to recognise that their narrative only resonates and has potency when it intersects with the very particular context and circumstances that some young Muslims in the West find themselves in today. The heady mix of increasing xenophobia and Islamophobia, alienation and cultural dislocation, socioeconomic marginalisation and political disenfranchisement that many young Muslims experience leads them to take solace in faux-religious identities proffered by welcoming jihadists. These new religious identities not only provide a sense of identification and belonging, but also serve as catalysts to transform young people's lives, lifting them from underachievement, marginalisation and criminality or simply even purposelessness and boredom, and in the process cast them as heroes and champions of the new reconfigured community of believers. The internet and its attendant new media environment, which has become the principal platform for the dissemination and mediation of the culture and ideology of jihadism,[59] are also largely responsible for the increasing resonance of these IS narratives. It is in these cloistered yet highly immersive web 2.0 environments that jihadist propagandists rely on emotive imagery and other affective content to venerate the hero, not just through polished jihadist video montages, stirring devotional songs and fawning hagiographies of martyrs, but also through appeals to video games like *Call of Duty* and *Grand Theft Auto* and other popular culture references. These strategies are tailored towards the newer generation of young, diasporic, non-Arabic speaking digital natives,[60] and so it is inevitable that these young people will not just continue to be drawn to the IS narrative, but will also continue to contribute disproportionately to the jihadist demographic.[61]

In light of the seismic events that have taken place in the MENA region and beyond, jihadist narratives have changed considerably over the last few years. However, these changes represent a gradual shift rather than an abrupt rupture, and the narrative has retained its overall cogence and coherence. In a sense, the establishment of IS's so-called Caliphate has simply followed al-Qaeda's narrative to its logical and inevitable conclusions, changing abstract utopian aspirations to tangible worldly realities. In the process, IS has resurrected the ailing jihadist narrative for a whole new generation.

NOTES

LIST OF CONTRIBUTORS

1. Both government officials are writing in a personal capacity and their views should not be taken as a representation of government policy.

PREFACE

1. See for example Patrick Cockburn, *The Rise of Islamic State: ISIS and the New Sunni Revolution*, London, New York: Verso (2015); Michael Weiss and Hassan Hassan, *Isis: Inside the Army of Terror*, New York: Regan Arts (2015); Jessica Stern and J. M. Berger, *ISIS: The State of Terror*, London: HarperCollins (2015); William Faizi McCants, *The ISIS Apocalypse: The History, Strategy, and Doomsday Vision of the Islamic State*, New York: St Martin's Press (2015); Andrew Hosken, *Rise and Fall of the Islamic State*, London: Oneworld Publications (2015); Abdel-Bari Atwan, *Islamic State*, London: Saqi Books (2016).

1. INTRODUCTION

1. Jean-Pierre Filiu, *The Arab Revolution: Ten Lessons from the Democratic Uprising*, Oxford, New York: Oxford University Press (2011), p. 111.
2. Daniel Byman, 'Al Qaeda's Terrible Spring: Why the Organization Might Not Survive', *Foreign Affairs*, 24 May 2011, https://www.foreignaffairs.com/articles/2011–05–24/al-qaeda-s-terrible-spring
3. Forum participant (10 December 2010), retrieved 16 January 2011 from www.as-ansar.com/vb/showthread.php?t=50676. Unless stated, all direct Arabic translations are the authors'.
4. Forum participant, Ansar al-Mujahideen Forum (21 December, 2011), retrieved 9 January 2012 from www.as-ansar.com/vb/showthread.php?t=482941
5. Forum participant, Ansar al-Mujahideen Forum (8 February 2011), retrieved 15 February 2011 from www.as-ansar.com/vb/showthread.php?t=87389
6. Scott Shane, 'Al Qaeda Finds Itself at a Crossroads—News Analysis', *New York*

Times, 27 February 2011, http://www.nytimes.com/2011/02/28/world/middle-east/28qaeda.html

7. Forum participant, Ansar al-Mujahideen Forum (8 February 2011), retrieved 15 February 2011 from www.as-ansar.com/vb/showthread.php?t=87389

8. Shane, 'Al Qaeda Finds Itself at a Crossroads—News Analysis'.

9. HSMPress (@HSMPress1), Twitter post, 4 July 2013, https://twitter.com/HSMpress_1

10. Bill Roggio, 'Zawahiri Rebukes Muslim Brotherhood for Trusting Democracy', *The Long War Journal*, 3 August 2013, http://www.longwarjournal.org/archives/2013/08/zawahiri_rebukes_muslim_brothe.php

11. William McCants, 'Slideshow: Black Flag', *Foreign Policy* (November 2011), available at https://foreignpolicy.com/slideshow/black-flag/

12. Abu Muhammad al-'Adnani, 'Peacefulness is Whose Religion?' (August 2013), retrieved September 2013, http://www.muslm.org/vb/showthread.php?518859

13. Abu Muhammad al-'Adnani, *This is the Promise of Allah* (29 June 2014), available at https://news.siteintelgroup.com/Jihadist-News/isis-spokesman-declares-caliph-ate-rebrands-group-as-islamic-state.html

14. Lawrence Wright, *The Looming Tower: Al-Qa'ida and the Road to 9/11*, New York: Vintage Books (2007).

15. Available at http://fas.org/irp/world/para/docs/980223-fatwa.htm

16. Akil N. Awan and Mina Al-Lami, 'Al-Qa'ida's Virtual Crisis', *RUSI Journal* 154, no. 1 (2009): 60.

17. Akil N. Awan, 'Spurning 'this Worldly Life': Terrorism and Martyrdom in Contemporary Britain', in Dominic Janes, ed., *Martyrdom and Terrorism: Pre-Modern to Contemporary Perspectives*, New York: Oxford University Press (2014), p. 245.

18. Available at http://media.clarionproject.org/files/islamic-state/islamic-state-isis-magazine-Issue-4-the-failed-crusade.pdf

19. 14 November 2015, https://twitter.com/abo_m_50/status/665479953568432128

20. Letter from Ayman al-Zawahiri to Abu Mus'ab al-Zarqawi (9 July 2005), Office of the Director of National Security, available at http://www.globalsecurity.org/security/library/report/2005/zawahiri-zarqawi-letter_9jul2005.htm

21. Aaron Zelin and Phillip Smyth, 'The Vocabulary of Sectarianism', *Foreign Policy* (29 January 2014), http://foreignpolicy.com/2014/01/29/the-vocabulary-of-sectarianism/

22. Ali Abdelaty and Suleiman al-Khalidi, 'Islamic State Urges Followers to Escalate Attacks in Ramadan', Reuters (23 June 2015), http://www.reuters.com/article/2015/06/23/us-mideast-crisis-ramadan-idUSKBN0P31YH20150623

23. Forum writer, 3 February 2014, http://alplatformmedia.com/vb/showthread.php?t=37073, retrieved 18 February 2014.

24. Rania Abouzeid, 'The Jihad Next Door', *Politico*, 23 June 2014.

25. *Healing of the Believers' Chests*, al-Furqan Foundation (3 February 2015).

26. Nineveh Province Media Office, *But If You Return, We Shall Return* (23 June 2015).

27. Akil N. Awan, Andrew Hoskins and Ben O'Loughlin, *Radicalisation and Media: Connectivity and Terrorism in the New Media Ecology* (London: Routledge, 2011).

28. Letter from Ayman al-Zawahiri to Abu Mus'ab al-Zarqawi, 9 July 2005.

29. http://www.bbc.co.uk/news/world-middle-east-26016318

30. Ayman al-Zawahiri statement posted 2 May 2014, retrieved 15 May 2014 from www.hanein.info/vb/showthread.php?t=678239

31. Available at: http://www.ctc.usma.edu/Management_of_Savagery.pdf

32. http://www.npr.org/templates/story/story.phpstoryId=5516640

33. Alistair Crooke, 'The ISIS' *Management of Savagery* in Iraq', *Huffington Post*, 30 June 2014, http://www.huffingtonpost.com/alastair-crooke/iraq-isis-alQa'ida_b_5542575.html

34. Hassan Hassan, 'Isis Has Reached New Depths of Depravity. But There Is a Brutal Logic Behind It', *Guardian*, 8 February 2015, available at http://www.theguardian.com/world/2015/feb/08/isis-islamic-state-ideology-shari'ah-syria-iraq-jordan-pilot

35. Jean Bethke Elshtain, *Just War on Terror*, New York: Basic Books (2003) p. 19; Cindy Coombs, *Terrorism in the Twenty First Century*, New Jersey: Prentice Hall (2006), Preface.

36. Letter from Ayman al-Zawahiri to Abu Mus'ab al-Zarqawi, 9 July 2005.

37. Akil N. Awan, 'Success of the Meta-Narrative: How Maintain Legitimacy', *CTC Sentinel* 2, no. 11 (2009).

38. Ayman al-Zawahiri, Message to the People of Egypt, 10, June 2012, retrieved 27 June 2011 from www.as-ansar.com/vb/showthread.php?t=63970

39. Ibid.

40. Ayman al-Zawahiri, statement, 13 September 2012, retrieved 15 May 2014 from www.as-ansar.com/vb/showthread.php?t=70528

41. Abu Sa'ad al Amili, forum post 15 October 2012, retrieved 18 October 2012 from www.as-ansar.com/vb/showthread.php?t=72712

42. Al-'Adnani al-Shami statement posted 30 July 2013, retrieved 2 August 2013 from www.hanein.info/vb/showthread.php?t=324301

43. Ayman al-Zawahiri, statement released 12 September 2013, retrieved 30 September 2013 from www.hanein.info/vb/showthread.php?t=678239

44. *Dabiq*, issue 1, p. 4. Michael W. S. Ryan, '*Dabiq*: What Islamic State's New Magazine Tells Us about their Strategic Direction, Recruitment Patterns and Guerrilla Doctrine', *Terrorism Monitor*, Jamestown Foundation (August 2014), available at http://www.jamestown.org/programs/tm/single/?tx_ttnews%5Btt_news%5D=42702#.VmQbvOOyOko

45. 'Why Islamic State chose town of Dabiq for propaganda', http://www.bbc.co.uk/news/world-middle-east-30083303

46. Ryan, 'Dabiq'.
47. Al-'Adnani, 'This is the Promise of Allah', available at https://news.siteintelgroup. com/Jihadist-News/isis-spokesman-declares-caliphate-rebrands-group-as-islam-ic-state.html
48. Ibid.
49. Ayman al-Zawahiri, *Knights Under the Prophet's Banner* (2001), available at http:// azelin.files.wordpress.com/2010/11/6759609-knights-under-the-prophet-ban-ner.pdf
50. See Moar Fahmy, 'Al Qa'ida calls Islamic State illegitimate but suggests coopera-tion', Reuters (9 September 2015), available at http://uk.reuters.com/article/ uk-mideast-zawahri-idUKKCN0R91LC20150909

2. THE 'ISLAMIC STATE' AND AL-QAEDA

1. This chapter is largely based on a section I authored as part of 'The Group that Calls Itself a State: Understanding the Evolution and Challenges of the Islamic State', by Muhammad al-'Ubaydi, Nelly Lahoud, Daniel Militon and Bryan Price, CTC Report (December 2014). My gratitude to my colleague Muhammad al-'Ubaydi for collecting some of the primary sources used in this chapter.
2. Abu Bakr al-Husayni al-Qurashi al-Baghdadi, 'Wa-Bashshir al-Mu'minin', *Shabakat Shumukh al-Islam* (April 2013), CTC Library. ISIL was meant to represent a merger between ISI and the Syrian-based jihadist group Jabhat al-Nusra (JN), a merger that was swiftly rejected by JN. To be discussed later in the chapter.
3. It should be noted that when al-Zarqawi's pledge of allegiance was accepted by bin Laden, the name of his group changed to al-Qaeda in Mesopotamia and not 'Qa'idat al-Jihad in Mesopotamia'. Nelly Lahoud remarked that the name 'Qa'idat al-Jihad' was not used by bin Laden in his public statements. See her 'The Merger of al-Shabab and Qa'idat al-Jihad', *CTC Sentinel* (16 February 2012), ftn 6.
4. al-Baghdadi, 'Wa-Bashshir al-Mu'minin'.
5. Ibid.
6. Ibid. It should be noted that on 12 June 2006 a short-lived coalition was put together under the name 'Hilf al-Mutayyabin', which was meant to replace the Advisory Council. See 'I'lan Hilfu al-Mutayyabin', 12 June 2006, https://nokbah. com/~w3/?p=533. It is not clear why it did not last and why Abu Bakr al-Bagh-dadi does not count it as part of the history of the group.
7. Ibid.
8. Abu Muhammad al-'Adnani, 'Hadha Wa'du Allah' (29 June 2014), CTC Library. Undoubtedly, the title is meant to echo Q. 24:55. Unless otherwise stated, trans-lations of Arabic in this section of the report are by Nelly Lahoud.
9. Ibid.
10. Al-Mawardi, *The Ordinances of Government*, translated by Wafaa H. Wahba, Reading: Center for Muslim Contribution to Civilization (1996), p. 4.

11. Tanzim Qa'idat al-Jihad—al-Qiyada al-'Amma, 'Bayan bi-Sha'ni 'Alaqat Jama'at Qa'idat al-Jihad bi-Jama'at al-Dawla al-Islamiyya fi al-'Iraq wa-al-Sham, Markaz al-Fajr li-al-I'lam', *Shabakat al-Fida' al-Islamiyya* (2 February 2014), CTC Library. For consistency, the article uses 'al-Qa'ida' instead of 'Qa'idat al-Jihad'. For the possible nuance between the two names, see Nelly Lahoud, 'The Merger of Al-Shabab and Qa'idat al-Jihad', *CTC Sentinel* 5:2 (2012), ftn 6.

12. Abu Muhammad al-'Adnani, "Udhran Amiru al-Qa'ida', May 2014, CTC Library.

13. Ibid.

14. Sayf al-'Adal, 'Tajrubati Ma' Abi Mus'ab al-Zarqawi', *Minbar al-Tawhid wa-al-Jihad*, http://www.tawhed.ws/r?i=ttofom6f. For further discussion on the ideological differences, see Nelly Lahoud, *The Jihadis' Path to Self-Destruction*, New York/London: Columbia University Press/Hurst (2010), pp. 205–11.

15. For studies that explore al-Maqdisi's jihadist ideology, see Nelly Lahoud, 'In Search of Philosopher-Jihadis: Abu Muhammad al-Maqdisi's Jihadi Philosophy', *Totalitarian Movements and Political Religions*, vol 10, no. 2, pp. 205–20 (June 2009); see also Joas Wagemakers, 'A Purist Jihadi-Salafi: The Ideology of Abu Muhammad al-Maqdisi', *British Journal of Middle Eastern Studies*, vol. 36, issue 2 (August 2009), 281–97.

16. Ibid. (Lahoud, 205–6; Wagemakers, 285–6).

17. Ibid.

18. Sayf al-'Adal, 'Tajrubati Ma' Abi Mus'ab al-Zarqawi'.

19. Abu Hammam Bakr Bin 'Abd al-'Aziz al-Athari, 'Ta'arraf ila Sirat al-Sheikh al-Mujahid al-'Adnani', *Shabakat Shumukh al-Islam* (26 May 2014), CTC Library.

20. Ibid.

21. Sayf al-'Adal, 'Tajrubati Ma' Abi Mus'ab al-Zarqawi'.

22. Lahoud, 'In Search of Philosopher-Jihadis', 205.

23. Abu Mus'ab al-Zarqawi, 'Bayan wa-Tawdih lima Atharahu al-Shaykh al-Maqdisi fi Liqa'ihi ma' al-Jazira' (12 July 2005), CTC Library.

24. Ibid.

25. Ibid.

26. Ibid. For an historical background about the Zangi legacy, see S. Heidemann, 'Zangi', *Encyclopaedia of Islam*, 2nd edn.

27. 'al-Baghdadi ikhtara Awwala Zuhurin lahu min al-Masjidi alladhi Banahu Nur al-Din Zangi', *Haqq*, http://www.dawaalhaq.com/?p=14591

28. The official announcement was made in April 2004 in two different releases, a statement signed Abu Mus'ab al-Zarqawi and a video release, entitled *Riyah al-Nasr*, featuring Abu Anas al-Shami, CTC Library.

29. On AQ being severely weakened in 2003, see Nelly Lahoud, *Beware of Imitators: al-Qa'ida through the Lens of its Confidential Secretary*, CTC Report, 4 June 2012, pp. 104–5.

30. Osama bin Laden, 'Risala ila al-Muslimin fi al-'Iraq Khasatan wa-al-Umma al-Islamiyya 'Ammatan', December 2004 (CTC Library).

31. See captured letters authored by Ayman al-Zawahiri and 'Atiyatullah al-Libi to Abu Mus'ab al-Zarqawi. These are available at www.ctc.usma.edu/posts/zawahiris-letter-to-zarqawi-original and www.ctc.usma.edu/posts/atiyahs-letter-to-zarqawi-original

32. The first statement announcing the formation of Majlis Shura al-Mujahidin is dated 15 January 2006, and was signed by Abu Maysara al-'Iraqi, CTC Library.

33. See 'Nafi 'Iraqi li-I'tiqal Qiyadi Murtabit bi-al-Qa'ida', BBC Arabic, 10 March 2007, http://news.bbc.co.uk/hi/arabic/middle_east_news/newsid_6436000/6436527.stm

34. It is reported that he is none other than Abu 'Umar al-Baghdadi, who would become the leader of the Islamic State of Iraq. See 'Nafi 'Iraqi li-I'tiqal Qiyadi Murtabit bi-al-Qa'ida', BBC Arabic, 10 March 2007, http://news.bbc.co.uk/hi/arabic/middle_east_news/newsid_6436000/6436527.stm

35. See for instance the statement announcing the martyrdom of al-Zarqawi, 'Bayan min Tanzim al-Qa'ida fi Bilad al-Rafidayn hawla Istishhad al-Sheikh al-Zarqawi', signed by Abi 'Abd al-Rahman al-'Iraqi, June 2006.

36. Umm Muhammad, 'Risala min Zawjat al-Sheikh Abi Mus'ab al-Zarqawi', June 2006, CTC Library.

37. Abu Hamza al-Muhajir, 'Sa-Yuhzamu al-Jam'u Wa-Yuwalluna al-Dubra', 13 June 2006.

38. Abu Hamza al-Muhajir, 'Inna al-Hukma illa li-llah', 10 November 2006. The ISI was announced on 15 October 2006. This discussion is partly based on the article by Nelly Lahoud and Muhammad al-'Ubaydi, 'The War of Jihadists against Jihadists in Syria', CTC Sentinel, 26 March 2014.

39. See the segment about Abu 'Umar al-Baghdadi on al-Iraq al-An, https://www.youtube.com/watch?v=2BN1oI32MgY; 'Zawjat Abu Ayyub al-Misri', al-Sharq al-Awsat, 25 July 2010.

40. 'al-Tashkila al-Wizariyya al-Ula li-Dawlat al-'Iraq al-Islamiyya', 19 April 2007, signed by Muharib al-Jaburi, CTC Library.

41. Ayman al-Zawahiri, untitled letter, 2 May 2014, CTC Library.

42. Ibid.

43. Harmony Document SOCOM-2012–0000011, 1.

44. Harmony Document SOCOM-2012–0000019, 19–23.

45. Harmony Document SOCOM-2012–0000005.

46. Tanzim Qa'idat al-Jihad, 'Bayan bi-Sha'ni 'Alaqat Jama'at Qa'idat al-Jihad bi-Jama'at al-Dawla al-Islamiyya fi al-'Iraq wa-al-Sham'.

47. Abu Hamza al-Muhajir, "Inna al-Hukma illa li-llah", November 10, 2006. Cited in: Nelly Lahoud and Muhammad al-'Ubaydi (2014), 'The War of the Jihadists against Jihadists in Syria', in CTC Sentinel 7(3): 1–5, https://www.ctc.usma.edu/posts/the-war-of-jihadists-in-syria

47. Ayman al-Zawahiri, untitled letter, 2 May 2014, CTC Library.

48. Harmony Document SOCOM-2012–0000004, 8.

49. Transcript of the founding statement/speech by Abu Muhammad al-Julani, *Shabakat al-Jihad al-'Alami*, posted on 12 February 2012, CTC Library.

50. See for example Riyad al-As'ad (interview), posted 19 March 2013, https://www.youtube.com/watch?v=RWrZhQG4leg&feature=player_embedded

51. Abu Bakr al-Baghdadi, 'Wa-Bashshir al-Mu'minin', *Shabakat Shumukh al-Islam*, April 2013, CTC Library; and Abu Muhammad al-Julani, 'Hawla Sahat al-Sham', *Shabakat al-Fida' al-Islamiyya*, April 2013, CTC Library.

52. al-Julani, 'Hawla Sahat al-Sham'.

53. See the letter authored by Abu Khalid al-Suri and Abu Mus'ab al-Suri, which was addressed to Usama bin Laden via Ayman al-Zawahiri, cited in Alan Cullison, 'Inside al-Qa'ida's Hard Drive', *The Atlantic*, 1 September 2004.

54. 'Al-Zawahiri Yulghi Damj 'Jihadiyyi' Suriya wa-al-'Iraq', al-Jazeera, 9 June 2013. It should be noted that Harakat Ahrar al-Sham is part of the Islamic Front (al-Jabha al-Islamiyya), one of the largest coalitions of militant groups operating in Syria under the banner of Islam. Ahrar al-Sham was a signatory to the charter that the Islamic Front released in November 2013.

55. See for example 'Mithaq al-Jabha al-Islamiyya', 22 November 2013, CTC Library. See also the one produced in March 2014 by the same coalition, which includes Kata'ib Ahrar al-Sham.

56. Muhammad al-Najjar, 'Abu Qatada Yuhajim Tanzim al-Dawla wa-Yu'ayyid Muhlat al-Nusra', al-Jazeera, 27 February 2014. See also Abu Qatada al-Filastini, 'Ma ba'da al-Muqaraba [Rabi' al-Mujahidin] ... Waqi' wa-Amal', *Shabakat al-Fida' al-Islamiyya*, February 2014.

57. See, for example, 'Nida' mina al-Dawla al-Islamiyya fi al-'Iraq wa-al-Sham', *Shabakat al-Fida' al-Islamiyya*, 4 January 2014.

58. The protagonists on the battlefield are many, but the main ones consist of ISIL (supported by Katibatu al-Muhajirin, led by Abu 'Umar al-Shishani) on the one hand, and on the other hand JN and its seeming allies (the Islamic Front coalition, particularly the group Ahrar al-Sham, Jaysh al-Mujahidin, and smaller militant groups).

59. The Islamic State of Iraq and the Levant, 'Bayan al-Dawla al-Islamiyya fi al-'Iraq wa-al-Sham—Wilayat al-Raqqa Hawla ma Tashhaduhu al-Madina min Ahdath', *Shabakat Shumukh al-Islam*, 13 January 2014.

60. Ibid.

61. See the statement by ISIL, posted 13 January 2014; and the statement by Jabhat al-Nusra, 'Raddan 'ala I'tiraf Jama'at al-Dawla bi-Qatli al-Sheikh Abi Sa'd al-Hadrami', 15 January 2014.

62. Abu Khalid al-Suri, 'Risalat Munasaha min al-Sheikh Abu Khalid al-Suri', *Shabakat al-Fida' al-Islamiyya*, 16 January 2014.

63. Ibid.

64. ISIL reportedly sent three suicide bombers on the mission. For details, see Abu

Yazan al-Shami, 'Qissat Istishhad al-Sheikh Abi Khalid al-Suri', February 2014, available at www.justpaste.it/eiv5

65. 'Abdallah al-Mhisni, 23 February 2014, available at www.twitter.com/mhesne

66. Abu Muhammad al-Julani, 'Laytaka Rathaytani', *Shabakat al-Fida' al-Islamiyya*, 24 February 2014.

67. On the importance of Abu Mus'ab al-Suri, see Brynjar Lia, *Architect of Global Jihad: the Life of al-Qa'ida Strategist Abu Mus'ab al-Suri*, New York: Columbia University Press (2008). One tweet by a certain Abu al-Bara' al-Zahrani reported that Abu Khalid was in fact the brother of Abu Mus'ab al-Suri. See Abu al-Bara' al-Zahrani, 24 February 2014, available at www.twitter.com/Braa73

68. Abu Qatada al-Filastini, 27 February 2014, available at www.youtube.com/watch?v=gem3m2bgGAA

69. The Islamic State of Iraq and the Levant, 'Bayan Mawqif al-Dawla al-Islamiyya min Maqalat al-Muftarin', 1 March 2014, available at www.justpaste.it/elax

70. President Barack Obama, 'Transcript of Obama's Remarks on the Fight Against ISIS', *New York Times*, 10 September 2014.

71. Abu Bakr al-Baghdadi, 'Risala ila al-Mujahidin wa-al-Umma al-Islamiyya fi Shahri Ramadan', 1 July 2014, CTC Library.

72. Abu al-Fadl Madi, twitter@sadeknimah, 30 June 2014.

73. 'Analysis of the State of ISI', Harmony Document NMEC-2007–612449, 17.

74. Ibid., 17.

75. Ibid., 19. For a discussion of the challenges faced by ISI, see Truls Hallberg Tonnessen, 'Training on a Battlefield: Iraq as a Training Ground for Global Jihadis', *Terrorism and Political Violence*, 20 (2008): 543–62.

76. For a detailed account of how the situations in Syria and Iraq propelled the Iraq-based group, see Nelly Lahoud, 'Metamorphosis: From al-Tawhid wa-al-Jihad to Dawlat al-Khilafa (2003–2014)', in Muhammad al-'Ubaydi, Nelly Lahoud, Daniel Milton, Bryan Price, *The Group that Calls itself a State: Understanding the Evolution and Challenges of the Islamic State*, CTC Report (December 2014), pp. 19–26.

77. Abu Muhammad al-'Adnani, 'Ma Kana Hadha Manhajuna, wa-lan Yakun', *Shabakat 'Arin al-Mujahidin*, http://www.al3aren.com/vb/showthread.php?p=267, accessed 18 April 2014. Sykes—Picot was the 1916 agreement between the United Kingdom and France in which they carved out their respective spheres of influence in the Middle East in anticipation of the fall of the Ottoman Empire, eventually leading to its division into nation-states.

78. Abu Muhammad al-'Adnani, ''Udhran Amiru al-Qa'ida', May 2014, CTC Library.

79. Ibid.

80. Ibid.

3. AYMAN AL-ZAWAHIRI AND THE RISE OF ISIL

1. Muntasir al-Zayyat, *The Road to Al-Qa'ida: The Story of Bin Laden's Right-Hand Man*, London: Pluto Press (2004), p. 17.

2. The chapter relies on translations of al-Zawahiri's communiqués provided by al-Qaeda or third parties, as well as professional translations of original content commissioned by the author.

3. Combating Terrorism Center, *Cracks in the Foundation: Leadership Schisms in Al-Qa'ida from 1989–2006*, West Point, NY: Harmony Project (2007).

4. Ayman al-Zawahiri, 'The Noble Knight Dismounted', published by As-Sahab and the Global Islamic Media Front (8 June 2011) via Ansar Al Mujahideen forum, https://ansar1.info, secured August 2011, since closed.

5. A. al-Zawahiri, 'Message of Hope and Glad Tidings to Our People in Egypt, Part 8: And What About the American Hostage Warren Weinstein', published by As-Sahab and distributed by al-Masadh Media (December 2011), available from https://azelin.files.wordpress.com/2011/12/ayman-al-e1ba93awc481hirc4ab-e2809ceighth-installment-of-a-message-of-hope-and-glad-tidings-to-our-people-in-egypte2809d.pdf, accessed February 2012.

6. Donald Holbrook, 'Al-Qa'ida's Response to the Arab Spring', in *Perspectives on Terrorism* 6:6 (2012); Jason Burke, *The 9/11 Wars*, London: Allen Lane (2011), p. 485; James F. Forest, 'Perception Challenges Faced by Al-Qa'ida on the Battlefield of Influence Warfare', *Perspectives on Terrorism*, vol. 6, issue 1 (2012): 18; Alex S. Wilner, 'Opportunity Costs or Costly Opportunities? The Arab Spring, Osama Bin Laden, and Al-Qa'ida's African Affiliates', *Perspectives on Terrorism*, vol. 5, issues 3–4 (2011): 55; Nellie Lahoud, 'Ayman al-Zawahiri's Reaction to Revolution in the Middle East', *CTC Sentinel*, vol. 4, no. 4 (2011); Analysis Intelligence, 'Al-Qa'ida's Democratic Conundrum' (March 2011), available at http://analysisintelligence.com/tag/yemen, as of 2 August 2012.

7. On the essence and substance of the Islamist extremist master narrative, see J. R. Halverson, S. R. Corman and H. L. Goodall, *Master Narratives of Islamist Extremism*, Basingstoke: Palgrave Macmillan (2013).

8. A. al-Zawahiri, 'Message of Hope and Glad Tidings to Our People in Egypt', Part 8 (2011).

9. A. al-Zawahiri, 'Message of Hope and Glad Tidings to Our People in Egypt, Part 9: Why did We Rebel Against Him?' published by As-Sahab (February2012), distributed by Global Islamic Media Front. Available at http://jihadology.net/2012/02/29/as-sa%E1%B8%A5ab-media-presents-a-new-video-message-from-al-Qa'idahs-ayman-al-%E1%BA%93awahiri-ninth-installment-of-a-message-of-hope-and-glad-tidings-to-our-people-in-egypt/, as of March 2016.

10. Osama bin Laden, 'The Last Speech of the Martyr of Islam—as we see him—to the Muslim Ummah', published by As-Sahab (19 May 2011), translated by the Global Islamic Media Front. See https://archive.org/stream/the-martyr-of-islam-last-speech-to-his-muslim-nation-imam-osama-bin-laden/he-martyr-of-islam-last-speech-to-his-muslim-nation-imam-osama-bin-laden_djvu.txt/, as of March 2016.

11. A. al-Zawahiri, 'Message of Hope and Glad Tidings to our People in Egypt, Part

7', distributed by As-Sahab (9 August 2011), translated by the Global Islamic Media Front. See http://jihadology.net/2011/10/05/the-global-islamic-media-front-presents-an-english-translation-of-ayman-a%E1%BA%93-%E1%BA%93awahiris-%E2%80%9Cseventh-installment-of-a-message-of-hope-and-glad-tidings-to-our-people-in-egypt/, as of March 2016.

12. A. al-Zawahiri, 'To Our People in the Place of the Revelation and the Cradle of Islam', distributed by As-Sahab (18 May 2012), translated by Fursan Al-Balagh Media. Available at https://archive.org/details/FursaanAlBalaagh ENGLISHTRANSLATIONTo OurPeopleInThePlaceOfRevelationAndCradleOfIs, as of March 2016.

13. A. al-Zawahiri, 'Message of Hope and Glad Tidings to our People in Egypt, Part 1', published by As-Sahab (19 February 2011), translated by the Global Islamic Media Front, available at https://archive.org/stream/AMessageofHope/A-Message-of-Hope_djvu.txt, as of March 2016; A. al-Zawahiri 'Message of Hope and Glad Tidings to our People in Egypt, Part 4', published by As-Sahab (4 March 2011), see http://jihadology.net/2011/03/04/as-sa%E1%B8%A5ab-media-presents-a-new-audio-message-from-ayman-a%E1%BA%93-%E1%BA%93awahiri-%E2%80%9Cfourth-installment-of-a-message-of-hope-and-glad-tidings-to-our-people-in-egypt%E2%80%9D/, as of March 2016; A. al-Zawahiri, 'Message of Hope and Glad Tidings to Our People in Egypt, Part 9 (2012); A. al-Zawahiri, 'Message of Hope and Glad Tidings to Our People in Egypt, Part 5', published by As-Sahab (14 April 2011), available at http://jihadology.net/2011/04/14/as-sa%E1%B8%A5ab-media-presents-a-new-video-message-from-ayman-a%E1%BA%93-%E1%BA%93awahiri-%E2%80%9Cfifth-installment-of-a-message-of-hope-and-glad-tidings-to-our-people-in-egypt%E2%80%9D/, as of March 2016.

14. A. al-Zawahiri, 'The Noble Knight Dismounted' (2011).

15. A. al-Zawahiri, 'Oh People of Tunisia, Support Your Shari'ah', distributed by As-Sahab (10 June 2012), available at https://archive.org/details/People-of-Tunisia, as of March 2016.

16. A. al-Zawahiri, 'Message of Hope and Glad Tidings to our People in Egypt, Part 7 (2011); A. al-Zawahiri, 'Message of Hope and Glad Tidings to Our People in Egypt, Part 6', distributed by As-Sahab (21 May 2011), available at http://jihadology.net/2011/05/21/as-sa%E1%B8%A5ab-media-presents-a-new-video-message-from-ayman-a%E1%BA%93-%E1%BA%93awahiri-%E2%80%9Csixth-installment-of-a-message-of-hope-and-glad-tidings-to-our-people-in-egypt%E2%80%9D/, as of March 2016.

17. Clark Lombardi and Nathan J. Brown, 'Islam in Egypt's New Constitution', *Foreign Policy* (13 December 2012).

18. A. al-Zawahiri, 'Unifying the Word toward the Word of Monotheism', produced by As-Sahab, distributed by al-Fajr Media Center (7 April 2013), available at

http://jihadology.net/2013/04/07/as-sa%E1%B8%A5ab-media-presents-a-new-video-message-from-al-Qa'idahs-dr-ayman-al-%E1%BA%93awahiri-unification-of-the-word-surrounding-the-word-of-taw%E1%B8%A5id/, as of March 2016.

19. Especially through Article 219 and Article 4 on the need to consult al-Azhar. Cf. C. B. Lombardi, 'Designing Islamic Constitutions: Past Trends and Options for a Democratic Future', *International Journal of Constitutional Law*, 11.3 (2013).

20. A. al-Zawahiri, 'The seventh interview with Sheikh Ayman al-Zawahiri', interview issued by As-Sahab (18 April 2014). See note 11 above.

21. A. al-Zawahiri, 'Emancipation from the Cycle of Failure and Frivolity', produced by As-Sahab and distributed by al-Fajr (24 January 2014), available at http://jihadology.net/2014/01/24/as-sa%E1%B8%A5ab-media-presents-a-new-video-message-from-al-Qa'idahs-dr-ayman-al-%E1%BA%93awahiri-emancipation-from-futility-and-failure/, as of March 2016 as 'Emancipation from Futlity and Failure'.

22. A. al-Zawahiri, 'Unifying the Word toward the Word of Monotheism' (2013).

23. A. al-Zawahiri, 'Emancipation from the Cycle of Failure and Frivolity' (2014).

24. Ibid.

25. Referring to Egypt's now president, Abdel Fattah El-Sisi.

26. A. al-Zawahiri, 'The seventh interview' (2014).

27. A. al-Zawahiri, 'Emancipation from the Cycle of Failure and Frivolity' (2014).

28. A. al-Zawahiri, 'Answers to the Esteemed Shaykhs' statement, issued by As-Sahab (24 May 2014), see http://jihadology.net/2014/05/24/as-sa%E1%B8%A5ab-media-presents-a-new-release-from-al-Qa'idahs-dr-ayman-al-%E1%BA%93awahiri-answers-to-the-esteemed-shaykhs/, as of March 2016.

29. A. al-Zawahiri, 'Testimony to Preserve the Blood of the Mujahidin in al-Sham', produced by As-Sahab (May 2014), available at http://jihadology.net/2014/05/02/as-sa%E1%B8%A5ab-media-presents-a-new-release-from-al-qaidahs-dr-ayman-al-%E1%BA%93awahiri-witnessing-the-bloodshed-of-the-mujahidin-in-al-sham/, as of March 2016.

30. Ibid.

31. A. al-Zawahiri, 'The seventh interview' (2014); Zawahiri expanded on these themes further in his series of statements titled 'The Islamic Spring', where he reiterated that 'our vision of what Abu Bakr al-Baghdadi declared is that it is not a caliphate on the method of Prophethood and it doesn't oblige Muslims to pledge their allegiance to it. This vision has nothing to do with our call for all the mujahedeen to stand in one rank in the face of the secular crusaders and Iranian-Alawite campaign.' A. al-Zawahiri, 'The Islamic Spring', Part 3, issued by As-Sahab (21 September 2015), available at http://jihadology.net/2015/09/21/as-sa%E1%B8%A5ab-media-presents-a-new-video-message-from-dr-ayman-al-%E1%BA%93awahiri-the-islamic-spring-3/, as of March 2016; A. al-Zawahiri, 'The seventh interview' (2014).

32. Ibid.

33. Ibid.

34. Ibid.

35. Hasaan Yusuf, 'A Step Towards Unity of Ranks', in *Resurgence: The Magazine for a Resurgent Muslim Ummah*, issue 1, Subcontinent: As-Sahab Media (2014), p. 19, available at https://archive.org/stream/As-sahaab/As-Sahab_Resurgence_Issue_djvu.txt, as of March 2016.

36. E.g. Shaul Mishal and Maoz Rosenthal, 'Al Qa'ida as a Dune Organization: Toward a Typology of Islamic Terrorist Organizations', *Studies in Conflict and Terrorism* 28:4 (July 2005): 275–93; J. Burke, 'Think Again: Al Qa'ida', *Foreign Policy* no. 142 (May/June 2004): 18–26.

37. ISIL, *Dabiq*, issue 9 (May 2014), p. 6.

38. ISIL, *Dabiq*, issue 6 (December 2014), pp. 17–25, 42–53.

39. ISIL, *Dabiq*, issue 7 (January 2015), p. 25.

40. A. al-Zawahiri, 'The seventh interview' (2014).

41. The *Kharijites* or *Khawarij* were a rebellious group in the first century of Islam (7th century CE), who are considered in mainstream Islam to have been heretical and extreme.

42. Ibid.

43. A. al-Zawahiri, 'Testimony to Preserve the Blood of the Mujahidin in al-Sham' (2014).

44. M. al-Zayyat, *The Road to Al-Qa'ida*, p. 30.

45. A. al-Zawahiri, 'General Guidelines for the Work of a Jihadi', statement issued by As-Sahab (14 September 2013), available at https://archive.org/stream/JihadGuidelines/guidelines_djvu.txt, as of March 2016.

46. Ibid.

47. A. al-Zawahiri, 'Exoneration: A Letter Exonerating the Ummah of the Pen and the Sword from the Unjust Allegation of Feebleness and Weakness', produced by As-Sahab and distributed via Ansar Al Mujahideen forum ansar1.info, since closed (2008).

48. A. al-Zawahiri, 'Realities of the Conflict between Islam and Unbelief', published by As-Sahab (22 December 2006), https://archive.org/details/AsSahab-RealitiesOfTheConflictBetweenIslamAndUnbelief, as of March 2016.

49. A. al-Zawahiri, 'The seventh interview' (2014).

4. FROM 25 JANUARY TO ISLAMIC STATE: TRANSITIONS IN EGYPTIAN JIHADIST NARRATIVES

1. I am grateful to Omar Ashour, Mokhtar Awad and Hisham Hellyer for their comments and suggestions.

2. William McCants, 'Al-Qa'ida's Challenge: The Jihadist's War with Islamist Democrats', *Foreign Policy* (September/October 2011).

3. See Samuel Tadros, *Mapping Egyptian Islamism*, Hudson Institute (2014); Mokhtar Awad and Mostafa Hashem, *Egypt's Escalating Insurgency*, Carnegie (2015); Chuck Fahrer, 'The Geography of Egypt's Islamist Insurgency', *Arab World Geographer*, no. 3 (2001): 160–84; Lawrence Wright, *The Looming Tower: Al-Qa'ida's Road to 9/11*, London: Penguin (2007).

4. Omar Ashour, *The De-Radicalization of Jihadists: Transforming Islamist Movements*, New York: Routledge (2009), p. 103; Paul Kamolnick, 'The Egyptian Islamic Group's Critique of Al-Qaeda's Interpretation of Jihad', *Perspective on Terrorism*, vol. 7, no. 5 (2013).

5. Lawrence Wright, 'The Rebellion Within', *New Yorker* (June 2008).

6. Samuel Tadros, *Mapping Egyptian Islamism*, Hudson Institute (2014), p. 76.

7. See Bruce Hoffman, *The Evolution of the Global Terrorism Threat*, NewYork: Columbia University Press (2011), p. 492.

8. Ali Abdel Aal, 'Jund Ansar Allah, al-Tariq ila al-imarat al-Islamia' (The Soldiers of Ansar Allah: The Road to the Islamic Emirate), *Arab Times*, available at http://www.arabtimes.com/portal/article_display.cfm?Action=&Preview=No&ArticleID=13129

9. See Hossam Tammam, 'Islamists and the Egyptian Revolution', *Egypt Independent*, 8 February 2011, available at http://www.egyptindependent.com/opinion/islamists-and-egyptian-revolution; Jonathan Brown, 'Salafis and Sufis in Egypt', *Carnegie Papers* (December 2011), available at http://carnegieendowment.org/files/salafis_sufis.pdf

10. Al-Zawahiri's series of statements is considered in detail by Donald Holbrook in Chapter 2.

11. http://www.egyptindependent.com/news/jihad-leader-arrested-nasr-city-allegedly-forming-terrorist-cell

12. Major Tariq Abu-al-Azm, 'The Salafi Vanguard for Jihad—Ansar al-Shari'ah', http://www.as-ansar.com/vb/showthread.php?p=562251. Unless stated otherwise, translations from Arabic are the author's. Many of the links for primary material are now broken; all texts referred to have been catalogued by the author.

13. 'Egypt to Aid Syrian Rebels', *Daily News Egypt*, 15 June 2013.

14. 'Founding Statement of the Army of Shari'ah Group', 31 July 2012, www.as-ansar.com/vb/showthread.php?s+e61601e464c2af8493bb, retrieved September 2012.

15. David Kirkpatrick, 'Clashes Kill 49 Egyptians on Uprisings Anniversary', *New York Times*, 25 January 2014.

16. David Kirkpatrick, 'Militant Group in Egypt Vows Loyalty to ISIS', *New York Times*, 10 November 2014.

17. See Mokhtar Awad and Samuel Tadros, 'Bay'a Remorse? Wilayat Sinai and the Nile Valley', *CTC Sentinel* (August 2015), available at https://www.ctc.usma.edu/posts/baya-remorse-wilayat-sinai-and-the-nile-valley

18. Abu Muhammad al-'Adnani, 'Peacefulness is Whose Religion?', released to jihad-

ist forums 31 August 2013. See David Barnett, 'Islamic State of Iraq and the Levant calls on Egyptians to wage "jihad" against army', available at http://www.longwar-journal.org/archives/2013/08/islamic_state_of_ira_6.php

19. See Georges Fahmi, 'The Struggle for Leadership of Egypt's Muslim Brotherhood', Carnegie Endowment, http://carnegie-mec.org/2015/07/14/struggle-for-lead-ership-of-Egypt's-muslim-brotherhood/idbr; Nathan Brown and Michele Dunne, 'Unprecedented Pressures, Uncharted Course for Egypt's Muslim Brotherhood', Carnegie Endowment, http://carnegieendowment.org/2015/07/29/unprece-dented-pressures-uncharted-course-for-egypt-s-muslim-brotherhood/ie2g

20. 'Insight—In Egypt, ex-military men fire up Islamist insurgency', http://uk.reuters.com/article/2015/04/07/uk-egypt-militants-military-insight-idUKKBN0MY1P P20150407

21. A. al-Zawahiri, statement released 12 September 2013, retrieved 30 September 2013 from www.hanein.info/vb/showthread.php?t=678239

22. Posted to ABM's Twitter account, @Ansar_B_Almqds, on 19 July 2014.

23. 'ISIL claim to have beheaded Croatian hostage in Egypt', http://www.telegraph.co.uk/news/worldnews/islamic-state/11798402/Isil-claim-to-have-beheaded-Croatian-hostage-in-Egypt.html

24. 'Three men found beheaded in North Sinai', *Cairo Post*, 29 January 2015.

25. Posted to ABM's Twitter account, @Ansar_B_Almqds, on 9 November 2014.

26. Nelly Lahoud, 'The Province of Sinai: Why Bother with Palestine if you can be Part of the "Islamic State"', *CTC Sentinel*, 19 March 2015, https://www.ctc.usma.edu/posts/the-province-of-sinai-why-bother-with-palestine-if-you-can-be-part-of-the-islamic-state

27. '2 rockets from Sinai hit Israel; Netanyahu blasts UNHRC over vote', http://edi-tion.cnn.com/2015/07/03/middleeast/israel-sinai-rocket-strike/

28. Posted to ABM's Twitter account, @Ansar_B_Almqds, on 9 November 2014.

29. 'Video Documenting the Egyptian—Zionist Alliance Crimes against the People of Sinai', tweeted on 5 December 2014 by 'Wilayah Sinai', @W_SINA55.

30. Ibid.

31. Tweet released 12 January 2015, via user @isis20166.

32. Mokhtar Awad and Samuel Tadros, 'Bay'a Remorse? Wilayat Sinai and the Nile Valley', https://www.ctc.usma.edu/posts/baya-remorse-wilayat-sinai-and-the-nile-valley

5. BEYOND NARRATIVE: HOW AND WHY ISLAMICALLY INSPIRED NARRATIVES OF POLITICAL VIOLENCE RESONATE IN CONTEMPORARY TUNISIA

1. The author wishes to offer special thanks to Simon Staffell and Tobias Borck for their assistance in the drafting of this chapter.

2. For discussion of Tunisian foreign fighter figures see the Soufan Group, 'Foreign

Fighters: An Updated Assessment of the Flow of Foreign Fighters in Syria and Iraq', December 2015, http://soufangroup.com/wp-content/uploads/2015/12/TSG_ForeignFightersUpdate3.pdf, accessed 1 April 2016.

3. For more on the evolution of, and the regime's policy of oppression against, political Islamism in Tunisia, see for example Gilles Kepel, *Jihad: The Trail of Political Islam*, London: IB Tauris (2009); or International Crisis Group, 'Tunisia: Violence and the Salafi Challenge', *Middle East/North Africa Report* 137 (2013).

4. See for example Aaron Zelin, 'New Video Message from the Islamic State: "Message from the Vultures to the Brave in the Islamic Maghrib—Wilayat al-Anbar"', *Jihadology*, 21 January 2016, available at http://jihadology.net/2016/01/21/new-video-message-from-the-islamic-state-message-from-the-vultures-to-the-brave-in-the-islamic-maghrib-wilayat-al-anbar/, accessed 27 January 2016; or Aaron Zelin, 'New Video Message from the Islamic State: "The Countries of the Islamic Maghrib: The New Mardin—Wilayat al-Barakah"', *Jihadology*, 21 January 2016, available at http://jihadology.net/2016/01/21/new-video-message-from-the-islamic-state-the-countries-of-the-islamic-maghrib-the-new-mardin-wilayat-al-barakah/, accessed 27 January 2016.

5. UN Office of the High Commissioner for Human Rights, 'Un groupe d'experts de l'ONU appelle à des mesures urgentes pour arrêter le flux de combattants étrangers de Tunisie' (A group of UN experts calls for urgent measures to stem the flow of foreign fighters from Tunisia), OHCHR Online, 10 July 2015, available at http://www.ohchr.org/FR/NewsEvents/Pages/DisplayNews.aspx?NewsID=16223&LangID=F, accessed 26 January 2016.

6. For example, see Jean-Pierre Filiu, *From Deep State to Islamic State*, Oxford: Oxford University Press, 2015.

7. For example, see Georges Fahmi and Hamza Meddeb, 'Market for Jihad: Radicalisation in Tunisia', Carnegie Middle East Center, 15 October 2015, available at http://carnegie-mec.org/2015/10/15/market-for-jihad-radicalization-in-tunisia/is5l

8. For example, see George Joffe, *Islamist Radicalisation in Europe and the Middle East: Reassessing the Causes of Terrorism*, London: I. B. Tauris (2012), pp. 315–17.

9. For an example of this kind of discourse, see 'After Kasserine, protests break out in 16 governorates', on Nawaat, 22 January 2016, available at https://nawaat.org/portail/2016/01/22/after-kasserine-protests-break-out-in-16-governorates/, accessed 26 January 2016.

10. For an overview of some of the AQ-affiliated battalions operating in Syria that primarily recruit from specific countries, see Aymenn J. Al-Tamimi, 'Muhajireen Battalions in Syria', 13 December 2013, available at http://www.aymennjawad.org/14144/muhajireen-battalions-in-syria, accessed 26 January 2016.

11. For further discussion of the role of Tunisians in international jihadist movements, see Georges Fahmi and Hamza Meddeb, 'Market for Jihad: Radicalization in

Tunisia', Carnegie Middle East Centre, 15 October 2015, available at http://carn-egie-mec.org/2015/10/15/market-for-jihad-radicalization-in-tunisia/ij5l, accessed 24 January 2016.

12. For the apparent pledge of allegiance, see SITE, 'Statement Attributed to Uqba Ibn Nafi Battalion in Tunisia Pledges Allegiance to IS', 19 September 2014, available at https://news.siteintelgroup.com/Jihadist-News/statement-attributed-to-uqba-bin-nafi-battalion-in-tunisia-pledges-support-to-is.html, accessed 27 January 2016. For an example of the group's reaffirmation of its affiliation to AQ and AQIM, see this video including a lengthy excerpt from a speech by AQ leader Ayman Al-Zawahiri: Aaron Zelin, 'New Video Message from Katibat Uqbah Ibn Nafi: "Indeed, God Does Not Like Traitors"', *Jihadology*, 11 November 2015, available at http://jihadology.net/2015/11/11/new-video-message-from-katibat-uqbah-ibn-nafi-indeed-god-does-not-like-traitors/, accessed 27 January 2016.

13. For some discussion of the importance of clandestine criminal networks in Tunisia, see Mehdi Mabrouk, 'Tunisia: the radicalization of religious policy', in G. Joffe, ed., *Islamist Radicalisation in North Africa: Politics and Process*, Abingdon: Routledge (2012), p. 66.

14. UN Office of the High Commissioner for Human Rights, 'Un groupe d'experts de l'ONU appelle à des mesures urgentes pur arrêter le flux de combattants étrang-ers de Tunisie' (A group of UN experts calls for urgent measures to stem the flow of foreign fighters from Tunisia), OHCHR Online, 10 July 2015, available at http://www.ohchr.org/FR/NewsEvents/Pages/DisplayNews.aspx?NewsID=162 23&LangID=F, accessed 26 January 2016.

15. This includes the highly publicised instances of teenage girls from the United Kingdom travelling to Syria and Iraq to join IS. See for example Tom Whitehead, 'Secret cell of British Muslim women encouraging others to join Islamic State exposed', Daily Telegraph, 23 November 2015, available at http://www.telegraph. co.uk/news/worldnews/islamic-state/12012683/Secret-cell-of-British-Muslim-women-encouraging-other-to-join-Isil-exposed.html, accessed 27 January 2016.

16. Bel Trew, 'Deliver your daughters to us, militants tell Libyan city', Times, 5 September 2015, available at http://www.thetimes.co.uk/tto/news/world/mid-dleeast/article4548001.ece, accessed 27 January 2016.

6. AL-QAEDA AND ISLAMIC STATE IN YEMEN: A BATTLE FOR LOCAL AUDIENCES

1. The word 'jihad' means 'striving' for the path of God and can be interpreted in a broad range of ways. In this chapter, it is used to refer to militant jihad.

2. 'Remaining and Expanding', *Dabiq*, issue 5 (November 2014), p. 24.

3. More information about the survey can be found in Elisabeth Kendall, 'The Mobilisation of Yemen's Eastern Tribes: al-Mahrah's Self Organisation Model', in Marie-Christine Heinze, ed., *Building the New Yemen*, London: I. B. Tauris (2016).

4. For a highly readable and well-researched account of al-Qaeda's history in Yemen, see Gregory Johnsen, *The Last Refuge: Yemen, al-Qaʻida, and the Battle for Arabia*, New York: Oneworld (2012).

5. Marc Sageman, *Leaderless Jihad*, Philadelphia: University of Pennsylvania Press (2008).

6. Although President Hadi in 2014 claimed that 70 per cent of AQAP were foreigners, the evidence suggests otherwise. Most of the hundreds killed in a major military crackdown in 2014 were Yemenis, many of them local tribesmen. Menas, *Yemen Focus*, 5: 5 (May 2014): 2.

7. A first basic step is to look for the official al-Malahim or al-Athir insignias and a recognisable concluding on-screen caption, usually 'Qadimun Ya Aqsa' ('O Aqsa, We are Coming', referring to Jerusalem's holiest mosque).

8. For those short of time, an excellent curated site for original primary source materials is jihadology.net, founded and run by Aaron Y. Zelin.

9. Some scholars are starting to recognise this and address the gap. Thomas Hegghammer of the Norwegian Defence Institute is currently editing a volume that promises to address a wide range of material largely ignored by analysts to date: Thomas Hegghammer, ed., *Jihadi Culture: The Art and Social Practices of Militant Islamists*, Cambridge: Cambridge University Press (forthcoming).

10. For more detail on this result, see Elisabeth Kendall, 'Yemen's al-Qaʻida and Poetry as a Weapon of Jihad', in Elisabeth Kendall and Ewan Stein, eds, *Twenty-First Century Jihad*, London: I. B. Tauris (2015), pp. 247–69, 251–3.

11. *Madad*, 1 (September 2011), p. 4.

12. *Madad*, 8 (December 2011), p. 1.

13. *Madad*, 10 (February 2012), p. 1.

14. For more detail on AQAP's brief attempt at Islamic rule, see Robin Simcox, 'Governance in Southern Yemen', Hudson Institute, 27 December 2012, available at http://www.hudson.org/research/9779-ansar-al-shari'ah-and-governance-in-southern yemen#

15. Abu al-Ḥasnaʼ al-Abyani, 'Limadha Ikhtarna al-Qaʻidah' (Why We Chose al-Qaeda), Part 1 (al-Hikma, 2015), http://justpaste.it/m5fi. Al-Hikma media was founded mid-2015 to replace al-Husam media, whose chief was allegedly discovered to be collaborating with Saudi intelligence.

16. *Madad*, 2 (October 2011), p. 2.

17. *Madad* News Agency, "Ayn ʻAla al-Hadath" (uploaded to YouTube 6 November 2011), https://www.youtube.com/watch?v=cSmH6YPBRcI

18. Note, for example, the IS Health Service video released on 24 April 2015; or videos of IS mujahidin repairing infrastructure around Palmyra in June 2015.

19. 'In the Words of the Enemy', *Dabiq*, issue 10 (June/July 2015), p. 67.

20. 'Jalal Balʻidi Yuʼlinu ʻan Taʼsis 'Daʻish' bi-Iftitah Muʻaskar Tadrib fi Sahraʼ Hadramawt Qurba al-Hudud al-Saʻudiyya' (Jalal Balʻidi Announces the Foundation of 'Daʻish'

with the Opening of a Military Training Camp in the Desert of Hadramawt close to the Saudi Border), al-Masdar Online, 27 June 2015, http://almasdaronline. com/article/72987

21. Al-Athir Media Agency—Hadramawt, 'Jawanib Min Taghtiyat Multaqa Qadimun Ya Aqsa bi-Madinat al-Mukalla' (Aspects of the Coverage of the 'O Aqsa, We are Coming' Gathering in al-Mukalla), 9 March 2016, https://justpaste.it/ AqsaComing

22. 'Qa'idat al-Jihad fi Jazirat al-'Arab Yudashshin (sic) Mawqi' Wikalat al-Athir al-Akhbariyya' (AQAP Inaugurates the Website of al-Athir News Agency), al-Masra, 3 (31 January 2016), p. 1.

23. Hasan Ba-Muhsin, 'Kayfa Tabdu Manatiq Saytarat Ansar al-Shari'ah Muqaranat-an bi-Baqi al-Mudun al-Yamaniyya?' (How Do Areas under Ansar al-Shari'ah Control Compare with the Rest of Yemen's Cities?), al-Masra, 7, 14 March 2016, p. 3.

24. 'al-Qa'ida Tastahdithu Sinama Mutajawwila li-Taghyir Wa'y al-Hadarim' (al-Qa'ida Introduces a Travelling Cinema to Change the Consciousness of Hadramis), Sada al-Mukalla, December 2016, http://www.sadaalmukalla.com/2015/12/blog-post_9.html

25. Abu Maysarah ash-Shami, 'The Qa'idah of Adh-Dhawahiri, al-Harari, and an-Nadhari', Dabiq, issue 6 (December 2014/January 2015), p. 18.

26. Elisabeth Kendall, 'Yemen's al-Qa'ida and Poetry as a Weapon of Jihad', in Elisabeth Kendall and Ewan Stein, eds, Twenty-First Century Jihad, London: I. B. Tauris (2015), pp. 247–69.

27. For a useful discussion of social media trends in the jihad movement up to 2013, see Aaron Y. Zelin, 'Jihad's Social Media Trend', Foreign Policy, 5 February 2013, http://foreignpolicy.com/2013/02/05/jihads-social-media-trend/

28. The text of the poem can be read here: https://ia902302.us.archive.org/32/items/ aimn.Zawahry.verse/aka.eslam.pdf/ The sung poem can be downloaded here: http://www.mp3searched.net/download/sc/177320426

29. 'Ibn al-Qamish Qad Ghada Maqhur', https://www.youtube.com/watch?v= FWI6FDdXWYQ

30. Yara Bayounmy, 'Al Qa'ida's Second-In-Command Vows to Strike America in New Video', Reuters, 16 April 2014, http://www.businessinsider.com/yara-bayoumy-al-Qa'ida-vows-to-strike-america-in-new-video-2014–4?IR=T

31. 'Wa-Yattakhidhu Min-kum Shuhada' (And He Takes Among You Martyrs), film series, no. 5. This video is now hard to locate, but can be found embedded in this longer flim: https:// www.youtube.com/watch?v=EYUt1W_za-Y&feature= youtube_gdata_player

32. See for example two poems under the title 'Malhamat Tarim' (The Massacre of Tarim), celebrating five young mujahidin killed by local police who stormed their house in Tarim in Hadramawt in August 2008. Sada al-Malahim, 10 (July 2009), pp. 45–6.

33. 'Atiyyat Allah al-Libi, 'Tawjihat fi al-'Amal al-I'lami al-Jihadi' (Guidelines in Jihadist Media Work) (Majmu'at Nukhbat al-Fikr, 2010; again 2015), p. 7, available at https://justpaste.it/klwe

34. A good example of this can be found one minute into 'Wa-Yattakhidhu Min-kum Shuhada': Hani al-Sha'lan' (And He Takes Among You Martyrs: Hani al-Sha'lan), 3 (August 2011?), https://videopress.com/v/7JMxtVEe

35. See, for example, the verses in *Sada al-Malahim*, 13 (April/May 2010), p. 34. These are an extract from an unattributed poem of over 70 verses that was already in circulation.

36. 'Wa-Yattakhidhu Min-kum Shuhada': 'Ali bin al-Aqra' al-Kazimi' (And He Takes Among You Martyrs: 'Ali bin al-Aqra' al-Kazimi), 7 (July 2015), https://www. youtube.com/watch?v=rduyrtN7ihM&feature=youtube

37. AQAP's Sa'id al-Shihri (d. 2013 in a drone strike) warned of a Houthi—US alliance in a video from February 2011 and in an audio message entitled 'And do not incline toward those who do wrong' (March 2012), extracts of which also featured in *Madad*, 12 (March 2012), p. 2. AQAP's current leader, Qasim al-Raymi, spoke about a 'Houthi—American alliance' facilitated by the UN, in an audio message in November 2014.

38. Jalal Bal'idi al-Marqashi (d. 2016 in a drone strike), for example, continued to claim a Houthi—US alliance in a video released by al-Malahim media in August 2015: 'Mujaz 'an 'Amaliyyat al-Mujahidin fi Jazirat al-'Arab' (Summary of Operations by the Mujahidin on the Arabian Peninsula), https://ia902307.us. archive.org/30/items/mojz_y/1435.mp4

39. Alleged US support for the Houthis made headlines in AQAP's newspaper in late March, 'Darabat al-Ta'irat al-Amrikiyya ... Tawatu' 'Ala Ahl al-Sunna fi al-Yaman wa-Da'm li-l-Tamarrud al-Huthi' (American Airstrikes ... Collusion Against Sunnis in Yemen and Support for the Houthi Rebellion), *al-Masra*, 8 (26 March 2016), p. 1.

40. Daniel L. Byman, 'Comparing Al Qa'ida and ISIS: Different goals, different targets', Brookings Institute, 29 April 2015.

41. *Madad*, 7 (December 2011), p. 1.

42. *Madad*, 9 (February 2012), p. 1.

43. *Madad*, 7 (December 2011), p. 1.

44. *Madad*, 9 (February 2012), p. 2.

45. Abu Maysarah ash-Shami, 'The Qa'idah of Adh-Dhawahiri, al-Harari, and an-Nadhari', *Dabiq*, issue 6 (December 2014/January 2015), p. 19.

46. Ibid., p. 20.

47. See Saud as-Sarhan, 'A House Divided: AQAP, IS, and Intra-Jihadi Conflict', King Faisal Center for Research and Islamic Studies, November 2014, http://rd-kfcris. com/all-commentaries-pdf/Commentaries-1.pdf

48. 'Bayt al-Maqdis fi Misr wa-Mujahidi al-Yaman yubayi'un al-Baghdadi' (Bayt al-

Maqdis in Egypt and Yemen's Mujahidin Swear Allegiance to al-Baghdadi), http://www.alghad.com/articles/835576. The audio file can be found here: https://www.youtube.com/watch?t=72&v=RAau476d1Gc

49. Foreword, *Dabiq*, issue 5 (November 2014), p. 3.

50. Abu Maysarah ash-Shami, op. cit., pp. 18–19.

51. Ibid., p. 23.

52. 'The Keys of Jannah: A Message from Shiekh [*sic*] al-Mujahid Abdullah al-Muhaysini', *Al-Risalah*, 1 (July 2015), p. 14; and Harith bin Ghazi al-Nazari, 'Statement on the Content of Sheikh Abu Bakr al-Baghdadi's Speech', video (21 November 2014).

53. AQAP recorded press conference from December 2014.

54. Untitled video from al-Malahim media, https://www.youtube.com/watch?v=NE4kJgQKV0Y (uploaded September 2009).

55. *Madad*, 13 (March 2012), p. 1.

56. A news release in July 2015 reporting the declaration of an Islamic Wilaya in Hadramawt actually refers to a declaration dated 12 August 2012. See http://yemen-press.com/news33296.html. Other reports date back to May 2013: 'Ansar al-Shari'ah al-Yamaniyya Tu'linu Hadramawt Wilayat-an Islamiyyat-an' (Yemeni Ansar al-Shari'ah Declares Hadramawt an Islamic Province), al-Sakina online, 25 May 2013, http://www.assakina.com/news/news2/25116.html

57. 'Atiyyat Allah al-Libi, op. cit.

58. Wa'il 'Isam, 'Al-Baghdadi Ya'muru bi-Waqf Taswir 'Amaliyyat al-Dhabh fi Isdarat "Da'ish"' (Al-Baghdadi Orders a Stop to the Depiction of Massacre Operations in Da'ish Publications), All4Syria Online, 17 July 215, http://www.all4syria.info/Archive/233218

59. AQAP recorded press conference with Nasr bin 'Ali al-Anisi (December 2014), https://www.youtube.com/watch?v=aNvxarFzey0

60. Al-Malahim media, 'Commentary on the targeting of the Ministry of Defence, Sana'a', video featuring Qasim al-Raymi (December 2013), https://www.youtube.com/watch?v=vPEMmorBhWk

61. The Arabic statement can be read here: https://azelin.files.wordpress.com/2015/03/al-qc481_idah-in-the-arabian-peninsula-22denying-a-relationship-with-the-bombings-of-the-e1b8a5c5abthc4ab-mosques-in-e1b9a3anac48122.pdf

62. 'Soldiers of Terror', *Dabiq*, issue 8 (March/April 2015), p. 19.

63. Ansar al-Shari'ah, Wilayat 'Adan, 'Bayan Nafy al-'Alaqa bi-Hadithat Dar al-Musinnin wa-Maqtal al-Shaykh 'Abd al-Rahman al-'Adani' (Statement Denying the Connection to the Incident at the Old People's Home and the Assassination of Shaykh 'Abd al-Rahman al-'Adani), 5 March 2016.

64. 'al-Qa'idah Tu'linu al-Hawta bi-Muhafazat Lahj Wilayat-an Islamiyyat-an' (Al-Qaeda announces al-Hawta in Lahj Governorate as an Islamic Province), *Aden Observer*, 1 March 2015, http://adenobserver.com/read-news/13548

65. Aimen Dean, cited in Sami Aboudi, 'Insight—In Yemen chaos, Islamic State grows to rival al Qa'ida', Reuters, 30 June 2015, http://uk.reuters.com/article/2015/06/30/uk-yemen-security-islamicstate-insight-idUKKCN0PA1T320150630. This author followed up with Aimen Dean in a public Twitter exchange which attributed the information to a Salafi cleric in Yemen, 26 July 2015.

66. Copies of the 24 February 2015 announcements of the creation of Wilayat Hadramawt, Aden and Lahj can be read on the blog of Aymenn Jawad al-Tamimi, 'Some Evidence for the Islamic State's Presence in Yemen (Part 2)', 3 March 2015, http://www.aymennjawad.org/2015/03/some-evidence-for-the-islamic-state-presence-in-1

67. Muhannad Ghallab (AQAP media strategist, d. 2015 in a drone strike), 'Atba' al-Khilafa fi al-Yaman: Haqa'iq wa-Tasa'ulat' (The Followers of the Islamic State in Yemen: Facts and Questions), 28 February 2015, http://justpaste.it/jo90

68. Ibid. This document freely confesses to defections from AQAP to IS, so it is unlikely that the statement about IS's lack of tribal support is mere AQAP propaganda.

69. Saud al-Sarhan, 'A House Divided: AQAP, IS, and Intra-Jihadi Conflict', King Faisal Center for Research and Islamic Studies, November 2014, http://rd-kfcris.com/all-commentaries-pdf/Commentaries-1.pdf

70. 'Ma'lumat Tuthbitu Tawarrut Hamid al-Ahmar wa-Qiyadat Ukhra fi al-Islah bi-Da'm Tanzim al-Qa'idah' (Intelligence Confirms the Involvement of Hamid al-Ahmar and Other Islah Leaders in Supporting al-Qaeda), *Lahj News*, 28 May 2012, http://www.lahjnews.net/news/news-20958.htm

71. In the first half of 2015 alone, drone strikes have killed the following prominent AQAP figures, alongside numerous less prominent ones: Abu Anas al-Libi, Harith bin Ghazi al-Nazari, Ibrahim al-Rubaysh, Abu Hafs al-Misri (Muhannad Ghallab), Ma'mum Hatim, Nasr bin 'Ali al-Anisi (often incorrectly transliterated as al-Ansi, which is a different tribe), Nasir al-Wuhyashi (overall leader of AQAP) and Abu Hajir al-Hadrami.

72. Muhannad Ghallab, op. cit.

73. Hidaya Media Foundation, 'Shahadat 'Antar al-Kindi, Amir Ihda Majmu'at al-Baghdadi—Far' al-Yaman—Sabiq-an' (Testimony of 'Antar al-Kindi, Former Commander of One of al-Baghdadi's Groups—Yemen Branch), https://archive.org/details/CertIFfic. Several dozen IS fighters in Yemen are also said to have rebelled against the centrally appointed leader of IS Yemen in December 2015. See Bill Roggio and Thomas Joscelyn, 'More Islamic State Members Reject Governor of Yemen Province', *Long War Journal*, 28 December 2015, http://www.longwarjournal.org/archives/2015/12/more-islamic-state-members-reject-governor-of-yemen-province.php

74. Thomas Hegghammer talking to Karl Morand, 'Studying Jihadi Culture', Middle East Week podcast, 6 May 2015, 17 minutes in.

75. See Elisabeth Kendall, 'The Mobilisation of Yemen's Eastern Tribes: al-Mahrah's Self Organisation Model', in Marie-Christine Heinze (ed.), *Building the New Yemen*, London: I. B. Tauris (2016).

7. INSIDE THE PROPAGANDA MACHINE OF AL-QAEDA IN THE ISLAMIC MAGHREB AND ITS EVOLUTION FOLLOWING THE RISE OF ISLAMIC STATE

1. See for instance Jean-Pierre Filiu, 'Al-Qaeda in the Islamic Maghreb: Algerian Challenge or Global Threat', *Carnegie Papers* 104 (October 2009): 1–10; Filiu, 'The Local and Global Jihad of al-Qaʿida in the Islamic Maghrib', *Middle East Journal* 63:2 (2009): 1–14; Filiu, 'Could Al-Qaeda Turn African in the Sahel?' *Carnegie Papers* 112 (June 2010): 1–10; S. Harmon, 'From GSPC to AQIM: The Evolution of an Algerian Islamist Terrorist Group into an Al-Qaʿida Affiliate', *Concerned African Scholars* (Spring 2010): 12–29; R. R. Larémont, 'Al Qaeda in the Islamic Maghreb: Terrorism and Counterterrorism in the Sahel', *African Security* 4:4 (2011): 242–68; G. A. Smith, 'Al-Qaeda in the Lands of the Islamic Maghreb', *Journal of Strategic Security* 2:2 (2009): 53–72.

2. See also Charlie Winter, 'The Virtual "Caliphate": Understanding Islamic State's Propaganda Strategy', Quilliam Foundation (2015), http://www.quilliamfoundation.org/wp/wp-content/uploads/publications/free/the-virtual-caliphate-understanding-islamic-states-propaganda-strategy.pdf

3. UN Security Council, Letter dated 13 May 2015 from the Chair of the Security Council Committee established pursuant to resolution 1373 (2001) concerning counter-terrorism addressed to the President of the Security Council, S/2015/338.

4. Notable exceptions include V. Bartolucci and S. Corman, 'The Narrative Landscape of al-Qaeda in the Islamic Maghreb', White Paper No. 1401, Arizona State University: Center for Strategic Communication (2014); A. Black, 'AQIM's Expanding Internationalist Agenda', *Combating Terrorism Center Sentinel* 1:5 (2008): 12–14; M. Lynch, 'Al Qaeda's Media Strategies', *National Interest* 83 (2006): 50–56; Manuel R. Torres Soriano, 'The road to media jihad: the propaganda actions of Al Qaeda in the Islamic Maghreb', *Terrorism and Political Violence* 23:1 (2010): 72–88; Torres Soriano, 'The evolution of the discourse of Al-Qaeda in the Islamic Maghreb: themes, countries and individuals', *Mediterranean Politics* 16:2 (2011): 279–98.

5. C. Winter, 'The Virtual "Caliphate"'.

6. 'Discourse' is a contested term. Here it is intended as 'a practice not just of representing the world, but of signifying the world, constituting and constructing the world in meaning'. See N. Fairclough, *Discourse and Social Change*, Cambridge: Polity Press (1992), p. 64.

7. Fairclough, op. cit.; T. A. van Dijk, 'Discourse, Ideology and Context', *Folia Linguistica* 30:1–2 (1992): 11–40.

8. Gilbert Weiss and Ruth Wodak, eds, *Critical Discourse Analysis. Theory and Interdisciplinarity*, London: Palgrave (2003).

9. Stephanie Taylor, 'Locating and Conducting Discourse Analytic Research', in M. Wetherell, S. Taylor and J. Y. Simeon, eds, *Discourse as Data: A Guide for Analysis*, Milton Keynes: Open University Press (2001), pp. 5–48.

10. CSC has developed a database of over 5,000 texts from Islamist extremist groups through the Department of Defense of Human Social Culture Behavior Research Program. Part of the research for this chapter has been made possible thanks to a Fulbright Research Scholar bursary by which the author could spend an academic year at CSC. I am very grateful to Professor Steve Corman for his advice on my research and for his support.

11. *JihadismAnalyzer*, developed by Stefano Pollio (2014).

12. This is largely motivated by the fact that after several months of 'silence', AQIM has attempted to find new ways to stay relevant in the jihadist environment by moving the core of its communication strategy to its Twitter account, in response to the growing global influence of the IS.

13. The choice to restrict the analysis to the materials available on the web is motivated by the fact that the internet is the main channel to propagate extremist violent discourses, even though it is not the only one. On the contrary, for the fact that violent jihadist communication targets multiple audiences (including Muslims in prevalently Muslim lands, diaspora communities, new converts) and thus is also multi-lingual, other channels are also used, in particular the radio, TV, local mail and, crucially, word of mouth. Despite this, the internet remains one of the principal tools to recruit for VEOs. See Rita Katz, *Terrorist Hunter: The Extraordinary Story of a Woman Who Went Undercover to Infiltrate the Radical Islamic Groups Operating in America*, New York: HarperCollins (2003). The choice of *Dabiq* is motivated by the fact that it is one of IS's key official media outlets and can arguably be seen as its most sophisticated attempt to recruit supporters worldwide.

14. These images have been selected as representative of the main trends which could be found in the visual propaganda of IS. The analysis was restricted to 152 images when it was found that other images did not add substantively to the analysis.

15. Shahira Fahmi, 'Visual Framing in the Islamic State', NATO Report (2015).

16. This section is largely based on a paper I co-authored with Steve R. Corman, 'The Narrative Landscape of al-Qaeda in the Islamic Maghreb', op. cit.

17. Teun A. van Dijk, 'War Rhetoric of a Little Ally', *Journal of Language and Politics* 4:1 (2005): 65 91.

18. Ruth Wodak, 'Language and Politics', in J. Culpeper, F. Katamba, P. Kerswill, R. Wodak and T. McEney, eds, *English Language: Description, Variation and Context*, New York: Palgrave, (2009), p. 302.

19. R. Wodak, R. de Cillia, M. Reisigl and K. Liebhart, *The Discursive Construction of National Identity*, Edinburgh: Edinburgh University Press (2009).

20. Sam Keen, *Faces of the Enemy—Reflections of the Hostile Imagination*, San Francisco, CA: Harper & Row (1986).

21. The majority of Muslim jurists consider dogs to be ritually unclean; see 'Dogs in the Islamic Tradition and Nature', *Encyclopedia of Religion and Nature*, New York: Continuum International (2004).

22. Van Dijk, 'War Rhetoric of a Little Ally'.

23. Roger Fowler, *Language in the News: Discourse and ideology in the press*, New York: Routledge (1991).

24. Paul Wolf, 'The Rhetoric of Terrorism', Leeds: University of Leeds Papers (2003).

25. See also Z. Laub and J. Masters, 'Al Qaeda in the Islamic Maghreb (AQIM)', Council on Foreign Relations (2015).

26. Caleb Weiss, 'AQIM commander threatens France in audio statement', *Long War Journal*, 24 December 2015.

27. Data available on the SITE Intelligence Group at www.siteintelgroup.com

28. Twitter @MEMRIReports, 8 December 2015.

29. Data available on the SITE Intelligence Group at www.siteintelgroup.com

30. See also Hamid Yess, 'Al-Qaeda in the Islamic Maghreb backs ISIS', *Al Monitor*, 2 July 2014.

31. See also Thomas Joscelyn, 'Al Qaeda in the Islamic Maghreb calls for reconciliation between jihadist groups', *Long War Journal*, 2 July 2014, http://www.longwarjournal.org/archives/2014/07/al_qaeda_in_the_isla.php

32. See also T. Joscelyn, 'AQIM Rejects Islamic State's Caliphate, Reaffirms Allegiance to Zawahiri', *Long War Journal*, 14 July 2014, http://www.longwarjournal.org/archives/2014/07/aqim_rejects_islamic.php

33. See also African Armed Forces, 'ISIS Divides Maghreb al-Qaeda (AQIM)', AAF Online, 19 August 2014, http://www.aafonline.co.za/news/isis-divides-maghreb-al-qaeda-aqim

34. The choice of *Dabiq* is motivated by the fact that 'Dabiq is—chronologically, technologically, and ideologically—the most recent and very well elaborated attempt of the Islamic State at winning support among the broadest public possible on a global level.' Christoph Gunther, 'Presenting the Glossy Look of Warfare in Cyberspace—The Islamic State's Magazine *Dabiq*', *CyberOrient* 9:1 (2015).

35. *Dabiq*, 'The return of Khilafah', issue 1, p. 3.

36. Figure 7.2: *Dabiq*, 'The Flood', issue 2, front cover.

37. *Dabiq*, 'From the Battle of Al-Ahzab to the War of Coalitions', issue 11, p. 22.

38. It is worth mentioning that even the name *Dabiq* as the title of the IS glossy magazine has a symbolic meaning which is in line with the theme of apocalyptic utopianism. Dabiq is in fact a small town in northern Aleppo in Syria, where, according to a well-known hadith, Muslims and 'Rome', representing the entire West, will clash in a definitive battle before the apocalypse.

8. BOKO HARAM AND ISLAMIC STATE

1. See for instance Emenike Ezedani, *Boko Haram. Chibok girls and all matters Nigeria security*, Amazon Kindle (2015).

2. Virginia Comolli, *Boko Haram: Nigeria's Islamist Insurgency*, London: Hurst & Co. (2015), pp. 38–42.

3. It is to be noted that the name 'Boko Haram' was given to the group by locals in Maiduguri by the media. Members of the group prefer the full name Jama'atu Ahlis Sunnah Lidda'awati w'al Jihad (People Committed to the Propagation of the Prophet's Teachings and Jihad): Abubakar Shekau, quoted in 'Nigeria: More Than 170 Perished in Kano Bomb Blasts', SaharaReporters.com, 22 January 2012.

4. For more detail on different explanations of the group's origin, see Comolli, *Boko Haram: Nigeria's Islamist Insurgency*, pp. 45–51.

5. Hussein Solomon, *Terrorism and Counter-terrorism in Africa. Fighing insurgency from Al Shabaab, Ansari Dine and Boko Haram*, Basingstoke: Palgrave Macmillan (2015), p. 90.

6. Freedom C. Onuoha, *Boko Haram: Nigeria's Extremist Islamic Sect*, Al Jazeera Centre for Studies, 29 February 2012.

7. Roel Meijer, ed., *Global Salafism: Islam's New Religious Movement*, New York: Columbia University Press (2009), p. 4.

8. Shaykh Muhammad Yusuf, 'Tarihin Musulmai' (History of Muslims), YouTube video, undated (estimated 2009).

9. Comolli, *Boko Haram: Nigeria's Islamist Insurgency*, pp. 96–8.

10. Mark Tran, 'Nigeria attack: Islamist militants claim responsibility for UN building blast', *Guardian*, 26 August 2011; Andrew Walker, 'Join us or die: the birth of Boko Haram', *Guardian*, 4 February 2016.

11. Jide Ajani, 'Nigeria: Trial of Mohammed Ashafa—the Making of Another Mohammed Yusuf, Boko Haram Leader', *Vanguard*, 11 March 2012.

12. Marc-Antoine Pérouse de Montclos, 'Boko Haram and politics: From insurgency to terrorism', in Marc-Antoine Pérouse de Montclos, ed., *Boko Haram: Islamism, politics, security and the state in Nigeria*, Leiden: African Studies Centre (2014), p. 140.

13. Comolli, *Boko Haram: Nigeria's Islamist Insurgency*, pp. 100–1; Abu Qaqa quoted in Monica Mark, 'Boko Haram vows to fight until Nigeria establishes shari'ah law', *Guardian*, 27 January 2012.

14. Raffaello Pantucci and Sasha Jesperson, 'From Boko Haram to Ansaru, The Evolution of Nigerian Jihad', RUSI Occasional Paper (April 2015), p. 28.

15. Comolli, *Boko Haram: Nigeria's Islamist Insurgency*, pp. 65–7; Jacob Zenn, Atta Barkindo and Nicholas Heras, 'The Ideological Evolution of Boko Haram in Nigeria', *RUSI Journal* 158:4 (2013).

16. Mark Doyle, 'Mali Islamists warned about Shari'ah in al-Qa'ida "manifesto"', BBC News, 26 February 2013.

17. Comolli, *Boko Haram: Nigeria's Islamist Insurgency*, p. 104.

18. See for instance 'Nigerian sect leader praises al Qa'ida, warns US', Reuters, 13 July 2010; Bill Roggio, 'Boko Haram emir praises al Qa'ida', *Long War Journal*, 30 November 2012.

19. Adepegba Adelani, Fidelis Soriwei and Umar Muhammed, 'Nigeria—Boko Haram Declares Caliphate in Gwoza', *Punch*, 25 August 2014; 'Sunni Rebels Declare New Islamic Caliphate', Al Jazeera, 30 June 2014.

20. P. J. W. and G. D., 'Daily Chart: Boko Haram's Rise', *Economist*, 11 September 2014; Suranjan Weeraratne, 'Theorizing the Expansion of the Boko Haram Insurgency in Nigeria', *Terrorism and Political Violence* (19 March 2015), p. 8.

21. 'Nigeria's Jihadists: The Other Caliphate', *Economist*, 6 September 2014; 'Special Report: North-east Nigeria on the Brink', *NSN*, 2 September 2014; Jack Moore, 'Boko Haram Receives Strategic Advice from ISIS as Caliphate Dream Grows', *International Business Times*, 9 September 2014.

22. Omar Mahmood, 'Nigeria: Boko Haram's Gwoza "Caliphate" Demonstrates Group's Increasing Power', *African Arguments*, 10 September 2014.

23. Michael Olugbode, 'Nigeria: 25 Towns Under the Control of Boko Haram—Catholic Church', *This Day*, 18 September 2014.

24. Madeline Grant, 'Boko Haram Seek to Imitate "Inspirational" Islamic State and Establish African Caliphate', *Newsweek*, 11 September 2014.

25. Michael Nwankpa, *Boko Haram: Whose Islamic State?* Houston, TX: James A. Baker III Institute for Public Policy, Rice University (May 2015), p. 4.

26. 'Analysts: Boko Haram's Bid to Join ISIS Could Internationalise Nigeria's Conflict', *This Day Live*, 10 March 2015.

27. Nathaniel Allen, 'The Islamic State, Boko Haram and the Evolution of International Jihad', *Washington Post*, 27 March 2015.

28. Heather Saul, 'Yazidi Sex Slaves Reveal Isis Militants Picked Who to Rape in Twisted "Lottery" in Distressing Accounts', *Independent*, 15 April 2015; Ariel I. Ahram, 'Sexual Violence and the Making of ISIS', *Survival* 57:3 (2015), pp. 50, 67–8; Adam Nossiter, 'Boko Haram Militants Raped Hundreds of Female Captives in Nigeria', *International New York Times*, 18 May 2015.

29. Nathaniel Allen, 'The Islamic State, Boko Haram and the Evolution of International Jihad'.

30. Simon Tisdall, 'Boko Haram—Isis Alliance is Nothing but Superficial Propaganda', *Guardian*, 8 March 2015; 'Is Islamic State Shaping Boko Haram Media?' BBC News, 4 March 2015.

31. 'Is Islamic State Shaping Boko Haram Media?', BBC News, 4 March 2015.

32. Hilary Matfess, 'How the ISIS—Boko Haram Alliance Will Alter Nigeria's Future', *Defense One*, 13 March 2015. In February 2015, for example, Boko Haram released a video showing militants' violence in Baga: a high-definition production with advanced graphics, audio effects and gratuitous brutality that reflects the style of

ISIS media propaganda. Tim Lister, 'Boko Haram + ISIS = Marriage from Hell', CNN, 25 February 2015.

33. For example, Boko Haram named a recent video series *Message from a Mujahid*, taking this title directly from an ISIS production, 'Is Islamic State Shaping Boko Haram Media?'

34. Heather Saul, 'Boko Haram Beheading Video Suggests Group is "Incorporating Itself into Islamic State" with "ISIS-Like" Production Techniques', *Independent*, 3 March 2015.

35. Examples of earlier execution videos can be found at Johnlee Varghese, 'Boko Haram Beheads Nigerian Air Force Office VIDEO', *International Business Times*, 25 July 2014; 'Boko Haram Beheads Christian Man—Very Graphic Video', *Nigeria News*, 28 January 2012.

36. Rukmini Callimachi, 'Boko Haram Generates Uncertainty with Pledge of Allegiance to Islamic State', *New York Times*, 7 March 2015.

37. 'Is Islamic State Shaping Boko Haram Media?'

38. Tim Lister, 'Boko Haram + ISIS = Marriage from Hell'; Lauren Ploch Blanchard, *Nigeria's 2015 Elections and the Boko Haram Crisis*, Washington, DC: Congressional Research Service (2015); Weeraratne, 'Theorizing the Expansion of the Boko Haram Insurgency in Nigeria', pp. 8–9.

39. Ruhi Khan, 'First Boko Haram Video Appears Under Wilayat West Africa Logo', *Terrorism Research and Analysis Consortium (TRAC)*, 2 June 2015, http://www.trackingterrorism.org/chatter/first-boko-haram-video-appears-under-wilayat-west-africa-logo

40. Ludovica Iaccino, 'Nigeria: Boko Haram changes name to Islamic State's West African Province after Isis alliance', *International Business Times*, 28 April 2015. Despite marked improvements, the quality of Boko Haram's media outputs lags behind that of the ISIS media package and it is clear that the same level of professionalism is yet to be achieved by the Nigerians, as indicated by spelling mistakes and delays in the release of videos. For example, a video featuring Shekau giving a speech in Arabic appeared online on 9 February but was not distributed via the new Twitter feed, indicating a lack of coordination between Boko Haram's media operatives. There were a number of spelling errors in the video's Arabic-language credits, including the name of the group itself and its new media group al-Urwah al-Wuthqa, and the overall quality of the footage was poorer than that of videos released via Twitter. Moreover, the release of propaganda videos has been affected by delays, indicating a lack of professionalism. For example, a Boko Haram-produced film titled *Ubat al-Daym* (Refusers of Justice) was only released after a fortnight's delay. 'Is Islamic State Shaping Boko Haram Media?' BBC News, 4 March 2015.

41. Tisdall, 'Boko Haram—Isis Alliance is Nothing but Superficial Propaganda'.

42. Ely Karmon, 'Islamic State and al-Qa'ida Competing for Hearts and Minds', *Perspectives on Terrorism* 9:2 (2015), p. 75.

43. 'ISIL Accepts Boko Haram's Pledge of Allegiance', Al Jazeera, 12 March 2015; Weeraratne, 'Theorizing the Expansion of the Boko Haram Insurgency in Nigeria', p. 14.

44. Karmon, 'Islamic State and al-Qa'ida Competing for Hearts and Minds', p. 75.

45. Adam Chandler, 'The Islamic State of Boko Haram?' *The Atlantic*, 9 March 2015.

46. See, for example, Karmon, 'Islamic State and al-Qa'ida Competing for Hearts and Minds', p. 75; and Chandler, 'The Islamic State of Boko Haram?'

47. Martin Ewi, 'What does the Boko Haram—ISIS Alliance Mean for Terrorism in Africa?' Institute for Security Studies, 17 March 2015.

48. Tomi Oladipo, 'Islamic State Strengthens Ties with Boko Haram', BBC News, 24 April 2015.

49. Ludovica Iaccino, 'Chad: 27 killed in suspected Boko Haram twin attacks on N'Djamena police', *International Business Times*, 15 June 2015; 'Nigeria's Boko Haram crisis: Eid prayer blasts hit Damaturu', BBC News, 17 July 2015.

50. Virginia Comolli, 'The regional problem of Boko Haram', *Survival* 5:4 (2015): 109–17.

51. 'Islamic State's 35 Global Affiliates Interactive World Map', *IntelCenter*, 19 May 2015.

52. Tisdall, 'Boko Haram—Isis Alliance is Nothing but Superficial Propaganda'; John Campbell, 'Nigeria's Boko Haram Moving Towards ISIS?' Council on Foreign Relations, 11 March 2015.

53. Thomas D., Williams, 'Boko Haram appeals to Somali al-Shabaab terrorists to join ISIS', Breitbart, 15 October 2015.

54. 'Security: Fall of Darul Hikma and the Rise of Islamic State West African Province', *Nigeria and Boko Haram Tracker*, 4 May 2015.

55. Comolli, 'Boko Haram: Nigeria's Islamist Insurgency', pp. 162–3.

56. For more on the subject, see Virginia Comolli and Kate Robertson, 'Boko Haram (ISWAP) and ISIS: two of a kind?' Terrorism Research and Analysis Consortium (TRAC), July 2015, http://www.trackingterrorism.org/article/boko-haram-iswap-and-isis-two-kind

57. 'Islamic State Take on Charles Darwin Banning Evolution from Curriculum in Iraq', *Huffington Post*, 16 September 2014; Simon Speakma Cordall, 'How ISIS Governs its Caliphate, *Newsweek*, 2 December 2014.

58. James Bwala, 'No Boko Haram Emir in Gwoza, Damboa—Locals Say Over 400 Insurgents Killed in Separate Attacks in Konduga, Ngamdu', *Nigerian Tribune*, 18 September 2014; 'Nigerian Army Repels Boko Haram, Kills Hundreds of Militants in Konduga', Sahara Reporters, 17 September 2014; 'Chad Troops Seize Nigerian Town of Dikwa from Boko Haram', Reuters, 2 March 2015.

59. Jack Moore, 'Boko Haram Receives Strategic Advice from ISIS as Caliphate Dream Grows', *International Business Times*, 19 September 2014; 'Boko Haram has Taken Over Most Parts of Borno—SSG', Sahara Reporters, 8 September 2014.

60. Iro Dan Fulani, 'Nigerian Troops, Mobile Police Unit Advance Towards Mubi to Flush Out Boko Haram', *Premium Times*, 6 November 2014.

61. Rotimi Akinwumi, Clement Ekong, Mohammed Abubakar, 'Boko Haram Implements Shari'ah in Mubi', *Daily Independent*, 4 November 2014.

62. John Campbell, 'Nigeria's Boko Haram Moving Toward Governance?' Council on Foreign Relations, 7 November 2014.

63. James Fromson and Steven Simon, 'ISIS: The Dubious Paradise of Apocalypse Now', *Survival* 57:3 (2015): 39–40; 'More than 10,000 People Flee Fresh Attacks in Nigeria, Seek Shelter in Cameroon and Niger', *UNHCR*, 2 September 2014; Omar Mahmood, 'Nigeria: Boko Haram's Gwoza "Caliphate" Demonstrates Group's Increasing Power', *African Arguments*, 10 September 2014; 'Special Report: North-east Nigeria on the Brink', *NSN*, 2 September 2014.

64. Comolli and Robertson, 'Boko Haram (ISWAP) and ISIS: two of a kind?'

65. Lauren Ploch Blanchard, *Nigeria's Boko Haram: Frequently Asked Questions*, Washington, DC: Congressional Research Service (2014), p. 3.

66. John Campbell, 'Nigeria's Boko Haram Moving Towards ISIS?' Council on Foreign Relations, 11 March 2015.

67. Meg Wagner, 'ISIS accepts pledge of allegiance from Nigeria's Boko Haram', *Daily News*, 13 March 2015.

9. LOCAL AND GLOBAL JIHADIST NARRATIVES IN AFGHANISTAN: THE IMPACT OF THE DECLINE OF AL-QAEDA AND RISE OF 'ISLAMIC STATE'

1. Alex Strick van Linschoten and Felix Kuehn, *An Enemy We Created: The Myth of the Taliban/Al Qa'ida Merger in Afghanistan, 1970–2010*, London: Hurst & Co. (2012), p. 326.

2. Daniel Byman, *Al Qa'ida, The Islamic State, and the Global Jihadist Movement: What Everyone Needs to Know*, New York: Oxford University Press (2015), p. 22.

3. In the late 1990s, following negotiations with the US, the Taliban offered to put bin Laden on trial inside Afghanistan. The US demanded his extradition to US soil. The Taliban offered to hand him over to a neutral Islamic country for trial. This was rejected by the US administration, with the situation remaining at an impasse until 2001.

4. Bin Laden released two fatwas during this time. In August 1996 he published 'Declaration of War against the Americans Occupying the Land of the Two Holy Places' from Saudi Arabia. It cited America and Israel as the source of all ills, with apostate regimes as their agents. In February 1998 he published his second fatwa, calling for jihad to 'kill the Americans and their allies—civilian and military'.

5. On 7 August 1998 AQ conducted near-simultaneous attacks on the US embassies in Kenya and Tanzania, killing 225 people and injuring over 4,000.

6. Omar's words about bin Laden are quoted in the AQ eulogies released in August 2015 following the Taliban announcement that he had died in 2013.

7. For more detail on the nature of the AQ/Taliban relationship, see Alex Strick van Linschoten and Felix Kuehn, *An Enemy We Created*.

8. For a copy of the full text, see 'Taliban agree to peace talks with US over Afghanistan—full statement', *Guardian*, 18 June 2013, available at http://www.theguardian.com/world/2013/jun/18/Taliban-peace-talks-us-afghanistan-full-text, accessed 25 June 2015.

9. Islamic Emirate of Afghanistan, 'Declaration of the Islamic Emirate about the suspension of dialogue with Americans, office in Qatar and its political activity', March 2012.

10. For the full text, see http://jihadology.net/2011/02/14/new-statement-from-the-islamic-emirate-of-afghanistan-response-regarding-the-victory-of-the-popular-uprising-in-egypt/, accessed 21 June 2015.

11. Ibid.

12. For further reading on the bandwagon effect and insurgent groups, see Daniel Byman, Peter Chalk, Bruce Hoffman, William Rosenau and David Brannan, 'Trends in Outside Support for Insurgent Movements', RAND Monograph (2001); Steven Metz and Raymond Millen, 'Insurgency and Counterinsurgency in the 21st century: Reconceptualising Threat and Response', Strategic Studies Institute Report (November 2004).

13. For the full interview, see 'Taliban Spokesman on Girls' Education, Al Qa'ida and Angelina Jolie', *Asharq Al Awsat*, 26 December 2013, available at http://www.aawsat.net/2013/12/article55325817, accessed 17 June 2015.

14. Exact figures are hard to find. For more information, see Niloufer Siddiqui, 'Sectarian Violence and Intolerance in Pakistan', Middle East Institute, http://www.mei.edu/content/map/sectarian-violence-and-intolerance-pakistan, accessed 12 August 2015.

15. On 7 September 1974, Pakistan's parliament voted overwhelmingly to declare the Ahmadis as non-Muslim through what is known as the Second Amendment. The amended text stated: 'A person who does not believe in the absolute and unqualified finality of The Prophethood of Muhammad (Peace be upon him), the last of the Prophets or claims to be a Prophet, in any sense of the word or of any description whatsoever, after Muhammad (Peace be upon him), or recognizes such a claimant as a Prophet or religious reformer, is not a Muslim for the purposes of the Constitution or law.' The Ahmadis do not believe that Mohammed was the final prophet sent to guide mankind, meaning that they are defined as non-Muslims by this amendment.

16. David Kilcullen, *Blood Year: Islamic State and the Failures of the War on Terrorism*, London: Hurst & Co. (2016), p. 181.

17. Ibid., p. 183.

18. Bill Roggio estimates the group is 1,000 strong, in 'State Department Lists Islamic State's "Khorasan Province" as Foreign Terrorist Organisation', *Long War Journal*, 14 January 2016, http://www.longwarjournal.org/archives/2016/01/state-department-lists-islamic-states-khorasan-province-as-foreign-terrorist-organization.php, accessed 6 April 2016. In *Blood Year*, Kilcullen describes '4,200 fighters in Nangarhar alone'.

19. See 'Islamic Emirate Leadership Council's Letter to Respectable Abdu Bakr al Baghdadi', released via *Voice of Jihad*, the Taliban's official propaganda website on 16 June 2015.

20. See ANF Twitter announcement entitled 'Statement Offering Condolences for the Death of Mullah Muhammad Omar Mujahid—May Allah have Mercy on Him'.

21. The eulogy, entitled, 'Steadfastness in the Time of Humiliation', was posted on the Deep Web jihadist forums Shumukh al-Islam and al-Fida' on 13 August 2015.

22. The eulogy, entitled 'Steadfastness in the Time of Humiliation. Condolences to the Islamic Ummah for the Death of the Emir of the Believes Mullah Muhammad Omar—May Allah have Mercy on Him', was posted on the Deep Web jihadist forums Shumukh al-Islam and al-Fida' on 13 August 2015.

23. Ayman al-Zawahiri statement, 'A Biography of Faithfulness', issued on 13 August 2015.

24. For more on this, see Jason Burke, *The New Threat from Islamic Militancy*, London: Penguin (2015), p. 102.

25. For more on this, see Alex Strick van Linschoten and Felix Kuehn, *An Enemy We Created*.

10. IN THE SHADOW OF THE ISLAMIC STATE: SHI'I RESPONSES TO SUNNI JIHADIST NARRATIVES IN A TURBULENT MIDDLE EAST

1. Shi'i Islam is divided into several different groups: (1) Twelver or Imami Shi'is, so-called because they believe in a line of twelve divinely guided leaders, the Imams; (2) Isma'ili Shi'is, who believe in the same line of Imams as the Twelvers up until the sixth, Ja'far al-Sadiq, who died in the eighth century C.E.; and (3) Zaydi Shi'is, whose beliefs and scholarly tradition lay between Sunni and Shi'i Islam. Unless otherwise noted, 'Shi'i' will be used throughout this chapter to denote Twelver Shi'is, the largest group of Shi'i Muslims.

2. Khamenei even delivered part of his Friday sermon (*khutba*) on 4 February 2011 at Tehran University (long a major political showcase for the Iranian state to broadcast its official religio-political positions) in Arabic in a transparent effort to win more supporters in the Arab world. Henner Fürtig, *Iran and the Arab Spring: Between Expectations and Dillusion*, working paper no. 241, German Institute of Global and Areas Studies, November 2013; Robert F. Worth, 'Effort to Rebrand

Arab Spring Backfires in Iran', *New York Times*, http://www.nytimes.com/2012/02/03/world/middleeast/effort-to-rebrand-arab-spring-backfires-in-iran.html?_r=0, accessed 2 February 2012; and Margaret Basheer, 'Hezbollah Supportive of Egyptian, Tunisian Uprisings, but not Syria's', *Voice of America*, http://www.voanews.com/content/hezbollah-supportive-of-egyptian-tunisian-uprisings-but-not-syrias-122348949/172965.html, accessed 19 May 2011.

3. See, for example, the following studies on sectarian identities, their creation, reification and use: Ussama Makdisi's seminal study on the political and social utilisation of sectarianism in Ottoman Lebanon, *The Culture of Sectarianism: Community, History, and Violence in Nineteenth Century Ottoman Lebanon*, Berkeley, CA: University of California Press (2000); Marc Lynch, 'The War for the Arab World', *Foreign Policy*, http://www.foreignpolicy.com/articles/2013/05/23/war_for_the_arab_world_sunni_shia_hatred?page=0,0, accessed 23 May 2013; Geneive Abdo, *The New Sectarianism: The Arab Uprisings and the Rebirth of the Shi'a-Sunni Divide*, analysis paper 29, Saban Center for Middle East Policy at Brookings (2013), http://www.brookings.edu/~/media/research/files/papers/2013/04/sunni%20shia%20abdo/sunni%20shia%20abdo.pdf, accessed 23 May 2015; and Mariz Tadros, 'Sectarianism and its Discontents in Post-Mubarak Egypt', *Middle East Report* (Summer 2011), http://www.merip.org/mer/mer259/sectarianism-its-discontents-post-mubarak-egypt, accessed 15 June 2015.

4. For good overviews of Sunni—Shi'i relations historically, see Ofra Bengio and Meir Litvak, eds, *The Sunna and Shi'a in History: Division and Ecumenism in the Muslim Middle East*, New York: Palgrave Macmillan (2011); and Brigitte Maréchal and Sami Zemni, eds, *The Dynamics of Sunni—Shia Relationships: Doctrine, Transnationalism, Intellectuals and the Media*, London: Hurst & Co. (2013).

5. I draw here on social movement theory literature about the framing process. See Quintan Wiktorowicz, ed., *Islamic Activism: A Social Movement Theory Approach*, Indianapolis: Indiana University Press (2004), pp. 15–19; Erving Goffman, *Frame Analysis: An Essay on the Organization of Experience*, Cambridge, MA: Harvard University Press (1974); David A. Snow, E. Burke Rochford, Jr, Steven K. Worden and Robert D. Benford, 'Frame Alignment Processes, Micromobilization, and Movement Participation', *American Sociological Review* 51:5 (1986): 464–81; David A. Snow and Robert D. Benford, 'Ideology, Frame Resonance, and Participant Mobilization', in Bert Klandermans, Hanspeter Kriesiand Sidney Tarrow, eds, *International Social Movement Research, Vol. 1: From Structure to Action: Comparing Social Movement Research Across Cultures*, London: JAI Press (1988); and Pamela Oliver and Hank Johnston, 'What a Good Idea: Frames and Ideologies in Social Movement Research', *Mobilization* 5:1 (2000): 37–54.

6. Ann Swidler, 'Culture in Action: Symbols and Strategies', *American Sociological Review* 51:2 (1986): 273–86; and Carrie Rosefsky Wickham, 'Interests, Ideas, and Islamist Outreach in Egypt', in Wiktorowicz, ed., *Islamic Activism: A Social Movement Theory Approach*, Indiana: Indiana University Press, (2004).

7. For detailed analysis of the rise of a politicised Egyptian Salafism, see Jonathan Brown, *Salafis and Sufis in Egypt*, occasional paper, Carnegie Endowment for International Peace (December 2011); Jonathan A. C. Brown, 'The Rise and Fall of the Salafi al-Nour Party in Egypt', *Jadaliyya*, http://www.jadaliyya.com/pages/index/15113/the-rise-and-fall-of-the-salafi-al-nour-party-in-e, accessed 14 November 2013; and Jacob Høigilt and Frida Nome, 'Egyptian Salafism in Revolution', *Journal of Islamic Studies* 25: 1 (2014): 333–54.

8. Khalil al-Anani, 'The Salafi-Brotherhood Feud in Egypt', *Al Monitor*, http://www.al-monitor.com/pulse/originals/2013/02/muslim-brotherhood-salafist-feud-in-egypt.html#, accessed 21 February 2013.

9. Maggie Fick, 'Egypt Brotherhood backs Syria Jihad, Denounces Shi'ites', http://www.reuters.com/article/2013/06/14/us-syria-crisis-sunnis-brotherhood-idUS-BRE95D0NL20130614, accessed 14 June 2013.

10. Al-Qaradawi is an *Ikhwan* affiliated religious jurist and one of the world's most influential Sunni religious scholars.

11. 'Top Egypt Cleric Condemns "Sectarian" Foes in Syria', Reuters, http://news.yahoo.com/top-egypt-cleric-condemns-sectarian-foes-syria-151654244.html, accessed 11 June 2013; Lee Keath, 'Hezbollah Entry in Syria Fans Shiite—Sunni Fires', Associated Press, http://bigstory.ap.org/article/hezbollah-entry-syria-fans-shiite-sunni-fires, accessed 7 June 2013; 'Al-Qaradawi Calls Upon the Able-bodied to Fight in Syria' (Arabic), *Qaradwi.net*, http://www.qaradwi.net/component/content/article/6666.html, accessed 1 June 2013; Griff Witte, 'New Wave of Foreigners in Syrian Fight', *Washington Post*, accessed 21 June 2013; and 'Sending of Egyptian Mujahideen to Syria Stirs Debate among Religious Scholars and Jihadi Organizations', *Azzaman*, http://www.azzaman.com/?p=35709, accessed 31 May 2013.

12. David H. Warren, 'The *'Ulamā'* and the Arab Uprisings, 2011–2013: Considering Yusuf al-Qaradawi, the "Global Mufti," between the Muslim Brotherhood, the Islamic Legal Tradition, and Qatari Foreign Policy', *New Middle Eastern Studies* 4 (2014); Frederic M. Wehrey, *Sectarian Politics in the Gulf: From the Iraq War to the Arab Uprisings*, New York: Columbia University Press (2013), ch. 5; CNN Arabic, 'Al-Qaradawi: Bahrain's Sectarian Revolution is Targeting the Sunnis' (Arabic), http://archive.arabic.cnn.com/2011/bahrain.2011/3/19/qaradawi.bahrain/, accessed 7 February 2013; and al-Sharq al-Awsat, 'Al-Qaradawi: What is Happening in Bahrain is not a People's Revolution but a Sectarian Revolution' (Arabic), http://archive.aawsat.com/details.asp?section=4&issueno=11799&article=613210#.VYRZRFPoa24, accessed 19 March 2011.

13. BBC News, 'Egypt Mob Attack Kills Four Shia Muslims near Cairo', http://www.bbc.com/news/world-middle-east-23026865, accessed 24 June 2013; Ahram Online, 'Egyptian anti-Sectarian Group Blames Morsi for Shia Attacks', http://english.ahram.org.eg/NewsContent/1/64/74811/Egypt/Politics-/Egyptian-

antisectarian-group-blames-Morsi-for-Shia.aspx, accessed 24 June 2013; Mada Masr, 'Suspect Arrested in June Shia Lynching', http://www.madamasr.com/news/ suspect-arrested-june-shia-lynching, accessed 20 October 2013; *Daily News Egypt*, 'Lynching of Shi'a in Giza Prompts Uproar', http://www.dailynewsegypt. com/2013/06/25/lynching-of-shia-in-giza-prompts-uproar/, accessed 25 June 2013; Human Rights Watch, 'Egypt: Lynching of Shia Follows Months of Hate Speech', http://www.hrw.org/news/2013/06/27/egypt-lynching-shia-follows-months-hate-speech, accessed 27 June 2013.

14. Al-'Alam, 'Who is Martyr Sheikh Hassan Shehata?' http://en.alalam.ir/ news/1487900, accessed 25 June 2013; and Press TV, 'Takfiri Extremists Kill Top Shia Cleric and 4 Others in Egypt', http://www.presstv.com/detail/2013/06/ 24/310617/prominent-shia-sheikh-killed-in-egypt/, accessed 24 June 2013.

15. For a detailed overview of the Salafi creed, see Bernard Haykel, 'On the Nature of Salafi Thought and Action', in Roel Meijer, ed., *Global Salafism: Islam's New Religious Movement*, New York: Columbia University Press (2009), pp. 33–57; Quintan Wiktorowicz, 'Anatomy of the Salafi Movement', *Studies in Conflict and Terrorism* 29:3 (2006): 207–39; Alexander Knysh, 'Contextualizing the Salafi—Sufi Conflict (from the Northern Caucasus to Hadramawt)', *Middle Eastern Studies* 43:4 (2007): 503–30; Ondrej Beranek and Pavel Tupek, *From Visiting Graves to Their Destruction: The Question of Ziyara through the Eyes of the Salafis*, Crown Paper no. 2, Crown Center for Middle East Studies, Brandeis University (July 2009); Guido Steinberg, 'Jihadi-Salafism and the Shi'is: Remarks about the Intellectual Roots of anti-Shi'ism', in Meijer, ed., *Global Salafism*, pp. 111–16; Bernard Haykel, 'Al-Qa'ida and Shiism', in Assaf Moghadam and Brian Fishman, eds, *Fault Lines in Global Jihad: Organizational, Strategic, and Ideological Fissures*, New York: Routledge (2011), pp. 188–9; and Cole Bunzel, *From Paper State to Caliphate: The Ideology of the Islamic State*, Analysis Paper no. 19, Brookings Project on US Relations with the Islamic World (March 2015), pp. 8–9.

16. Fanar Haddad, 'Sectarian Relations and Sunni Identity in Post-Civil War Iraq', in Lawrence G. Potter, ed., *Sectarian Politics in the Persian Gulf*, London: Hurst & Co. (2013), pp. 67–116; and Thomas Pierret, 'Karbala in the Umayyad Mosque: Sunnite Panic at the 'Shiitization' of Syria in the 2000s', in Maréchal and Zemni, *The Dynamics of Sunni—Shia Relationships*, pp. 99–116.

17. Raphaël Lefèvre, *Ashes of Hama: The Perilous History of Syria's Muslim Brotherhood*, London: Hurst & Co. (2013), chs 4–6; Itzchak Weismann, 'Sa'id Hawwa: The Making of a Radical Muslim Thinker in Modern Syria', *Middle Eastern Studies* 29:4 (2007): 601–23; Itzchak Weismann, 'Sa'id Hawwa and Islamic Revivalism in Ba'thist Syria' *Studia Islamica*, no. 85 (1997), pp. 131–54; Sa'id Hawwa, *Khumayni: Aberrations in Creed, Aberrations in Positions: First Edition* (Arabic), Amman: Dar 'Ammar li-l-Nashr wa al-Tawzi'a (1987); and Steinberg, 'Jihadi-Salafism and the Shi'is', pp. 117–21.

18. Haykel, 'Al-Qa'ida and Shiism', pp. 189–90.

19. Al-Qaeda Central, *Meeting with the Mujahid Shaykh Ayman al-Zawahiri: The Realities of Jihad and the Fallacy of Hypocrisy* (Arabic), film, released August 2009.

20. Ayman al-Zawahiri, 'General Guidelines for Jihadi Action' (Arabic), September 2013.

21. Ibid.

22. Joas Wagemakers, 'Invoking Zarqawi: Abu Muhammad al-Maqdisi's Jihad Deficit', *CTC Sentinel* 2:6 (June 2009), pp. 14–17; Haykel, 'Al-Qa'ida and Shiism', pp. 190–98.

23. For an in-depth discussion of this tension, see Brynjar Lia, 'Jihadis Divided between Strategists and Doctrinarians', in Moghadam and Fishman, eds, *Fault Lines in Global Jihad*, pp. 69–87; and Bryjar Lia, '"Destructive Doctrinarians": Abu Mus'ab al-Suri's Critique of the Salafis in the Jihadi Current', in Meijer, ed., *Global Salafism*, pp. 281–300.

24. AQAP is careful to differentiate between mainstream Zaydis and the Houthi movement, alleging that the Houthis and their supporters have: adopted Twelver Shi'i beliefs and rituals including the cursing of the Prophet Muhammad's companions (*Sahaba*) and wives revered by Sunnis, are proxies of Iran, and are engaged in attacking Yemen's majority Sunnis. See Abu al-Bara' al-San'ani, 'The Houthis, *Rawafid* (Twelver Shi'is)', in Zaydi Masks, *Sada al-Malahim* (e-magazine of al-Qaeda in the Arabian Peninsula, AQAP), issue 12 (Feb. 2010), pp. 20–21; and al-Qaeda in the Arabian Peninsula (AQAP), '*Fatwa* (juridical opinion) of the *Shari'a* Council of Al-Qa'ida in the Arabian Peninsula concerning Fighting the Shi'i Houthis in the South of the Arabian Peninsula' (Arabic), 18 Jan. 2012; Anwar al-'Awlaqi, *You Should Make It Clear to People and Not Conceal It* (Arabic), AQAP film, released Nov. 2010; *Meeting with Commander Jalal Bal'aydi al-Murqashi about the Recent Events of the War with the Houthis in Yemen* (Arabic), AQAP film, Nov. 2014; *Your Victory, O' Sunnis*, part one (Arabic), AQAP film, released March 2011; and Sa'id al-Shihri, *Your Victory, O' Sunnis*, AQAP audio message, released January 2011.

25. Jama'at al-Tawhid wa'l Jihad/Group of Absolute Monotheism and Struggle (2003–4); al-Qaeda in the Land of the Two Rivers (2004–5); the Majlis Shura al-Mujahidin (Mujahidin Consultative Council) umbrella (2006); the Islamic State of Iraq (2006–13); and the Islamic State of Iraq and al-Sham (2013–14).

26. Al-Zarqawi's recorded messages and writings are full of anti-Shi'i rhetoric and are too numerous to list. Representative messages are 'Has the Story of the *Rafida* (Shi'is) Reached You?' 3 parts (June 2006); and a letter he wrote that was intercepted by the US government in Feb. 2004, available in English translation at http://2001–2009.state.gov/p/nea/rls/31694.htm, accessed 20 June 2015. The title of these audio lectures plays off Qur'an 20:9.

27. For detailed background information on the career and role within the Islamic

State of al-Bin'ali, see Cole Bunzel, 'The Caliphate's Scholar-in-Arms', *Jihadica*, http://www.jihadica.com/the-caliphate%E2%80%99s-scholar-in-arms/, accessed 9 July 2014; and Cole Bunzel, 'Bin'ali Leaks: Revelations of the Silent Mufti', *Jihadica*, http://www.jihadica.com/binali-leaks/, accessed 15 July 2015.

28. ISIL also distributes copies of Muhammad ibn 'Abd al-Wahhab's writings in territories it controls as part of its *da'wa* campaign.

29. ISIL's public and media discourse is full of anti-Shi'i invective and polemic, with nearly every media release and public declaration including it. What follows is a small representative sample of these materials. These primary sources have been collected and archived. Because of the constant shift of jihadist websites, Twitter accounts and blogs (most of which are quickly shut down, some for good while other re-open relatively quickly), providing active URLs for these sources is difficult since many if not most of the links will be 'dead' by the time of publication. Islamic State films and audio messages (Arabic): *Holocaust of the Safavids in Wilayat Saladin*, parts 1–5, released March–April 2015; *Liquidation of a Safavid Criminal (safawi mujrim)*, released April 2015; *The Rattling of Sabers*, parts 1–4, released July 2012–May 2014; *Breaking the Borders*, released June 2014; *Assault of the Monotheists against the Dens of the Safavids*, released May 2015; *Upon the Prophetic Methodology*, released July 2014; *Punish Them Severely so That Those Who Follow Disperse Fearfully*, parts 1 and 2, released Aug.-Sept. 2014; Abu Muhammad al-'Adnani, *So They Kill and are Killed*, released March 2015; Abu Muhammad al-'Adnani, *Iraq, Iraq, O' Sunnis*, released Feb. 2012; Wilayat Najd, *Expel the Rafida Polytheists from the Peninsula of the Prophet, peace and prayers be upon him*, released May 2015. Islamic State written publications and statements (Arabic): 'Two Martyrdom-seekers, a German and a Syrian, and Two Car Bombs in Baghdad and Killing Dozens in the Ranks of the Army, Police, and the Volunteers of al-Sistani and the Army of the Antichrist (*Dajjal*)', 19 July 2014; 'Two Martyrdom-seekers from the *Ansar* (Iraqis) in the Heart of Baghdad and Killing and Wounding Nearly 200 Members of the Repressive Government Bodies, the *Rafidi* Mobilization Units, the Army of the Dajjal', 12 Oct. 2014; and 'Revenge for Our People in the Mus'ab ibn 'Umayr Mosque in Diyala: A Martyrdom Operation with an Explosive Belt against a Temple (*ma'bad*) used by the Rejectionist Militias (*al-milishiyyat al-rafidiyya*) in the War on Islam and Its People, Killing More Than 100', 25 Aug. 2014.

30. Al-Zarqawi, 'Has the Story of the *Rafida* Reached You?' parts 1–3; and Abu Anas al-Shami, *The Shi'a* (Arabic), n.p., n.d.

31. Islamic State film, *Destruction of the Idols* (Arabic), released Feb. 2015. Most of these hadith are drawn from the collection of the famous hadith compiler and jurist Ibn Hanbal (d. 855), his *Musnad*; a *musnad* is a hadith collection organised by the name of the Prophetic companion narrating each hadith rather than by topic.

32. Islamic State film, *Although the Unbelievers Dislike It* (Arabic and English), released

Nov. 2014. Sunnis are described as the 'descendants of Abu Bakr and 'Umar', the first two Rashidun caliphs.

33. Ian Black and Dan Roberts, 'Hezbollah is Helping Assad Fight Syria Uprising, says Hassan Nasrallah', *Guardian*, http://www.theguardian.com/world/2013/apr/30/hezbollah-syria-uprising-nasrallah, accessed 30 April 2013; Loveday Morris, 'Hezbollah Chief Defends Group's Involvement in Syrian War', *Washington Post*, http://www.washingtonpost.com/world/middle_east/hezbollah-chief-admits-and-defends-groups-involvement-in-syrian-war/2013/05/25/3748965a-c55e-11e2–9fe2–6ee52d0eb7c1_story.html, accessed 25 May 2013; Reuters, 'Top Egypt Cleric Condemns "Sectarian" Foes in Syria', accessed 11 June 2013; Keath, 'Hezbollah Entry in Syria Fans Shiite-Sunni Fires'; Fick, 'Egypt Brotherhood backs Syria Jihad, Denounces Shi'ites'; and Qaradawi.net, 'Al-Qaradawi Calls Upon the Able-bodied to Fight in Syria' (Arabic).

34. 'El-Qazzaz: Egypt says Citizens Free to Join Fight in Syria', Arab News Agency, http://www.anaonline.net/news/default/view/id/133014/lang/en#.Ucdx0l1CL3C, accessed 14 June 2013; Hamza Hendawi, 'Mursi Pulls Egypt Deeper into Syria Turmoil with Apparent Nod to Jihad', Associated Press, http://www.dailystar.com.lb/News/Middle-East/2013/Jun-18/220718-mursi-pulls-egypt-deeper-into-syria-turmoil-with-apparent-nod-to-jihad.ashx#axzz2X4upLH4G, accessed 18 June 2013; Aya Batrawy, 'Egypt says Citizens Free to Join Fight in Syria', Associated Press, http://news.yahoo.com/egypt-says-citizens-free-join-fight-syria-180118807.html, accessed 13 June 2013; and Matthew Barber, 'Clerics in Egypt Call for Global Jihad against Regime's Shiite Allies, Egypt Cuts Syria Ties', http://www.joshualandis.com/blog/clerics-in-egypt-call-for-global-jihad-against-regimes-shiite-allies/, accessed 17 June 2013.

35. Haykel, 'Al-Qa'ida and Shiism', pp. 186–7.

36. Ibid.

37. Aron Lund, *Syria's Salafi Insurgents: The Rise of the Syrian Islamic Front*, occasional paper no. 17, Swedish Institute of International Affairs, March 2013; and Aaron Y. Zelin and Charles Lister, 'The Crowning of the Syrian Islamic Front', *Foreign Policy*, http://mideast.foreignpolicy.com/posts/2013/06/24/the_crowning_of_the_syrian_islamic_front?wp_login_redirect=0, accessed 24 June 2013.

38. Usama al-Rifa'i, 'The *Shaykh* Usama al-Rifa'i, may God protect him, Implores the Free Syrian Army and Cautions against the Safavid Magian Shi'a (*al-Rawafid al-Safawiyin al-Majus*)' (Arabic), video statement, released 22 May 2013, available at https.//www.youtube.com/watch?v=gBzJg6AyFNQ

39. Usama al-Rifa'i, 'Lecture of Shaykh Usama al-Rifa'i on the Topic of the Realities of the Shi'a on Nov. 11, 2014' (Arabic), lecture, available at https://www.youtube.com/watch?v=78VSiQot9CA

40. Qays al-Kha'azli, 'Speech Commemorating the Tenth Anniversary of the Founding of 'Asa'ib Ahl al-Haqq', (Arabic), 5 May 2013, http://ahlualhaq.com/index.php/

permalink/3322.html. Al-Khaz'ali is the secretary general of 'Asa'ib Ahl al-Haqq, an Iraqi group closely aligned with Iran that fields a powerful paramilitary wing. The group actively targeted US and other coalition forces in Iraq during the occupation of the country and now is one of the main paramilitary groups that make up the Popular Mobilization Units (*al-Hashd al-Sha'bi*), a paramilitary umbrella sanctioned by the Iraqi government.

41. Press TV, 'Nasrallah Defends Hezbollah Fighting Extremists in Syrian Town of Qusayr', http://www.presstv.com/detail/2013/05/25/305392/nasrallah-backs-fighting-syria-extremists/, accessed 25 May 2013.

42. Alison Meuse, 'Syria's Minorities: Caught between Sword of ISIS and Wrath of Assad', National Public Radio, http://www.npr.org/sections/parallels/2015/04/17/400360836/syrias-minorities-caught-between-sword-of-isis-and-wrath-of-assad, accessed 18 April 2015; Ruth Sherlock, 'Syrian Shias Flee to Lebanon to Escape Sunni Militias', *Daily Telegraph*, http://www.telegraph.co.uk/news/world-news/middleeast/syria/10031492/Syrian-Shias-flee-to-Lebanon-to-escape-Sunni-militias.html, accessed 1 May 2013; and Patrick J. McDonnell and Nabih Bulos, 'Syria's Shiites Offer Different Picture of War', *Los Angeles Times*, http://articles.latimes.com/2013/mar/26/world/la-fg-0326-syria-shiites-hezbollah-20130326, accessed 26 March 2013.

43. 'Asa'ib Ahl al-Haqq statement, 'The Islamic Resistance, 'Asa'ib Ahl al-Haqq, Condemns the Heinous Crime against the Shrine of the Prophet's Companion Hujr bin 'Adi, may God bless him, in Syria' (Arabic), 3 May 2013; AhlulBayt News Agency, 'Senior Shia Cleric 'Seyyed Naser al-Alawi Assassinated in Syria', http://www.abna.ir/data.asp?lang=3&Id=308518, accessed 14 April 2013; AhlulBayt News Agency, 'Holy Shrine of Hazrat Holiness Sakina (AS) Damaged by Terrorists in Syria', http://abna.ir/data.asp?lang=3&Id=390320, accessed 12 Feb. 2013; and Associated Press, 'After Threats to Shrine, Iraqi Shiite Fighters Prepare for Sectarian Strife at Home, in Syria', http://www.foxnews.com/world/2012/10/25/after-threats-to-shrine-iraqi-shiite-fighters-prepare-for-sectarian-strife-at/, accessed 25 Oct. 2012.

44. Jafria News, 'Head of Hawza E Zainabia Martyred by Target Killing in Syria', http://jafrianews.com/2012/04/16/head-of-hawza-e-zainabia-martyred-by-target-killing-in-syria/, accessed 16 April 2013; and Council of European Jamaats, 'Desecration of Shrine of Hujr bin 'Adi al-Kindi', http://www.coej.org/secretariat/statements/2639-hujr-bin-adi-al-kindi-statement, accessed 3 May 2013. The last is a statement from the European representative body of Khoja Shi'i Muslims, an affluent and influential sub-group within Twelver Shi'ism.

45. See, for example, threads on a popular English-language Shi'i internet discussion board, ShiaChat, such as 'Terrorists Assassinate a Sayyid in Damascus', http://www.shiachat.com/forum/index.php?/topic/235001124-terrorists-assassinate-a-sayyid-in-damascus/, accessed 20 June 2015; and 'Nawasibs Responding to Their

Loss in Qusair', http://www.shiachat.com/forum/index.php?/topic/235014497-nawasibs-responding-to-their-loss-in-qusair/, accessed 20 June 2015. *Nawasib* (singular: *nasibi*) is a derogatory term used by Shi'is to describe critics of Shi'ism who allegedly hate the Prophet Muhammad's family. The term, which appears in Shi'i juridical discourse, appears today frequently in Shi'i polemics against Salafis and other Sunni groups opposed to Shi'ism.

46. Paulo G. Pinto, 'Pilgrimage, Commodities, and Religious Objectification: The Making of Transnational Shiism between Iran and Syria', *Comparative Studies of South Asia, Africa and the Middle East* 27:1 (2007): 109–25.

47. Edith Szanto Ali-Dib, 'Following Sayyida Zaynab: Twelver Shi'ism in Contemporary Syria' (PhD dissertation, University of Toronto, 2012), pp. 52–3.

48. Pinto, 'Pilgrimage, Commodities, and Religious Objectification'.

49. Edith Szanto, 'Contesting Fragile Saintly Traditions: Miraculous Healing among Twelver Shi'is in Contemporary Syria', in Andreas Bandak and Mikkel Bille, eds, *Politics of Worship in the Contemporary Middle East*, Leiden: Brill (2013), pp. 33–52. There is also a major shrine dedicated to Zaynab in Cairo; built by the Fatimids, it is a popular site among Egyptian Sufis who revere and perform rituals to honor the *Ahl al-Bayt*, the Prophet Muhammad's family. See Nadia Abu Zahra, 'Love and Light in the Imagination of al-Sayyida Zaynab's Pilgrims', *Alif: Journal of Comparative Poetics*, vol. 8 (1988), pp. 118–32; Valerie J. Hoffman-Ladd, 'Devotion to the Prophet and His Family in Egyptian Sufism', *International Journal of Middle East Studies* 24:4 (1992): 616–37; and Caroline Williams, 'The Cult of 'Alid Saints in the Fatimid Monuments of Cairo Part I: The Mosque of al-Aqmar', *Muqarnas*, vol. 1 (1983), pp. 37–52; and 'The Cult of 'Alid Saints in Fatimid Cairo Part II: The Mausolea', *Muqarnas*, vol. 3 (1985), pp. 39–60.

50. Szanto Ali-Dib, *Following Sayyida Zaynab*, p. 50; Stephennie Mulder, 'Shi'ites and Shi'ism in Medieval Syria', *Syria Comment*, http://www.joshualandis.com/blog/shi%E2%80%99ites-and-shi%E2%80%99ism-in-medieval-syria-by-stephennie-mulder/, accessed 19 June 2015; and Stephennie Mulder, *The Shrines of the 'Alids in Medieval Syria*, Edinburgh: Edinburgh University Press (2014).

51. Lay Shi'is follow a *marja' al-taqlid* (literally 'reference for emulation', a grand jurist/*mujtahid* qualified to deliver juridical opinions) on issues of ritual practice and interpretation of tradition and creed. There is no consensus among Shi'i *maraji'* (plural of *marja'*) as to whether the laity should also follow the political opinions of their *marja'*. See Robert Gleave, 'Conceptions of Authority in Iraqi Shiism: Baqir al-Hakim, Ha'iri and Sistani on Ijtihad, Taqlid, and Marja'iyya', *Theory, Culture and Society* 24: 2 (2007): 59–78. The *maraji'* are frequently referred to by the Shi'i laity and in the news media as 'grand ayatollahs' (singular: *ayatollah al-uzma*).

52. Szanto Ali-Dib, *Following Sayyida Zaynab*, p. 56.

53. Ibid., pp. 56–62.

54. Ibid., p. 56; and Edith Szanto, 'Beyond the Karbala Paradigm: Rethinking Revolution and Redemption in Twelver Shi'a Mourning Rituals', *Journal of Shi'a Islamic Studies* 6:1 (2013): 75–91. The Shirazi *maraji'* permit and even encourage the performance of *tatbir*, while Khamenei has prohibited the practice, as has Hizbullah. Its performance, in addition to symbolically rejecting the religious authority of its critics, also has political implications as regards the competition between the Shirazis and Khamenei over the structure of political authority.

55. Christopher Anzalone, 'A Few Notes on Shi'ism in Syria and the Emergence of a Pro-Asad Shi'i Militia, Liwa' Abu'l Fadl al-'Abbas', *Al-Wasat*, http://thewasat. wordpress.com/2013/05/21/observations-on-shiism-in-syria-and-the-emergence-of-a-pro-asad-shii-militia-liwa-abul-fadl-al-abbas/, accessed 22 May 2013.

56. BBC, *Freedom to Broadcast Hate*, documentary film, released 2013. For background on the al-Anwar television channels, see Rafid Fadhil Ali, 'Religious and the Sectarian Divide in Iraq', in Khalid Hroub, ed., *Religious Broadcasting in the Middle East*, New York: Columbia University Press (2012), pp. 155–71.

57. Szanto Ali-Dib, *Following Sayyida Zaynab*, p. 51. For a history of Iraq's shrine cities, see Yitzhak Nakash, *The Shi'is of Iraq*, Princeton, NJ: Princeton University Press (1994).

58. Representative videos, all in Arabic, saved in the author's archives and originally uploaded to YouTube and other video-sharing websites include *The Prayer over the Martyrs in the Shrine of Sayyida Zaynab, peace be upon her*, released Sept. 2012; *Presentation to the Souls of the Martyrs of Sayyida Zaynab, peace be upon her, and to the Souls of the Martyrs of al-Asad's Syria*, released Sept. 2012; and *Presentation to the Souls of the Martyrs of Sayyida Zaynab*, released Sept. 2012. Many of these videos have since been taken down.

59. Suadad al-Salhy, 'Iraqi Shi'ite Militants Fight for Syria's Assad', Reuters, http://www.reuters.com/article/2012/10/16/us-syria-crisis-iraq-militias-idUSBRE89F0 PX20121016, accessed 16 Oct. 2012.

60. Estimates of the composition of LAFA are based on collected photographs and documents published by the group online and the national and ethnic origins of individual fighters. The Shi'i militias, unlike Sunni militant organisations such as Islamic State and al-Qaeda groups, do not distribute nearly as much media operations material and other literature, nor do they generally produce many polished propaganda films. They do, however, produce and distribute (online as well as on the ground) photographs, recruitment and martyr posters, and short videos seemingly recorded, on cell phones, from their graininess. The visual productions of Shi'i armed groups in Syria and the Hashd al-Sha'bi groups in Iraq are particularly rich. Examples representing only a very small sample are referenced throughout this chapter and are available for viewing online. See Figures 12 and 34 in 'Visual References', *Views from the Occident*, http://occidentblog.wordpress.com/2013/06/24/visual-references/, as well as news media reports, including Russia Today,

'Syria … National Defense Brigades' Specific Tasks', TV broadcast, 26 March 2013.

A number of Afghan Shi'i seminary students expelled by the Iraqi Ba'thist government in the 1970s settled in the *Sayyida* Zaynab district where many of them re-started their studies at the Zaynabiyya Hawza. See Laurence Louër, *Transnational Shia Politics: Religious Networks in the Gulf*, New York: Columbia University Press (2008), p. 196.

61. See Figure 1 in 'Visual References', *Views from the Occident*, https://occidentblog. wordpress.com/2013/06/24/visual-references/; and Jonathan Steele, 'Sunni Tribes Joining Shia Militias as War against IS Heats Up in Iraq', *Middle East Eye*, http:// www.middleeasteye.net/news/sunni-tribes-joining-shia-militias-war-against-heats-iraq-1175770052, accessed 1 April 2016.

62. Mona Alami, 'Iraq's Sunni Fighting Force Still Months Away', *Al-Monitor*, http:// www.al-monitor.com/pulse/originals/2015/05/iraq-isis-sunnis-anbar-mosul-tikrit-nouri-maliki.html#, accessed 1 April 2016; Hamza Hendawi and Qassim Abdul-Zahra, 'Fears in Iraqi Government, Army Over Shiite Militias' Power', Associated Press, http://bigstory.ap.org/article/9696d8589a774c33a2e29aaf96 99330c/fears-iraqi-government-army-over-shiite-militias-power, accessed 1 April 2016; Robin Wright, 'In War against ISIS, Numbers Don't Always Tell the Story', *Wall Street Journal*, http://blogs.wsj.com/washwire/2015/03/13/in-war-against-isis-numbers-dont-always-tell-the-story/, accessed 1 April 2016; and Mustafa Saadoun, 'It's Official: Sunnis Joining Iraq's Popular Mobilization Units', *Al-Monitor*, http://www.al-monitor.com/pulse/originals/2016/01/iraq-sunnis-join-shiite-popular-mobilization-forces.html#, accessed 1 April 2016.

63. For various estimates, see Richard Barrett, *Foreign Fighters in Syria*, occasional paper, Soufan Group, June 2014; and Aron Lund, 'Who are the Foreign Fighters in Syria? An Interview with Aaron Y. Zelin', blog post, Carnegie Endowment for International Peace, http://carnegieendowment.org/syriaincrisis/?fa=53811, accessed 5 Dec. 2013.

64. Associated Press, 'After Threats to Shrine, Iraqi Shiite Fighters Prepare for Sectarian Strife at Home, in Syria', http://www.foxnews.com/world/2012/10/25/after-threats-to-shrine-iraqi-shiite-fighters-prepare-for-sectarian-strife-at/, accessed 25 Oct. 2012; al-Salhy, 'Iraqi Shi'ite Militants Fight for Syria's Assad'; Yasir Ghazi and Tim Arango, 'Iraqi Sects Join Battle in Syria on Both Sides', *New York Times*, http://www.nytimes.com/2012/10/28/world/middleeast/influx-of-iraqi-shiites-to-syria-widens-wars-scope.html?_r=0, accessed 27 Oct. 2012; and Russia Today, TV broadcast, 26 March 2013.

65. Nicholas Blanford, 'Hezbollah Readying for Qalamoun Offensive', *Daily Star*, http://www.dailystar.com.lb/News/Lebanon-News/2015/Mar-20/291498-hezbollah-readying-for-qalamoun-offensive.ashx, accessed 20 March 2015; Nour Samaha, 'Why Qalamoun Matters for Hezbollah', Al-Jazeera English online, http://www.aljazeera.com/news/2015/05/150511085809867.html, accessed

11 May 2015; *Daily Star*, 'Hezbollah, Syrian Army Destroyed 40 Militant Bases, 4 Operation Rooms in Qalamoun Offensive', http://www.dailystar.com.lb/News/Lebanon-News/2015/May-19/298593-hezbollah-syrian-army-destroyed-40-militant-bases-4-operations-rooms-in-qalamoun-offensive.ashx, accessed 19 May 2015; and *Daily Star*, 'Hezbollah Takes More Qalamoun Highlands from Nusra; Jihadis Clash Nearby', http://www.dailystar.com.lb/News/Lebanon-News/2015/May–25/299227-hezbollah-takes-more-qalamoun-highlands-from-nusra-jihadis. ashx, accessed 25 May 2015.

66. Associated Press, 'After Threats to Shrine, Iraqi Shiite Fighters Prepare for Sectarian Strife at Home, in Syria'. Representative early statements, all in Arabic, include Kata'ib Hizbullah (Brigades of the Party of God), 'Statement: The Martyr, Ahmad Mahdi al-Shuwayli', 15 April 2013; and Kata'ib Hizbullah, 'Rida Khudayr al-Khalidi, 6 May 2013, and a representative video in which the group affiliations of Shi'i fighters killed in Syria are listed is 'Martyrs of *Liwa' Abu al-Fadl al-'Abbas*' (Arabic), released June 2013. The group affiliations listed include the Sadr Movement, 'Asa'ib Ahl al-Haqq (League of the Righteous), and Kata'ib Hezbollah. The video also purports to show martyred fighters from two other militias, the Liwa' Jund Allah (Brigade of God's Soldiers) and Liwa' Quwat Haydar (Brigade of the Force of Haydar), using an honorific meaning 'lion' in Arabic used by Shi'is for the first Imam, 'Ali ibn Abi Talib. See also Figures 13–15 in 'Visual References', https://occidentblog.wordpress.com/2013/06/24/visual-references/. The martyr posters and artwork produced by Iran and the Iraqi political parties and paramilitary organisations both within the Hashd umbrella and outside it are quite similar to the output of the militias in Syria. See Figures 54–61 in 'Visual References', https://occidentblog.wordpress.com/2013/06/24/visual-references/

67. See Figures 16–18 in 'Visual References', https://occidentblog.wordpress.com/2013/06/24/visual-references/

68. Russia Today, 'News Report: Formation of a Shi'ite Brigade composed of Iraqis and Lebanese for Defending the Shrine of Sayyida Zaynab South of Damascus', http://arabic.rt.com/news/609264, accessed 4 March 2013. See also Figures 2–6 and 37–39 in 'Visual References', https://occidentblog.wordpress.com/2013/06/24/visual-references/; and a militia video, *Clashes of the Al-Qasim Brigade of Liwa' Abu al-Fadl al-'Abbas* (Arabic), April 2013.

69. Ibid. and Figure 1 in 'Visual References', https://occidentblog.wordpress.com/2013/06/24/visual-references/

70. Al-Nahar, 'Exhumation of the Grave of Hujr bin 'Adi and Hezbollah: It was a Terrorist Crime', http://www.annahar.com/article/31061, accessed 2 May 2013; Ramin Mostaghim and Patrick J. McDonnell, 'Iranians Protest Desecration of Syrian Shrine', *Los Angeles Times*, http://www.latimes.com/news/world/world-now/la-fg-wn-iran-protest-syria-shrine-desecration-20130510,0,4871059.story, accessed 10 May 2013; and AhlulBayt News Agency, 'Holy Shrine of Hazrat Sakina

(AS) Damaged by Terrorists in Syria', http://abna.ir/data.asp?lang=3&Id=390320, accessed 12 Feb. 2013.

71. See Figure 10 in 'Visual References', https://occidentblog.wordpress.com/2013/06/24/visual-references/

72. See Figure 11 in 'Visual References', https://occidentblog.wordpress.com/2013/06/24/visual-references/

73. I do not mean that the months of importance to all Muslims, such as Ramadan, are not central also to the Shi'i religious calendar, but that 'Ashura and 'Arba'in are the centres of the distinctly Shi'i Islamic lunar year and annual ritual practice.

74. See Figures 24–27 and 40–44 in 'Visual References', https://occidentblog.wordpress.com/2013/06/24/visual-references/

75. Referring here specifically to the family line revered by Shi'is.

76. See Figures 31–33 in 'Visual References', https://occidentblog.wordpress.com/2013/06/24/visual-references/

77. The Karbala tragedy is re-enacted annually in passion plays (*ta'ziyat*) and gatherings in Shi'i mosques and centres in which the events leading up to the battle, the battle and its aftermath are recalled and discussed. The mourning rituals for Husayn and his party vary from locale to locale and from community to community. For details, see Peter Chelkowski, ed., *Eternal Performance: Taziyeh and Other Shiite Rituals*, Chicago: Seagull Books/University of Chicago Press (2010).

78. For English translations of her orations, see Mehdi Jaferey, *The Orations of Hazrat Zainab after Kerbela*, Karachi: Ishtiaq Ahmed Romi (1960).

79. Abir Hamdar, 'Jihad of Words: Gender and Contemporary Karbala Narratives', *The Yearbook of English Studies* vol. 39, no. 1/2 (2009): 90–96; Rachel Kantz Feder, 'Fatima's Revolutionary Image in *Fadak fi al-Tarikh* (1955): The Inception of Muhammad Baqir al-Sadr's Activism', *British Journal of Middle Eastern Studies* vol. 41, no. 1 (2014): 79–96: Edith Szanto, 'Sayyida Zaynab in the State of Exception: Shi'i Sainthood as "Qualified Life," in Contemporary Syria', *International Journal of Middle East Studies* vol. 44 (2012): 286; Lara Deeb, 'Emulating and/or Embodying the Ideal: The Gendering of Temporal Frameworks and Islamic Role Models in Shi'i Lebanon', *American Ethnologist* vol. 36, no. 2 (2009): 252–3; and David Pinault, 'Zaynab bint 'Ali and the Place of the Women of the Households of the First Imams in Shi 'ite Devottional Literature', in Gavin R. G. Hambly, ed., *Women in the Medieval Islamic World: Power, Patronage, and Piety*, New York: St Martin's Press (2008), pp. 73, 83–94.

80. Syed Akbar Hyder, *Reliving Karbala: Martyrdom in South Asian Memory*, Oxford: Oxford University Press (2006), p. 96.

81. See Figures 7 and 8, 20–23 and 28–30 in 'Visual References', https://occidentblog.wordpress.com/2013/06/24/visual-references/; and videos, all in Arabic, *O' Zaynab: Operations of Liwa' Abu al-Fadl al-'Abbas, designated to Protect the Shrine*

of Sayyida Zaynab, peace be upon her, released December 2012; and Baraq al-Khaqani and 'Ali Abu Kiyan al-Muwali, 'Ya Zaynab', *nashid*; the music video is viewable at https://www.youtube.com/watch?v=zHcEiDjmDss, accessed 20 June 2015.

82. For Abu Sakkar's reported cannibalism, see Drishya Nair, 'Syria's Cannibal Commander Abu Sakkar: Why I Ate My Enemy's Heart', *International Business Times*, http://www.ibtimes.co.uk/articles/467780/20130515/syria-rebel-abu-sakkar-bites-heart-interview.htm, accessed 15 May 2013. See Figure 35 in 'Visual References', https://occidentblog.wordpress.com/2013/06/24/visual-references/; the image of Hind kneeling over the fallen Hamza is taken from the late director Moustapha Akkad's classic 1976 film *The Message* about the Prophet Muhammad and the origins of Islam. According to Islamic historical writings, Hind later converted to Islam after the fall of Mecca to the Muslims in 630 CE, was forgiven by the Prophet Muhammad, and is today considered one of the many of the revered 'companions' (*Sahaba*) of the Prophet.

83. Sayyid Najmulhasan Karravri, *Biography of Hazrat Abbas*, Karachi: Peermahomed Ebrahim Trust (1974), pp. 49–51 and 78–90; and *Karbala: When the Skies Wept Blood*, film, viewable at https://www.youtube.com/watch?v=QIQQ_ODKMWE, accessed 19 June 2015.

84. Yitzhak Nakash, *The Shi'is of Iraq*, Princeton, NJ: Princeton University Press (1994), p. 45.

85. See Figures 14 and 48–53 in 'Visual References', *Views from the Occident*, https://occidentblog.wordpress.com/2013/06/24/visual-references/

86. See Figures 48–53 and in 'Visual References', *Views from the Occident*, https://occidentblog.wordpress.com/2013/06/24/visual-references/

87. http://www.kt-im-ali.com/, accessed 19 June 2015.

88. http://saidshuhada.com/, accessed 19 June 2015.

89. Hyder, *Reliving Karbala*, p. 47.

90. The tragic story of al-Qasim's battlefield marriage was likely first included in the sixteenth-century, Persian-language elegiac martyrology of Husayn Va'iz Kashifi, *Garden of the Martyrs*. See Hyder, *Reliving Karbala*, p. 28; and David Pinault, *Horse of Karbala: Muslim Devotional Life in India*, New York: Palgrave (2001), p. 68. It has been published numerous times in various languages. See Husayn Va'iz Kashifi, *Garden of the Martyrs*, Qum: Daftar-i Nashr-i Navid-i Islam (2000).

91. Pinault, *Horse of Karbala*, pp. 66–7.

92. *The History of al-Tabari*, vol. 17: *The First Civil War*, trans. by G. R. Hawting, Albany, NY: State University of New York Press (1996), pp. 145–6.

93. Myriam Ababsa, 'Les mausolées invisibles: Raqqa, ville de pèlerinage chiite ou pôle étatique en Jazîra syrienne', *Annales de Géographie* 622 (2001): 647–64; and 'Significations territoriales et appropriations conflictuelles des mausolées chiites de Raqqa (Syrie)', in *Les pèlerinages au Maghreb et au Moyen-Orient: Espaces Public,*

Espaces du Public (Pilgrimages to the Maghreb and Middle East: Public Spaces and Spaces of the Public), Damascus: Presses de l'Ifpo (2010).

94. Myriam Ababsa, 'The Shi'i Mausoleums of Raqqa: Iranian Proselytism and Local Significations', in Fred H. Larson, ed., *Demystifying Syria*, London: Saqi (2009), pp. 85–104.

95. Ibid., p. 89; and Pinto, 'Pilgrimage, Commodities, and Religious Objectification'.

96. Ababsa, 'The Shi'i Mausoleums of Raqqa', p. 92.

97. Ibid., pp. 99–100.

98. I differentiate here between the movement led by Muhammad Sadiq al-Sadr's son, Muqtada, and a broader set of groups who base their legitimacy in large part on their supposed connection to the late ayatollah, referring here to the latter.

99. Sadiq al-Sadr's cousin, the famous Iraqi Shi'i *mujtahid* and intellectual Muhammad Baqir al-Sadr (1935–80), who was tortured and executed by the Iraqi government, is known as 'the first martyr al-Sadr' (*al-shahid al-Sadr al-awwal*).

100. This change in name was not official but the collective decision of the district's residents, who began to call it Sadr City soon after the toppling of Saddam's regime in April 2003.

101. Centres where rituals to commemorate the *Ahl al-Bayt* are held.

102. Juan Cole, 'The United States and Shi'ite Religious Factions in Post-Ba'thist Iraq', *Middle East Journal*, vol. 57, no. 4 (2003): 543–66.

103. Justin Jones, *Shi'a Islam in Colonial India: Religion, Community and Sectarianism*, New York: Cambridge University Press (2012), particularly ch. 5.

104. For background on 'Asa'ib Ahl al-Haqq, see Sam Wyer, *The Resurgence of Asa'ib Ahl al-Haq*, Middle East Security Report no. 7, Institute for the Study of War, Dec. 2012, http://www.understandingwar.org/sites/default/files/Resurgence ofAAH.pdf, accessed 21 June 2015.

105. A representative view is that of Husayn al-Qazwini in a lecture entitled 'Analaysis of Sistani's Fetwa [*sic*] on Jihad' during the month of Ramadan in 2014 (1435 *hijri*), https://www.youtube.com/watch?v=Tn2NsnCBgbc, accessed 19 June 2015. Note the focus solely on the targeting and persecution of Shi'is and the essential neglect of the many non-Shi'is who were also killed during the Arab uprisings. Al-Qazwini describes the wave of protests and uprisings as the 'Arab Winter' and portrays the Syrian opposition as being largely foreign, though he focuses almost entirely on the Islamic State and Jabhat al-Nusra.

106. Muhammad al-Jaburi, (official) *Biography of the Marja' Qasim al-Ta'i, may God protect his shadow* (Arabic).

107. 'Advice to the Mujahidin who are Defending the Shrine of Sayyida Zaynab, during the Pilgrimage (*ziyarat*) to the Shrine' (Arabic), released May 2013; 'Word of His Eminence, Shaykh al-Ta'i, during His Reception of a Group of Mujahidin' (Arabic), released June 2013; 'The Mujahid Shaykh Qasim al-Ta'i at the Blessed Shrine of Sayyida Zaynab' (Arabic), released April 2013; and 'Shaykh Qasim al-

Ta'i Opens an Office in Syria, Sayyida Zaynab' (Arabic), video, released Dec. 2012. See also Figures 45–47 in 'Visual References', *Views from the Occident*, https://occidentblog.wordpress.com/2013/06/24/visual-references/

108. 'Shaykh al-Ta'i's presents a Eulogistic Ceremony for the Martyrs of Zaynab, peace be upon her' (Arabic), released April 2013; 'Letter of His Eminence Shaykh al-Ta'i to the Leader of Liwa' Abu al-Fadl al-'Abbas, *Sayyid* Muhammad al-'Askari' (Arabic), released April 2013; Liwa' Zulfiqar (Brigade of Zulfiqar), 'Statement from the Leadership of Liwa' Zulfiqar Defending the Holy Shrines in Beloved Syria' (Arabic), 16 June 2013.

109. Kazim al-Ha'iri, *fatwa* (Arabic), 18 Nov. 2013 (14 *Muharram* 1435 *hijri*); and *fatwa* (Arabic), 25 May 2013 (14 *Rajab* 1434 *hijri*).

110. The questioner, however, does specifically ask about them.

111. Al-Ha'iri, *fatwa*, 25 May 2013.

112. Muqtada's position on dispatching fighters to Syria remained unclear in 2013, though at least one Iraqi Shi'i armed group in the country, Liwa' al-Imam al-Husayn (Brigade of Imam Husayn), invoked him and his father, displaying their photographs prominently in propaganda photography in the field.

113. Mohamad Ali Harissi, 'Iraq Attacks Kill 15 as Election Looms', *Agence France-Presse*, http://reliefweb.int/report/iraq/iraq-attacks-kill-15-elections-loom, accessed 26 April 2014; Martin Chulov, 'Controlled by Iran, the Deadly Militia Recruiting Iraq's Men to Die in Syria', *Guardian*, http://www.theguardian.com/world/2014/mar/12/iraq-battle-dead-valley-peace-syria, accessed 12 March 2014; and Liz Sly, 'Iranian-backed Militant Group in Iraq is Recasting Itself as a Political Player', *Washington Post*, http://www.washingtonpost.com/world/middle_east/iranian-backed-militant-group-in-iraq-is-recasting-itself-as-a-political-player/2013/02/18/b0154204–77bb-11e2-b102–948929030e64_story.html, accessed 18 February 2013.

114. Jeremy Bowen, 'The Fearsome Iraqi Militias Vowing to Vanquish ISIS', BBC News, http://www.bbc.com/news/world-middle-east-28199741, accessed 7 July 2014.

115. Babak Dehghanpisheh, 'The Fighters of Iraq who Answer to Iran', Reuters, http://www.reuters.com/article/us-mideast-crisis-militias-specialreport-idUSKCN0I-W0ZA20141112, accessed 12 Nov. 2014; Matthew Hilburn, 'One-time US Prisoner Now Key in Battling IS', *Voice of America*, http://www.voanews.com/content/qais-khazali-onetime-us-prisoner-now-key-in-battling-islamic-state/2679431.html, accessed 16 March 2015; and Mohammed al-Zaidi, 'Interview with Militia Leader, Qais al-Khazali', *Niqash*, http://www.niqash.org/en/articles/politics/5080/, accessed 19 Aug. 2015.

116. Samia Nakhoul, 'Iraqi Militia Leader says U.S. Not Serious about Fighting Islamic State', Reuters, http://www.reuters.com/article/us-mideast-crisis-iraq-khazali-idUSKCN0Q22ED20150728, accessed 29 July 2015; Raf Sanchez, 'Iran-backed

Shia Militia says It Will Fight US Marines Deployed to Iraq', *Daily Telegraph*, http://www.telegraph.co.uk/news/worldnews/middleeast/iraq/12200172/Iran-backed-Shia-militia-says-it-will-fight-US-Marines-deployed-to-Iraq.html, accessed 22 March 2016; and 'Asa'ib Ahl al-Haqq communiqué, 'Statement of the Islamic Resistance Movement 'Asa'ib Ahl al-Haqq Concerning the Entrance of American Marines into Iraq', 21 March 2016.

117. Al-Kha'azli, 'Tenth Anniversary of the Founding of 'Asa'ib Ahl al-Haqq'.

118. Ibid.

119. 'Asa'ib Ahl al-Haqq communiqué, 'The Islamic Ahl al-Haqq Movement Condemns the Three Bloody Bombings on Tuesday and Calls for Unity in Foiling the Plots Designed to Ignite Sectarian Discord (*fitna*)', 21 March 2013, http://ahlualhaq.com/index.php/permalink/3185.html; and 'Asa'ib Ahl al-Haqq news report, 'Ahl al-Haqq's Foundation for Students and Youth Holds a Seminar, an Analytical Speech by the Secretary-General of the Ahl al-Haqq Islamic Movement concerning the Tenth Anniversary of Its Founding', 2 June 2013, http://ahlualhaq.com/index.php/permalink/3342.html

120. Suadad al-Salhy, 'Syria War Widens Rift between Shi'ite Clergy in Iraq, Iran', Reuters, http://www.reuters.com/article/2013/07/20/us-iraq-politics-syria-idUSBRE96J04120130720, accessed 20 July 2013; *Al-Sharq al-Awsat*, 'Syrian Conflict Increases Shi'ite Divisions', http://www.aawsat.net/2013/07/article55310611/syrian-conflict-increases-shiite-divisions, accessed 21 July 2013; and Ali Mamouri, 'Shiite Seminaries Divided on Fatwas for Syrian Jihad', http://www.al-monitor.com/pulse/originals/2013/07/syria—jihad-fatwas-shiite-clergy-iran-iraq.html#, accessed 29 July 2013.

121. This sweep culminated in ISIL's capture of Mosul and Tikrit and advances on Samarra, home to a revered Shi'i shrine complex in which the tenth and eleventh Imams, 'Ali al-Hadi and Hasan al-'Askari, are buried.

122. 'Ali al-Sistani, 'Call of the Supreme Religious Authority (*al-marja'iyya al-diniyya al'Ulya*) to Defend the Nation (*al-watan*)' (Arabic), 10 July 2014; 'Ali al-Sistani, 'Statement from the Office of His Eminence *Sayyid* al-Sistani, may God protect his shadow, in Najaf concerning the Latest Security Developments in the Governorate of Nineveh' (Arabic), 10 July 2014; Bashir Najafi, 'Statement from the Office of His Eminence Grand Ayatullah, the *Marja'* Shaykh Bashir Husayn al-Najafi, may God protect his shadow, concerning the Year since the Issuance of the Fatwa of Blessed Defensive Jihad in Iraq' (Arabic), 2 June 2015, http://www.alnajafy.com/list/mainnews-1-444-2713.html; Bashir Najafi, 'Statement from His Eminence Grand Ayatullah, the *Marja'*, Bashir Husayn al-Najafi, may God protect his shadow, about the Obligation to Defend the Nation and the Holy Sites' (Arabic), 13 June 2014, http://www.alnajafy.com/list/mainnews-1-444-2713.html; Muhammad Ishaq al-Fayyad, 'Statement concerning the Events in Nineveh' (Arabic), 11 July 2014; BBC News, 'Iraq Conflict: Shia Cleric Sistani

Issues Call to Arms', http://www.bbc.com/news/world-middle-east-27834462, accessed 13 June 2014; Luay Al Khatteeb, 'What Do You Know about Sistani's Fatwa?' *Huffington Post*, http://www.huffingtonpost.com/luay-al-khatteeb/what-do-you-know-about-si_b_5576244.html, accessed 10 July 2014; Rachel Kantz Feder, 'A Call to Arms: What Lies Beneath Sistani's Potent Fatwa?' *openDemocracy*, https://www.opendemocracy.net/arab-awakening/rachel-kantz-feder/call-to-arms-what-lies-beneath-sistani%E2%80%99s-potent-fatwa, accessed 10 July 2014; Juan Cole, 'Enter the Ayatollah: Sistani Calls on Iraqis to Enlist in Fight against "Terrorists"', *Informed Comment*, http://www.juancole.com/2014/06/ayatollah-against-terrorists.html, accessed 14 June 2014; Loveday Morris, 'Shiite Cleric Sistani Backs Iraqi Government's Call for Volunteers to Fight Advancing Militants', *Washington Post*, http://www.washingtonpost.com/world/middle_east/volunteers-flock-to-defend-baghdad-as-insurgents-seize-more-iraqi-territory/2014/06/13/10d46f9c-f2c8–11e3–914c-1fbd0614e2d4_story.html, accessed 13 June 2014; and Buwaba Saida, 'Al-Sistani Refuses for a Third Time to Issue a Fatwa for Jihad in Syria,' (Arabic), http://www.saidagate.net/Show-29376, accessed 15 May 2013.

123. Suadad al-Salhy, 'Iraqi Sunnis Join Shia Militias to Fight IS Militants', *Middle East Eye*, http://www.middleeasteye.net/news/iraqi-sunnis-join-shiite-militias-fight-militants-520291754, accessed 15 June 2015.

124. Concerning difficulties in mobilising Iraq's Sunni Arab tribes, see Raed El-Hamed, 'The Challenges of Mobilizing Sunni Tribes in Iraq', *Sada*, carnegieendowment.org/sada/index.cfm?fa=show&article=59401&solr_hilite, accessed 17 March 2015.

125. Martin Chulov, 'Kurds and Shias Face Off Over Kirkuk in Vacuum Left by Iraqi Army', *Guardian*, http://www.theguardian.com/world/2016/jan/22/kurds-and-shias-face-off-over-kirkuk-in-vacuum-left-by-iraqi-army, accessed 22 January 2016; Sam Dagher and Ben Kesling, 'Arabs Accuse Kurds of Exploiting War with Islamic State to Grab Land', *Wall Street Journal*, http://www.wsj.com/articles/ethnic-tensions-flare-in-iraqi-city-of-sinjar-after-kurdish-led-offensive-pushes-islamic-state-out-1448361003, accessed 25 Nov. 2015; Tim Arango, 'Sinjar Victory Bolsters Kurds, but Could Further Alienate U.S. from Iraq', *New York Times*, http://www.nytimes.com/2015/11/14/world/middleeast/sinjar-iraq-kurds-isis.html, accessed 13 Nov. 2015; Sofia Barbarani, 'Inside Sinjar: Suspicion and Anger Thrives in the City Broken by Islamic State', *Daily Telegraph*, http://www.telegraph.co.uk/news/worldnews/middleeast/iraq/12028113/Inside-Sinjar-Suspicion-and-anger-thrive-in-the-city-broken-by-Islamic-State.html, accessed 2 Dec. 2015; Adnan Abu Zeed, 'Arab-Kurd Conflict Heats Up after Tuz Khormato Incidents', *Al-Monitor*, http://www.al-monitor.com/pulse/originals/2015/12/iraq-kurdistan-region-tuz-khormato-arabs-kurds-conflict.html#, accessed 8 Dec. 2015; Sharon Behn, 'Kurds Warn of Post-IS Fight with Shi'ite

Militias', *Voice of America*, http://www.voanews.com/content/kurds-warn-of-post-is-fight-with-shiite-militias/3256998.html, accessed 27 March 2016; and BBC News, 'United Nations "concerned" about Sunni abuse in Iraq', http://www.bbc.com/news/world-middle-east-35010363, accessed 4 Dec. 2015.

126. Fanar Haddad, 'The Hashd: Redrawing the Military and Political Map of Iraq', *Middle East Institute blog*, http://www.mei.edu/content/article/hashd-redrawing-military-and-political-map-iraq, accessed 9 April 2015; Joel Wing, 'Will the Hashd al-Shaabi Change the Face of Iraqi Politics? Interview with Fanar Haddad', *Musings on Iraq*, http://musingsoniraq.blogspot.ca/2015/05/will-hashd-al-shaabi-change-face-of.html, accessed 26 May 2015; Associated Press, 'Iraqi Shia Cleric Calls for Unity after Militia Pullout', http://timesofindia.indiatimes.com/world/middle-east/Iraqi-Shia-cleric-calls-for-unity-after-militia-pullout/articleshow/46717421.cms, accessed 27 March 2015; Associated Press, 'Sistani Urges Help for Militias Battling ISIS', http://www.dailystar.com.lb/News/Middle-East/2015/Mar-13/290666-sistani-urges-help-for-militias-battling-isis.ashx, accessed 13 March 2015; Hendawi and Abdul-Zahra, 'Fears in Iraqi Government, Army Over Shiite Militias' Power' and Erika Soloman, 'Iraq's Shia Militia Leaders See Opportunity in Baghdad Paralysis', *Financial Times*, http://www.ft.com/cms/s/0/007b882c-ef8a-11e5–9f20-c3a047354386.html#axzz44Vh6OJKp, accessed 29 March 2016.

127. Ned Parker, 'Power Failure in Iraq as Militias Outgun State', Reuters, http://www.reuters.com/investigates/special-report/iraq-abadi/, accessed 21 Oct. 2015; Renad Mansour, 'The Popularity of the Hashd in Iraq', *Syria in Crisis* (Carnegie Endowment for International Peace), http://carnegieendowment.org/syriaincrisis/?fa=62638, accessed 1 Feb. 2016; Maher Chmaytelli, 'As Iraqi Civilian Rule Weakens, Shi'ite Clerics Call the Shots', Reuters, http://www.reuters.com/article/us-mideast-crisis-iraq-politics-idUSKCN0WM0U2, accessed 20 March 2016; Saif Hameed, 'Sadr Supporters Rally in Baghdad, Press Abadi to Form New Cabinet', Reuters, http://www.reuters.com/article/us-mideast-crisis-iraq-politics-cabinet-idUSKCN0WD1JO, accessed 11 March 2016; and Amnesty International, 'Absolute Impunity: Militia Rule in Iraq', https://www.amnesty.org/en/documents/MDE14/015/2014/en/, accessed 14 Oct. 2014.

128. 'Ali al-Sistani, 'Advice and Guidelines to the Fighters in the Fields of Jihad' (Arabic), 12 Feb. 2015, http://www.sistani.org/arabic/archive/25034//

129. Kirk H. Sowell, 'Badr at the Forefront of Iraq's Shia Militias', *Sada* (Carnegie Endowment for International Peace), http://carnegieendowment.org/sada/?fa=61016, accessed 13 Aug. 2015; Press TV, 'Full Interview with Hadi al-Ameri', http://217.218.67.231/Detail/2015/05/08/410035/Hadi-al-Ameri-interview, accessed 7 May 2015; Hamza Mustafa, 'Hadi al-Ameri: A Militia Leader Torn between Washington and Tehran', *Al-Sharq al-Awsat*, http://english.aawsat.com/2014/09/article55336936/hadi-al-ameri-a-militia-leader-torn-between-

washington-and-tehran, accessed 25 Sept. 2014; and Bill Neely, 'Hadi al-Ameri on Shiite Militias Fighting ISIS: "We Expect More" from U.S.', NBC News, http://www.nbcnews.com/storyline/isis-terror/hadi-al-ameri-shiite-militias-fighting-isis-we-expect-more-n379571, accessed 23 June 2015.

130. Al-Sistani, 'Advice and Guidelines'.

131. Ibid.

132. Ibid.

133. Najafi, 'Statement concerning the Year since the Issuance of the Fatwa of Blessed Defensive Jihad in Iraq'.

134. Ibid.

135. Ibid.

136. Ibid.

137. Najafi, 'The Obligation to Defend the Nation and the Holy Sites'.

138. Muhammad Sa 'id al-Hakim's website, 'His Eminence, the Religious Authority *Sayyid* al-Hakim, may God protect his shadow, Calls for the Fighters to Uphold the Unity of the Word the Qur'an, of Islam and of the Homeland, the Holy Sites, and Properties', n.d. (uploaded on or around 8 April 2015), http://alhakeem.com/arabic/pages/news.php?nid=1428&gid=18&sw=%D8%A7%D9%84%D8%AC%D9%87%D8%A7%D8%AF

139. Islamic State film, 'The Most Evil of Creation The Shi'a', released 30 Jan. 2016 (Arabic).

11. THE IMPACT OF EVOLVING JIHADIST NARRATIVES ON RADICALISATION IN THE WEST

1. The Soufan Group, 'Foreign Fighters: An Updated Assessment of the Flow of Foreign Fighters into Syria and Iraq' (December 2015), http://soufangroup.com/wp-content/uploads/2015/12/TSG_ForeignFightersUpdate1.pdf; ICSR, 'Foreign fighter total in Syria/Iraq now exceeds 20,000; surpasses Afghanistan conflict in the 1980s', *ICSR Insight*, 26 Jan. 2015, http://icsr.info/2015/01/foreign-fighter-total-syriairaq-now-exceeds-20000-surpasses-afghanistan-conflict-1980s/

2. http://www.un.org/press/en/2014/sc11580.doc.htm

3. David Chazan, 'Brussels Museum Shooting Suspect "Beheaded Baby"', *Daily Telegraph*, 7 September 2014, http://www.telegraph.co.uk/news/worldnews/middleeast/syria/11080079/Brussels-museum-shooting-suspect-beheaded-baby.html

4. BBC News, 'Paris Attacks: Who Were the Attackers?' BBC News, accessed 21 December 2015, http://www.bbc.co.uk/news/world-europe-34832512

5. Akil N. Awan, 'What Happens When ISIS Comes Home?' *The National Interest*, 29 September 2014, http://nationalinterest.org/feature/what-happens-when-isis-comes-home-11363

6. Akil N. Awan, 'Jihadi Ideology in the New Media Environment', in Jeevan Deol

and Zaheer Kazmi, eds, *Contextualising Jihadi Thought*, London: Hurst & Co. (2012).

7. Michael Scheuer, *Imperial Hubris: Why the West is Losing the War on Terror*, Nebraska: Potomac (2008); Lawrence Wright, *The Looming Tower: Al-Qa'ida and the Road to 9/11*, New York: Vintage Books (2007).

8. Osama bin Laden, 'Declaration of War against the Americans Occupying the Land of the Two Holy Places', 1996, http://www.mideastweb.org/osamabinladen1.htm

9. Michael Scheuer, *Through Our Enemies' Eyes: Osama Bin Laden, Radical Islam, and the Future of America*, Washington, DC: Brassey's (2002), p. xxv.

10. Abdullah Azzam, *Join the Caravan* (1987). Available at: https://archive.org/stream/JoinTheCaravan/JoinTheCaravan_djvu.txt

11. Akil N. Awan, 'The Virtual Jihad: An Increasingly Legitimate Form of Warfare', *CTC Sentinel* 3, no. 5 (2010).

12. Letter from Osama bin Laden to Mullah Omar, 5 June 2002, US Military Academy Counterterrorism Center website, document AFGP-2002–600321.

13. Abu al-Harith al-Ansari, *Irshad al-Sa'ul ila Hurub al-Rasul* (2008). Available at: http://pdfdatabase.com/download/abu-al-harith-al-ansari-irshad-al-saul-ila-hurub-alrasul-d8a5d8b1d8b4d8a7d8af-d8a7d984d8b3d8a4d988d984--d8a5d984d989-d8add8b-1d988d8a8-d8a7d984d8b1d8b3-doc-4571909.html

14. Muhammad bin Ahmad al-Salim, *39 Ways to Serve and Participate in Jihad* (2003). Available at: http://www.archive.org/stream/39WaysToServeAndParticipate/39WaysToServeAndParticipateInJihad_djvu.txt

15. Anwar al-'Awlaqi, *44 Ways of Supporting Jihad* (2009). Available at: https://ebooks.worldofislam.info/ebooks/Jihad/Anwar_Al_Awlaki-_44_Ways_To_Support_Jihad.pdf

16. Abu Mus'ab al-Suri, 'Theory of Media and Incitement in the Call to Global Islamic Resistance', in *The Global Islamic Resistance Call* (2005). Available at: https://archive.org/stream/TheGlobalIslamicResistanceCall/The_Global_Islamic_Resistance_Call_-_Chapter_8_sections_5_to_7_LIST_OF_TARGETS_djvu.txt

17. Pew Research Center, 'Islamic Extremism: Common Concern for Muslim and Western Publics' (2005) and Pew Research Center, 'Confidence in Obama Lifts U.S. Image Around the World', Washington, DC: Pew Research Center (2009).

18. Ayman al-Zawahiri, 'Letter to Abu Musab Al-Zarqawi', 9 July 2005, http://www.globalsecurity.org/security/library/report/2005/zawahiri-zarqawi-letter_9jul2005.htm

19. Ayman al Zawahiri statement, 13 September 2012, retrieved from www.as-ansar.com/vb/showthread.php?t=70528

20. Abu Muhammad al-'Adnani, *This is the Promise of Allah*, 29 June 2014, available at https://news.siteintelgroup.com/Jihadist-News/isis-spokesman-declares-caliphate-rebrands-group-as-islamic-state.html

21. The term *jahilliyya* literally means the age of ignorance, and traditionally refers to

the pagan pre-Islamic Arabian peninsula; however, the term was redeployed by Sayyid Qutb during the 1960s to critique contemporary Egyptian society as having regressed to the level of pagan society, and it is this usage that is employed by *Takfir wal-hijra*; John Calvert, *Islamism: A Documentary and Reference Guide*, Westport, CT: Greenwood Press (2008).

22. Indeed, the *Takfir wal-hijra* group was viewed by most contemporary Egyptians as a secretive religious cult that converted and brainwashed Egyptian youth, forcing them to withdraw from society and disassociate from their families. Gilles Kepel, *Muslim Extremism in Egypt: The Prophet and Pharaoh*, Berkeley, CA: University of California Press (1985).

23. Robert Mackey, 'A Dutch ISIS Fighter Takes Questions on Tumblr', *New York Times*, 20 November 2015, http://www.nytimes.com/2015/11/21/world/middleeast/a-dutch-isis-fighter-is-taking-questions-on-tumblr.html

24. For a detailed snapshot of ISIL's media production, see Charlie Winter, 'Documenting the Virtual "Caliphate"', Quilliam Foundation (October 2015), http://www.quilliamfoundation.org/wp/wp-content/uploads/2015/10/FINAL-documenting-the-virtual-caliphate.pdf

25. Scott Atran, 'The Moral Logic and Growth of Suicide Terrorism', *Washington Quarterly* 29, no. 2 (2006): 127–47, doi:10.1162/wash.2006.29.2.127; Akil N. Awan, 'Transitional Religiosity Experiences: Contextual Disjuncture and Islamic Political Radicalism', in Tahir Abbas, ed., *Islamic Political Radicalism: A European Comparative Perspective*, Edinburgh: Edinburgh University Press (2007); Akil N. Awan, 'Dual Cultural Alterity: The Ummah and Fictive Kin—Narratives of Vicarious Victimhood amongst Jihadists', paper delivered at Understanding Terrorism and Political Violence: The roles of Victims and Perpetrators, University College Cork, Ireland, 2015.

26. 'Transcript: Read Abdulmutallab's Statement on Guilty Plea', *Detroit Free Press*, 12 October 2011.

27. This term is borrowed from S. Atran, 'Genesis of Suicide Terrorism', *Science* 299, no. 5612 (7 March 2003): 1534, doi:10.1126/science.1078854.

28. Available at http://news.bbc.co.uk/1/hi/uk/4206800.stm

29. Cited in Akil N. Awan, 'Antecedents of Islamic Political Radicalism Among Muslim Communities in Europe', *Political Science and Politics* 41, no. 1 (2008): 222, doi:10.1017/S1049096508080013.

30. Harriet Alexander and Anna Mees, 'Dutch jihadi bride: "Is she a victim or a suspect?"' *Daily Telegraph*, 23 November 2014.

31. Awan, 'Transitional Religiosity Experiences', p. 219.

32. Awan, 'Transitional Religiosity Experiences', p. 217; Home Office Working Groups, 'Preventing Extremism Together', London: Home Office (2005), p. 15.

33. http://www.nytimes.com/2015/01/08/world/two-brothers-suspected-in-killings-were-known-to-french-intelligence-services.html

34. John C. Turner, *Rediscovering the Social Group: A Self-Categorization Theory*, Oxford: Basil Blackwell (1988); Penelope J. Oakes, *Stereotyping and Social Reality*, Oxford, UK and Cambridge, MA: Blackwell (1994).

35. Peter Gottschalk, *Islamophobia: Making Muslims the Enemy*, Lanham, MD: Rowman & Littlefield (2008).

36. Awan, 'Transitional Religiosity Experiences', p. 219.

37. Available at http://media.clarionproject.org/files/islamic-state/islamic-state-isis-magazine-Issue-4-the-failed-crusade.pdf

38. Sam Mullins, 'Re-Examining the Involvement of Converts in Islamist Terrorism: A Comparison of the U.S. and U.K.', *Perspectives on Terrorism* 9, no. 6 (15 December 2015), http://www.terrorismanalysts.com/pt/index.php/pot/article/view/474

39. Adam Nossiter, 'Lonely Trek to Radicalism for Terror Suspect', *New York Times*, 16 January 2010.

40. Olivier Roy, *Globalized Islam: The Search for a New Ummah*, New York: Columbia University Press (2004).

41. See for example Sunan A-Tirmidhi (1663) and Sunan Ibn Majah (2799).

42. http://news.bbc.co.uk/1/hi/uk/4206800.stm

43. 'Transcript: Read Abdulmutallab's Statement on Guilty Plea', *Detroit Free Press*.

44. See also Anne Speckhard and Khapta Akhmedova, 'The Making of a Martyr: Chechen Suicide Terrorism', *Studies in Conflict and Terrorism* 29, no. 5 (2006): 25, doi:10.1080/10576100600698550.

45. http://www.theguardian.com/uk-news/2014/dec/05/two-britons-jailed-13-years-joining-jihadi-group-syria

46. http://www.liberation.fr/societe/2005/02/21/un-ticket-pour-le-jihad_510275

47. Steven Hopkins, 'Paris Terrorist Smoked "Alarming Amount of Cannabis", Drank Alcohol, and Never Went to a Mosque, Ex-Wife Claims', *Huffington Post*, 18 November 2015, http://www.huffingtonpost.co.uk/2015/11/18/paris-terrorist-smoked-alarming-amount-of-cannabis_n_8589508.html

48. Awan, 'Transitional Religiosity Experiences', p. 220.; Martha Crenshaw, 'Explaining Suicide Terrorism: A Review Essay', *Security Studies* 16, no. 1 (2007): 153.

49. Marc Sageman, *Leaderless Jihad: Terror Networks in the Twenty-First Century*, Philadelphia: University of Pennsylvania Press (2008), p. 152.

50. BBC News, 'Profile: Anthony Garcia', 30 April 2007, http://news.bbc.co.uk/1/hi/uk/6149798.stm

51. BBC News, 'Who Is Richard Reid?' 28 December 2001, http://news.bbc.co.uk/1/hi/uk/1731568.stm

52. Scott Atran and Nafess Hamid, 'Paris: The war ISIS wants', *New York Review of Books*, 16 November 2015, http://www.nybooks.com/daily/2015/11/16/paris-attacks-isis-strategy-chaos/

53. P. Neumann, ed., *Prisons and Terrorism. Radicalisation and de-radicalisation in 15 countries*, London: International Centre for the Study of Radicalisation and

Political Violence (2010); A. Silke, ed., *Prisons, Terrorism and Extremism: Critical issues in management, radicalisation and reform*, Abingdon: Routledge. (2014).

54. Johnlee Varghese, 'ISIS Hails Charlie Hebdo Shooters as "Heroes" for Avenging "Allah"', *International Business Times*, India Edition, 9 January 2015, http://www.ibtimes.co.in/isis-hails-charlie-hebdo-shooters-heroes-avenging-allah-619883

55. Available at http://news.bbc.co.uk/1/hi/uk/4206800.stm

56. Ayman al-Zawahiri, *Fursan Taht Rayah Al-Nabi* (Knights Under the Prophet's Banner) (2001), www.scribd.com/doc/6759609/ Knights-Under-the-Prophet-Banner

57. Farhad Khosrokhavar, *Suicide Bombers: Allah's New Martyrs*, London: Pluto Press (2005), p. 133.

58. Available at http://news.bbc.co.uk/1/hi/uk/4206800.stm

59. Akil N. Awan, 'Virtual Jihadist Media: Function, Legitimacy and Radicalizing Efficacy', *European Journal of Cultural Studies* 10, no. 3 (1 August 2007): 389–408.

60. This term is adapted from Prensky, by which I mean a generation of young people who, having been born and raised in an omnipresent digital world, are so comfortably immersed in this virtual environment that they no longer make significant distinctions between it and the 'real' world. See also Marc Prensky, 'Digital Natives, Digital Immigrants', *On the Horizon* 9, no. 5 (2001).

61. Awan, 'Jihadi Ideology in the New Media Environment', p. 114; Akil N. Awan and Mina al-Lami, 'Al-Qa'ida's Virtual Crisis', *RUSI Journal* 154, no. 1 (2009): 62, doi:10.1080/03071840902818605.

INDEX